5938 8651

W9-BPJ-326

Shortly after graduation from university, Steve Van Beek left the U.S. to serve as a Peace Corps volunteer in a small village in the torrid Nepalese Terai. While on his way home in 1969, he stopped in Bangkok and was so captivated by its people and culture that it has since been his home. A writer and a filmmaker, he has traveled extensively in Asia, not always by boat but usually to remote areas. In 1988, he was elected a Fellow of the Explorers Club for his solo river expeditions. More of his writing can be found at www.stevevanbeek.com

WITHDRAWN

BEAVERTON CITY LIBRARY
BEAVERTON, OR 97005
MEMBER OF WASHINGTON COUNTY
COOPERATIVE LIBRARY SERVICES

3

Slithering
South
Steve Van Beek

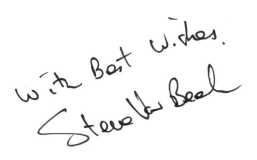

With Best Wishes.

Steve Van Beek

Wind & Water

Copyright Steve Van Beek, 2002. All rights reserved.

This book or parts thereof may not be reproduced in any form without permission in writing from the publisher.

Published by
Wind & Water
Room 1202, 12/Fl.
Jubilee Centre,
42-46 Gloucester Road,
Wanchai, Hong Kong

Designer: Barry Owen
Maps: Gundh Supasri

With grateful thanks to:
Anong Lertrakskul, Robert Burrows, Bob Halliday Maia Hansen, Alex Kerr, Jude Sullivan, Peter Sullivan, Thongchai Nawawat, Bill Young.

Printed in Bangkok, Thailand

ISBN Number: 974-619-074-1

Cover illustration, photograph by the author.

To my parents, Donald and Lucille Van Beek, who never quavered when I embarked on an adventure, remaining supportive even when they were fearful for my safety.

And to all the Thais who, when they recovered from the shock of seeing a strange foreigner suddenly appear in their village, went out of their way to welcome, shelter, and speed me on my way.

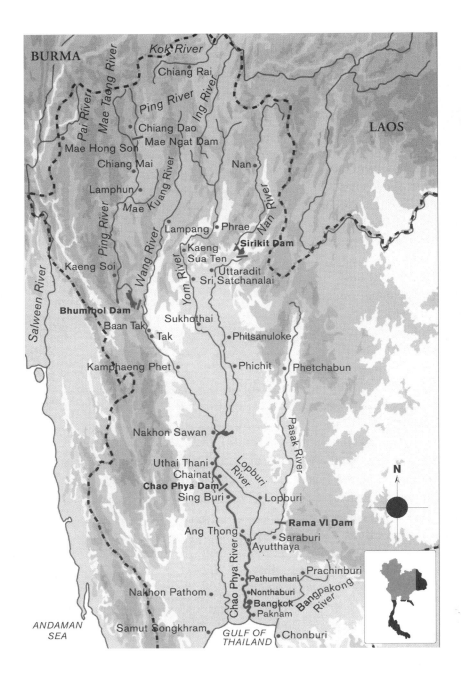

Prologue

For eleven years I lived in a stilted wooden house perched heron-like above Thailand's Chao Phya River. The liquid road that cleaves the royal city into Bangkok and Thonburi coursed under and–during the monsoon floods–through my home. Past my balcony, people and boats glided in their daily pursuits, a never-ending panoply of movement, color, and minor dramas.

The river so intrigued me that I tore out my bedroom wall, and filled the space floor to ceiling with glass. Still not satisfied, I sawed a window in the floor so I could watch fishermen scooping nets in the dark waters beneath my house, surprising fish confident they had found refuge in the shadows. And then I built a bay window over the water so I could look up, down, and across the river, my box seat on its activities.

The river swarmed with life every hour of the day, the tumult ceasing only after the neighborhood watchman had struck his iron gong twelve times. A few hours later, long before the sun illuminated the Temple of Dawn a few yards downriver, the din resumed. Sampans piled high with vegetables, double-decked riverboats, elephantine barges, freighters, water taxis, and river buses noisily dodged each other, their propellers churning the river's surface to a froth in the dark, damp, gelid air.

Across the river from my Thonburi home, the sky would lighten. The sun would peer between the needle spires of the Emerald Buddha Temple, gilding them before painting a molten path across the river's broken surface to melt my glass wall and fill my room with golden light. Lambent flames, reflected by the river's shattered mirror, danced on my wooden ceiling. I lay beneath the flickering tongues, reluctant to begin the day.

Throughout the morning, I would hunker over a typewriter, my back to the river, ignoring its distractions, intent on my day's work. But in the torpid afternoon, when the dying sun stirred the sodden air to the semblance of a breeze, I would push aside my work, splash lime and soda into a glass, and wander out to the verandah. Settling into my wicker rocking chair I would watch ferries and fishermen, vendors and freighters as if from a sidewalk café in an Oriental bazaar. Immense rice barges with rounded teak hulls lumbered along the central channel. Like water skimmers, motorboats darted among these queenly matrons, their wakes breaking against open boats bearing half-naked fishermen, their torsos glowing in the ochre evening light as they cast nets in perfect circles.

Small sampans paddled by elderly women in indigo shirts and straw-colored, volcano-shaped hats paused before houses like mine, offering an array of sweets blended from bananas, cane sugar, coconut milk, tapioca, and other savory ingredients. Other vendors sold cups of mule-kick Thai coffee flavored with chicory, or bowls of noodle soup boiled on charcoal stoves set amidships. Men in loincloths donned crude helmets to dive 60 feet to the muddy riverbed, linked by hoses to life-giving compressors chugging noisily on sampans. At the river bottom, they retrieved whatever they could sell to a junk dealer. Small boats carried vats of bright colors to dye clothes on the customer's doorstep.

Each day, something new floated across this vast stage spread before me: a new type of boat, a new business venture, new ways of using the rolling brown band. As one season melded into the next, the river rose and fell. In April, it would drop 10 feet, exposing the rocks beneath my house. Barefoot children armed with bamboo fishing poles would scamper gingerly across them. Or dart after tiny crabs in the shallows.

From June through August, light rains freshened the air but it was only a prelude to the real violence of the monsoon. From September, when rain fell in torrents, to November, when it began to taper off, the swollen river collided with the incoming tides. Burgeoned with the sky's largess, it overspilled its banks, flooding my low-lying kitchen and bathroom with knee-deep water. Late November brought cool air that lasted only too briefly before the March sun boiled the air, plastering shirts to bare skins.

As I rocked in my chair, the river murmured messages I couldn't decipher. The northern stream, clear when it emerged from the mountains, had become muddy as it journeyed south, its silt a record of lives experienced in the flat valleys through which it had passed as it slid towards marriage with the sea. But the silty rubric in which it spoke was an enigma.

As I watched from my rocking chair, questions formed in my mind: what had given birth to the river? How had its malleable waters been molded by diverse geography? How had it shaped the villages dependent upon its life-giving waters, and the lives of the people past whose doorsteps it flowed?

Equally important, how had the farms, villages, towns, and factories waters altered it? During the rainy season, the river that passed my verandah was a polluted, garbage-choked mess that mirrored the chaos of Bangkok itself. For last dozen miles of its journey–from Bangkok's port to the Gulf of Thailand–the river was biologically dead, devoid of life. What had happened during the last stages of its life to change it so radically?

At the time, I was experiencing my own spiritual pollution. In 1966, I had begun my Asian incarnation as a Peace Corps volunteer in a small Nepalese village. I lived in a cow shed and ate rice and curry yet I savored the purity of the experience, an emotion common among uncompromising children of the 1960s. On my way home in 1969, I paused in Bangkok to visit a Thai friend, and forgot to leave. For 18 years, I had supported myself by writing.

But something had gotten lost along the way. When I started traveling, I had ridden wooden buses, slept in rude inns, and eaten local food in order to experience unique cultures unburdened by concerns for comfort. In recent years, however, my writing and my life had become routine, bland. I had become jaded. Asia had become so familiar that I no longer appreciated the miracles unfolding around me. Too often I traveled with companions, on fixed schedules, or at someone's behest. I no longer rode in bullock carts or slept in villages; I rode in taxis and slept between linen sheets in fine hotels. In my writing, I was covering ground already trodden and tilled by other writers.

Something had to change or there would no longer be a reason for me to remain in Asia. Since I was reluctant to return home, my salvation lay in striking out in a new direction, going where other travelers had not gone. I craved an adventure that would be mine alone, perceived through the filter of my twenty-one years in Asia. It was at this point that my yearning for new experiences and my curiosity about the river collided. I resolved to travel the entire length of the river that flowed past my door.

At first, these thoughts were nothing more than idle reveries on hot afternoons. The Chao Phya was a mystery to most people, even Thais. Over the years, I had searched in vain for information about it in books. Thai friends knew little more than I. Perhaps if I started at its source and worked my way towards the sea the river would reveal what it was murmuring as it rolled past my verandah. Perhaps the journey would revitalize me.

What conceit! I was 43 and had never rowed a boat more than a pond's length. And while I knew Thailand and felt I was mentally and physically tough, I was reluctant to set off on my own because the far North was jungled and remote. A friend had disappeared while trekking and his body was never found. I talked with friends about joining me but few had the five weeks I calculated it would take. Even fewer found the quest interesting. I pushed the idea from my mind.

Or so it seemed. For months, I sat on my balcony, trying to convince myself that I was wise in staying put. Yet, deep in my heart, I knew I was rationalizing, focusing on the "what ifs" that keep one on the shore, reluctant to embark on a perilous sea. But soon I found myself sketching a boat, and idly tracing a route down a map, a blind man trying to read terrain from contour lines as flat as those on his finger pads. It was then that I realized I was too far down a mental road to turn back. I began jotting plans and equipment lists, uncertain what I would encounter or how I would contend with obstacles.

I wanted it to be a clean journey with no outside help, my success or failure hinging on my ability to use my wits. As much as possible, I wanted to travel like early Thai river men, sleeping in the jungles or villages, and eating local food.

After considering each of the four rivers that fed the Chao Phya, I settled on the Ping, the second-longest but most interesting tributary. The Ping rose in a remote corner of the Golden Triangle where the borders of Burma, Thailand, and Laos meet. It rolled south through Chiang Mai, northern Thailand's largest town; southwest through the rugged mountains separating Thailand and Burma; then southeast to Nakhon Sawan where it joined the Wang, Nan, and Yom tributaries. From there, it flowed due south as the Chao Phya River through Thailand's former capital of Ayutthaya, then Bangkok, the present capital, and on to the sea. In all, it would be a journey of 720 miles, roughly the length of the Rhine or the St. Lawrence.

I searched old books for a hint of what I might encounter. But 19th-century travel journals were written by Europeans riding in large boats poled or paddled by Thais. Nowhere did they talk about currents or topography. Their pages provided no ideas on the type of boat would I need, the supplies I should carry, to what extent could I live off the land, or the people I would meet. And none of the early travelers had traveled the rivers north of Chiang Mai.

I scoured Thai-language libraries, but boatmen seldom write memoirs. And, like the foreigners, most Thais had traveled as passengers. I sought out elderly rivermen, but most had used motorized craft, or were familiar only with a short stretch of the river; nobody had run it from top to bottom. For two years I searched for information, convincing myself that I needed mounds of data to prepare for all contingencies.

And still I dawdled. Until I remembered a lesson I thought I had learned in Sumatra ten years before. One afternoon, hoping to view the countryside surrounding Lake Toba, I began climbing a hill with little thought about how I was going to get down. The steps cut by someone–a ranger?–should have alerted me to the steepness of the slope but I was in a hurry to reach the top. Just below the summit, I had to pull myself over a rough rock perhaps four feet high and hemmed by thick grass.

After an hour marveling at the view, I peered down the path I'd just ascended. A trail always looks more precipitous when viewed from above but a peek over the edge revealed a path sloping at an alarming angle. One misstep and I would plunge 1,000 feet to the rocks below. I searched along the rim for another path down, but found none.

For an hour I sat, paralyzed by fear, hoping a voice would emerge from the clouds with a solution. "Do something," I exhorted myself. "You can't stay here; night is coming on." And still I sat.

Then, a strange realization came to me: "You're trying to descend the entire mountain in one go, working out every move beforehand. But that's not the way you got up here. You reached the top one step at a time. You'll get down the same way; step by step."

The first step was over the large rock over which I'd just crawled. Lying on my stomach, I wriggled down its surface, my hands grasping tufts of grass for anchorage, my flailing feet searching for a foothold. Inch by inch I descended, hearing the tiny pops of the grass being torn from their roots by the stress of my weight. Long moments later, as my shirt was losing its grip on the rough surface, my foot struck a tiny dirt platform capable of supporting me. I had solved the first problem. Step by tortuous step, I worked my way down until, after nearly an hour, my weary feet rested on flat ground.

The same technique would get me down the river: encounter and solve a problem, then move to the next obstacle, over and over until I could move as fluidly as the river itself. Bereft of excuses, I began to work out logistics with the data I already had.

As I calculated supplies and itineraries, I envisioned the journey as a contest of wills between me and flowing water. While I would mingle with villagers–only they could help me understand how people interacted with their river–they were secondary to my main goal of figuring out how the river thought and using that knowledge to get me down it in one piece.

By the end, it would become a different journey altogether. The physical obstacles would recede. People would come to the forefront, both as my salvation and the bane of my existence.

Journey to the Source

Naam Khun Hai Riip Tak
(When the water rises, rush to catch fish)
Seize opportunity when it presents itself

A tropical sun filtering through the trees did little to warm a chill December wind that blew through the windows of the *songtaew* bus. A high passenger compartment burdening the bed of a battered pick-up truck, the *songtaew* had bussed villagers through remote northern hills for so many years that it was no longer a match for the rough roads. Its whining, straining engine was barely audible above the groans and squeals of its tortured body as it lurched from deep rut to deeper pothole that pitted the red mud moon-road that wound through the jungled hills.

In the dim interior, two cramped rows of silent Lahu tribesmen faced each other across a narrow aisle. These were not the colorfully-clad tribesmen of tourist brochures but farmers in dun clothes that, like their owners, were prematurely aged by the dust impregnating them. Impassive, unseeing, their bodies jerked in unison, rag dolls spasmodically tensing to keep their heads from banging the vehicle's ceiling.

I bounced with them, hunkered just behind the cab window, not so much to preserve warmth as to be inconspicuous. Through the smudged glass, the driver ricocheted between a barely-cushioned seat and a low ceiling, but my attention was concentrated on the scene beyond his grimy windshield. Down the narrow corridor between the trees stood the squat, black silhouette of yet another police checkpost. I had already slipped through three guardposts without incident. Could I get past this one as well?

"The Border Patrol Police are monitoring road traffic," a friend had warned as I boarded the *songtaew* in Chiang Mai, 60 miles to the south. "You may not get through."

This lawless corner of the Golden Triangle was the fiefdom of shady figures who floated back and forth across the porous Thai-Burmese border carrying contraband jade and antiques, but it was opium and heroin the Thai army and police worked to intercept. Their efforts were stymied by the opium warlords' firepower and their unabashed willingness to use it. Add to it the impenetrability of the jungle, and the connivance of their own compatriots, and the police–those who were interested in carrying out their duties–were battling heavy odds. The drug trade was lucrative and there were too many empty pockets to fill for authorities to make more than token raids against the smugglers. To maintain the fiction of controlling traffic through their area, the paramilitary Border Patrol Police had erected checkpoints along this dirt road to the Burmese frontier.

I was enduring this punishing ride to locate a Lahu hilltribe man I had befriended two years earlier. He lived in a border village called Muang Na and I hoped to persuade him to guide me through the mountains to the Ping's source. Although I was not planning anything illegal, my mere presence in this military zone could be construed as trespassing. At worst, I would be held until I could establish my identity and purpose. More likely I would be sent to Bangkok to spend endless days getting proper authorization, and probably be turned down despite my efforts.

Years of living in Thailand had taught me that to avoid being told "no", don't ask in the first place. Thus, I had not wasted time arming myself with official permits. I'd rather take my chances locally–relying on my knowledge of Thai and Thais–than have my venture closed down before it started.

As we approached the horizontal barrier, the smudged windshield revealed one militiaman raising his hand and the other shifting his M-16 to his opposite shoulder. This time, there would be no blithe wave as the driver gunned the *songtaew* past the checkpoint. We were going to be searched.

The driver braked, shut off the engine, climbed out of the cab, pulled out a cigarette. His slamming door rang in the sudden silence. A silvery female voice floated out of the guardhouse radio, a melodious lament of a lover lost. Intertwining with wood smoke rising from the chimney, it evaporated in the towering trees.

The policemen, M-16's slung over their camouflaged combat fatigues, walked with the calm assurance of absolute authority, heels scuffing the mud. One talked with the driver in a low, flat voice; the other positioned himself at the tailgate, examining the contents of a tattered burlap bag a tribesmen had tossed on the litter-strewn floor. When he looked up to ask the tribesman a question, he spotted me and stepped back, momentarily confused. He recovered his composure and, forgetting the bag, asked me in Thai where I was going. His tone suggested he was not expecting an answer, and I found it expedient to forget I spoke his language.

"Muang Na," the driver said helpfully, adding "he speaks Thai," as if to clear himself of any complicity since he was not sure what I was up to either.

"Oh? Why there?" the policeman asked, swelling perceptibly, secure in the knowledge that he could interrogate me in a familiar language.

"To visit a friend," I replied with a non-committal smile.

"What's his name?"

"Ca-Ui."

"Second name?"

"He doesn't have one. He's a Musur (hunter, the name by which ethnic Thais refer to Lahu tribesmen)."

The policeman, clearly dubious, turned to the other passengers. "Anybody know this Ca-Ui?"

The tribesmen, few of whom spoke Thai, shuffled uneasily for a moment before someone volunteered that he thought he knew him. "He lives in Muang Na Tai (south Muang Na)."

When I had met him two years earlier, Ca-Ui was working in Chiang Mai for a friend who assured me that he would be a good guide through the northern hills. Ca-Ui had gone home to reap Muang Na's winter rice but I had no idea if I might find him there. My explanation seemed to satisfy the policeman but he wanted to see some identification. I pulled my passport and residence permit from my beltbag. He ignored the passport but seemed intrigued by the lifetime residence permit with the gold royal *garuda* (a mythical bird associated with Vishnu, and symbolic of Thai royalty) emblazoned on its hard cover. Foreigners with Thai residence permits are rare but to the guard–who had apparently never seen one–it suggested that I was someone important or that I had special connections.

"Are you an official?" he asked.

"More or less," I answered.

In that case, I was somebody else's responsibility and he was off the hook. A foreigner on this road, speaking Thai and carrying an official document had to be legit. He didn't even look at me as he handed it back and, in the same motion, signaled the second policeman to raise the barrier. As we resumed our tortured journey, I breathed normally again.

In the monsoon-softened red clay goo, passing tires had imprinted deep ruts like negative train tracks. The driver continually spun the wheel to avoid melding with them or sliding over the cliff. Visible on the downside of the road, were the remains of a truck crumpled like foil around a huge boulder. Above it, as if in compensation, was a stunning archipelago of mountain peaks floating in a cerulean sky. On their precipitous, moss-green flanks limestone encrustations jutted like brown watchtowers. As we descended into the valley, the peaks' long shadows reached across the floor to touch a thin, silver ribbon winding among rice paddies yellowing in the dying sun. The Ping, the river of my quest.

When the tribesmen disembarked at a small settlement, I moved to the front seat, listening as the driver discussed directions with the townspeople, most of whom stared at me, mouths agape. Nobody could agree on the exact location of Muang Na Tai; some pointed up the road and others indicated a spot barely discernable on the opposite hill. Night was coming and the village had no inns. "Let's continue until we find something recognizable," I suggested. This was normally the driver's last stop and it was obvious from his fatigue-lined face that he wanted to get rid of me and head back to Chiang Mai, but he shifted into gear and we pulled away.

In the next village was a checkpoint manned by a half dozen soldiers. Even worse than police, soldiers could simply order me out without any formalities or appeals. But they were busy talking and we passed unnoticed.

Farther on, I spotted an opening between the houses and a dirt track threading across the valley floor towards the silver ribbon. "Could that be it?" I asked, pointing to a distant hillside where tan squares of brown thatched roofs dotted the green. Without answering, he turned right and the pickup trundled down the hill. At the stream, the driver shut off the engine. I took this as a signal that we'd arrived. "The Ping?" I asked. He shrugged; he drove on roads, streams had no meaning for him.

I paid him and watched him drive away trailing city sounds, leaving me to enjoy the evening's quiet. Ravens wheeled among powder puff clouds, their cries mingling with those of children at play in the village above me.

The stream seemed so small, barely burbling over brown-and-gray-striped pebbles whose every striation was visible beneath the clear water. But the map insisted that this was the Ping. On smooth stones forming a causeway, I took six hops and began climbing the dirt track.

Like many hilltribe villages, Muang Na Tai was a half-hearted concession to settled life by a nomadic people who for centuries had ignored national boundaries. They wandered through Burma, Thailand, Laos, and southern China in search of land on which to plant corn and upland rice. They carved it from virgin rainforest, felling trees and burning undergrowth, the "slash and burn" method of cultivation common among primitive peoples. Once the soil's fertility was exhausted, they abandoned their makeshift houses to trek over new hills to find fresh land.

Many historians claim that proto-Thais migrated south from China's Yunnan province around 1,000 A.D. Population pressures and Genghis Khan's Mongol armies pushed them into remote valleys in northern Thailand. In the 13th century, their leaders established the Sukhothai kingdom in the upper Chao Phya Valley and laid the foundations for the modern Thai nation.

The six main tribal groups didn't arrive until the 20th century. Professing allegiance to nothing but their stomachs, the Lahu had arrived via Burma, seeking forests to hunt and land to till. Calling themselves, "children of blessing" their lives were anchored in dozens of complex rituals designed to ensure continuance of that blessing through good health, long life, wealth, and numerous children.

The tribes' disregard for borders and forests had led the Thai government to insist that they settle permanently, setting up hamlets for them in the 1960s. The tribes' idea of farming was to grow opium, thereby creating a major headache for government administrators. Rather than punish them, King Bhumibol offered technical and marketing assistance to encourage them to cultivate more socially acceptable (and ultimately more lucrative, since the opium warlords kept most of the profits) crops like mushrooms, peas, strawberries, coffee, and other produce never before grown in Thailand. Nonetheless, many still farmed secret plots of opium for their own use.

The change to a blander lifestyle was reflected in their clothes. Women had once worn black blouses and skirts marked by broad red, horizontal stripes, the vests festooned with silver ornaments. Now, these bright costumes were reserved for festive occasions. For daily tasks, women wore blue blouses and black sarongs. The men dressed in faded black pants and dark shirts.

Like its neighbors, Muang Na Tai looked undecided about the benefits of domestication, displaying the impermanent mien common to nomads rooted against their will in a single site. A tribal settlement was little more than a cluster of woven bamboo walls anchored by stout columns and capped by grass roofs grayed by rain. Raised waist-high above the ground on short stilts, the houses resembled shy maidens about to lift their skirts and scamper on stubby legs into the hills.

I climbed the path between plots of pea plants poking their heads above protective blankets of straw. At the top, I entered a broad expanse of hard earth, a communal meeting ground of some kind. Boys kicked a ragged soccer ball across the sun-hardened clay and children squabbled over a game played with rubber bands. Women staggered under clay pots of water hauled from a nearby pond. The older men were nowhere in sight.

The adults and children ignored me; I was an apparition, invisible to all, an odd reception since I had attracted so much attention in the lower village.

"Where can I find Ca-Ui?" I asked.

They halted their game and looked at each other, speaking an alien language. Of course, I thought, none speaks central Thai; they're shy about responding. But someone had caught the name "Ca-Ui", and pointed down a path. I walked to the house but nobody was home. To an elderly woman at a neighboring house I pantomimed "where is he?" and pointed to Ca-Ui's locked door. With her left hand, she grasped an imaginary bundle, and with her right hand made short circular motions parallel to the ground. Ca-Ui was harvesting rice. But where? She shrugged.

Dropping my pack on Ca-Ui's porch, I climbed to the top of the village. From a tired bamboo pole, a soiled, gauze prayer flag inscribed with black, mystical letters snapped and popped in the brisk breeze. I scanned the roof ridges. In ethnic Thai villages, the headman's house would normally be the most affluent-looking but there was a curious uniformity to Muang Na's houses. Neither was there a Buddhist temple; since the Lahu were animists, most houses would contain shrine rooms filled with ancestral bones.

Scanning an adjacent valley beyond the rooftops, my eye was arrested by movement in a yellow field that could only be people harvesting rice. I glanced at the mountains to see that the sun was nearly gone. A tropical evening does not fade gently as in northern climes but is an unromantic custodian of the hours, compelling darkness to descend like a black curtain, ending the day in a matter of minutes. I would have to move quickly.

Zigzagging down the hill between stands of elephant grass and hopping over a rushing brook, I climbed a bluff tonsured by bamboo trees to arrive at a patchwork of golden stubble gridded by low, grass-covered earthen walls. A procession of straw figures with human heads and legs–men buried in tall bundles of rice stalks–moved across the open ground towards a mountainous haystack on the edge of the threshing floor. When they were thoroughly dry the rice straw ropes fastening each bundle would be loosened; threshing would coax the stalks to release the fat golden seeds burdening their flowering heads.

Emerging from a clump of trees, Ca-Ui saw me and whooped. With a big smile on his handsome face, he trotted up to me.

"Are we going to do it?" he asked in Thai. When two years earlier I had told him my plans, he had asked to go with me. I nodded, adding, "but first we have to find the river's source." He frowned momentarily but said nothing, brightening when I said we would then head south, "to Chiang Dao, if necessary".

"That could be 40 miles," he said. "It's jungle most of the way. We'll have to sleep in the open."

"No problem," I replied.

"When do we leave?"

"Tomorrow morning. Can?"

"Can," he replied.

Our conversation carried us up the hill and into the village. While Ca-Ui organized dinner, I looked around his house. It was a dwelling on its way to becoming a home, like a shambling youth entertaining the idea of combing his hair and spiffing up his clothes. Typical of tribal houses, it comprised two woven bamboo buildings–a living area and a small kitchen–set on three-foot-high log columns and linked by a wide wooden verandah. In many cultures, men are barred from the kitchen but although they tittered as they shot shy glances at me, the women seemed not to mind my presence. On one end, an open fire smoldered, its smoke seeped through the roof thatch. Pots and pans hung on pegs along the walls. Women got to sleep around the fire, stoking it through the cold night. They, of course, also cooked and did the heavy chores so the benefits of gender were not as attractive as they might first appear.

The wide, unroofed verandah served as a workplace and meeting area. The living quarters were raised 18 inches higher so that the feet of those walking on the verandah would not be above the head of someone sleeping inside. In a culture that regards the head as sacred and the feet as filthy, this arrangement overcame a potential insult of enormous magnitude. Built of two thick teak planks hinged, hasped, and hung with a lock, the narrow door opened into a large room which, like the kitchen, was enclosed by windowless, split-bamboo walls. Sunlight forced its way between the bamboo slats; a sooty kerosene lamp illuminated it at night. To one side, a small bedroom was partially shielded from prying eyes by a dingy curtain hanging limply from a wire strung across the doorway.

Furnishings were limited to the straw mats on which family members slept, each covered by a single thin blanket. A trunk against one wall held their clothes. Two walls were festooned with baskets, tools, and farm implements. No attempt had been made to beautify it nor to make it more comfortable. "Home" meant walls and a roof to shelter one from the rain; nothing more.

The gloominess was offset by a wonderful feature that melded the house with its environment. Hinged at the top, the two long walls could be propped open by stout sticks to admit the breeze on hot days. The side facing the houseyard allowed the owner to monitor movements around the front gate and the other side opened on superb views of the valley and the distant hills. Now, as the day was ending, families sat cracking castor bean shells and enjoying the last light.

Sun-crowned peaks glowed like beacons over darkened valleys now faintly blurred by the blue smoke of cooking fires. A full moon was rising above the far rim as Ca-Ui brought in two plates of sticky rice and dried, salted fish. In Central Thailand, fluffy white rice is the staple food. In the North and the Northeast, it is a glutinous, or sticky, variety. We sat on the floor, talking of life in Muang Na. Ca-Ui was an uncomplicated man, seemingly at peace with himself and the world. He'd seen the big towns and wasn't impressed.

"Good for making money but also good for spending it," he laughed, "here is better." It was hard to disagree. Life in Muang Na flowed at a languid pace, the seasons regulated by the sun and the rains according to a predictable, comforting pattern. "I spent 18 months in Chiang Rai," he said, shaking his head in disbelief. "If I could make money here, I'd never go to town." Though I nodded in agreement, I wondered how long I would be able to contemplate the mountains and rivers in a village setting. I was too restless, needed too much external stimulation to sit in one place for long.

We talked until the late hour of 9 p.m., normal bedtime in a Thai village. I was a city boy, seldom in bed before 11 p.m. and too excited about the coming day to be sleepy. As the village bedded down for the night, I sat on the verandah hugging my knees to keep warm. Far below, ground fog was phosphored by the moonlight giving the valley an ethereal, dream-like quality, the perfect setting for contemplating the adventure that lay before me. No more languishing in Bangkok, speculating blindly about the journey's feasibility. After so many years, I was about to embark. The moon watched me silently, distantly. And–it seemed– doubtfully.

The Spirit That Stops Clocks

Jab Maew Jaew Rua, Jab Sua Thai Naa
(To force the cat to row the boat
To make the tiger plow the field)
Don't force someone do something
he doesn't want to do

Slivers of pale light were squeezing through the split bamboo wall when I awoke. Throughout the night, the porous walls and the cracks between the wooden floor boards had admitted every chill gust blowing across the valley penetrating my sleeping bag as if it were mesh. Although it was only 40 degrees, I kept adding pieces of clothing and, when I had emptied my pack, stuffed my feet into it but could not get warm. More than once I wished I were a woman so I could sleep by the fire.

Through the night, moonbeams piercing the tattered thatch roof had dappled the floor in whitewash puddles. By dawn, the sieve-like roof was admitting fat drops of dew which splattered on my head and soaked my sleeping bag making a frosty night even colder. No wonder the villagers were early risers.

I emerged into a village enveloped in a sea of white, the trees dripping as though after a heavy storm. Audible deep in the fog-cloaked hillsides were the bells worn by invisible cows. Wrapped in thin blankets, tribesmen huddled over straw fires, absorbing their heat, blinking smoke-stung eyes, waiting for the sun to melt the frozen sky. Noisy children darted out of the murk, teeth chattering, to warm themselves before dashing away, swallowed up by the mist, their laughter ringing out from nowhere. A pretty brindle mongrel with fur too short for winter shivered with the rest of us.

Several neighbors squatted on our porch, chewing the ends of twigs until they shredded, and with them, brushing their teeth. The saliva was aimed into cracks between the thick, rough-hewn wooden planks, where in the stygian darkness below, chickens scratched and pigs rooted noisily. Softening the grayness was the scent of burning pine from the kitchen stoves; the smoke percolated through the thatched roofs like rain evaporating in a hot sun.

Breakfast was the same dried fish and glutinous rice of the previous night. Since rice is invariably sprinkled with a liberal dose of the small pebbles that always seemed to leap off the threshing floor, I chewed gingerly, waiting to hear a tooth shatter on an unyielding stone. We ate, more to acquire the food's warmth than to satisfy hunger.

Addressing the rice he was kneading into small balls, northern style, Ca-Ui said, "I don't know the way to the headwaters." I was startled, not by his ignorance but by his confession. Unwilling to admit a lack of knowledge, Thai guides had often told me what I wanted to hear, and prayed for a miracle to bail them out. When providence failed them, they were surprised to find me more annoyed than if they had simply confessed beforehand.

Taken aback, I readily agreed to Ca-Ui's suggestion that we hire another, more knowledgeable, Lahu. In the circumlocution that serves to ameliorate an unpleasant situation, what Ca-Ui actually said was: "We could take along a friend so we would have someone to talk with as we walked." Couched so charmingly, how could I refuse? We'd already agreed that Ca-Ui would receive 200 *baht* ($8) per day plus food. Ca-Hpeu, he said, would be more than happy with 100 *baht* and food. Neither expense would put a serious dent in my budget. Besides, if the two of them were talking, I'd be free to study my surroundings without seeming impolite.

Unlike the husky Ca-Ui, Ca-Hpeu was wiry, bandy-legged, and spoke no Thai. They made an odd pair, the larger one listening attentively to the diminutive one describing how we would proceed. When they talk, Lahus sound like they are laughing. Half-listening to them, I watched the brindle bitch I'd thought so pretty wash my breakfast plate.

By mid-morning, the sun had boiled away the mist. Men lounged in small groups chatting, and women slipped tumplines across their foreheads and hoisted heavy baskets to their backs, the first of many they would tote to the market across the valley. Ca-Ui, Ca-Hpeu, and I filled our packs with dried fish and glutinous rice wrapped in banana leaves.

The Ping's headwaters lay a day north. Two other men tagged along, curious to see what the foreigner was up to. Or perhaps to safeguard us in these hostile hills. Long knives hung from leather waist thongs and the heavy shoulder bags bulged with what I assumed were guns.

At the edge of the valley, we passed through Muang Na Nua (northern Muang Na), the last outpost on Thai territory; over the ridge lay Burma. Two stout bunkers reinforced with concrete blocks served as vantage points up the path leading to the border, suggesting that insurgency was not unknown.

Half an hour later, the jungle swallowed the path and the breeze-blown bamboos creaked like ethereal doors. Conversation quieted and the men watched the slopes for signs of movement. There was a better trail higher up the hill but "we don't want to be up there," Ca-Ui said. Strangers who stumbled upon opium or heroin mule trains were often killed. Too much money was at stake for the warlords to be squeamish about dispatching would-be informers. As a consequence, we struggled through shoulder-height brush that shushed like a rushing stream, the thorns tearing clothes and bare arms, negating any attempts at concealment. Ten minutes later, a man higher on the hill shouted in a hoarse whisper that could be heard for some distance. We clambered up to find him standing with a puzzled expression next to a concrete post. It took a moment to realize that it was a border marker and we were looking at it from the wrong side. A few steps put us back in Thailand, heading along a ridgetop with a spectacular view into an uninhabited Burmese valley.

Shortly before noon, we reached the Ping, crashing down a steep slope. An hour's climb along its banks brought us to a waterfall spattering into a pool it had sculpted in large plates of smooth black rock. The men in the lead hunkered down to inspect something. Pocking the rock's pig iron surface were a half dozen large holes like those left by trees incinerated in a lava flow. The tribesmen seemed to regard them with some awe.

"*Teen Chang*. The footprints of ancient elephants," Ca-Ui said softly as though fearful of offending someone. "Powerful spirits."

With solemn ceremony, they placed lighted candles along the "footprint" rims while they prayed to hovering spirits to protect them. I did the same.

The waterfall flowed copiously over a ledge 70 feet above the pool, the thin rope of water hinting at the nearness of the headwaters. Savoring the tang of discovery, I began climbing the rock face framing the waterfall, grabbing for handholds on the water-polished stone heading for what I imagined would be a spring bubbling out of the ground.

Nearing the top, I realized that the tribesmen were still below, huddled beside the pool, regarding me silently.

"What's the problem?" I called down to Ca-Ui.

"It's dangerous," he said above the water's din.

"How so?" I asked, puzzled. The rocks looked solid enough. What could be dangerous?

"The warlords have mined the upper riverbed."

"Why?" I demanded, unwilling to believe that something so beautiful could be threatening.

"To keep the Border Patrol Police from following them into Burma. This is an opium route. I'd come back down if I were you."

I now understood the reason for Ca-Ui's frown when I had suggested tracing the river to its source. Damn. So close it was tantalizing. Thailand is awash in rumors; should I listen or risk it? I looked up the rock face for long moments, weighing, considering.

It wasn't worth it. The Lahus had shown no reluctance to forge ahead when they encountered other obstacles, so they must know what they were talking about. The headwaters weren't worth the price of a leg. I banged my fist gently against the rock in frustration, and then worked my way back down. There was no point in getting angry, I reasoned, but a residue of irritation simmered. The impotence of not being on top of a situation is familiar to anyone living in a country not his own.

Seated by the "elephant footprints," I watched the water hurtle by me on its long journey to the sea. Like an infant, a stream gives little hint of its potential. It flows swiftly, full of itself, heedless of obstacles, unconcerned that it might disappear into the ground a few miles on or be absorbed into a larger river. Like a salmon in reverse, it knows only its distant objective, blindly moving towards it until, engorged, it is swallowed by the sea. Here, it was untamed, untainted, innocent of a wider world.

What lay ahead was a mystery. I knew I'd have to walk down it until, thickened by tributary streams, it was deep enough to float a boat. I slipped my hand into its cold, rushing waters, letting them buffet my fingers, feeling its strength. I formed my fingers into a cup, raised it to my lips and drank deeply as a symbolic token of the start of a journey. Then, rejoining the others , I set off on the path that would lead us back to Muang Na Tai.

It was late afternoon before we reached Ca-Ui's home. The sky was free of clouds and the valley was bathed in a warm autumnal light. Each year when the monsoon rains washed the sky and land of dust, it was as if cataracts had been stripped from one's eyes. Contours were sharply etched and colors were rich. Now that the rain clouds had exhausted their cargoes, the hills were solid green blocks towering over golden rice squares, the warm browns of bamboo house walls set against the rust red soil, all under a vault of Dutch blue. Winter is a rare and all-too-short season in the tropics, one to be savored like a deeply-drawn breath of mountain air.

"Let's take a bath," Ca-Ui suggested. With sarongs and towels, we walked down a gently-sloping lane, threading a corridor bounded by split bamboo fences set vertically to protected gardens from marauding goats and pigs. Villagers had tapped the Ping a mile upstream to flow along a high ridge and into Muang Na Tai. The technique had eliminated the risk of encountering the bad spirits the Lahus believe infest rivers. Halfway down the hill, the stream cascaded into a pond, a natural shower in the communal bathtub and laundromat. Pegged to the banks, worn boards lightly slimed by algae projected over the water. On them sarong-wrapped women squatted, scrubbing and rinsing clothes, detergent foam clouding the water. As the stream exited the pool it frothed with suds, a gift to the next village along the Ping's course.

Ignoring and being ignored by the bare-breasted women and splashing children, we toweled off and returned to Ca-Ui's house to look at my maps. Produced by the U.S. Air Force during the Vietnam war, they had been re-issued with minor updates by the Thai Army. No roads built in the intervening 20 years had been recorded and villages seemed to have been chosen at random. Because the military mappers were interested in land routes they had devoted little attention to rivers. A village name appeared here and there along the river but on a 1:250,000 scale, half a dozen miles separated the dots.

The idea of using a two-dimensional sheet of paper to represent topography was novel to the tribes. Ca-Ui and Ca-Hpeu clucked and sighed, struggling to translate squiggly lines and varying colors into terrain and contours. We would travel by feel anyway, working our way down the valleys, following the stream's flow.

Dinner was rice and rocks, fish and eggs. I had vowed to eat what the villagers ate but it was obvious their choice was dictated by budget and availability. While they looked healthy, I knew that most of them suffered from stomach ailments. How long would my metabolism stand up to such a meager diet? It might be wise to carry a few high-nutrition health supplements.

After dinner, we retired to the verandah and two of Ca-Ui's children plopped down either side of him, sitting cross-legged like their father.

"How many do you have?" I asked.

"Five," adding "by the same wife."

He readily talked about his sons and daughters, but when I asked about his wife, he became reticent. Twice during the day, his attention had wandered and he'd been terse in his replies. Something told me not to press him. To my surprise, my silence prompted a torrent of words delivered with a scowl.

"When I came back from Chiang Rai, I found out she'd been sleeping with other men," he said. "She'd also become an opium smoker and a liar. And a thief," he spat out. As he talked, he poked a stick at the floor planks with a vehemence to match his words. His candor and sharpness were unusual; Thais normally papered over their difficulties with a smile. His objections seemed odd since he earlier intimated he had been dallying with the women of Chiang Rai. But in a male-oriented society, a double standard was in force and her behavior was unacceptable.

"A bad woman," he concluded, disgustedly. "Marriage is stupid. It just costs money, and all for nothing. Being single is better."

This was a side of Ca-Ui I'd not seen. Obviously, there was turmoil beneath that placid, sunny exterior. I'd do well to tread lightly.

A long night lay ahead. The village lacked electricity and the winter sun set at 5:45. The kerosene lamp's feeble flame barely lit the interior. The lamp–a wick jammed in an old medicine bottle–was a mixed blessing, pouring forth as much thick, inky smoke as light. The smoke cloyed, made me cough and coated the bamboo and thatch roof—and likely my lungs—with lampblack.

As I unpacked, several children silently filtered in and gathered around me. Shy, they whispered their questions to a teenage girl student who conveyed them to me. The questions were those asked by Asians elsewhere: What was my name, my country, my job, was I married, how much money did I earn, how much did my pack, my book, my camera cost? The lamplight caught their rapt faces and bright eyes as they hung on every word. When I asked them about school or family members, all heads swiveled as they fixed their eyes on the girl. Hands shielding mouths, they giggled and consulted with each other before answering.

Gradually, I filled in a picture of a village to which change was coming slowly but inexorably. Most children had four or five brothers and sisters. A few traveled across the valley to school, studying up to the sixth grade; only a few teenagers had made it as far south as Chiang Mai. They liked Thai pop singers on the radio, knew Thai film stars and were both intrigued by and frightened of the big cities. They'd likely heard stories of village girls taking jobs as waitresses and being lured into prostitution. Less educated than their lowland sisters, hilltribe girls were particularly susceptible to procurers, their innate trust leading them to believe the job offers were sincere. Within a few years, AIDS would become a full-blown epidemic in the North with the brunt of the attack borne by the tribes. So rampant would it become that some experts would predict the tribes' eventual extinction.

When they ran out of questions, I began writing the day's events in my journal. They knelt in a circle around me, elbows on the floor, chins in their cupped hands, watching fascinated as my pen scratched strange curlicues. A few knew some English but my handwriting is so bad that only occasionally would they recognize a word. Then would come an excited whispering of the sound or an argument over correct pronunciation; always subdued, always respectful. Each time I emptied my glass, it was silently refilled with bitter Chinese tea, the leaves swirling in the glass. The scene, the children, and the smell of the lamp carried me back 20 years to nights in my Nepalese village where I read by the light of a kerosene lamp as the children tugged at my book to get a better look.

Eventually, they drifted away to bed. It had been years since I'd slept on a floor; the wooden boards seemed to have become harder. I knew I would adjust in a day or so, but I spent a fitful hour before dozing off, disturbed not by noise but by the absence of it. I blew out the lamp and discovered the room zebra-striped and spotted. Stepping onto the verandah, I found the moon dusting the grass roofs and ground with snow. A few howling dogs and crickets of every pitch were competing for the airwaves. It had been a good day. At last, I knew something about the Ping, had a real picture to replace all the imaginings. Tomorrow, to give dimension to those images, I would trace the river's southward path to the sea.

Like crystal prisms, the diamond dewdrops hanging in trailside cobwebs sparkled as Ca-Ui, Ca-Hpeu and I dropped down the hill out of Muang Na Tai and moved across the valley. The road led directly to the army outpost. Only as we were approaching it did Ca-Hpeu mention that he had gone the previous evening to talk with the soldiers.

"They told me not to leave the village," he announced.

"What?" Lulled by the beauty, Ca-Hpeu's words startled me. "Why?"

"King's birthday."

Of course. December 5th, a national holiday. This year was special because King Bhumibol had turned sixty, completing his fifth twelve-year cycle. It was an auspicious year in a Thai's life, the year in which a man retired to enjoy the fruits of his toils, letting the children he had labored to support, support him. So the soldiers' objection to our traveling was minor. Or was it?

"If they wanted us to stay put, why are we leaving?" I wondered aloud.

"You're a *farang* (foreigner)." Ca-Hpeu was a man of maddeningly few words.

"So?"

"You can change their minds." George Orwell in his short story "Shooting an Elephant " talked of the expectations Asians had of the foreigners' abilities to accomplish miracles and of the problems this often caused. I hoped Ca-Hpeu was right.

In Thai fashion, we did not directly confront the soldiers; just let them know we were in the vicinity. Under their watchful eyes, we bought supplies at a general store. It may have been national day of rejoicing but the store owners had not allowed royal pomp to interfere with commerce.

The shop had been hammered together from unfinished wooden planks. Like 19th century American stores, the proprietor served his customers, handing us rice and foodstuffs taken from rough shelves across the back wall. Packets of laundry detergent, snacks, dried meats, crispy bacon rind and even children's toys dangled from threads hung from the glassless front window like a beaded curtain. Ca-Ui chose rice, egg noodles, canned fish, a dozen red and green chilies, and a box of matches.

After paying, Ca-Ui and I strolled across to the guardpost. The soldiers invited us to sit down while one went to find the commander. Spotting Ca-Hpeu lingering by the store, they beckoned him over. It was obvious that we had not heeded their instructions.

Ca-Ui did not help matters by fidgeting. One soldier casually asked where we were going and why. Ca-Ui faltered for a moment, our reason for the journey suddenly sounding implausible under interrogation. As the silence began to lengthen, I quietly continued the explanation. My interruption, in Thai, had an immediate effect on the soldiers. Their tension dissipated, their boots scuffing on the wooden floor as they relaxed, the air suddenly more breathable. What I said seemed less important than that I was saying it in their language. They began asking about our itinerary, but casually, not as a formal interrogation.

By the time the lieutenant arrived, the ice had been broken. He gruffly asked the same questions but Ca-Ui had no sooner begun to explain when the soldiers began stumbling over each other to give us a handsome introduction. The lieutenant turned to me.

"What are your plans?" he asked.

In reply, I took out my maps. Although available to anyone for a small fee, few civilians knew of their existence. Their appearance seemed to give me a special imprime which I found useful to exploit. And once again, the residence permit had the desired effect.

The lieutenant spread out my map among cups of tea that had appeared on the table. Glancing out the window, he aligned the map according to the topography. At the far end of the valley, the Ping disappeared into the trees. We worked out the path we must take to reach it. If there had been real opposition to our departing on this auspicious day it was no longer apparent.

But the lieutenant hadn't forgotten.

"Why did you choose today to start?" Since he asked the question conversationally, I decided to be very Thai.

"Today is the King's birthday," I said solemnly. "By beginning what will undoubtedly be a momentous journey on his birthday I am honoring him."

They bought it. The lieutenant had no objections, only a warning.

"Be on the alert for robbers. Don't be afraid to use your guns," he said.

"Uh, we don't have any," I said. Remembering yesterday's bulge in the bag, I glanced at Ca-Ui, wondering if, in fact, we did.

The soldiers looked at each other. "No weapons whatever?" the officer asked, frowning.

"Some long knives. And a pocket knife."

The lieutenant looked at the ground. Uh, oh, I thought. I held my breath as he looked at me and then at Ca-Ui.

"Then, be smart. If you hear someone coming or hear gunshots, move off the path and into the jungle. Don't ask for trouble."

He signaled to one of the soldiers to return my residence permit.

"Good luck," he said with a rueful smile.

I ruminated over the latest information as we exited the guardpost. Guns? I thought we only had to worry about gunmen along the border. I quelled a rising anxiety.

As we descended into the valley, the air seemed so benign that I soon forgot my concern. The path wound between split rail fences enclosing corn fields and an occasional hut. A few miles on, the fences were replaced by tall elephant grass bearing fat fluffy flywhisk heads. An hour later, as the sun-drenched sky clouded and the air turned cold, we rounded a bend. Blocking our path was the Ping.

Although shin deep and 20 feet wide, human hands had already interrupted it. Having driven a two-foot-tall line of bamboo stakes across the flow, a family was now toiling to fill the upstream side with stones. From the resultant reservoir, they would cut a small channel to lead water to a field they had carved from the thick forest. I realized I was gazing on living history.

The weir-based irrigation system called *muang fai* had originated 2,000 years ago in southern China. A thousand years later, it had been carried into northern Thailand, ultimately forming the basis for the modern Thai political system. Until the mid-20th century, the *hua na fai* or weir administrator had been the most powerful man in the village. He adjudicated water disputes, conducted spirit propitiation rites, and determined the amount of each villager's annual corvee labor contribution to repair the weirs and channels. Laws written on the same palm leaves as Buddhist scriptures dictated punishments for misdeeds like accidentally destroying the dams or their protective spirit houses, or allowing one's cows or elephants to stray into them. Water theft was considered a crime against society, much as cattle or horse rustling was regarded in the American West. If a farmer caught a neighbor channeling into his fields more than his allotted share of water, he could kill him and be exonerated by the law.

Overpopulation had changed public perceptions. Thirty years ago, this family would have been regarded as hardy pioneers, hacking a livelihood from the pestilential jungle. Now, driven here by a search for land, they were regarded as illegal squatters. Government attempts to remove them had divided Thai society. Some felt that biodiversity–the small amounts that hadn't already been obliterated by dams and developers– was being compromised by migrants concerned only with their own interests. Other critics centered on alleviating immediate needs and felt that poor people were being sacrificed to national policies formulated by uncaring urban officials.

Leaving these pioneers/desecrators to their labors, we reached the hills at the lower end of the valley. In its long journey, the Ping winds through a series of valleys separated by mountain walls, what boaters call a "pool and drop" topography. To a bird, the terrain resembled stairsteps, the river meandering along a flat valley, then rushing down a deep V-notch gorge into the next valley. We now entered one of these thickly-treed canyons.

Like most rainforests, its vegetation varied enormously. The dominant teak trees shared space with semi-tropical montane varieties like Ironwood, Coffinwood, Rosewood, Blackwood, *Takhien, Shirea, Turpinia, Lac,* and a dozen dipterocarps whose rotor-bladed seed pods helicopter the seeds to new homes in distant glades. Trees 100 feet tall shared space with creepers, chest-high brush, vines, rattan lianas, the pale green-hair of Spanish moss; wild orchids and rusty bracket fungi clung to their trunks.

Like most tropical species, the trees did not agree on what constituted "autumn" and dropped their leaves at differing times. The forest floor was carpeted in moldering leaves, including teak leaves two feet long.

The trail zigzagged back and forth across the river as though it had been scraped by meandering cattle. After entering and exiting the river more than 30 times–each time removing my shoes–I switched to rubber sandals. The Ping broadened and deepened and by noon, my pants were wet to the crotch.

The surging water was beginning to feel less like a brook and more like a river. The soil along the banks was soft, the accumulated leaves and duff of a thousand years. It was easy to picture gigantic reptiles stalking through the dank tropical forest, their great feet tamping the Carboniferous forest into oil, peat, then anthracite.

To my surprise, aside from a few bird calls and rustling leaves, the jungle was bereft of natural sound. At intervals, gunshots, unnerving in the silence, emanated from the thick tangle of trees. Despite our caution, we eventually stumbled into trouble. Rounding a bend, we came face to face with two hunters, both of them carrying long, slender rifles which they lowered to point at us. When Ca-Ui began speaking in Lahu, the men shouldered their guns and dropped to their haunches to chat.

As they talked, one reloaded, dropping a cap down the barrel followed by gunpowder, and by ball shot. He then tamped it with a ramrod, technology as antique as the concept of a rifle. It was as if I had stumbled across two pilgrim fathers in a Pennsylvania wood.

"Have they shot any game today?" I asked.

"There's nothing to shoot, only birds."

I had read of tigers, deer, elephants, wild boar and dozens of other mammals populating the Thai forests in the 1920s, providing travelers with their chief source of food. Now, except for a few isolated pockets along the borders, they had been hunted to extinction.

At points, the path entered stands of bamboo which appeared to have been flattened by a giant foot, hundreds of trees, each shattered and split into a dozen strands, broken at waist height. To pass, we had to duck walk for 300 feet at a time. I felt like the hunchbacked crone in Hansel and Gretel's forest.

When the trail disappeared entirely, we walked down the riverbed. Underwater stones, now slicked with slime and obscured by the shadows of the forest canopy, robbed us of firm footing. We blundered on, stumbling and sliding. Within an hour, my feet were cut and bruised with dark blue patches that oozed blood. Not an auspicious start.

By mid-afternoon, the sun had already set in the deep ravines.

"Ca-Hpeu is not sure how far we are from Baan Pong Ang, our night stop," Ca-Ui said uneasily. We discussed our situation and, realizing that our only other option was to camp in the jungle, we decided to push on.

Half an hour later, we emerged into the bright sunlight. Just downriver a fisherman in patterned pants was winding a net around his forearm. As we drew closer, however, I saw that below his short pants his bare legs were black with tiny tattoos laid down in thick rows like needle-point patterns which time and imperfect needles had smudged.

"He's a Palaung," Ca-Ui replied to my quizzical look. Palaungs were a minor tribe, of which only two settlements remained in northern Thailand.

"Why the tattoos?" I asked.

"Protection," he replied. "Sometimes they cover the entire body." Like medallions to Catholics, the tattoos protected their wearers, their potency emanating from the animal exemplifying that quality. For example, invincibility came from the gall bladder of a Slow Loris monkey–considered extremely difficult to kill–whose gall was mixed into the ink injected to create the tattoo.

As we passed, the Palaung planted his legs on the bank, twisting his torso back and forth like a discus thrower. With a mighty swing, he released a seine net that arced over the water and dropped in a circle, the weighted rim smacking the water with a light "plack". As he carefully pulled the pursed net from the water, sunlight flashed on the silver sides of struggling fish no longer than six inches. A few steps down the path, we startled a cloud of backlit yellow butterflies, brilliant against the dark green jungle. I was at peace. This was the Thailand I had come to see: pristine, beautiful.

As we moved from a defile of tall grasses and into a bamboo grove, we were startled by rustling to our left. We froze, listening intently. A wizened old man with silver hair, more an apparition than a person, emerged. Ca-Ui uttered a cry of recognition.

"He's a shaman who lives near our village," he said, advancing towards him. A moment later, a similarly wrinkled woman stepped from the grove. From behind her peeked a small boy, the couple's grandson. The old man dropped his bulky bag on the ground and talked quietly with Ca-Ui.

"He says Pong Ang is three hours down the valley. Maybe we should camp here. It is better if many people sleep together," he said. "Safer."

We set up camp beneath bamboos that rose like cathedral arches 45 feet above our heads. Ca-Ui and Ca-Hpeu unsheathed their long knives. I had watched them sink the 20-inch blades deep into tree trunks to clear a path but now they wielded the swords like surgical knives. They cleared an area of spindly bamboo, laying them on the forest floor to serve as carpeting. Touching a match to dried bamboo leaves cupped in his hands, Ca-Ui blew steadily until the leaves ignited. Placing the glowing leaves on the ground, he built a small enclosure of the dead bamboo logs Ca-Hpeu had hacked into firewood, With a few deft cuts, bamboo saplings were transformed into a rack to dry our wet clothes.

Now came the true artistry. With minimal strokes, the pair felled an arm-thick bamboo at ground level. Two sections became jars which I carried to the river to fill with water. One was placed in the embers as a teapot; the other was set aside as a rice pot. A third section, split lengthwise, was crafted into a curry bowl. A few quick strokes turned the other half into a ladle for stirring the rice. The remainder was whittled into chopsticks.

Glutinous rice was poured into the rice pot; the noodles and fish were prepared in my canteen cup. Into yet another bamboo section, they poured more rice and water. They set this next to the "teapot" to boil *khao lam*. This wonderful dessert, normally sweetened with coconut milk and black beans, became the perfect finale to a delicious meal.

As an encore, they whittled bamboo scraps into toothpicks. I applauded this masterful performance and was rewarded with bashful smiles. As we sipped our tea, I asked Ca-Ui about the old man and his family.

"They spend the winter in the jungle gathering special herbs," Ca-Ui said. As he spoke, the old man pulled one plant after another from the burlap bag. Each tree or shrub had its specific purpose. "The acacia stem heals both wounds and dysentery," he said as he examined a sprig.

"Strange isn't it? And the seeds alleviate scabies." Candlebush leaves healed skin diseases; the boiled stem cured yaws and the roots, bronchitis. Shamans used the roots of the Chung Ching woody climber to treat cerebral malaria while the flowers remedied diseases of the oral and ear cavities. Many plants were reputed to enhance longevity.

It was difficult to attach curative properties to any of them, so ordinary did they look. In these hills where life seemed very basic, it came as a surprise to discover that herbal medicine had a long tradition and a complex pharmacology with highly-refined disease concepts and detailed explanations of the causes and cures of a wide number of ailments. There were even strictures on the proper times for collecting herbs.

"In the cold season like this," the shaman said, "we collect only bark and stems." Collections were regulated to the hours of the day when regenerative sap flowed. In other seasons, six-to-9 a.m. were the hours for collecting leaves, flowers, fruits, and pods, while 9-to-noon was reserved for branches and twigs. On Sundays and Tuesdays, shamans collected herbs to the east of their village while on Thursdays they foraged to the north.

With his silver hair and slow but precise movements, the old man seemed the embodiment of something ancient and arcane, intelligence animating his bright eyes and gentle manner. His paramount role in the village was evident in the way that Ca-Ui and Ca-Hpeu hung on his words, reverently helping him return the herbs to the bag.

The moon's pale blue light now filtering into our bamboo cave contrasted with the orange firelight glowing on the ceiling. Exhausted, we settled in for the night, the silence broken only by the crackling of the fire and the old man's wracking cough.

The not-yet-risen sun was haloing the far ridge at the end of a long night made longer by the moonlight. Sleeping under a full moon may be romantic but the world's largest nightlight interferes with sleep. In wakeful moments, I could hear the old medicine man coughing horribly, each outburst followed by a grating groan to stifle another bout. Would he survive the winter? Perhaps the herbs he sought were to cure himself.

When the sun had risen high enough to touch the steaming river, we bade the shaman and his wife goodbye and set off. Past a waterfall, we entered a treeless tract littered with charred logs and derelict houses.

Timber dealers working in collusion with corrupt officials had shorn huge areas of the North, but it was the tribes that were normally blamed for forest destruction. Somehow, the tribe's clearing land to feed themselves seemed more acceptable than businessmen's destroying them to line their pockets.

It was only part of the disturbing lack of environmental awareness I was encountering. Perhaps I was naïve but I'd thought that environmental destruction was an urban failing. Maybe I assumed that it happened on such a small scale in the hills as to be unnoticeable, yet, already, I was seeing a profligacy in the use of natural resources. Although the morning was already warm, Ca-Ui and Ca-Hpeu had continued to heave logs on the fire as if we were settling in for another day. They threw empty cans into the bushes. Out of habit, I fished them out and dropped them in my pack, and tossed the plastic noodle bags into the fire. Ca-Ui watched me and then put the breakfast debris in his pack, more to mollify me than from environmental awareness. Farther down the trail he would heedlessly flip a spent cigarette packet into the brush.

It was probably a residual habit from the days when garbage was organic and degraded within days. Waste had changed; plastic and metal lasted forever but it was thoughtlessly tossed left and right. It was especially odd because for Thais, personal cleanliness was of paramount importance. In the city, I had long ago given up saying anything, my protests dismissed as *farang* raving or, worse yet, as nagging that ultimately created resentment. I wasn't prepared for pollution in these remote hills but I wasn't going to let it destroy my enjoyment of the landscape.

After a morning of fighting through thick vegetation, we emerged onto a valley so radically altered that I came to a dead halt. The valley spread at my feet was utterly devoid of trees. Instead, fields of ripening rice and corn covered its floor and flanks. Suddenly to move from green to buff was a shock, more so because I had expected to be sheltered by trees for another week. Yet, here, after only two days, we were in cultivated fields.

In the 1920s, Reginald Campbell, an employee of a British timber company, wrote of northern hills covered in teak as far as the eye could see. In his book, *Teak Wallah*, he described hundreds of miles of virgin forests that he and his compatriots were determined to fell as quickly as possible. His tone betrayed a sense of manifest destiny. I wondered what Campbell would have said had he stood with us on the ridge.

Halfway down the valley lay Baan Pong Ang, a clutch of wooden buildings in a hard-scrabble plain dotted with scraggly scrub baking under a sun that seemed to burn with greater intensity. It was so offensive that after pausing for glasses of bitter green tea I suggested that we move on.

Our exit from the village took us along a dirt path hemmed by eight-foot-tall elephant grass that gave me elephantine sneezes. In the next valley, old and new agricultural collided in fields of yellow beans and tobacco. Rototiller engines were lifting river water into a flume made of hollowed-out logs, each section perfectly chamfered to create a watertight fit with the next log. It was pleasing to see the craftsmanship. Once again, I was observing the demise of local technology. Soon farmers would adopt the blue PVC pipes already snaking through the Chiang Mai valley just south of us.

Mid-afternoon, we entered Baan Huai Pao, a village of relative affluence strung along a dirt road. Houses were fronted by proper gardens. Many homes had glass windows and some were painted. In the space of two days we had witnessed the evolution of a Thai village from simple jungle huts to something approaching a town. Ca-Hpeu gawked like a tourist in a big city.

As we emerged from Baan Huai Pao, I began to detect signs of a mutiny. South of the village, a paved road ran across the fields towards a hill. As the road was 300 feet from the river, I turned right and started towards the Ping. A few steps in, I realized that Ca-Ui was still standing on the road.

"Come on," I said, waving him on.

He didn't move. "Why are you going that way?" he asked.

"I want to follow the river."

"But the road is easier," he protested.

"But we came to look at the river," I said.

"You can see it from the road," he persisted, petulantly. "It's harder to walk through the fields," he added. True, but that wasn't the point. But it was equally clear that he wasn't going to budge. And he wasn't prepared to discuss it. What to do?

An outsider can insist on doing things his way but in the end, a local, armed with myriad ways of making life difficult by carping or half-cooperating, always wins. Since I needed Ca-Ui to translate the hilltribe dialects I couldn't fathom it was impossible to continue on my own. In the end, we did it the Thai way; we compromised. Instead of paralleling the river, we would walk across the fields towards a distant hill, crossing the winding river whenever we met it.

After a half hour, however, it became apparent this was not going to work either. The river was now too deep and too swift to cross easily. We altered our path to touch the Ping tangentially at various points so I could observe it. I consoled myself that by now I had seen enough of its character to understand how it behaved. When we again encountered the paved road, we followed it to the town of Mae Ja, arriving just as the sun was setting behind the hills.

One of the pieces of advice Thais had given me was that when seeking rural accommodation, I should start with the *phu yai baan's* (village headman's) house, then the village monastery, then a villager's house, and then, as absolutely the last resort, a police station. The headman was sacrosanct in his village; anyone under his protection was safe from harm. A temple offered no refuge, and an ordinary villager might have his own agenda or be embarrassed by his inability to provide hospitality befitting a guest's status. No explanation was necessary for the police's position at the bottom of the rankings; unless they were personally acquainted, most people simply didn't trust them.

A village headman was not only the village's titular chieftain, he was its prime mover. His title translated literally as the "big man of the village" and in former days, he would have been the scion of the village's most important family. Although in today's democratic society, he was elected from among his peers, he usually descended from the richest family because it gave the village more clout in negotiating with district authorities for development funds. The headman was poorly paid and was required to spend long hours bookkeeping and report filing. Despite the burden, most worked hard, taking pride in their jobs and the progress they brought to their villages. By tradition, the headman was also obliged to entertain visitors, providing food and shelter if necessary.

Mae Ja's headman, however, was not home. His stern wife asked us what we wanted.

"Shelter," Ca-Ui said.

"Why are you here?" she asked.

Ca-Ui explained our mission.

"He's not here," she said.

We discussed our options and decided to wait for him, slumping against a house wall to talk of the day's events. The courtyard was deserted except for a few chickens and a man sweeping it in long, deliberate strokes. I said hello but he did not reply.

Twenty minutes went by before Ca-Ui asked me the plan for the following day. "Keep walking to Chiang Dao," I replied. The by-now-familiar frown flashed briefly.

The sweeper completed his work and leaned the broom against a wall. After washing his hands at the well and drying them on his sarong, he walked slowly across the yard to us. To our surprise, he asked, "Why are you seeking the headman?"

He had been close enough to overhear our conversation with the woman but we repeated it anyway. At the end, he leaned on his broom, lost in thought. "I am the headman," he said at last. "You can sleep in a room in the outer courtyard." He then walked into the house. The look on Ca-Ui's face told me I wasn't the only one jarred by his odd reticence.

His children more than made up for our strange reception. Foreigners were a novelty, those who had walked from Muang Na even more so. The children commented on the distance we had covered and asked what we had seen along the way; a half hour passed pleasantly. Once the family had eaten its dinner, we took over the kitchen. Ca-Ui cooked another noodle, fish, and sticky rice meal that was delicious when washed down with Chinese tea.

It was going to be another cold night. Ca-Ui and I huddled over the map in a circle of lamplight, planning the next day's route. While I was busy plotting a course along the river he was running his finger down the road. Would I have to go through the same nonsense and grumbling as today?

We bedded down in a room separated from the rest of the house by a stout wall. The family bade us good night but we did not see anything more of the headman. When, four months later, I read a brief newspaper article about three men found shot dead for unknown reasons just outside of Mae Ja, I would understand the headman's wariness.

No fog had settled in the valley during the night–a bad sign because it underscored the harm done by deforestation-which meant we could get an early start. Or so I thought.

As we were folding our bedrolls, I heard Ca-Ui's low mutter. There was enough urgency in his tone that I turned to look. He was holding his wrist to his ear and then dropping it to look at his watch.

"It's stopped," he said.

"Yes, I once had one like it," I said. "You have to shake your wrist to wind it."

"No, this is something else."

"What?"

"Bad spirit."

I thought he was joking and laughed. He looked at me, and his face said that levity was uncalled for.

"A spirit has killed the watch."

"Maybe. So?"

"It means someone will be hurt, or will die. The spirit will harm him."

I tried to cajole him but could feel a growing sense of what was coming.

"Sooo, how do we pacify this spirit?" I asked.

"We can't. He's angry over something we've done and we have to stop doing it."

"What might that be?"

"We can't go any farther."

"My watch is fine," I said.

"No, your watch is *farang*."

"It's Japanese, like yours."

"But the spirit is a Lahu spirit. You don't believe in it so it cannot harm you. But it can harm us," he said, pointing to Ca-Hpeu who sat blankly, listening to our Thai, unaware of what was going on.

I was tempted to tell Ca-Ui he was full of crap and was only looking for an excuse to go home. But a sharp word, once uttered, can sour a relationship for a lifetime.

"I'm going down to the bridge to look at the river. Wait for me," I said.

It was a half mile down to the bridge. I hung over the parapet and watched the dark Ping course by. In a foul mood, I reviewed the morning's events and once again found myself in a no-win situation. Taking his obstinacy as a given, how should I proceed? The river looked deep enough to drop in a boat but this was December and already the monsoon-swollen waters were subsiding. Whether it would still be deep enough in a month was questionable. What was certain was that the walking portion of the journey was over.

Back at the house, I thanked my guides for their help and paid them. Ca-Hpeu immediately set off north, back to Muang Na. Ca-Ui hesitated.

"Where are you going?" he asked, the most animated I'd seen him all morning.

"Chiang Mai," I replied.

"I'll go with you," he said. "To see my friend."

I considered suggesting that from here on, I would travel by myself. But what was the point of being churlish? I nodded and we waited by the road, eventually flagging down a *songtaew* that was even more rickety than the one I'd ridden north. When we arrived in Chiang Mai, he strode across the bazaar and was lost in the crowd.

That evening, I sat in the kitchen of the friend who had introduced me to Ca-Ui, drinking coffee and reviewing the events of the previous days.

"What's this about Lahu spirits stopping time?"

"What?" he replied, setting down his cup.

I told him the story. He smiled. "Ca-Ui is a crafty one."

"But smarter than me," I replied. "He got what he wanted."

"Isn't it usually that way?" he asked, eyebrows cocked.

So it seemed. Pushing aside my coffee cup, I thanked him and left. The first part of the journey was over. Now all I needed was a boat.

Searching for a Boat

Thor Phae Lai Sua, Thor Rua Lai Chorakhee
(To pole the raft to catch a tiger,
to pole the boat to catch the crocodile)
Avoid undertaking an impossible task

On the banks of Rangsit Canal just north of Bangkok, new sampans were stacked five high, waiting for buyers. I walked among the boats, like a shopper in a car lot, knocking on hulls, putting myself in the driver's seat as it were, and mentally stowing gear to see how it would fit. But nothing looked right. These were built for flat water; in a rapid, they would tip. One collision with a rock and they'd shatter.

I'd briefly considered a bamboo raft. Centuries before, rafts had conveyed the first immigrants down Thai rivers to their new homes. Like those pioneers, I could lash together bundles of arm-thick bamboo, and at obstacles, could cut the lashing, move the bundles past the barrier, and then reassemble them. It was a romantic, Huck Finn way to travel.

But completely impractical. I needed a proper boat, something small enough to pull around weirs without herniating myself. It also had to be large enough to be stable in the fast, rock-strewn waters of the upper Ping. On the other hand, a broad-beamed, untippable boat capable of holding a lot of gear would drag in the river's flat lower reaches; to slice through draggy currents, I required something narrow and sleek. Near Bangkok I would need a craft that would hold its own against larger vessels. From my porch, I'd seen small sampans swamped by the wakes of larger boats. High gunwales would eliminate the problem but would impede paddle strokes. The more I factored in insurance against contingencies, the more unwieldy my imaginary boat became. Perhaps a carpenter familiar with the river could suggest something suitable. I caught a train north.

Standing on the Ping's banks near Chiang Mai's main bazaar, I surveyed a river empty of all craft except for one leaky, weather-beaten boat. A fisherman squatted on its bow pulling in a net while his partner paddled slowly or bailed furiously to avoid sinking. I asked the fishermen about boatbuilders.

"There's one about two miles upriver...no, wait, he died." He pondered a bit and then admitted surprise that an era had passed without a murmur. Others expressed similar sentiments. "I guess no one uses boats anymore," was the common refrain, often spoken with chagrin as if remembering a long-deceased friend.

I motorcycled to distant villages where carpenters were said to live, only to be greeted by puzzled looks and suggestions that I try elsewhere. An old man told me of an entire village of boatbuilders at a place called Baan Tak, 200 miles downriver, a dozen miles north of the provincial town of Tak. I caught a bus south.

The serpentine main street of Baan Tak limned the twisting curves of the Ping. The town owed its genesis and its existence to the river. It had once been a way station for cargo boats traveling up and down the Ping, flourishing between 1880 and 1930 when the timber industry engorged its economy. In the far north, elephants nudged teak logs into the rivers where they would begin the long float to Paknampoh, now known as Nakhon Sawan, the juncture of the four major rivers and the beginning of the Chao Phya. There, the logs were bound into rafts for the journey to Bangkok's sawmills. With the fading of the logging industry, Baan Tak had returned to somnolence, becoming a supply center for nearby farms. Now, it snoozed in the midday sun, the balconies of the two-story wooden houses drooping over the streets like the nodding heads of napping men. Boatbuilding had died with the passing of the logging era.

"I think there's a carpenter living off the main highway," a shopkeeper ventured. "What is it, two or three miles from here?" He turned to several loiterers for confirmation but they were as vague as he. "Anybody know his name?" he asked no one in particular. General consternation, head scratching, murmuring.

"I think its Sirichai," one finally said. General assent. "Yeah, look for Sirichai," he concluded uncertainly. "Why don't you ask from house to house until you find him?

One man volunteered his son to drive me there on his 50 cc motorcycle. The son at that moment was cruising by with his girlfriend and seemed less than pleased at this interruption to his courting. His displeasure was palpable as we set off, the tiny motorbike's engine straining, its nose nearly in the air from the weight freighting its stern. I tried to make conversation but his mind was elsewhere. An uncomfortable two miles passed in silence.

At the first few houses we drew a blank but at the fifth, there was a glimmer of recognition. "Try down about six or seven houses on the left." The eleventh house belonged to Sirichai. The boy, still chaffing at being dragooned asked sullenly, "Can I go now?" and did.

Sirichai was a muscular, affable man in his mid-30s. "I've built boats before; no problem," he assured me. We walked through his compound to the porch of a brooding two-story wooden house. His wife–a tiny woman half sinewy strength and the rest a huge smile–scurried with the energy of a terrier. Slinging a tiny leg over an ancient motorcycle triple her size, she threw her weight on the starter, and roared away to the market. A few moments later, she returned with soft drinks and bananas.

Children and dogs tumbled about the houseyard. When I asked how many children he had, Sirichai seemed perplexed but his wife immediately said "eight," eliciting gales of laughter from the children, whose energy and sunny exuberance mirrored their mother's.

"What kind of boat do you want?" he asked.

I told him my multitude of requirements. He picked up a stick and in the hard-clay yard inscribed two lines about 16 feet apart. "This long?"

"Shorter. About here." With my toe, I scuffed a line five feet back from the first. We did the same for the width, sketching a boat about 2.5 feet wide and pointed at each end. We stepped back and looked at the brownprint etched on the hard earth.

"How will you propel yourself?"

"Paddle."

"So you need to sit here just back from the center," and he drew a seat with twin lines.

"I also need storage space to keep my gear."

Eyes still on the ground, he pondered his drawing, walking around it several times. Amidships he drew a compartment. "You can also sit on it," he said. He then drew a line across the bow and one across the stern, twin lockers "to balance the weight," he explained. His easy confidence was reassuring.

"Teak planks, they'll be solid enough," he said. We made a few more modifications, and settled on a price of 5,700 *baht* (US$ 230). He would contact me in three weeks. I gave him 4,000 *baht* for materials and, after another soft drink, found myself standing on the highway shoulder waiting for anything that could carry me south. Soon, I was at the Phitsanulok station on the main north-south line, boarding the midnight train to Bangkok.

On reaching the city, I began buying supplies, knowing little or nothing about what I would require: nylon cord for securing gear, a plastic sheet to shelter from rain, soft cloth bags, canteens. They joined a small alcohol-fueled stove, candles, raw rice in soft plastic jars, clothes, and other items I thought essential. I was prepared for any contingency.

But could there be that many contingencies? I wanted to travel light but the huge heap on the living room floor mocked me. There is a fine line between over-burdening oneself and finding oneself in the middle of nowhere with an essential item missing. With grave misgivings, I began paring back, removing items that seemed superfluous, replacing two items with one that would do the same job.

Two weeks passed while I completed projects in Bangkok and attempted to get in shape. I've always lacked upper body heft, my primary strength being in my legs. Rowing a boat in Lumpini Park for half an hour every morning then jogging, plus afternoon laps in the pool seemed to increase stamina if not bulk. I plodded on, waiting for Sirichai's call, wondering how much the river had dropped. I put to the back of my mind the possibility that I might have to delay the journey for another year.

Two days before Christmas, the telephone rang. Sirichai's Bangkok friend read me a telegram he had just received: "Boat finished. Come soon. Sirichai." Five words that made my spirits soar. I was finally on my way.

The next two days were a mad scramble to assemble remaining supplies. It seemed so strange to fight through Christmas shoppers in a large department store, the muzak Christmas carols, plastic fir trees, and twinkling lights so alien to Thailand, and even more so to my impending adventure. On December 26, three bags, a waterproof camera/map/document box, and my pack were lined up by the door. On the 27th, they were in the hold of a bus pulling out of the northern bus terminal for the seven-hour drive up Highway 1.

It was late afternoon when the bus pulled into Tak, leaving me just enough daylight to reach Baan Tak. I dropped my bags in a back street hotel, and moments later was seated in a wooden rural bus. Only half-full, it made a maddeningly slow round of the town, horn honking, trawling for passengers. But the waters were empty at this late hour so the driver turned onto the highway, hoping to improve his luck.

With frequent stops to load and unload people, chickens, pigs, and other market purchases, the 12-mile journey took over an hour. It was nearly dusk before I reached Sirichai's gate. The house was eerily quiet. No giggling children. No dogs. Deserted. I called once, twice. No reply. Half an hour until sunset; I decided to wait. The air was cool, perhaps 65 degrees, a contrast to Bangkok's warmth. I leaned against a tree and listened to the cicadas shrill in the teak trees. Gradually a new sound intruded into their rasping song. Squeaking and wrenching, five bamboo-laden wooden carts pulled by pairs of white bullocks were working their way down the road.

Something thumped on the upper floor of the house.

"*Aoiii!*" said an angry voice. "Put some grease on the axles," it bellowed.

A moment later, the voice was followed by a form as Sirichai staggered onto the verandah. He was preparing to launch another blast at the unheeding carters when he spotted me.

"You're here," he cried, his voice overflowing with holiday spirit.

He stumbled down the stairs, barely able to maintain his balance. Eyes glazed, he assailed my nostrils with a blast of whiskey fumes and seeing me recoil, said with some chagrin, "*lao khao* (white lightning)". "Get the *farang* some *lao khao*", he shouted in the vague direction of the upstairs door. Silence. "Gone to her mom's," he said to himself. "Kids too." "Never mind," he shouted joyously, "I'll get it myself," and–whirling, almost falling–clambered up the stairs on all fours.

"No need," I called.

"Need. Need," he shouted back.

He plunged into the dark interior and a moment later re-emerged strangling the neck of a bottle holding a milky liquid. "No *lao khao. Ka-chae* (palm toddy). Better," he shouted joyously, and began the same precarious journey back down the stairs. "Worse," I thought, eyeing the cloudy brew that could double as paint stripper.

The bottle was opaque with grime; hopefully, the alcohol sterilized it. I protested but Sirichai wouldn't hear of it. He began to pour until it dawned on him that he was pouring it into the empty air between his cupped fingers.

"Glass." His eyes alighted on one sitting on a stump across the yard and, leaning forward like a sailor fighting a wind, reeled across to it. It was even filthier than the bottle. I was still laughing and saying, "no need" but he was pushing me away with the hand holding the bottle and attempting to purse his lips to blow the debris out of the glass. On one hard blow, he let go the bottle which landed on perhaps the only rock in the entire yard. It shattered and the whiskey spread in a dark stain on the hard dun earth. He looked stricken. "Ehhhh," was all he said.

He observed it a moment and then tried to shove his free hand into his voluminous shirt pocket. After several misses, he made it. I couldn't figure out what he was after but with another triumphant grin, he extracted a box of matches. Fumbling it open, he removed one, struck it, dropped it onto the dark patch causing an enormous flame to leap up, nearly singeing both of us. We leapt back and the flame blazed blue and then yellow for several minutes. Sirichai appeared transfixed by the spectacle, his face flush and sweating. When the fire had died, he looked up at me and whispered hoarsely, "gone."

He now seemed disoriented, looking around his feet for something.

"Boat," I prompted.

"Boat!" he recalled, face alight. "Under the house."

The under-house area was Sirichai's workshop. In the twilight, I could see a familiar shape. I peered closer. Uh oh. This was not the boat we had drawn in the dirt three weeks earlier. My confusion must have been evident because through his fog, Sirichai nodded his head vigorously up and down, "Yes. Your boat."

It wasn't the sleek-lined, pointed-prow boat that would glide through the water. It was a bulky fat tub, a foot wider than we had discussed and with a pointed prow but a squared-off stern. No commodious storage areas amidships, and two tiny compartments built into the bow and stern. Neither would hold more than a sleeping bag and a few clothes. Gear would have to be lashed to the deck, in open view, vulnerable to the elements and to theft. This was a catastrophe.

He looked at me expectantly. "Good?" It was hard to fault the workmanship; it was beautiful. The seams were perfectly aligned, and it had been finished superbly, some of the best work I'd seen in Thailand. I measured it and found it to be 11 feet long and three feet wide. I hefted the stern and barely got it off the ground. Teak is not a light wood and with all the admirably-wrought studding and cross-studding to strengthen it, the boat weighed somewhere in the region of 180 pounds, too heavy for me to pick up and portage. Moreover, its girth and flat bottom meant I'd have to paddle hard in slow water. I looked at it in dismay. Once again, I had been second-guessed by an artisan after clearly specifying what I wanted.

"Good," I croaked, trying not to sound as upset as I felt. "But it is too heavy."

He looked from me to it. "No problem," he said dismissively. "Once you attach the engine, it'll go really fast."

"But I told you I was going to paddle it."

"Yes. Paddles. Here." He picked up two broomsticks which ended in narrow blades. He swept one back and forth to mimic paddling. The effort nearly toppled him.

"Oh, and chain." He shuffled to the bow. A few chain links protruded from a steel-ringed hole. Like a man pulling a bucket from a well, he tugged on the chain, hand over hand until he had extracted about 18 feet.

"See?" he said. "All fits in the bow," and threaded it back down the hole.

I didn't want to upset Sirichai–assuming that were possible given his inebriated state–but this was not what I ordered or needed. I was now the owner of an ungainly, overweight, completely impractical boat. But I was stuck with it. Smiling weakly, I paid him the balance of the price and he stuffed the bills in his pocket, unconcerned if they were the correct amount.

"I'll be back in the morning to pick it up," I said

"Spend the night here," he offered, but the mosquitoes were swarming and he would probably end up frying himself if he tried to prepare a meal.

"Thanks, but I'll head into town. You should get some sleep."

He considered this, then nodded. "Good boat," he said, satisfied. He was somewhat subdued by this point and made it up the stairs unaided.

On the highway, I waited for nearly an hour for a vehicle to pass. I flagged down a pick-up which weaved to the side of the road but didn't stop until it was well past me. A head poked out of the window. "Tak?" it said fuzzily. Oh hell, they're drunk, too. But I didn't have much choice; I could either ride or sit here by the road and be eaten by bugs. Deciding that he could navigate safely, I squeezed into the front seat to ensure he stayed on the road. We crawled to Tak at 15 mph, whiskey fumes and drunken words spewed into my face the entire way. I'd seldom been more depressed.

I was awakened by the din of the market below my hotel window. As I sat up in the dim light, the memory of my disaster of a boat swept over me. I sank down again, and stared at the flies and the *chinchoks* (house lizards) moving along the ceiling. I lay for a long while, overwhelmed by a confusion of ugly thoughts. At last, I rose, slid into jeans and shirt, slipped into my flip-flops, and walked downstairs, not bothering to shave.

In the market, I plunked down on a wobbly stool at an equally wobbly wooden table. A chunky vendor, her faded sarong hitched high and folded into rolls so that she resembled a sumo wrestler in mufti, regarded me with concern. "Coffee," she said, a statement, not a question. A moment later, a glass of Thai coffee, the color of Guinness but with the cream at the bottom, landed with a sharp thud on the table. Thai coffee is a treacly, chocolately brew whose ingredients I've never known or wanted to know. All I know is that it would stir the dead and at this moment, I qualified. It is so thick it is served with a weak tea chaser. After half a glass my heart was pounding.

I reviewed my situation: I had a boat. Sort of. It was beautiful but useless. What to do? Bail out now, find another builder? He'd never finish it before the end of winter when the river would be too shallow to navigate. Refurbish an older boat? That wouldn't work either. Thai river boats were too tippy, too leaky, and too small for my purposes. What then?

I was overwhelmed with despair as I watched my dream become unglued before it even began. The boat was supposed to have been a given, a certainty; the journey was to have been devoted solely to sorting out river obstacles. Now, I was stuck with a great teak lump that might prove to be the biggest obstacle of all. What to do? I ran the loop again. None of the options seemed particularly palatable and I was wasting time. I wanted to push off, to set paddle in water, and begin moving downstream.

Maybe I could modify the boat in Chiang Mai. It would delay me by a few days but I could gain greater familiarity with it. Perhaps with time I would grow to like it, seeing its positive rather than its negative points. Fat chance, I thought. Let's just get it north and sort out the rest later.

In rural Thailand, the pick-up truck is the transport of choice. Those at the market shuttled vegetables to and from surrounding towns; taking two days off for a long-distance trip was out of the question. Long-haul goods were carried by ten-wheeled trucks, big lumbering diesel vehicles far too large for my boat. Something smaller was required. A songtaew.

I walked a half-mile east to the Highway. Huge trucks roared by, their wash creating dust devils that tornadoed the litter. A pair of motor-cycles passed, each drawing an open, homemade trailer housing a fat pink pig on its way to market. A pick-up resembling a gypsy wagon–every surface bristling with baskets, brooms, fish traps and dozens of other rattan and wattle items–crawled along the road, a blaring loudspeaker advertising its wares. Tiny children in tidy blue-and-white uniforms chatted as they walked to school, swinging bookbags half as large as themselves. But no *songtaew* passed.

Gradually, the morning traffic thinned. A large orange bus hove up on the horizon, blasting its horn, the driver's subtle way of asking if I wanted a ride. But I knew he would not wait in Baan Tak while I wrestled the boat to the roof rack so I waved him on.

And sat. Down the highway, a *songtaew* slowed to turn onto the road I'd just walked from the market. I waved to him.

"Where's the boat?" Boonchoo asked when I explained what I wanted.

"In Baan Tak."

"3,000 *baht* ($ 120)."

"Jeez, that's nearly the price of the boat!"

"2,000 *baht*."

"How long do you think it will take to reach Chiang Mai?"

He looked at his *songtaew* which appeared to sag at strategic points. "The hills would slow us, and there are a lot of them. Let's see. If we take the road around Mae Phrik, around Thoen, Ko Kha, avoiding Lampang..."

"Wait. Why such a circuitous route? Those are all backroads. Why not just stick to the highway?"

"Your boat's too big."

"But we'll tie it down well."

"No. Police."

"Police?"

"They'll ask why I don't have a permit to carry something this big."

"It's not that large."

He looked at me as if I were a country bumpkin.

"It could be any size, it doesn't matter. If they see it, they'll stop me, and find an excuse to fine me," he said, rubbing two fingers against his thumb.

Ah. So that's why the price is so high.

"If I take care of the payoff, how much?"

"1,200."

"Fine. Let's go. Up the main road," I added.

After a brief stop at the hotel to grab my gear, we were eating up the 12 miles to Baan Tak. The *songtaew* was a very slow eater. "Don't want to overheat it," Boonchoo cautioned.

Sirichai was nowhere in sight but his diminutive wife was. When Boonchoo and I started to lift to boat, she put her shoulder under the stern and helped to hoist it. Like most Thai vehicles, the *songtaew* was studded with burrs and jagged metal bits, souvenirs of encounters with inanimate objects. When the boat left the ground it was pristine; by the time we were tossing nylon ropes over the top to secure it, it had a gouge the length of its hull.

Sent off by Sirichai's entire brood, we pulled onto the highway and a short way on, turned left onto a side road.

"Where are we going?"

"Police."

"Where?"

"You never know."

"But I said I'd take care of the payoff."

He ignored me, eyes intent on the road ahead with furtive glances into the rearview mirror. I resigned myself to a very long, very slow journey through what turned out to be the scenic backwaters of northern Thailand.

After numerous stops to pour water over a boiling engine, we reached Chiang Mai at dusk. I rang a friend for advice on where I might put the boat while I was modifying it.

"Moses would be your best bet," he said.

"Moses?"

"He's a Wa from northern Burma, an old friend with a big yard. He won't mind the company for a few days."

Moses and his family lived on the outer edges of Chiang Mai and his broad yard was perfect for boat repairs. We unloaded the boat and sent the driver back to Tak. I checked into a small riverside hotel and sank into a dreamless sleep, undisturbed even by the mosquitoes.

Alarms

Mai Lak Pak Leen
(The mooring pole not stuck
firmly in the river bed floats away)
Someone who lacks resolve creates problems for himself

As I opened the mossy gate into Moses's yard, I could hear him talking into his tape recorder in an inner room. Each morning, he recorded religious programs in the Wa language and mailed the cassette to the Philippines. A Christian radio station in Manila broadcast his homilies to fellow Wa tribesmen living in Burma's northern Shan States along the Sino-Burmese border.

Centuries before–for reasons not entirely clear–Wa farmers became convinced that the only way to make their crops grow was to impale human heads on posts set along the margins of their fields. As late as the 1940s, British officials considered it dangerous to travel into their realm without armed escorts. At special peril were the Sikhs whose long flowing hair and beards could command 300 silver rupees among the Wa cranium connoisseurs.

Eventually, the Wa were converted to Christianity by missionaries skilled in their own brand of headhunting. Moses provided the converts with sermons to guide their daily lives. The tape squealed in rewind as he listened again and again to the cadences of a language that beat on my ear drum but conveyed no meaning. Not wanting to disturb him, I turned to the boat. It sat in a wide, unkempt yard beneath a tall palm. A light breeze rattled the dried fronds high overhead and fluffed up the magenta bougainvillea blossoms; a peaceful setting for the work at hand.

The boat needed drastic alteration. With a little work, I could expand the tiny aft locker, attach hasps for locks, and install floor boards to raise the gear above the bilge. To make room for it, I'd remove one of the two seats that Sirichai had inexplicably installed, moving the other one forward a few inches to center me better and provide proper purchase for paddling. Taking measurements, I made a shopping list, and set off for the market.

Musty, murky, junk-jumbled hardware stores crammed with arcane treasures mesmerize builders the way antique shops attract collectors. This one was just off Charoen Muang Road, the main thoroughfare through eastern Chiang Mai. Windowless and doorless, the store's open front allowed the slanting sun free entry into its gloomy interior. The same sun also illuminated the scarlet signboard over the entrance; "Wonderful Fortune" it read in gilded Chinese and Thai characters that ran from one jamb to the other. Beneath it sat its Cerebus, a slender Chinese man of the Taew-chiew clan, his bushy eyebrows, gray hair, shaved sides and burred crown sitting proudly above his white singlet, and pajama bottoms. Like the stone lions before Chinese shrines, he guarded his shop, more engrossed in glaring at passersby than in pursuing business.

"What d'ya need?" he barked to the fire hydrant, poking at his gold teeth with an ivory toothpick.

"A hammer, and a saw to begin with."

"There." He flung a careless arm towards the dim recesses of the shop, not bothering to follow it with his eyes.

I plowed through the debris until I found the saws.

"I need something with more teeth, to make lengthwise cuts."

"Behind the paint buckets," still without looking my direction. Almost as an afterthought, he asked, "What're you building? Shelving?"

"A boat."

The head came about, uncertain it had heard me correctly.

"A what?"

"A boat. For the river."

Pedestrians were ignored as he swiveled suspiciously on his po-lished wooden stool, peering into the interior to see what I was doing. He unhinged himself slowly from the stool and shuffled over to where I was rummaging through heaps of C-clamps.

"Try behind the planes."

Shoving aside several block planes made of a hardwood only slightly denser than the planks they were to smooth, I found my saw.

"Uhhh," he said in approval. "What else?" He peered closely at my head for a clue to my motives.

"Latches, nails, screws, urethane lacquer."

He began scurrying, locating in his private filing system each item I needed, as if visualizing the contours of the boat from the description of the implements I required. Finally, his struggle ceased.

"A boat, huh? Why?"

"I'm going down the Ping." As I said it, I realized how foolish it sounded.

"A motorboat? For tourists? You have a travel agency?"

"No, for me."

"Who's paying you?

"Nobody."

"Nobody's paying you? So why go?"

"Curiosity."

"Curiosity," he said, almost to himself, incredulously, seeing no commercial value whatever in it.

"I've always wanted to go down this river. So I'm going."

"Who with?"

"By myself."

Forever the pragmatic Chinese shopkeeper, rooted firmly in the here and now, the tangible that he could see, touch, or sell, he suspected I was leaving out some key facts, my real reasons for setting off on such a pointless, profitless journey.

"Ahh," he said, the light dawning, "*Shee-ai-aa.*" Wagging his finger and his downturned head, he shuffled toward the counter, smiling and congratulating himself on his perspicacity.

I snorted in surprise. "CIA? No way." The abruptness of my response erased his smile.

"Not? Then what?"

"Just to do it."

He stood for a moment, looking at the floor. Then, deciding that either I was lying or determined not to tell him, he lost interest in me, becoming almost curt as he snapped the beads of his abacus to sum up my purchases. I watched him closely; the amount shown by the beads did not tally with the total he announced to me. I pointed out the discrepancy, which had erred in his favor, of course. He glanced up at me, his face registering shock. He pondered the bead frame a moment and then reached under the counter and extracted a dusty, grease-smudged pocket calculator. It took him a moment to find the "On" switch. Stubby fingers punched the buttons with a modicum of the grace he had used to send the beads flying.

"OK, OK," he said, his only concession to English.

I peeled a few 100-*baht* bills off the wad I had in my pocket, and he wrapped each purchase in an old newspaper, fastening the packet with a rubber band. By the time I placed them in my hilltribe shoulder bag he had retreated to his stool to glare angrily down the street. As I passed, he muttered in barely-muffled irritation, "*Shee-ai-aa. Shee-ai-aa*," tagging a choice Taew-chiew dialect epithet to the end.

Finding wood to match Sirichai's teak proved more difficult, and after the third lumber yard, I gave up. I would use some of the flooring as raw material for the alterations, and the extra seat to widen the lid of the rear compartment.

As the afternoon warmed, I pulled the boat into the shade, noting how heavy it was. The palm crown overhead laid a star shadow on the hull as I set to work.

Carpentry had always held a special appeal for me; the heady scent of sawdust, the shaping of wood to imbue new life in a formerly live material. Growing up in rural Oregon, I'd been taught the wood butcher's art by a father who had radically modified our home with the simplest of tools. The love of woodworking had never left me. But the pine and fir, cedar and hemlock softwoods of the high Cascades were quite unlike tropical hardwoods that defied sawtooth and nail. It took all my concentration to cut a straight line through the cranky grain and to strike a nailhead perfectly to sink it into the hull. I was so intent on sawing a board that I didn't hear someone approach until his voice startled me.

"Heard about your boat. Looks good," he said in English.

The tones were British but the face was that of a Thai man in his 60s.

"Jack Bain," he said, expending a hand instead of pressing it against the other in a prayer-like *wai*. "Where're you going?" When he heard, he whistled, a decidedly un-Thai response. "My father used to spend lots of time on this part of the Ping. Many other rivers too."

I must have looked perplexed because he said, "My father was British. Came out with the Borneo Company to manage a big timber concession north of here."

Like many foreigners resident in Thailand early in the century, Jack's father had never returned home. But while disease had spurred many to take premature residence in Chiang Mai's cemetery, the elder Bain had lived to an old age. After marrying a Thai woman and working for the Borneo Company for 55 years, he'd used his accumulated wealth to build a fine teak house in a huge, treed compound, a home which Jack inherited. Jack was now retired and took a lively interest in neighborhood activities. "You're the strangest activity the neighborhood has seen in some time," he said, chuckling.

Jack provided good company while I worked, detailing the town's history as described to him by his father. Aside from breakbone fever, malaria, tuberculosis, leprosy, and other debilitating diseases, Chiang Mai in the late 19th century sounded idyllic. It was a comfortable town built on a habitable scale. The Ping provided a central axis and Doi Suthep temple watched over it from the brow of a tall hill on the sunset side of town. The dirt track leaving Chiang Mai's northern gate had entered tall forests where tigers prowled and elephants worked the teak forests.

The city owed its genesis to elephants. In the 13th century, a monk had placed a broken relic on an elephant's back and set the beast loose, decreeing that wherever it halted to rest, a Buddhist *wat* (monastery or temple) would be built. It is easy to imagine the muffled ire of the pious prelates as they sweated and puffed their way up the steep slopes the perverse elephant had chosen to climb. Finally, high above the town, the beast stopped, trumpeted three times, and lay down. There, Wat Phra That Doi Suthep was built, and a city soon mushroomed in the valley below.

When I first visited it in 1969, the town's avenues were still lined with two-story wooden houses whose balconies overhung the streets like opera boxes. There were tall trees everywhere and the air seemed cooler...and quieter since most people rode bicycles and *samlors* (trishaws). The foot-powered trishaw conveyed passengers through narrow lanes and along the broken city wall, its leisurely passage reflected in the protective moat. Even then, elephants still roamed the streets. The region's timber industry depended on them, but by 1980, they had retreated to the hills, driven out by the clamor of cars and a growing population.

Jack was Thai in his politeness and European in his directness, and in his pleasant company the afternoon passed quickly. As the light was dying, he left and I finished expanding the aft compartment. The day had given me a better feel for the boat. It just might work after all.

The next morning, I was working on the latches when his now-familiar voice asked, "you're going alone?"

"Hi, Jack. Yes, I am."

"I don't want to alarm you but I've been thinking about your trip. And talking with some people. I don't think you know what you're getting yourself into." The concern in his voice was palpable.

"I think I have a pretty good idea. I'd prefer to have more detailed and more recent maps but..."

"No," he cut me off. "I mean people."

"What people?"

"There are many rascals in the hills. They're dangerous."

"Surely they are a tiny minority..."

From his pocket he pulled a story torn from the *Bangkok Post*.

"This appeared this morning. Read it."

It was a police report of a young Australian woman who had gone trekking with friends near Mae Hong Son, 70 miles to the west. In the afternoon, she had returned to her cabin. Her body was later found 500 feet from the door. The authorities could not posit a motive or a suspect.

I silently handed back the clipping.

"You see?" he said.

"Yes, and no."

He sighed. "You don't know the dangers in unpopulated areas. Even Thais don't go there. And if they have to, they go in groups."

He reminded me that the hills hid opium smugglers, poachers, and bandits who would find me an unwelcome intruder or a tempting target. "They know they can harm you and escape into the wilderness and never be caught. I think you should consider taking along a friend."

"I want to go alone," I insisted. "And besides, no one is available."

"I mean a 'friend'."

I just looked at him.

"A pistol, something that will put a large hole in someone, or at least discourage him," he said. "Otherwise, and pardon me for saying it, but you'll reach the sea face down."

Having delivered his grave message, he departed, leaving me to spend an uneasy afternoon. I tried to brush off his warning but he'd planted a seed and it began to grow. He was right: What did I know about these hills? Not much. The Lahu hunters had carried guns. And everyone wore a longknife. I recalled the lieutenant's hesitation when I told him we weren't armed, Ca-Ui's quickness in establishing kinship with strangers we met, and the wariness of the Mae Ja headman. Yet none of these incidents had struck me as personally threatening. An odd, vague discomfort was gripping me.

I hadn't been blind to the possibility that there might be dangers, but I thought it would be a simple matter of skirting trouble, avoiding the wrong people. I'd lived for a while in a tough New York neighborhood and learned that when in hostile territory, it was best to act like I knew what I was doing and keep moving. By the time people reacted to my presence, I would be out of range. Yet Jack was telling me it wasn't a question of "if" I would encounter miscreants but "when".

The *Post* story and Jack's concern jogged memories of a friend who had disappeared while trekking across the southern peninsula. I began recalling other stories involving foreigners in areas more populated than those I would be exploring: the American wife of a U.S. Drug Enforcement Administration official shot on a downtown Chiang Mai street; a Japanese cyclist robbed and killed near Tak; the shooting and robbing of trekkers in the northern hills. But as one always does, I'd dismissed these incidents as things that happened to other people. Was I being too casual about the potential dangers?

No Thai wanted to go with me and I'd already considered and rejected the idea of traveling with another foreigner. While Asians would strike up a conversation with a single foreigner, two *farangs* presented a wall. And at the end of a tiring day, it would be too tempting to relax with my friend instead of doing the hard work of talking with strangers in their language. I wanted riverine villagers to tell me about their lives, how they regarded the river and interacted with it. I could do that best alone. Now with Jack's warnings ringing in my ears, I wondered if I had been too blasé about the dangers I might face. Long before the workday was over, I put aside my tools and sought the advice of another friend, a Thai who had worked in the hills for many years as a road surveyor.

I rode a motorbike to his house at the opposite side of town. He welcomed me, asking his second wife–a Hmong hilltribe woman–to bring me a glass of cold water. His first wife was preparing dinner. I laid out my dilemma.

"Jack's right, you know," he said, after hearing me out. "Anything can happen in these hills, especially in the remote areas. Nobody travels the river. Anybody wandering the area probably doesn't belong there."

"Anybody?"

"Outlaws, poachers, anybody who makes his living by his wits. There aren't enough police to keep track of them, even if they were interested. And you know that the King had just granted amnesty to 50,000 prisoners to celebrate his 60th birthday. Many of them will be out there as well."

"I just don't like the idea of carrying a gun."

"Carrying doesn't mean using." He saw my brow furrow. "Think of it as life insurance; you don't want to collect but its nice to know it's there."

"Aren't guns hard to buy?"

"It might take a day or two. I have some hilltribe friends who have access to them. It will be a copy but it will have the same firepower. Just keep it oiled and out of the water and it will work fine."

"What size are we talking about?"

"A *ship-sham* sounds about right," he said, using the Chinese word.

"A 13?"

"Yeah, that's what the Chinese call them. Thirteen rounds to a clip. It uses a 9 m.m. bullet."

"Expensive?"

"3,000, 4,000 *baht*."

"Let me think about it."

"I'd also suggest that you pick up a farmer's *moh hom* blue shirt and a straw hat in the market. Disguise yourself as a farmer. It'll buy you a bit of time before they discover who you really are."

"Any more life-saving tips?" I asked it sardonically but he ignored my tone.

"Stick to the middle of the river, cook during the day so there's no fire light to attract anyone. Just expect that someone's going to be out there and don't let your guard down."

I spent the afternoon in a small riverside cafe in a deep funk about the turn of events. Something awful was happening to my journey. The focus of my concern was shifting from contending with the river to the possibility that I would find myself in the wrong place at the wrong moment and pay for it. A simple adventure, already fraught with logistical problems, was turning into a ride through a shooting gallery with me as the tin duck.

And then there was the matter of the pistol. Despite his years in the Oregon forests, my father hadn't been a hunter so we never had guns around the house. To me, guns represented a surrender to paranoia. Instead of being open to villagers, I would have to be suspicious of every-one, questioning all motives. Was this the Thailand I had come to find? Maybe I should skip the upper portion and start farther down. Or maybe just chuck the idea altogether.

I watched the sun sink over Doi Suthep and ordered a very spicy *kaeng khiew wan* green curry, as if to burn out the bad thoughts. The rest of the evening, I wandered through the market, ostensibly looking for supplies but mostly walking to wear out my brain. When the last vendor had packed up his goods and the last shopfront metal shutter had come clattering down, I plodded through the deserted streets, dotted with pools of light from the occasional street lamp, and crawled into bed.

Swirling water, foam, and nausea as the boat is tossed by tower-ing waves, slammed against rocks. A roar in my ears, which block, un-block, block as I sink, bob, sink. Struggling to stay afloat, gagging on water, pulled down by a weight wrapped around my leg. Men's faces grin down at me each time I break the surface, smothered by water and fighting for breath.

I was panting as I broke from one blackness into another, a throb-bing sound. Clammy and cold, I wore a corpse's skin. A faint light filtered by the window screen entered the room like mist. The ceiling fan whirled and bumped slowly to blow away mosquitoes. Tangled thoughts–twisted like the tortured bedclothes–fogged my brain, a wild profusion of filaments leading into darkness. I instinctively reached to the watch lying on the floor, a compass to orient me in the night: 4:15 a.m. I lay back. Two voices were endlessly repeating: "What are you doing? Aside from row-boats across park lakes, you've never paddled a boat," and "Knowing, caring people are warning that you are paddling your coffin to the sea."

In the shower, chill water coursed like a braided river down my torso, cauterizing irrational thought. In shirt, shorts, and sandals, I slipped into the night. Crystal shards speckled an ebon sky. A fluorescent tube over the guest house door illuminated the yard, a graveled expanse that held motorcycles strange in their silence, a clothesline, bits of broken engines; the derelict backyard of a city house anywhere. On the street, a few trishaws swished past me, their riders straining to overcome the weight of heaping vegetable baskets that burdened protesting springs. I walked aimlessly, eventually reaching the river. I sat the bank, facing the liquid companion that had become my nemesis. Were I a smoker, this would have been the time to light up.

The scene along the Ping was reminiscent of nights long ago in my Bangkok river house. Diesel ferry boats would cease operation at midnight and the only way to cross the quiet river was in a small sampan. It was rowed by an old man standing at his single oar; his wife sat in the bow, her face glowing in the lantern light that served as a warning beacon. No matter where I was in the river, reflections laid across the water from shore lights seemed to radiate out from me as if I were the source rather than the black hole sucking the light from them.

Across the Ping, the silhouette of a boat glided along the far shore, its calcium carbide lamp laying a willowy white line across the water to me. Perched on the bow, a fisherman slowly drew the river towards him, pulling hand over hand a barbed line. At intervals, he paused to rip hooks from mouths that moments before had been doing their own fishing among the watery reeds. The water was satiny, with a few rippling creases ironed in by the fisherman's boat. Nothing could have been more peaceful.

But it was a deceptive calm. Thais had told me that *nguak*, spirits of the deceased, lurked far below the river's skin, waiting for the unwary. Were there malevolent beings deep beneath the surface of everyday thought? Had they been there all along, buried beneath the belief that if I didn't provoke them, they wouldn't bother me? Probably. But I could no longer ignore them. They'd been loosed and they snarled in the darkness.

Why am I doing this? Why am I deliberately putting myself in danger? Is it the lure of a new venture and the urge to satisfy a curiosity, or is it some weird form of midlife crisis, something I have to prove? I hadn't exactly lived a normal, sedentary life. I'd been free to travel, to live at my own pace, unencumbered by family or possessions. I wanted to recapture the emotions I had felt in 1969 when I had hitch-hiked for four months from Kathmandu to Istanbul and back. There had been no itinerary, no time frame; I had experienced each place until its air permeated my being and its rhythms became my own, and then I'd moved on.

It was what I had hoped this trip would be. But something else was now happening. Philosophically, I knew that experiences most valuable to me had been those in which I had been frightened to death. Only then would all my senses operate at full capacity to decipher a dilemma, and find a solution to it. Yet here I was, apprehensive of danger, debating whether to pull out. Had I lost the courage of youth, the bravado that treats threats as abstractions and distractions? Maybe I'd become more cautious with age, more aware of the precariousness and brevity of life. I was still willing to take a risk, but against physical obstacles, not against strangers whose motives I couldn't fathom, whose moves I couldn't calculate.

The river's silky surface slowly purpled, then melded into orange, then pale yellow to mantle the sun now edging over the horizon. Buddha had sat on a river bank and faced a rising sun as he meditated to reach enlightenment. I was sitting in the same position but I wasn't gaining clarity of purpose; I was only getting wet from the dewy grass.

I rose to my feet, understanding that I was less driven by the challenge than by a realization of the depression I would feel later if I bailed out. I would be angry at myself for having surrendered to fear, abandoning something towards which I'd been moving for some time. But was that necessarily bad? Many human acts had been impelled by the same motive.

There was also another emotion at work, something deeper than a rational reckoning of risks and rewards. It was no longer a matter of questing towards a goal, it was one of being pulled by an inexorable current, something others would call obsession, a hook set in my mouth by an unseen fisherman. To combat my paranoia, I would compartmentalize the experience and not think beyond it, reverting to my original strategy of solving each problem as it occurred. The least I could do was stack the odds in my favor. After a heart-jolting cup of coffee, I telephoned my Thai friend and asked him to begin searching for a "friend."

I spent the next two days completing the modifications to my boat. After painting several protective coats of urethane on exposed surfaces, I turned my attention to the paddles. Sirichai had carved two lower-river paddles with blades the width of a hand. I carried one to the river. Kneeling on a dock, I tried it out; it slipped through the water like a butter knife. Wrong implement. I needed a ladle if I was to propel a boat of this size. Back at Moses's, I cut a six-inch-wide strip from one of the discarded floorboards and bolted it to the original blade. It was heavy, it looked ugly, but it would work. I'd keep the second paddle as a back-up.

After squeezing thin gelatinous beads of silicone between the planks to waterproof the hull, I headed into the market for the supplies I'd been too dispirited to buy the previous evening. I planned to spend the nights in villages, eating whatever the villagers prepared, and paying them for their hospitality. For the mid-day meal and for those nights in the wilds between villages, I would carry raw rice and canned vegetables, cooking them on my stove. Dried fruit and meats would round out my diet.

The covered market filled my nostrils with rich aromas: the pungency of shrimp paste, the mustard gas tang of frying chilies, the heady aroma of shredded tobacco for roll-your-own smokes. Fresh produce beaded with water was heaped two feet high, oranges piled like cannon balls burned under light bulbs whose newspaper shades were fastened with rubber bands. Catfish flopped in moistened tubs while crabs stacked in tall columns struggled silently in pink plastic string trusses, tiered sages with their claws folded neatly in front of them. Meat chunks hissed in a hot wok, coconuts were shaved in the sawmill whine of an electric shredder. With a few cleaver blows, hog carcasses were reduced to spareribs and cutlets.

I slid along the wet concrete floor past clover-leafed coriander, lemon grass, spiky durians (reputedly Asia's stinkiest fruit but a personal favorite), chubby pumpkins, pyramids of pink eggs, stalks of turmeric and cloves of garlic until I came to the dried meats. Slabs of red pork lacquered in honey hung from strings, fatty chops lay in rows. Sheets of sun-dried beef one can chew for hours and still extract a rich, gamy flavor lay in piles. Five pounds of beef would last me a while.

Down another aisle were the dried and sweet preserved fruits to supply quick energy; I would supplement them with groundnuts. Elsewhere I bought 20 pounds of rice, and fish sauce to flavor it. Provisions stores carried canned curries but I was reluctant to take them because it would be difficult to dispose of the cans.

On my way out of the market, I bought a dark blue *moh hom* farmer shirt. I wasn't going to fool anybody into thinking I was a Thai peasant but it was loose, the cotton fabric "breathed" in the moist air, and it had big pockets. It was well worth 50 *baht* ($2.00).

On Chang Klang Road, vendors' wares were sprawled across the sidewalk. One man sold boards spread with linoleum glue to enmire a mouse for later dispatch. Others repaired shoes, lighters, or watches and still others sold brooms, buckets, and farm household utensils. Yet another man had erected a small table to hold small shiny black rectangles; he was absorbed in etching on one of them.

"I.D. pins," he said, looking up.

Each had a small symbol in one corner and blank space for the owner's name. Police, military, civil servants, doctors were all represented and the pins looked very official. In a land where a uniform carries weight and an I.D. badge signifies importance, a pin could come in handy. I picked one designed for a civil servant, had him engrave my name on it, and for 35 *baht* became a Thai government official. Thailand had a long history of employing foreigners in official capacities; I was the newest recruit.

The last day of the year found me in the guesthouse packing. This time, I was merciless. The discard pile grew until it filled one bag. Now I would carry only two bags, the pack, and the large map box. If I really needed an item, I could pick it up when the river carried me through Chiang Mai.

As I was finishing, the desk clerk called me to the telephone. "Your friend has arrived," said the voice.

"I'm on my way."

I kicked my motorbike to life and drove the narrow lanes. He was waiting for me under a tree in front of his house.

"I was afraid it wouldn't get here before you left. A man brought it in from the hills this morning," he said, leading me inside and closing the door.

From a shoulder bag hanging on a peg, he extracted something wrapped in a tattered *Thai Rath* newspaper. Inside was a black chunk of iron, its gray metal showing through the worn spots. Nothing in its appearance suggested it was lethal, yet it was obvious it had been around for a while. I wondered briefly who it had killed.

"Its a copy of a Smith and Wesson 9 m.m."

I hefted it. "Heavy."

"But solid. Single shot, cockable hammer, safety catch between the trigger and the hammer."

He took it from me. "If you have a bullet in the chamber, just pull back the housing like this to eject it. I'd keep it loaded with the safety on. Put a round in the chamber only when you need it. Flip this to remove the clip," he said, doing so.

He handed the two pieces back to me and I shoved the clip into the handle and heard it click home.

"5,000 *baht*."

I looked up.

"It comes with a second clip and two dozen rounds, that's worth the extra money."

"Jeez, these are dum-dums," I said, looking at the cross-cuts on the lead points.

My friend was no stranger to violence; highway builders had often been ambushed by bandits and others who feared that the road would allow the police easy entry into their territory. He must have wondered about my resolve.

"You may not get a second shot," he said. "Besides, the gun is illegal to begin with."

"Yeah, but..."

He shook his head to cut me off. "Just take it."

I fished 10 purple 500-*baht* notes from my pocket and gave them to him.

"Here, take the shoulder bag as well. It will disguise it."

I thanked him and left, my cargo weighting my shoulder and reminding me of the responsibility I'd just assumed. Would I really be able to use this? And what had happened to my concerns about maintaining the purity of the journey? What was I getting myself into?

I'd never left Chiang Mai without making an offering at the temple atop Doi Suthep and I usually traveled there by motorbike. Motorbiking through the late afternoon air is my way of clearing the pipes of mental garbage. The wind through my hair frees me from constraints, helps me think clearer. I climbed aboard and headed west.

The sun was already setting on the other side of the hill, plunging the road into darkness. At the end of the steep, seven-mile climb, I parked the bike and ascended the 304 stairs between the twin ceramic *nagas* (dragons)–potent river symbols–undulating along its balustrades, making merit with each step. Above me, the gilded *chedi (stupa)* gleamed in the last of the day's light. In the chapel, orange-robed monks chanted evening prayers. Bathed in ethereal murmurs, I felt peace for the first time in days. As dusk settled, I climbed on my motorbike and, without starting it, coasted silently down the hill. It would be many days before I would again travel at this speed.

On the final evening of the year, I dined at a restaurant on the banks of the Ping whose waters I would join in the morning. Tomorrow was the birth of 1988; a new year, a page turned to a new chapter. I was now on a track, responding to the instinct that pulls birds across barren winter oceans or makes a cat walk a thousand miles to its home. All I had to do was step into my boat and paddle south, my salty, iron blood pulled along a broad artery towards a distant, briny lodestone. It seemed too easy.

The Launch

"Do not set your boat sideways to a strong current"
–King Ramkamhaeng (1275-1317)

There's something symbolic about starting a journey on the birth of a new year. Symbolic, yes; practical, no. The town was hung over from the previous night's festivities and was not inclined to move. Even vendors who worked 364 days a year rested on New Year's Day.

A silent, still Thai town is an anomaly. Morning fog seeped through the empty streets, making the deserted town even spookier. Even the hounds that normally roamed the streets were nowhere to be seen. Dozens of *songtaew* slumped by the roadsides, their drivers slumbering far away. I was not going to get away as early as I'd planned.

When, after a few hours, a handful of drivers stumbled into the streets, they knew their worth and charged accordingly. A man with a boat would fetch a very high price. By mid-morning, and with no hope of hiring a *songtaew* for anything less than its purchase price, I resigned myself to several more nights' stay. Maybe my friend Bill would have a solution.

Born in Chiang Mai, the son of missionary parents, Bill Young knew the northern hills intimately, spoke several hilltribe languages, and counted tribesmen among his best friends. He was nearly 60 years old and the steady, quiet rhythm of the hills was instilled in his bones. One of the most knowledgeable and perceptive men I had met, more than once he had generously pointed me in the right direction when I had hit dead ends. I biked over to see him. Over a cup of coffee, I told him of my fruitless search for transportation to Mae Ja.

"Why not wait a few days?" he asked, smiling.

"You know the answer to that," I laughed.

"True. Well, I'm not doing anything this morning. How about if I drive you up in the Landrover?"

"Thanks but I came to you for suggestions, not transport."

"But you're here, you need a ride, and I'm not busy. Rover hasn't had a decent run in a long time. It would do her good."

Despite its 20 years and several paint jobs, the Landrover turned over on the first try. We tied on the boat, loaded in the gear, and headed north on Highway 107 that ran through rice fields interrupted by the occasional small town. Past Mae Taeng, we climbed from the valley to the hills, the highway curving gently to follow the gorge walls. By 3 p.m. we were looking down a long slope at the Mae Ja bridge. Only four weeks earlier, I had peered over the bridge parapet at a glassy river and its dimly-perceived rounded stones. Now, the stones were etched in sharper relief; was it still deep enough? Shucking my boots at the bottom of the slope, I waded in. It was strong, swift, cold...and runnable. In moments, we were sliding the boat off the Landrover's roof and into the water. Despite the silicone caulking, it began to sink.

"We'll let it seal itself before we load it," I said, praying that the water, now seeping through the cracks, would soon stop.

"Why not camp here tonight and set off tomorrow morning?" Bill asked.

"No. I'm here and I want to go. I'll camp wherever I end up when the sun goes down."

Bill laughed, and then walked to the Rover. "I almost forgot. I have something for you." From behind the driver's seat, he drew out a long, red object bound together with braided grass. "Here, insurance."

The scabbard was made of a light pithy wood and from it protruded a rounded, pitted metal haft. Clasping the sheath, I drew out a knife blade two feet long and three fingers wide. It was not Toledo steel but a serviceable hunk of metal honed for hacking.

"It's Lahu. Should keep you out of trouble."

I briefly considered mentioning the pistol in my pack but thought better of it. I was still having trouble explaining it to myself.

"Thanks. I'm sure it will come in handy."

The boat was still leaking but if I detained Bill, he'd arrive home after dark. Dropping the lid on the bag-filled locker and lashing the pack to the deck just ahead of the map box, I turned to him.

"See you when I reach Chiang Mai."

"Good luck," he said, clasping my hand. His grip seemed a bit firmer than warranted by a casual goodbye.

The Rover climbed the slope and was gone, leaving me very alone, the river's soft burbling the only sound. I felt a tingle of something I couldn't identify, a combination of trepidation and excitement. Now it was just me, the boat, and the river. Taking a deep breath, I pushed off.

At first, I simply drifted, drinking in the exhilaration of the moment. After years of thinking about it, I was finally embarked on my journey to the sea. I dipped my fingers into the cold water; fingerlings nibbled fingers. The tree boughs closed over my head as I floated into a green corridor.

The Ping was less than 15 feet wide and about two feet deep but it was swift and full of mischief. Paddling hard, I passed the first bend effortlessly. But when I failed to withdraw the paddle quickly I collided with the opposite bank. Struggling to correct my course, I overcompensated and found myself heading downriver stern first. I no sooner straightened out then I banged into another riverbank. Each corrective stroke invariably pushed the bow too far around, like a novice driver who turns too hard. And in swinging the wet paddle from side to side, I soaked my pack which held my dry clothes. My lack of skill was alarmingly evident and my tub of a boat was not helping.

To add to my woes, the river held partially submerged rocks. I'd avoid one and hit another. Worse yet, I'd slide over it, tipping the boat and forcing me to throw my weight to the opposite side to counterbalance. It was taking all my concentration just to stay upright. Half a mile earlier I'd briefly pictured myself as a Thai explorer a millennium ago bravely descending the river in search of a new home. But if he'd been as clumsy as me Thailand would still be virgin territory. By the end of the first hour, I was exhausted.

The afternoon introduced me to a plant I would quickly grow to despise. Blanketing the banks was a briar that bristled with thick, sharp thorns. Each time I hit the riverbank, thorns entangled my clothes and raked my unprotected skin. Within minutes my arms were gouged; blood streamed down my forehead. Time out for a re-think; I ground the boat into a gravel bar.

The droplets seeping into my pack had soaked my sleeping bag. A wet sleeping bag on a cold night is a bad idea so I removed it, placing it atop the back locker to dry. Donning a sweatshirt to armor me against the thorns, I pushed into the mainstream but my first strokes put me among the brambles again. Thorns snagged my sweatshirt, holding me firmly while the boat tried to continue the journey on its own. Since it was impossible to remove the tendrils one by one while the boat was moving, I tugged sharply, tearing the shirt and my fingers. And rotated the boat, sending me into another bramble-infested bank. At this rate, it was going to take me a year to get down the river, assuming I had any skin left.

The next half hour was not pretty. Instead of trying to maneuver the boat, I allowed it to go where it would and used the paddle to fend off the bushes. Gradually, I gained a modicum of control but it took all my concentration. I know I passed some lovely scenery–shafts of afternoon sunlight piercing my leafy roof–but pre-occupied with my struggles, I recall it only as brief freeze frames.

Two miles later, the trees thinned and the swift current became sluggish. When I shoved the paddle straight down to test the depth, my arm disappeared beneath the surface. The river had suddenly become six feet deep. What was going on? Around the next bend, I found a huge weir blocking the flow.

Dams are deceptive when viewed from upstream. From a boat, one sees only a horizon line and, above it, the downstream hills. It is as if a photograph had been sliced into thirds horizontally, the middle third removed, and the remaining two thirds pasted together again. It is that missing portion that one must "read". It could be a gentle drop or a ten-foot waterfall. I paddled to shore for a closer look, pulling the boat onto solid ground.

Six feet high and sloping 100 feet to the downstream river, the *muang fai* weir stretched from shore to shore, a tangle of stones, bamboo stakes, and broken trees which had drifted in during the monsoon floods. To pass it, I would have to unload the boat and manhandle it 100 feet down the weir face, my first test of how portable it was.

The water rushing down the face denied me firm footing. As I plotted a path, a branch cracked behind me. I froze. Five men in sarongs, armed with longknives were ranged along the bank, a few feet away silently observing me.

Bain's warning flashed in my brain. Eager to establish that I spoke Thai–as if that was going to save me–I lamely asked, "Where is your village?"

One spoke to the others in a tribal language I couldn't identify, then pointed with his sheathed knife over a hill to the east. The others eyed my gear tied to the deck. One leaned down to tap the boat, turning to another to say something. Both snickered. It occurred to me that the best way to break the ice would be to involve them in getting me to faster water.

"Can you help me get the boat over the weir?" I asked.

They conferred a moment. Then, in one swift motion, they moved to the sides of the boat, brushing me away. I scrambled backwards nearly losing my footing on the loose stones but ready to run the moment the first knife left its scabbard. Lifting the boat a few inches off the ground, they moved it to the face of the weir, and set it down.

"Heavy," the leader said, panting.

"Yes, heavy," I replied.

A moment later, they reset and tried again, moving it a few feet farther down the weir. I lifted the stern and we moved in several stages to the river below. As we set it into the lower pool, all of us were puffing and sweating.

I offered them 20 *baht* each for their help but they backed away, wagging their hands. Instead, they turned and moved swiftly up the trail into the trees and were gone as mysteriously as they'd arrived. I stood by the river feeling enormously relieved.

And disturbed. I had given in to my paranoia; the longknives had unhinged me. I was also dismayed by their stealth and my slowness to react. True, the rushing water had muted their footsteps but they had been on me before I was even aware of them. My vulnerability did not feel good.

And my gun? Nestled deep inside my pack, lashed to the deck, useless. With shaking hands, I untied the pack. Making sure I wasn't being watched, I slipped the gun into my shoulder bag and placed both in the more-accessible map box. The sleeping bag was returned to its place on the aft cover to dry.

I now understood what a liability this boat was. Not only wouldn't it track, it was too heavy to maneuver or carry. This weir was not the largest barrier I would encounter, yet it took six straining men to get past it. What would happen at the next dam when I'd be on my own?

It was a more somber paddler who quietly moved downriver, a man more alert, more apprehensive. I checked the boat for damage and found as many gashes and gouges as my body bore from the brambles. Thrusting my hand into the cold water and running it over the hull, I discovered that the urethane had cracked in several places. A sudden sharp pain on the right side told me the wood had splintered. At this rate, the boat would be as solid as a chewed toothpick by the time I reached Chiang Mai. If.

A mile downstream, I entered a dense, dark forest whose trees reached long fingers over the river, forcing me to duck. Turning my head upstream to avoid being poked in the eye, my attention was caught by a large rock that I hadn't recalled passing. It's shape seemed strangely familiar. My sleeping bag! Backpaddling, I fished out a sodden mass. I'd expected to solve problems one by one but they seemed to be ganging up on me. Add one more precaution to the list: If I was going to be inept and unaware, I would have to tie down anything I put on the locker lid.

An hour later and tired of paddling, I crunched onto a bank that lay in the deep shadows of a 10-foot bluff. The shore seemed large enough for a camp and the trees would shelter me from the dew. Quietly stowing the paddle, I stepped ashore...and sank to my knees in thick mud. Lying on the bow, I strained for long moments before they left the muck with a moist sucking sound.

My pants and shoes were covered in thick goo so I shucked them, dropping them into the boat before poling to firmer ground. Leaping out, I grabbed the chain, which exited the housing with such a racket that anyone within a half mile could have heard me. So much for stealth.

Deciding it would be wise to check what lay beyond the bluff, I wrapped the chain around a tree root and, still in my underwear, I scrambled upwards to peer over the rim. Across a broad expanse of fields lay a village.

While Central Thais build their homes on the very banks of the river and depend on it to irrigate their crops, Northerners site their villages hundreds of feet from the river and rely on rainfall and the streams pouring down the hills. Whoever had founded this village had shown complete disinterest in the river by building a quarter mile from it, a long distance, even for a northerner.

The village seemed ordinary but my nascent paranoia was in high gear so I kept to my original plan of camping on the riverbank. In the waning light, I groped in my belongings for my flashlight before realizing that switching it on would reveal my location. Neither, for the same reason, could I light a cooking fire. I slumped down, my back to the bank wall, afraid to move because I couldn't see anything, and unable to rouse the courage to walk to the village.

"This is nuts," I thought. "Your fears are irrational." But my rational brain needed something more to push me towards the village. The wet sleeping bag. Without its warmth, I would spend a miserable night. "Just do it," I thought. "You came out here to meet people; so go meet them." I pinned my government badge to my shirt for insurance.

Donning dry pants and rubber sandals, I hid the paddle in the underbrush, slicing my hand on swordgrass. Hoisting my pack to my back, I walked as nonchalantly as possible towards the village, waiting for the change in the faint voices which would tell me I'd been spotted. Although the sky was aglow with dusk light, I was well inside the village and still hadn't been seen. Just down the road, a farmer was slopping pigs.

"*Sawasdee, khrap* (hello, sir), " I said.

"*Oi!*", he yelped, jumping as if he had seen a phantom. His head swiveled around, either to figure out where I'd come from or to find the fastest escape route.

"*Sawasdee, khrap,*" I repeated.

"*Oi!*" he said again. "*Oh, khun phuut Thai dai luh* (you can speak Thai)," he said, visibly relaxing.

"Yes."

"Where did you come from?" he asked, peering closer at me.

"The river."

He looked that direction, skepticism in his eyes. "And where are you going?" he asked, finally.

"To the other side of the valley," I said. I decided against telling him about the boat. "Where is the *phu yai baan's* house?" I asked.

"Over there," he said, pointing with his chin behind my shoulder. "Wait a minute. I'll go with you," he added, putting down his mash bucket, prompting cries of protest from the pigs inside the bamboo sty.

The village was like most in the North. At one end stood the Buddhist *wat*, its gleaming white walls covered by a steeply-angled roof of green tiles that framed an inscription in red tiles noting the date of its construction, "2517," signifying the years since Buddha's birth and corresponding to 1974.

A dirt track overhung by teak, *takhien*, and *mai daeng* trees, ran past two dozen yards, each enclosed by a tall, split-bamboo fence broken by a central, ungated entrance. Within each family compound was a well, a garden, a raw-hewn, unpainted house, and a granary, the latter two raised to head-height on stout pillars. Word of my arrival quickly spread and as we walked men and children fell into step behind us, discussing my presence in loud whispers. Anticipating a meal somewhere, several stray mutts joined the parade, seemingly unconcerned by the stranger in their midst.

As we entered one large compound a powerfully-built man descending the narrow stairs of his house, looked up briefly, did a double take, and missed the last step altogether. My effect on the villagers seemed as unsettling as theirs on me. These were not people to be feared.

"Are you the headman?" I asked.

He turned to the others. "He speaks!" They nodded eagerly.

Then, as if remembering that I had addressed him, he said, "Oh, yes. I'm the headman. I'm Chutam."

I introduced myself and began telling who I was and where I was going, ending with, "Any ideas where might I spend the night?"

"Where are you coming from?"

"Uh, over there," I pointed behind me. All heads turned. "Near Mae Taeng." The heads swung to the right. Apparently, I had missed my bearings.

He looked me up and down and I followed his eyes. I looked a complete mess from my matted hair to my scabbed arms and muddy legs.

"You've been out there several weeks?" he asked.

"Yeeessss...."

"Where are the others?" he asked, looking into the now-dark fields.

"Just me."

"Oh. Then, stay with me."

There were cheers from the children. As I shed my pack, several boys darted forward to drag it up the wooden stairs into Chutam's house.

"What happened to your sleeping bag?" he said as I disassembled myself on his living room floor.

"It fell in the river," I answered, hastily adding, "while I was crossing it."

"It will be cold tonight. We have extra blankets," he said. He handed my sleeping bag to his wife to dry near the cooking fire. "Do you have a *pakoma* (sarong)? You can shower under the trees." Such was my introduction to the village of Huay Sai Khao.

I wrapped a *pakoma* around my waist, and from beneath it, removed my pants. The *pakoma* is a wonderful multi-purpose cotton tube no village man would be without. It serves as a loin cloth, head wrap, pillow, a sack to carry goods, even a hammock. Every man has two. One he wears while bathing, washing it as he washes himself. While still wet, he wraps the dry one around him and wriggles until the wet one drops to his feet. In a few hours the thin cloth will dry, ready for whatever use the man then devises for it.

Watched by half the village, I drew water from the open well with a rope and bucket. Twenty years in Asia had erased my shyness about bathing in public. Almost. At one point, one must loosen his sarong and grope with a bar of soap among his privates, watched by several dozen eyes. I'd never lost the fear that while manipulating the soap and pouring the bucket, the sarong would unwind and slip to the ground. Other than gasping as the icy water sluiced over me, I maintained my grip and my dignity.

Still shivering, I sat cross-legged on Chutam's living room floor made of teak planks polished to satiny smoothness by years of use. A rush mat was spread on the floor as a dinner table. I looked around the room, noting that a tall, glass-door cabinet holding family heirlooms was the only furniture. The walls were unpainted, revealing the backsides of the siding that clad the house's exterior. A single fluorescent tube cast its arctic light over the room. I often wondered whether, in lieu of air-conditioning, rural Thais used fluorescent light to impart a frigid coolness to a home. How much greater warmth an incandescent lamp would have lent these bare rooms.

Chutam's wife placed several curry plates on the mat and the male relatives ringed themselves around them. As was customary in rural households, Chutam's wife served us but did not eat with us. Northern wives were treated more democratically than in the south but they still hovered in the background. Seldom was I even given their names, and I ended up referring to them as *phii* (sister) or *paa* (aunt), or for elderly women, *yai* or *ya* (paternal or maternal grandmother).

With the other diners, I pulled a bit of sticky rice from a congealed mass, kneaded it and then dipped it into a brown dried chili sauce or one of the curry sauces, before popping it in my mouth. From time to time, I used a thumb to press a bit of meat or vegetable into the rice ball. The curries, while appetizing, were designed solely to encourage one to consume more rice; the rice itself was the main course. Central Thais are convinced it is impossible to live on a steady diet of sticky rice but these people seemed hardy.

"What's in the curry?" I asked.

Pointing from one dish to the other with his spoon, Chutam said. "Well, that's clotted pig blood. That's banana flower. That's cobra. These are noon (kapok) buds. And that's chicken giblets." Nothing that moved escaped the pot. Fortunately, hunger is a wonderful stimulus to overcoming prissiness.

Drinking water was drawn from a huge clay jar positioned to catch nam fon (rainwater) streaming off the roof. Since the days when cholera had been the scourge of the land and the *wat* overflowed with corpses–the air thick with cremation smoke or vultures–Thais had learned the value of clean water. The river was clear but the farmers took no chances. They drank only rainwater and used the river for washing clothes.

Although Thais considered rainwater "pure", it could be clouded by dust and rotted leaves that had settled on the roof. No one seemed to ask who or what was on the roof when the rain began; on a pre-monsoon roof, I'd once seen a dead rat.

I had intended to purify my drinking water with tablets but it seemed insulting to drop them into my glass and there was no way to do it surreptitiously. I breathed a prayer for luck and gulped down the rainwater, knowing that it was probably alive with wriggling mosquito larvae.

As his wife cleared the dishes from the mat, Chutam said, "So, tell me about your journey so far."

"Uh, well, I started from Pai and followed paths through the hills. I stayed in hilltribe villages along the way," I began inventing.

"And where do you go from here?" Was he questioning me out of politeness or suspicion?

"Um, well, I'm headed towards Chiang Rai. I'm meeting a friend there."

"Did you fight with a cat?" The others hooted.

"Cat?"

"You have scratches all over your face and arms."

"Oh, yes–no, these are brambles. By the river."

"Ah, *don mayarap yaak*."

I flipped through my dictionary and found it described as "giant mimosa", or "cat's claw," the *yaak* translating as the giant demons which guard the doorways at Bangkok's Emerald Buddha. Highly appropriate. The mimosa I remembered from childhood was a shy retiring lass that hugged the ground submissively, folding its fronds when touched. I would later learn that the river variety grew 20 feet tall. In a sense I *had* battled with a cat.

"You are American?" Chutam asked.

I nodded.

"Americans are good. I've seen them in the markets in Chiang Mai and have friends who know them."

"Thais are good too," I said.

He smiled indulgently. "There are many bad people in Thailand. You can't trust anyone," he said.

Most Thais knew America from magazines or movies. In them, everyone had money and everyone was good. If I suggested that America also had people they wouldn't want to meet on a dark night, that "*every country has good people and bad people*," they smiled, convinced I was pulling their legs.

The Thais' love affair with America extended back 150 years. The U.S. had not attempted to colonize Thailand as had European powers and Japan and, in the 1960s it had protected the country from Communists. America was also the fount of new ideas. Thais have seldom rejected new concepts on the basis of ideology, or concerns that they would corrupt their culture. And they welcomed foreigners because they believed strongly in their own culture.

I'd noticed that Chutam and the others spoke Central Thai.

"Why don't you speak *kam muang*?" I asked, referring to the northern dialect. "Aren't you from here?"

"No one is," he replied. "In the 1960s, the government moved us here from a village down the Ping. They were building a dam."

"Bhumibol Dam?" It is the largest in Thailand.

"Yes. Our old houses are now at the bottom of the reservoir. Fish homes," he giggled. That explained the recent date on the *wat* roof.

"Are you better off here than you were there?" I asked.

"When we came, there was nothing except jungle. It was really *baan nawk* (backwards). We had to clear the trees but the soil was black and rich. In fact, we're doing better up here than in our old village."

They were lucky. Later farmers/fishermen removed from dam sites had been resettled on inferior land, far from fish-filled rivers. Huay Sai Khao supported itself on rice, onions, and garlic and its self-sufficiency grew out of a strong communal bond, its remoteness shielding it from disruptive forces, new arrivals, or emigration to the cities in search of work. It had not had to sell its daughters into prostitution as many poor northern villages now did.

Contact with a farther world came in the form of the merchant who appeared at harvest time to buy their produce. He transported it to markets a few dozen miles away where he sold it for double and sometimes triple the farm price. The farmers were aware of the price differences but they were not sufficiently organized to market their own produce. Still, it was heartening to find that this village was prospering despite the constraints.

We talked until 9 p.m. when lights were extinguished and retired for the night. Exhausted though I was, my internal clock said there were still two hours until bedtime. It was a long time before I finally descended into a dreamless sleep.

I awakened in darkness to the sound of voices and movements of villagers already well into their day. I rose, folded the blankets and mat, and strolled into the chilly air. The sun was still only a dim halo on the hills but cattle shuffled in their byres, awaiting fodder. Pigs rooted and squealed in bamboo pens, impatient for the women to boil their rice-and-husk mash. Men warmed themselves around straw and leaf fires, and dogs roamed on morning expeditions, crossing each other's paths but seldom barking or even pausing. Their calm demeanor reflected the village's contentment.

Chutam was ringed by farmers discussing the business of the day. Spotting me, he asked, "Tea?" A moment later, his wife appeared with tea steaming in drinking glasses set on an enameled tray painted in bright red hibiscus. We sat on the floor, sipped and talked as the rectangles in the walls gradually brightened. Draculean mosquitoes buzzed off to hide from the encroaching sun.

While awaiting breakfast, I shaved near an ixora bright with its rich red florets and was quickly enveloped in villagers discussing this strange foreign ritual. Children giggled as the lather created a clown face. Elderly women, teeth betel-stained and gray hair cropped short in the proper old woman style, examined my razor.

Thais are late-morning farmers, up at dawn but not into the fields until the dew has evaporated. Breakfast was warmed-up leftovers, salty fish, sticky rice, and a greasy omelet. "Foreigners like omelets," Chutam said. He admitted that he'd never met a foreigner, but this bit of folklore was believed religiously by all Thais. Although never particularly fond of omelets, especially not one swimming in oil, I smiled and swallowed.

Eventually, the isinglass fog filling the windows dissipated. The sun warming the green banana leaves outside slanted onto the polished teak floors, its reflection filling even the dimmest corners with bright light. It was time to go. I'd planned to pay each of my hosts for the food I consumed but when I handed Chutam 100 *baht*, he pushed away my hand.

"I'm the headman, you are my guest," he said.

"Sweets for your children, then," I insisted.

He just smiled, backed away, and shook his head. I thanked him and turned to go to the river.

"I thought you were going this way," Chutam said. Two dozen villagers awaited me at the village's eastern exit. Uh-oh. How to get out of this one?

"I wanted to look at the river again. To see if it had risen. Or fallen. During the night," I said none too convincingly.

"All right, we'll walk with you," offered Chutam and the people began moving towards the river.

"No, no, it's all right," I said, a bit too hurriedly. "There's something I have to do."

The villagers conferred and Chutam took my arm and pulled me gently to one side. "It's o.k. We have a toilet here," he murmured.

"No, I, uh, want to walk along the river before I turn east," I said.

"But it is marshy down that way."

"I know," I said, remembering the muck. "I want to try it anyway."

I wonder now why I didn't just tell them. At the time, it seemed too late to admit that I'd lied. I could feel confused eyes on my back as I shambled along the path to the river. I looked back and waved, and they waved. Fifty feet on, I turned and dozens of waving hands came up in unison. And again, another 50 feet, until I dropped over the bluff to the river. As I descended the bank, my hand brushed against a sharp edge on my shirt; my government official name tag. Nobody had even mentioned it. Like Dumbo the Flying Elephant's feather, perhaps I hadn't needed it. Some insurance!

I was relieved to see that the boat was still there. I brushed away fallen leaves that had been dew-plastered to the deck, tied down the pack, and prepared to set off. A sudden premonition prompted me to climb back up to peek over the bluff. In the far distance, dozens of hands rose to wave. I waved back and scrambled down to the boat. As I pushed off, I was determined not to repeat the mistakes of the previous day. This time the boat was going to go where I wanted it to go.

It was not to be. I'd halted just above a rapid, hoping that its noise would muffle my movements; a good idea at night, a bad idea in the morning. Without sufficient time to warm up, I was immediately spun by the roiling waters and thrown into a large rock. I corrected just in time to collide with another before being shoved towards the opposite bank. There, the bow lodged, pivoting the boat so I was heading downstream backwards and into an eddy. I sat, stewing. If this was the best I could do in a small rapid, what would happen when I encountered a large one?

The answer was lurking a few miles south. Rounding a bend, I saw a low bridge. It comprised fat bamboo sections the thickness of a man's arm, lashed together with vines, mere inches above the rushing water. It was impossible to pass beneath or around it, but I surmised that it wouldn't take much for me to lift one of the spans and let the boat slip through.

But then the river accelerated and, to my consternation, the paddle wouldn't bite off enough water to steer me. A second later, I slammed into the bridge sideways and it responded with a loud shriek. The powerful current pinned the boat against the span and, to my horror, the upstream gunwale began to rise, jamming the downstream edge under the bridge. Throwing my weight to the upriver side, I tried to use the paddle as a lever to pry myself away from the bridge but the current pressed me firmly against it.

Jumping to the boat's downstream side, I pushed against the bridge with all my strength, trying to hop the boat towards the banks. Instead, the downstream edge tipped farther and water began pouring in. I leapt to the upstream side to counterbalance it but it was too late. The boat filled, loose gear floating out of it and downstream.

Leaping onto the bridge, I jerked up one of the spans. The boat broke free and rushed through the gap. Dropping the span, I dove into the water and swam hard to the boat's stern. When my hands touched wood, I kicked hard, pushing for shore. The moment I felt the bow lodge in the gravel, I leapt back into the river and caught up with the spare paddle and the sleeping bag. Several more trips salvaged the other items but my sandals were swept away.

On shore, I hurriedly unloaded, noting that the map box was suspiciously heavy. I tore away its lid and found a wash basin; the silicone sealant had failed. Opening the camera bag was a mere formality; I already knew what I'd find. The lenses were swimming in their compartments. I put them in the sun to dry but water trapped between the prisms evaporated and the lenses instantly fogged. The waterlogged camera body was a write-off. A bilious fluid seeped from the film canister containing photos of Chutam's family.

Both bags sloshed as I removed them from the back locker. All the sealable plastic bags were filled with water. The gauze and the Band-Aids were soaked; even if they dried, they would no longer be sterile. The sopping jerky and other foods would be risky to eat; who knew what pathogens the river water contained? The books had become pulp novels. Only the pistol escaped a wetting and, ironically, the fishing gear. Only my second day out, and deep in trouble. It was depressing, not simply for the serious dent in my supplies but because it was such a spectacular display of my ineptitude.

Fortunately, the sun burned hot on the river and a light breeze blew down the banks. I spread everything on the sandy shore, pinioning blowables with stones. Clothes I hung from the mimosa branches, by now their natural home. The riverbank looked like a meadow after a rock concert.

The wading pool boat was too heavy to tip so I bailed with a canteen cup. What a shame it no longer leaked and could drain on its own. When it was empty, I collapsed onto the sand. High above, columbine clouds drifted by unconcerned. The warm sun was rejuvenating. If I could just lie here for a year, I'd be fine.

I had hoped to gain experience in small chunks as I went; not a lifetime's worth in 20 seconds. I reflected on the preceding minutes to figure out where I'd erred. Seven centuries before, King Ramkamhaeng had written, "Do not set your boat sideways to a strong current." He was speaking metaphorically but his advice was apt. The moment the current pinned the boat against the bridge, I should have jumped onto the bridge and pulled up the span instead of adding my weight to the boat's downstream edge. A small lesson and one of many I needed to learn.

The ruined food seriously compromised my plans. I'd chosen dry foods for their low weight but the plastic bags weren't waterproof. Maybe canned goods were better after all. The boat couldn't get much heavier than it was.

To a passerby, had there been any, the scene would have looked ridiculous: in the middle of an otherwise deserted riverbank covered in damp underwear, Band-Aids, pulpy books, and soggy fruits, a white man clad in a towel stood holding a longknife. The knife seemed necessary just to maintain a semblance of dignity.

I'd never watched clothes dry but would rate it somewhere down around observing rocks being eroded by glaciers. Two hours passed. Then three. As soon as an item dried, I would stuff it in the now-dry nylon bags, one step closer to getting underway, a charcoal stroke on a prison wall marking progress towards freedom.

By early afternoon, only a few stubborn items remained wet. Impatient, I shoved off, paddling south into a new valley with wider, less angular bends. The bones of trees long ago ripped from the earth by floodwaters lay along the banks, dry-docked on their journey to the sea until the next rainy season. A snake sunning itself on a log slithered into the water with a plop and disappeared; a tranquil scene in sharp contrast to the morning.

It should have been a leisurely afternoon but after half an hour, the clouds drifting slowly across the sky stopped dead and others rear-ended them. The breeze picked up and turned cold. As if inspired by the storm-burdened air, the river began accelerating and within a few hundred feet, it was moving so fast that it was no longer necessary to paddle, only to steer. I hugged the left bank to avoid mid-stream rocks, a bad tactic, as it turned out. Paralleling the bank was an ancient, downed tree whose unseen, upstream end was anchored to the river bottom. It announced its presence by thunking the underside of the boat. The swift current carried my boat in a long skid up the slick, barkless surface at an alarming rate. I struggled to push away and into deeper water, all to no avail. Suddenly, the bow stuck and the stern swung around, dipping beneath the water's surface. The river poured in and this time I didn't hesitate. Hurling the paddle upstream, I leapt over the stern and kicked for the opposite shore, my fury with myself providing most of the propulsion. When the nose slid over the bank, I jumped back into the river to retrieve the paddle.

I returned to shore, shouting my rage at having been upended by something so simple and stupid. The river was playing with me and I slammed the paddle on it to punish it. But it flowed on unprotesting. My anger was all-encompassing, embracing myself, the boat, the world, my helplessness, and my ignorance of how it happened and how I might have prevented it. Of all the things I had imagined going wrong, today's events were not among them. I had anticipated heroic encounters, not something so inane. In Bangkok's I'd envisioned this journey as the consummation of a love affair between me and the river, never anticipating that an irascible boat would come between us.

Once again, I surveyed the damage. Nearly everything was soaked but now there was no sunshine to dry them. Instead, dark clouds filled the sky and the wind was cold. Teeth chattering, I changed into damp pants, a T-shirt, and a pullover, and after re-packing, I pushed off again.

To my relief, the clouds moved west and the sun returned to warm me. The valley narrowed and soon teak and takhien trees began crowding the riverbanks. Their foliage hid invisible song birds; trees that sang. The cicadas rasped a subdued afternoon song, the chill having taken the crispness from their manic sawing.

With the sun spackling the river's Appaloosa surface, my thoughts turned towards the night's lodging. The jungle seemed sufficiently remote; I might not be disturbed if I camped. No trails led to the water's edge and there were no signs of cattle or herdsmen. But the steep banks were heavily overgrown or wet with mud. I paddled on, searching. The river was broadening, the water was turbid, sluggish. I plunged the paddle downwards but before it touched bottom, its buoyancy popped it back to the surface. Another dam, I concluded.

When I heard falling water dead ahead, I paddled to the right bank and pulled the chain from its housing, its clanking breaking the silence. Wrapping it around a tree, I slipped along the wet bank towards the barrier: a dam built of old railway ties and standing 10 feet tall. It appeared impassable. I surveyed the banks: too steep to portage, which left only one possibility: lowering the boat down the dam's vertical face. That involved unloading the gear.

"*Aow alai* (what do you want)?" a voice above me barked. Two men with assault rifles stood atop the bank about 15 feet away, the barrels pointing directly at me.

"To get past this damned dam," I muttered.

A hoarse, excited whisper passed from one to another. "It's a *farang.*"

"Yes, it's a *farang.* And who are you?" I heard my hard-edged voice ask.

"Soldiers," came the reply. "You're in an army base. Trespassing."

Peering closer, I saw their camouflaged fatigues.

"Then help me get out."

"Can't. Regulations."

"So I suppose I can't camp here?"

"We have orders to arrest anyone who crosses the perimeter. You have to go." They were young; the corporal in his early 20s, the private in his late teens. This was a remote area so they weren't conscripts; they were part of a forward unit of seasoned soldiers watching the border.

"I'm moving," I said.

They watched, guns still at the ready, as I carried the gear below the dam. Now came the hard part. Bow forward was not going to work because I couldn't control it with the chain. The only way was to back it over until the stern rested on the lower river, then to work the bow down the dam face.

With foreboding, I gently nudged the stern towards the dam rim, planting my feet on the bank, paying out the chain like a fishing line. At the rim, the stern lodged, refusing to move past it. Wrapping the chain around a tree, I went to inspect. The only way to get the boat past it was to stand on the two-inch-thick rim and lift the stern over it, a tricky proposition at best.

The soldiers were now engrossed in watching my struggles. Back at the tree, I paid out two feet of chain. and re-secured it to the trunk. At the dam, I gingerly braced my feet on the rim, and wrapping my arm and one leg around a tall post to steady myself, I curled my bare toes over the boards–talons to give me purchase–and slid the stern across the algae-slicked rim so that it overhung the rocks below.

Back at the tree, I released the chain in short lengths and watched the hull disappear over the rim. When the boat moved past its center of balance, it teetered momentarily and then the stern dropped, the links singing as the chain snapped taut and then, to my horror, was ripped from the tree by weight of the boat. The hull hit the rocks with a sickening crunch. I winced, the soldiers snickered. But other than a small gouge amidships, there appeared to be no damage. I'd done it, not very elegantly but successfully, one triumph in an otherwise dismal day.

Bathed in perspiration, I re-stowed the bags. A sound behind me told me the soldiers had climbed down the bank after me. As I turned, the corporal handed me a welcome glass of water.

I was re-tying the pack when he asked: "Where are you going?"

"To the sea."

"The sea? I've never been to the sea," he said with barely-suppressed excitement. "*Klai* (Far)."

I stood up. "Any idea where I can spend the night?"

"I think there's a buffalo herder downstream. You can stay with him."

"Thanks."

I had returned the chain to its housing when the private spoke again.

"Wait a minute. What do you have in the bags."

Damn. These were the wrong people to find the gun. "Wet clothes, rotten food," I replied. "You wouldn't want to smell the stench."

The private standing above me said, almost beseechingly, "We're under orders to search everyone," he said. "We have the right."

A tense moment passed. Then, the corporal waved him away and turned to me.

"Go," he said quietly. "Good luck."

Sin the Buffalo Man

Naam Rorn Plaa Pen, Naam Yen Plaa Taay
(Hard to catch in warm water, its natural element,
a fish is easy to catch in chilly water)
Be cool and you will prevail

In the dusk light, a half-naked man stood in silhouette, blocking the trail through the thick vegetation. The moment I said a tentative "*Sawasdee, Khrap*?" he pulled a longknife and set his feet in a defensive stance.

It was a logical reaction for an old man deep in the jungle where few strangers strayed, but it caught me by surprise. In the pale evening light the longknife, freed from its bamboo sheath, glowed with deadly intent. Its owner eyed me suspiciously and barked, "What do you want?" I explained that a soldier upstream had told me I might find a night's accommodation in the herder's hut.

"Why'd he tell you that?" he muttered in an agitated voice. "He had no right saying that. Go away. Get out of here."

The sight of the knife should have compelled me to leave but there was nowhere to go. Although I towered over him, I was certain that a lifetime of hacking through everything imaginable had made him faster than me. To calm him, I explained quietly that I was on my way down the Ping and had gotten soaked trying to wrestle my way over a six-foot-high weir. I had paddled this far in search of shelter; the herder's hut was the only thing I'd found.

His voice altered almost imperceptibly, a note of curiosity creeping into it.

"Paddled? Paddled what?" he demanded.

"A boat. Paddled a boat," I said, repeating the words *'pai rua'* (paddled).

"Nobody paddles a boat in this jungle," he said, scoffingly. "Where is this boat?"

"Down at the riverbank," I said, pointing down the thickly-treed slope.

He peered for a long moment the direction my finger pointed but could see nothing. But his hostility had abated. The knife blade dropped a few inches and he shifted nervously from one leg to the other, his curiosity piqued.

"Let's go see," he said, finally. "You first." He sheathed his knife and I breathed easier.

At the riverbank, he ran a gnarled hand over the teak hull. "Nice boat," he said, nodding approvingly. "Don't see any this far north." I told him I'd had it made in a village 200 miles to the south. "Figures" he said, enigmatically. Straightening up, he said, "Stuck, huh? I don't have much out here. This is the jungle. You can sleep in a lean-to. I only have curry and rice, you can eat that." Home free.

Walking back up the hill, he said. "You startled me. Nobody comes out here at night except to make trouble. I have nine water buffalo and they are worth a lot of money." He said it, not in apology for his actions, but as a statement of fact about a precarious life.

For most of the year, Sin Promma, an ethnic Lao, lived with his wife and three grown sons in Muang Ngai two valleys away. While he waited for the garlic to ripen, he spent three months in this jungle glade fattening his buffalo on grass made luxuriant by monsoon rains. "My eldest son is here. Somewhere," he said, squinting as his eyes tried to penetrate the now-dark jungle wall. "Went hunting. He'll sleep in the jungle and be back tomorrow morning."

Like many hill men, Sin was short and sinewy, browned by years in the sun. He was clearly used to taking care of himself. In a small patch hacked out among the tall trees, he had erected bamboo walls on posts four feet off the ground and capped it with a thatch roof. He climbed a notched log to its door. It was obvious from his exertions that he was no longer young.

"Sixty-three," he said with a smile when I asked him. "Old already. That's why I have to be careful of strangers. There are black-hearted people in these hills" he said, sweeping his arm across the silhouetted ridge. "They wouldn't hesitate to kill me to steal my buffaloes."

Water buffalo were rapidly disappearing in the Central Plains, replaced by small tractors that didn't get sick; that fed on reliable, readily-available fuel, and could power irrigation pumps and small farm trucks. Here in the North, buffalo were still valuable draft, milk, and meat animals.

Across the yard from his house was a smaller thatched structure raised two feet off the ground, a hay rick with one side open and just wide enough to sleep two people in cramped comfort. Like a manger, it was filled with straw which softened the hard wooden floor and covered the cracks between the planks. It would not bar the cold but would shelter me from the dew. "You sleep here," Sin said.

On the hard dirt yard separating the manger from the main house a small fire was burning. Sin dumped more logs on it and I began unpacking my gear, hanging the sleeping bag to dry by the fire. It would stink of wood smoke but I didn't care; smelly beat wet. Sin fingered its material and asked what I used it for. He was intrigued by my reply. "That would be useful in the hills," he said. "Wouldn't have to worry about the blanket slipping off in the middle of the night and exposing you," he said. Sin seemed to judge everything in terms of its utility in the wilds.

"When we came up here years ago, it was all jungle," he explained. "It was a long time before we had cleared sufficient land to grow food. Before then, we foraged for everything. In the old days, it was easy; the forests were full of game. Today..." he looked wistfully into the blackness, "...there are still fruits but the animals...I guess most of them have been shot."

The fire was warm and I huddled close to dry myself. Sin squatted nearby for a long time. Then, unhinging his legs and sighing, he got up. "I guess we should have some dinner. I don't have much... Can you eat Thai food?" "Yes." "*Phet* (Spicy)?" "Can."

He disappeared into the house. Hidden by the bamboo lattice that enclosed his porch, I could hear him clanking pans, and saw a momentary gleam as he lit a cooking fire. "Sticky rice?" he shouted. "Can," I answered. "Good. Good."

I knew it would be a meager meal but I didn't care. It had been a tough day and I was very hungry. While he was making dinner, I recorded the day's events in my journal. Finally, as hunger was beginning to gnaw at me, Sin invited me inside to eat. The dingy interior was lit only by the fiery embers of the cooking fire in its firepit, and a wick stuck in half a tin can of kerosene. In the darkness, two ragged cats prowled, the lamp occasionally illuminating a broken tail or a glinting eye. We dined on the floor.

As I suspected, dinner was an unidentifiable mass of vegetables and something which crunched and from which I had to extract bones. Perhaps the dim lamp was not without its benefits. Uncertain of what to do with the bones, I set them on the floor. Sin reached over, picked them up and, without looking, threw them in the general vicinity of the cats who immediately pounced on them, each growling at the other to keep clear. Some of the leftover sticky rice was also dumped on the floor for the cats to fight over. The pan holding the remainder was set beside the fire.

We returned to squat by the outside fire. Sin threw a large *mai daeng* log on it, angling it to reflect heat into my lean-to. The cats continued to slink around the fire, jumping nervously each time a burning log popped. They soon curled up on my now-dry sleeping bag and seemed determined to spend the night there.

Over the next hour, in a leisurely manner Sin questioned me about my journey and my life in Thailand. Listening intently but gazing into the fire, he paused after each question to absorb my answers, like his buffalo ruminating before digesting.

"Why are you going down the river?" he asked.

It was a question I had fumbled a hundred times. Whatever answer I gave sounded ludicrous. I was exploring the river, I was studying the river, I was trying to understand the people who lived along it...

"Ah," he interrupted. "*Samruat*."

I'd not heard the word before but henceforth, it would answer all questions, stifle all further interrogations. My dictionary defined "*samruat*" as "survey". It was a vague but useful word that had a ring of officialdom to it. It stood by itself without need for further explanation, suggesting that I worked for the government. I would soon find that *samruat* imbued its speaker with special properties. When asked my mission, all I had to say was "*samruat*" and smile knowingly. The listener's eyes would reflect a mental retreat, the suggestion that he was in the presence of someone performing official duties and with the authority of a distant government; someone who should not be meddled with. I used it sparingly but with effect when required.

Sin said nothing for a while. A few hardy crickets provided music in the crisp air. Then, as if to himself, he said: *"Farang* women," again directing his comment at the fire. What? *"Farang* women. They're so big." I'd heard this before; Thai men were intimidated by the height and bulk of foreign women. As in much of Asia, there was a fascination with the blondness and the–as perceived from movies–seeming sexual promiscuity of foreign women; their willingness to jump into bed in a instant. Thai males were intrigued but hesitant about what to do with all that mass of flesh.

"Thai women..." Ah, here we go, I thought. Thai women were best, didn't I agree? "Thai women," he repeated. "Too small, too thin," he snorted dismissively. *"Farang* women. That's the size women should be," he said chuckling to himself. Here was a man for whom size was a challenge, not an obstacle. I had to smile at the intensity and certainty with which he said it. Not obscenely, not lecherously. Just plain fact.

Sin lapsed into silence again. *"Jai lai* (evil hearts)," he said to the fire. He pointed with his chin to the riverbank. "When you get farther down the river, there are bad people, especially around Chiang Mai. Plains people. You'll have to be on your guard," he warned ominously.

The antipathy between hill and plains people seems to be universal. While living in Nepal, I'd found that plains dwellers regarded hill people as backward and impious while hill people felt plains people had lost touch with the important things of life and had become soft and corrupt. Moreover, farmers distrusted strangers, a perception I'd encountered throughout Asia, a suspicion founded on experience. There was a sense of lawlessness and a mistrust of the authorities to do anything but exploit their weakness. Thus, they clustered in villages as much for protection as for a sense of community. Until he proved otherwise, an outsider was suspect, a threat whose motives needed scrutinizing lest he present a danger to the village.

As a foreigner, I occupied a third category. Hill and plains people alike weren't sure how to deal with me but assumed that I was benign. Traveling alone made me even less of a threat. Almost. Unlike Chutam who had invited me to sleep in his house, Sin had placed me outside. He climbed the notched log, bade me good night, closed the door firmly behind him and shot the bolt. He wasn't taking any chances.

It had been a cold night and dawn revealed a yellowish sky. With the straw beneath me, I had slept warmly, awakening only once when I had difficulty breathing. In my half-coma I was aware of fur covering my face and slowly realized that both cats had snuggled up next to my head. They were probably covered in vermin and groggily I had tried to push them away. Half asleep, they growled menacingly, a guttural warning that I thought it best to defer to. But when I awoke at first light, they were stalking something in the murk beneath the house.

Water buffaloes were stamping their feet and Sin was making clucking sounds as he fed them. When he saw I was up, he came over to warm his hands by the dying embers of the *mai daeng* log. Barefoot, he wore short pants and a flimsy cotton shirt yet, aside from his hands, appeared not to feel the cold.

We talked for a few minutes and then he went inside to prepare breakfast. It was too cold for a shower, so I shaved and began packing my gear. It was a beautiful morning and I wanted to get an early start.

Sin, however, had other ideas. "I want you to meet my son. He should be here soon," he said, peering into the jungle hopefully.

In Thailand, "soon" can mean anything up to half a day. Sin was unclear about his son's whereabouts let alone his arrival time; I could be in for a long wait.

It was apparent that Sin had been living as a bachelor for some time because his idea of preparing breakfast was to warm up the sticky rice of the night before. The cold air had congealed it to a hard mass, the grains nearly as firm as they had been before being boiled. To flavor it, he stacked the plate with slabs of salted fish the thickness of crepes, added two fresh young bananas, and handed it to me. I had only sipped the water he had given me the night before because I was unsure of its purity. But with this mass, it was going to take a great deal of liquid just to get the food to chewing consistency. I smiled graciously as I accepted the glass which looked as though it had last held a paint brush and thinner.

During breakfast, he continued to announce his son's imminent arrival as if his words might lure the phantom to quicken his pace. By the end of the meal, the sun was just beginning to clear the hill and we were still alone. It was apparent that this man–who couldn't wait to get rid of me the night before–could not bear to have me leave. He probably didn't get many visitors and certainly none as exotic as a foreigner, and paddling a boat to boot.

"Come look at my garden," he said, and then looked at my feet. "Where are your shoes?" I explained that they had been stolen by the river. He chuckled and went into the house, returning with a pair of sandals that looked like they'd barely survived a stampede. They were gouged, the thongs kept pulling loose, and they were about four sizes too short, but they would do. "Thanks," I said and we set off, me hobbling behind him like a bound-foot Chinese wife.

Most of the clearing was occupied by a pen: rough-hewn, wooden-slab fence posts supporting long bamboo poles. Within it, nine black, bulky water buffalo with scimitar horns sweeping back over their broad shoulders sniffled and exhaled vapor blasts as they stamped to keep warm. Beyond the pen was a forest of papaya trees, a half dozen other fruit trees, and a vegetable garden.

I traipsed behind him as he gave me a botany test. "What's that?" he asked, walking by a tree, not even stopping to look at it. "Jackfruit," I dutifully answered. "Um, um," he said, pleased. "And that?" "Teak", "Um, um. *Geng* (Clever)." We must have gone through 15 plants and still had not exhausted the possibilities. In a Thai jungle there can be 300 varieties of plants, creepers, trees, bushes, vines in addition to everything he'd planted in his garden. I could see my legs being walked off before we'd cataloged even half of them. Where in hell was that son?

After a few moments we'd completed a circuit and his pupil seemed to have passed the test. I'd mis-identified only one, probably the simplest plant in the world, and one I'd seen at least a million times. He pointed at a knee-high sapling, two stems fanning into broad, pleated leaves. "Uh," I ventured, baffled. "Is it a kind of banana?"

He seemed surprised by my ignorance and almost scoffed in answering: "Coconut." My god, I really was slipping.

We arrived back at his buffalo pen where he began introducing me to each of the placid beasts. They chewed their cud and regarding me with what I can only describe as wary disinterest. Like a good schoolboy, I repeated each of the names as he spoke them.

But then Sin seemed to run out of steam. We returned to the

shed where my pack lay and he seemed bereft of conversation topics. "Where is he?" he said, looking into the pathless jungle. He was so eager to have me stay that I decided to heck with an early start; he obviously can tell me a lot of valuable things about the jungle.

I had slipped the pack onto my shoulder but now laid it down again. When Sin saw that I intended to stay a while longer, he perked up, entering the house to get me another glass of water. As he emerged, we heard sticks crackling among the trees.

A younger version of Sin with a shotgun barrel sticking above his shoulder and rubber boots shodding his feet strode resolutely into the yard. In his belt was an unsheathed hatchet. Had I met him in the jungle I might have run. He seemed not the least bit surprised at my presence, even after Sin had explained who I was and what I was doing there. The son set down his gun and squatted by the fire. His had been a fruitless hunt; no game to be found, not even edible birds.

He and Sin talked for a few moments. As they conversed, the son walked to the house and began searching along the wall. He stopped at a rough teak pillar festooned with feathers. Still talking quietly, he selected one, laying it against the house pillar. He pulled the hatchet from his belt and with a swift blow, chopped the long end from the feather. I was puzzled. Was he about to perform a rite to call the game to him? Replacing the hatchet in his belt, he grasped the quill in his large fingers and began twirling it to clean his ear, all the while talking with his father.

From his pocket, Sin pulled a dried leaf cut into a square and flattened it with his thumb against the shed wall. He saw me watching him and, breaking off his conversation abruptly, held it up for me to see and said "*bai thong gloy*", a leaf I'd seen growing near his garden. From a small tin box whose once-shiny surface had long ago corroded, he extracted a few chopped tobacco leaves, also grown in his garden. He mixed them with a lighter tobacco from another pocket ("*Chaiyo* tobacco," he said, "makes the hill tobacco burn smoother").

He spread the shredded leaves on the wrapper, rolling and tightening it as he went. Using a small pair of rusty scissors to snip both ends off the tube, he slid a bamboo sliver stuck with what appeared to be wetted glutinous rice along one edge of the wrapper to seal his cheroot. I marveled at this bit of hill technology that made the man a walking cigarette factory. He offered it to me, reaching into the fire for a glowing brand to light it. The *Chaiyo* had done little to refine the tobacco's rough flavor. Down the valley, the Thai farmers grew a fine tobacco prized by American connoisseurs for its mildness. Up here, it was rejected for a rough, raw leaf; a straw fire would have produced a smoother smoke. The son borrowed his father's scissors to complete the same operation, touching the brand to the green wrapper and inhaling contentedly. Two men with creosote lungs.

Abruptly, the son rose to his feet, re-shouldered the rifle strode towards the river as unceremoniously as he'd arrived. Even Sin seemed surprised, looking down the path after him as the underbrush swallowed him up.

"He wanted to get back to Muang Ngai," he said, almost apologetically. Now, I felt almost duty-bound to stay around for a while longer. But he surprised me by saying, "Well, I guess you want to get on your way as well."

Sin's eyes lit up when I handed him a 50-*baht* ($2.00) bill. Exceptionally pleased, he hoisted my heavy pack onto his thin shoulders and almost ran downhill to the river with it.

He stood on the bank, watching me prepare the boat. As I lashed the pack to the deck, Sin said: "It was fate."

"What was?" I asked.

"Our meeting. Fate isn't always kind," he said, *waiing* me from the bank.

Tying the last knot, I *waiied* in return and pushed off.

The Abbot and the Amulet

Jai Khwaang Muan Mae Naam
(A heart as wide as the river)
A very generous person

One of the lessons one learns when trekking in the Himalaya is the ephemeral nature of victory. Each time one tops a ridge thinking he's gained a major foothold in his quest for the summit, he finds himself looking down into another valley, all the day's gains erased. And at the bottom, he must begin another demanding ascent to a new ridge with another stunning valley view. I found myself in a similar position as I pushed away from Sin and his buffalo.

Despite the lessons of the previous day, I was immediately embroiled in problems, none of them new. I had vowed not to moor overnight above a rapid, and then had done so because it had looked like a safe haven. Like a car on a winter morning, unflexed muscles and a fogged brain need time to idle before shifting into gear. Once again I bounced off the banks and grated over rocks. When the paddler cannot control his boat, the river controls it for him.

The Ping had begun to lose its clarity. Bedrocks were algae-slicked, a sign of phosphates. The new agriculture called for chemical additives to enhance growth and in their quest to improve yields, farmers gave little thought to long-term soil damage or bestowing chemical-laden irrigation water on downstream villages. Below Huay Sai Khao, farmers cleaned spray cans in the river. The chromed tanks were emblazoned with orange skulls and crossbones, but did the farmers really understand their meaning?

An hour later, the river emerged from thick foliage and its bends flattened. The rocks were still there, however, lurking just beneath a surface opaqued by the sky's reflection. Thinking I saw a shoal, I stood up to get a better look. Instantly, I could see beneath the water, the abrupt angle change revealing light patches indicating shallow water, and dark areas hinting at deep water. Ripples showed me where the river flowed around hidden rocks. It was as though filters had been removed from my eyes. My navigating skills improved dramatically.

Standing also gave me leverage to take more powerful strokes. And keep the boat dry. With the paddle's pendulum sweeping between 9 and 3 o'clock, the arc of droplets fell on the bow, not the deck. I was paddling a new boat.

The next obstacle, however, was visible from any vantage point. Lying across the river was a yard-thick fallen tree with two feet of daylight between its lower surface and the waterline, not enough to slip beneath. Beaching the boat I set to work with my longknife, holding a branch with one hand and twisting so I could chop away the crown branches. The blade was dull and the foliage was so thick that I failed to see that I was hacking at a supporting branch. After several dozen blows, the branch broke free, causing the trunk to drop. Instinctively, I grabbed for another branch and narrowly avoided tumbling into the swirling water. Moments later, the swift current rocketed my boat through the gap. My straw hat, which I had laid on the locker lid while I chopped, was neatly snagged by a branch as I passed, collected as toll.

The trees and mimosa thinned and were replaced by thick bolsters of elephant grass that covered the high banks, obscuring everything beyond them. Their feathery plumes waved in the breeze, and the morning was filled with bird calls. Yellow-breasted wagtails flitted across the river, saffron wedges alternating with the metallic blue flash of kingfishers. The tall mud banks were pitted with dark holes, entrances to kingfisher burrows that ran six feet into the hardened soil. The straight tunnels protected kingfisher fledglings from cobras and other predator snakes unable to undulate along the narrow passages.

Here, the monarch of the bird realm was the ungainly, black-bodied, brown-winged coucal. In the upper river, I'd been fooled by its distinctive call, a series of soft hoots that ascended the scale. They were reminiscent of the female gibbon, whose mournful whoops haunt the central Thailand jungles, the call trailing off in anguished sobs. Thais believed that the gibbon was once a maiden who was transformed by a magus into a long-limbed, shaggy, leathery-faced gibbon as punishment for betraying her lover. Karen and Hmong hilltribes had once believed that her song helped their crops flourish. Each time I heard the coucal, I instinctively looked high in the trees for a gibbon. But they had long ago disappeared from the northern forests, hunted down or deprived of their homes by deforestation.

The coucal, or "crow pheasant" wasn't a bird of romance. It was the size of a crow, and like him, a survivor. Lord of the riverbank, it was immune from destruction, shunned by hunters because it was too bony to eat. Fleshier birds must have envied him.

As the trees receded, the birds were replaced by hundreds of iridescent green butterflies floating just above the water. From time to time, houses appeared but they were set a hundred yards from the Ping, indicating the degree that their owners distrusted the river. At a landing, a woman dipped a bucket into the river, but did not see me. Alerted by giggling, I stood to peer over the grass-covered banks where women chatted as they hoed chartreuse plots of soybeans.

Soon, the water clouded and slowed, sure signs of another weir. Long and narrow and punctuated by sharp bamboo retaining spikes, it gently bent to the left. The angle down its face was so shallow that the water slid 300 feet to drop into a pool that was only five feet lower than the weir crest. The steepness of the riverbanks ruled out portaging; I'd have to find a way down the weir face.

Sin's sandals slid on the slick rocks. Thinking that bare feet might give me better purchase on the stones, I tossed the sandals in the boat. But when my weight tipped a stone, my unprotected foot wedged between two large rocks; I withdrew it bruised and bleeding. At the weir crest, I sliced the other foot on a bamboo stake. If I didn't shod my feet, they'd soon be in tatters.

I'd chosen to stow my running shoes so my feet would be warm and dry at night. Deciding that cold feet were better than damaged feet, I withdrew them from the locker and slipped them on. Not having to watch my step allowed me to concentrate on the task and within moments I had pulled the boat safely down the weir face.

In a calm stretch before the next weir, I saw my first boat, a narrow, unpainted dugout carved from a single log. When I'd asked Chutam why there were no boats on the upper river, his reply was absurdly simple: "It's easy to float down a river but how do we get back up?" Boats were used by flat water fishermen or cross-river ferrymen. Even the bamboo rafts that once hauled goods from Chiang Mai to Bangkok had been replaced by trucks. A farmer could now lug his produce four or five miles to a road and hire a passing pick-up to carry it to market.

Just as the sun at its zenith was heating the air, the forest mercifully closed around me. It was so peaceful that I stopped paddling. At a shady shoal I stripped and plunged into the cold, invigorating water. The river flowed past me, and for the first time I was the unmoving obstacle. I watched how it formed eddies on the downstream portion of my body and sought to carry me away in its liquid embrace. At last, I soaped up, washing wood smoke and grime from my hair and skin. The sun was a balm, drying and warming my sore body.

The afternoon was a duplicate of the morning's pleasures. The sun smoldered in the pale green canopies. A long series of rills and rapids echoed the burbling brook of boyhood summers. Lulled by the Ping's quiet rhythms, I frequently lost concentration. When it sensed I wasn't paying attention, the river would play with me, pulling me into an eddy where I would be jolted to wakefulness by the hull crunching into gravel.

The trees thinned again, and I entered another valley carpeted in small farms. I slipped unnoticed past farmers absorbed in their work and unaccustomed to seeing someone in a boat. I felt like a voyeur but my invisibility allowed me to experience them as they lived naturally.

As I rounded a bend, my ruminations were cut short. Four bare-chested men in sarongs, stood thigh-deep in the water ahead. Long knives hung from their belts and seine nets were wrapped around their arms. The fear that had riveted me when surprised by the tribemen flooded over me. I was in a remote area and as Bain's warnings rang in my ears, I briefly considered pulling over until they moved elsewhere. I then recalled the farmers I'd passed unnoticed. These men were working in two pairs about 30 feet apart, their eyes peering into the depths. I might be able to slip by them undetected.

With the river's babble muffling my paddle strokes, they were unaware of my approach until I was nearly on them. One suddenly backed up, reaching for his knife. Hearing the noise, the others swung around to look at me and one lurched forward to grab the bow. I looked at him, shaking my head and at the same time asked him the distance to the next village.

"About a mile," he said startled, his halting Thai betraying him as a tribesman. But I had the advantage of surprise and they stood unmoving until one asked, "Why are you here?".

"*Samruat,*" I replied, remembering Sin's word for "survey."

"*Samruat,*" he repeated slowly, as I passed him. "How many are there?"

"There's another boat following me," I said. Four pairs of eyes followed my finger pointing upstream into the forest as the current had carried me downstream past their reach. Had I been in danger or was my imagination overactive? I'll never know–they may still be waiting for the second boat to come by. Jack Bain's words had taken root and there was no shaking them. By there was also no denying the magic of the word *samruat.*

After a mile, lime-green tobacco plants crowded the riverbank, tumbling into it where the river had undercut the fields. Behind them was the hazy outline of Chiang Dao, at 7,201 feet, Thailand's third-highest peak; I must be nearing the town of the same name, my first town in days. If I was reading my map correctly I would arrive there shortly past noon but by mid-afternoon, I was still deep in trees. When, two hours later, the high hills reached up to intercept the sun's descent, I realized I had to choose between continuing or camping. Although my hands sported half a dozen burst blisters and were aching from the weight of the paddle, I decided to push on.

Almost immediately I encountered a steep weir. In working my way down its face, I slipped and lost my grip on the boat. It shot down the channel and–to my horror–into a fast current that swiftly carried it downstream. Gashing my ankles on the rocks, I scrambled down the weir face, leapt into the water and began swimming after it. But in the fast river, it grew smaller and smaller and finally disappeared around a bend.

In shock, I stumbled to the bank and slumped on the sand. The shock of what had just happened registered long moments later. In an instant, my journey had ended. And in such a stupid manner. Stunned and trying to process what had happened, I walked a dozen yards downriver to retrieve a towel which had snagged on a branch. As I stood up, I glanced downstream and was amazed to see the boat circling gently in a distant eddy. I crashed through the underbrush to it, ripping the chain out of its housing and wrapping it around a tree in the same motion. For several moments, I stood panting with the growing recognition of how lucky I'd been. How many times had I cursed the boat for putting me into yet another eddy, yet this time its contrariness had saved me.

As I pushed into the current, the sun was hovering on the hill crest. A breeze was blowing and, soaking wet, I was shivering; camping was out of the question. I had to reach shelter.

The river was running so rapidly that it took me only minutes to move two miles downstream. I knew I was nearing civilization when from somewhere high on the bank a boy shouted in clear English: "Where you go?" Around the next bend, the Chiang Dao bridge appeared. I tried to head in but the bridge foot was blocked by trees and debris. I shot past it and only by putting my last ounce of strength behind the paddle did I avoid being swept past the town and into the forest again.

Posted on the tall bank above me was a sign inscribed "Wat Indraram." Beneath it, several young monks watched me tie up.

"We were trying to guess whether you were going to stop or were trying to get some place downriver," one said.

"By the time I got to the bridge, I wasn't sure myself," I replied, to their laughter. "Is there room at the *wat*?" I asked.

"You'll have to find your own food," said one, reminding me that monks eat their daily meal before noon. I glanced into the distance. The low buildings of Chiang Dao were a half mile in from the river, an easy walk. I needed to buy sandals and Band-Aids anyway.

The monks ran to the abbot's *kuti* (a one-man hut used by a monk for habitation and meditation), then back to tell me I had his permission to spend the night in an abandoned *kuti*. The room had not been dusted in months but several young monks set to work with whisk brooms, the dust billowing into the air and then immediately settling back. There was a sleeping mat and a candle but no mosquito net and already the winged beasts were swarming in through the cracks between the wall laths. I showered, hung my wet clothes to dry, and limped to town.

Chiang Dao was once a remote hill village straddling the trail to Fang and the Burmese border. Over the decades, a dirt path had become a logging road and eventually a two-lane asphalt highway that wound among tall trees. The village had grown into a settlement but had not yet acquired the concrete buildings that would mark its decline into another anonymous district town, one of thousands dotting the kingdom. Two-story houses built of hazel-stained planks lined the main street. The lower story held dry goods, hardware, implements, and other farm necessities that spilled out the wide doorways. The upper stories, some with board balconies, were family homes. Chiang Dao's electricity was channeled through dim 40-watt bulbs; moths batted against the globes to reach the flames within.

My first task was to repair the damage to my hands. They were a mess; abrasions, scratches, broken blisters, cuts, the hands of a very old and battered man. I was barely into my journey; if I didn't take better care of them, they wouldn't last another week. I had considered gloves but bare hands gave me a firmer grip and more intimate contact with the boat. It was psychological conceit and I was paying dearly for it.

Chiang Dao offered few services but one shop was a joy. More than any so-called convenience store I'd seen, this one was crammed with everything one could need. Utterly without organization, tables and shelves overflowed with canisters of motor oil, cheap perfumes, canned foods, clothes, sewing needles, plowshares, bamboo scoops, clay water jars, galvanized buckets, fish traps, rope, chewing gum; all the products of a country general store. Open-fronted, it would have benefited from glass panes. Instead, the owner walked around, flicking goods with a duster of chicken feathers, erasing grit blown in by passing trucks. I bought a dozen Band-Aids, a pair of rubber sandals, and oil for the locks which had been seizing up. To replace the one the branch had snatched, I bought a broad-brimmed straw hat.

In another shop, I sat at a marble-topped round table like those in Bangkok's Chinese restaurants, and ordered rice and a pork curry. I was so thirsty, I downed four bottles of Vitamilk, a sweetened soybean drink. Thirst had plagued me throughout the day and my two one-quart canteens had been insufficient to slake my dry throat. I would have to buy more in Chiang Mai.

It was only 7 p.m. and I was sagging. The long hours in Bangkok lifting weights, swimming, running, and rowing seemed to have done little good. Muscles I didn't even know I had were being strained to the limit.

My shoulders, mid-back, and abdomen ached with each movement, special muscles that had little use in other endeavors. (I would later return to Bangkok and discover to my dismay that I could not swim any farther nor lift more weight than I had before I left.) I bought a small jar of Tiger Balm liniment and trudged back to the *wat*.

Except for the mongrels scrapping under the houses, the *wat* was deserted. A passing farmer told me the monks had been invited to a neighboring village to chant at the funeral of a mahout who had been crushed by an elephant. They wouldn't return until late.

In my room, I lit a candle. While the mosquitoes hummed around me, I applied antiseptic cream to my hands and bandaged the worst of my wounds. In minutes, all 12 Band-Aids were gone and several cuts remained undressed.

In a corner, I found a discarded mosquito coil. Touching my lighter to it, I watched the tip glow orange like an incense stick and hoped that the thin tendril of pungent smoke might disperse the mosquitoes. I lit a candle and, placing it close to my map I traced the day's journey. I had traveled more than 13 miles, winding around several hills to emerge into this gorge, yet my straight-line distance totaled only five miles. Five miles! Such a lot of work for such a short gain. At this rate, the journey would take months.

I noted the lessons of the day. My journal read:

Rule One: When you make a rule, heed it. I'd told myself to secure all gear. When I ignored the rule, I lost my hat. Replacing it had been easy but what would happen when I entered wilderness areas without markets?

Rule Two: Stay alert. Twice I had been distracted by something on the bank and immediately I'd gotten into trouble. The boat was like a young child; leave it alone for a moment, and it would get into mischief and take me with it.

I reviewed the river I'd experienced that day: Although I was still in the hills, the Ping moved through this valley like a sluggish old delta river limping towards the sea. The clear waters and wild rapids of the upper river were gone. The once-clean bottom was now covered with fern-like plants that waved mesmerizingly like a maiden's hair. There had been more obstacles than I'd imagined, fallen trees and weirs. And bamboo bridges.

I was startled by a crackling. An sharp scent told me I'd drowsed and singed my hair in the candle flame. Time for bed. The map suggested that the new day would bring sharp descents and, perhaps, some excitement. I needed sleep to cope. In a distant village, a watchman tolled the hour: 8 p.m. The last time I had gone to bed at 8 p.m., I had been seven years old. After crawling into my sleeping bag, I pinched the candle wick between two moistened fingers and sank beneath a silent ocean.

Through the unglazed window, the frosted, forested mountains echoed with the sharp caws and fluty songs of a half dozen birds foraging for seeds and fruits. Unfortunately, the night had not been cold enough to discourage the mosquitoes that had used the coil as a beacon to zero in on whatever extremity protruded from my sleeping bag. Any skin not covered in Band-Aids was swollen with bites. My hands seemed to belong to an ancient mummy.

I opened the *kuti* door to give entry to the cold wind that had been nudging it. Through the fog, an undulating ribbon of saffron assumed a shape and became a line of silent monks returning from collecting alms at a nearby village. As they entered the compound, a few broke rank and ran to the porch to invite me to breakfast. Monastery breakfasts generally take place at 8 a.m. after the *luang paw* (abbot) has eaten his fill. Staying for breakfast meant setting off late but I'd be violating hospitality if I refused an invitation.

I shaved, packed, and checked the day's route. Then, as I sat on the top step watching the sun disperse the fog from the ravine, a young monk beckoned me to follow him. Oblivious to the cold, his bare feet padded on the hard earth as he led me to the porch where the abbot was eating breakfast. I folded myself into a modified lotus at the edge of his straw mat. An elderly man with cropped gray hair and sagging flesh, the abbot said nothing. Indifferent to my presence, he dipped curries and condiments from a half dozen dishes, dropping them on the small mountain of rice in his own plate. A *luang paw* is not obliged to address a lay person directly; he is aloof from daily considerations and my existence was my own business, not his. This one ignored me completely for several moments.

At last, he cleared his throat loudly and I prepared myself for the usual questions.

"Are you a Buddhist?"

"No. I am a Christian," I replied, though I couldn't recall when I'd last been in a church, much less what brand of Christian I was.

"How long have you lived in Thailand?"

"18 years."

"And you're not a Buddhist?"

"I believe in some of the tenets of Buddhism. Avoiding suffering is a good formula for living."

"If that's so," I saw him puckishly smile, "why are you paddling a boat down the river?"

Touché. "I'm not sure, but you're right, I'm not avoiding suffering."

"Yes, your hands..." This was uncanny. I'd been watching him the whole time and he still had not even glanced my direction.

"Minor problems," I said. "They'll heal."

The spoon continued its circuit between rice plate and mouth, his eyes concentrated on his task as a form of meditation. "Do you have protection?" That word again.

"From...?"

"*Jai dam* (black hearts)."

"I carry a longknife..." I said.

"I mean something more powerful."

"No..." Had someone gone through my pack?

He pointed with his spoon to a rusted tin box in a corner. A young monk brought it over. Its faded label said it had once held a salve to heal buffalo hide. The monk extracted a small tan object, showing it to the *luang paw* who shook his head. The monk then withdraw a dark, slightly larger triangular tablet. The abbot nodded and the monk handed it across to me.

"This is your protection."

I lay the small baked-clay amulet in my palm. Enclosed in a flame-like halo was a badly-worn bas relief of a meditating Buddha.

"This has special powers to turn away knife blades and bullets. Do you have a necklace?"

"No."

"You can buy one in Chiang Mai. And have this framed. In gold. Wear it around your neck at all times. For now, put it in your shirt pocket and do not, at any time, let it go below your waist line." Asians believe that the head is holy, the feet profane; putting the amulet below my waist would be blasphemy.

"Thank you," I said, raising my hands in a *wai*.

He motioned me away with his spoon, ending the conversation. If he glanced at my back as I descended the stairs, it was the only time he acknowledged my presence with his eyes. The monks motioned me to follow them and in a side room I found other curries spread on a mat. In contrast to the laconic abbot, the monks were gregarious. They asked many questions about wild animals, whether I was afraid, how much the boat cost, if I'd met any bad people along the way.

They came from nearby villages and their knowledge was of the world of hills and farms. I asked about the mahout at whose funeral they had chanted the previous evening.

"He was stupid."

"Why?"

"Everyone knows you don't go near an elephant when it is in musth."

"Musth?"

"In heat," one monk said. "You can tell by the stream of tears that come from glands beneath the eyes; they mean he is *baba-bobo* (crazy). He'll kill anyone who gets in his way. The mahout was foolish." The others grunted in agreement.

We talked about elephants. Although they were still the best vehicles in steep terrain–especially during the monsoon when the rains turned the roads to mush–their role in logging was declining. It would cease altogether the following month when the government imposed a ban on logging.

"What will happen to the elephants if the ban goes into effect?"

Shrugged shoulders. "Carry tourists, I guess. Go back to the Northeast where the mahouts come from. Walk around in Bangkok so that women can get pregnant."

"What?"

"You know, let women walk under the bellies."

"Ah," I said, remembering. Elephants regularly walked Bangkok's streets, their wall-like sides serving as billboards advertising their services. For 30 *baht*, barren women could walk under the great beasts' stomachs in hopes of becoming pregnant, an act of courage considering how easily the mammoth animals spooked. The belief stemmed from a legend that said Buddha's mother conceived in a dream in which a white elephant touched her side with his trunk, the Buddhist version of Mary and the immaculate conception. The belief still had currency among rural women. In the city it was the migrant laborers who pursued this course; rich women consulted expensive obstetricians.

The sun had cauterized the ravine and the fog was gone. Tiny diamonds hung from the trees or sped like shooting stars to the ground. As I watched, the monks wrapped rice and roasted pork in banana leaves and fastened them with slivers of bamboo. "Lunch," they said, handing the bundles to me. After hiking to town to buy three dozen Band-Aids, I once again pushed into the swift current, watched by the monks until I disappeared from sight.

The morning was stunning. The sun backlit the pale green bamboo leaves and sparkled off the water. The river ran strongly and was now broad enough so I didn't bump into the banks. After a mile, I entered a long gorge. Set in a deep "V," the river ran through a series of rapids, providing the first true whitewater I had encountered. Two days before, I might have capsized due to inexperience, but today it was a clean run. Maybe I was learning something at last.

At noon, I pulled to shore and climbed the high banks to eat my rice and pork. Glancing downstream my breath caught; two hundred feet below my boat, the river was strewn with huge rocks. I searched for a passage and saw only a four-foot breach between two house-sized boulders through which the river gushed, dropping five feet into a churning pool. If I failed to hit the channel dead center, the boat would be smashed by a boulder, or turn sideways and lodge between the boulders, dumping me into the boiling water.

I was strangely calm as I sat in the shade, sipping water, plotting my approach. In casting off, I would paddle hard to the middle, swing the bow to point into the gap, and shoot through. The longer I looked at it, the more difficult it seemed. Better to move quickly before I had second thoughts.

I slipped the chain from the tree. Several Thais stood on a nearby bluff, watching silently. As I exited the eddy, the current sucked me towards the opening. Paddling hard, I reached the middle but a cross-river current carried me to the left and out of range. As the river relentlessly propelled me toward the left-hand boulder, I swung the bow to the right and dug hard for the river's center. No sooner had I re-aligned myself then the boat shot through the gap, scraping the rock on the right and landing with a whump in the pool below.

The churning water exited the pool in a dozen directions, turning and twisting the boat, soaking me with spray, sucking me backwards into the gap. With all my strength, I paddled rapidly, hoping the cataract would not fill the boat before I could break free. Long moments later, the river decided to let me go, shoving the boat roughly into the mainstream, swiftly carrying me out of danger. Above the roar of the falls, I heard the Thais cheering. My boat might be a bathtub but it responded superbly when coaxed by hard strokes. For the next half hour, I slalomed on a wild sleigh ride in and out of the big rocks, my nerves keening. As the white water thundered around me, I whooped in excitement, the adrenaline rushing through my veins faster than the river through the gorge.

When at last I emerged into calmer water, my heart was thumping and all my senses were electrified. "Yes!" I shouted in triumph. For a brief moment I had figured out how the river thought and used its strength to my advantage. Might I actually become a boatman after all?

Guns and Ghosts

Naam Ning, Lai Luk
(Still water runs deep)
Don't underestimate quiet people

"Snow."

It was the first word he had uttered in several minutes and it was so unexpected that I involuntarily tipped forward, my chair legs banging the porch floor.

"Snow? Where?"

"In America."

"Ah yes. In the northern states."

"And ice."

"Sometimes."

He pondered this, nodding, his sturdy body as calm as his words.

"Cold, working in the fields."

"Oh, when the snows come that's the end of work 'til spring."

"No crops?"

"Ground's too hard. The plants can't stand the cold. They die. It's like that for four or five months."

A flicker of surprise. "The winter here is so chilly. Painful."

In the mauve light, the distant fields were hedgehogs, pale rice stalks bristling in the evening sky. Crickets rubbed their legs together as much to warm themselves as to herald the approaching night.

A day of paddling had brought me to Mr. Mun's porch. The winding river had meandered across a flat valley of soybean fields, like a dog lazily sniffing his way across a yard. I should have rejoiced at the quieter pace but I missed the rapids. My field of vision had also narrowed to three hues: blue-black water, azure sky, and the six-foot grass wall that concealed fields and muffled sounds. I was blind, orienting myself by the sun, and giving shape to an unseen world by listening to aural clues filtering through the whispering screen.

Most of the afternoon's journey had been in stillness, the sky dotted like a musical score by bands of twittering birds. The occasional gong and the shushing of rumination among the tall grasses betrayed the presence of cows. Young herdsmen neglected their charges to prowl among the trees, exploding sibilants and hushed shouts telling me they had spotted a bird. Sounds enabled me to picture a small boy drawing a sun-dried clay pellet from his shorts pocket, cradling it in a homemade slingshot. And then, the sharp thwack as the projectile smacked into dense mango leaves, followed by hoarse accusations and exasperations if the bird fled unscathed. The recriminations ceased only when another bird was sighted. For the boys, it was both sport and–if the quarry was large enough–protein supplement to a spare farm diet.

Occasionally, the gusts that ran fingers through the tall grass carried the giggles and murmurs of farmers and their wives weeding onions in distant fields. I reveled in my isolation the way a child tingles to think he might be invisible. If nothing else, it provided privacy for private thoughts.

The river undulated through the fields like a prowling snake, at times appearing to travel in circles. It was disconcerting to have the sun at my back, then at one side, and then blinding me, only to have it appear at my other side, then my back again. It was discouraging to pass a large tree and half an hour later creep ashore to find it still only a stone's throw away. In the afternoon, however, the river finally made up its mind where it wanted to go and etched a straighter path across the valley.

The sinking sun was igniting the breeze-blown grass plumes like candle flames when I called to a fisherman to ask the location of the next village. "Baan Ba Jee," he replied, "about two kilometers downriver." I paddled steadily for half an hour and was beginning to think I had passed it when the grass shutter slid away to reveal a slick plank landing nearly level with the water. Tying up at a bamboo stake, I climbed the dirt steps and nearly bumped into a very startled elderly farmer standing in his kitchen garden. Naked except for a checkered sarong, he had apparently been on his way to the river for a bath when this apparition leapt into his back yard. When I asked the name of the village, it took him a few moments to recover his composure and confirm that I had landed in Baan Ba Jee. The old man was joined by an equally wizened, equally short wife, their leathery skins crinkled by myriad suns.

"Where did you come from?" he asked, looking up at me.

"Mae Ja."

"Where to?"

To the sea? It sounded too foolish. "Chiang Mai," I said.

"And where are you staying tonight?"

Behind them was their small hovel. I weighed imposing on their meager abode and resources.

"I don't know..." I said hesitantly.

"You should stay with the *phu yai baan*," said the woman, wearing the same beatific smile as her husband. "He has a nice, big house." Village telegraph soon announced my arrival and within moments, I was engulfed by children. Circumspect with Northern reserve, they ran their eyes rather than their hands over my boat, exchanging their discoveries in excited murmurs.

"Where's the village from here?" I asked them.

Arms pointed a dozen directions. Technically they were all correct. Beyond the dry fields, I could see that the village was spread over a wide area.

"Where is your house?" I asked, and the arms pointed another dozen directions. A voice at my elbow came to my rescue.

"The *phu yai baan*'s house is down the path and over there," the old man said, his bony arm tracing a track along the river and then jigging left across the fields to a house that looked more prosperous than its neighbors.

Locking the boat and entrusting my paddles to the couple, I set off down a road bathed in orange sunlight. Several children sped on ahead, skipping sideways and backwards, torn between watching me and spreading the news in the village. I would discover that children were my keys to a warm welcome in a village: if they were determined that I should stay, their elders were loathe to refuse them.

Solid wooden houses set on high stilts were arrayed along the first graveled road I'd seen since Mae Ja. The headman's house differed from the rest in that its ground floor, normally open, was enclosed by walls of concrete blocks. The headman was standing before his house with a reception committee of half a dozen farmers; their wives peeked out from doorways. The children danced around the fringes of my entourage or ran back to take my hand and pull me towards the headman.

Mun Kiankham was a stocky man. Unlike the shuffling, baggy-panted, blue-shirted farmers surrounding him, his body–clad in a tan shift and khaki pants–was planted like a teak tree in the solid earth. He was pleasant but unsmiling, his gravity betraying shyness.

"Where are you coming from?"

"Chiang Dao. I stayed at the *wat*."

"Where are you staying tonight?"

"Not sure. Any suggestions?"

"Here," the children shouted.

"How many of you are there?"

Again the children answered for me. He shifted as if shaking out stiffness, visibly relaxing.

"I don't have much space...and you'll have to sleep on the floor. What do you eat?"

"Whatever you eat."

For the first time, he showed surprise. "Anything?" I thought I detected the hint of a sly smile. "Do you have any baggage in the boat? You should bring it all up here. Thieves," he added ominously.

I thanked him and set off for the boat. The drove of children was augmented by several farmers anxious to see the boat.

The elderly couple was standing at the same spot I had left them. "What did he say?" Two pairs of anxious eyes watched me.

"He said it was alright to stay with him." Visible relief.

While the men watched from above, the children scampered down the riverbank and grabbed whatever I untied, two or three of them team-ing up to drag the heavy items up the bank. Several men came down to look at the boat, running their hands over its hull, patting it approvingly. Locking it, I climbed up the dirt stairs to find that my gear was already trundling down the road, large bugs scurrying uncertainly on a multitudes of legs silhouetted against the dying light.

At the house, the headman told the children to put my belongings on a raised concrete platform which I realized would be my bed. His wife was preparing dinner, he said, so I should shower quickly and join them. Farm families dine shortly after sundown while there is still daylight to prepare the meal, but even in villages like this that had electricity, the habit had persisted.

After dinner, I laid my map on the floor to check my progress for the day. A dozen small bodies flopped down to peer excitedly at it. Tracing my route on the map, I calculated the distance by bending a twist-tie to the contours of the winding river, then straightening it and measuring it against the scale in the map's margin. Boys and girls watched me intently, wondering in loud whispers what I was doing. Before I had a chance to answer, one little girl had sounded out the name, written in Thai, of a village near the river. The others immediately leapt to that section. Suddenly the map had r elevance to their lives. Another village name was deciphered. They began moving rapidly across the map towards the village at the end of my red twist-tie. Finally, one child pounced on Baan Ba Jee and the whispers erupted into cries of delight as a dozen more children crowded in. Their excited cries attracted the older men who knelt down to confirm the discovery.

The air was electric. It was as though their remote village's appearance on a government map conferred legitimacy. "We are on the map, therefore, we exist." I remembered the excitement I had felt in the city hall of a small Dutch town when in the registrar's ledger I found my grandfather's name and details of his birth. The black ink on the sepia page seemed to signify bureaucratic recognition of my grandfather and, by extension, me. Here, half a world away, a map had the same effect. I could hear echoes of the discovery rolling from house to house. Feet ran to my room, new villagers crowded in to see for themselves. It seemed incredible that such a small item could generate such enthusiasm.

When most of the crowd had filtered home, the headman invited me to the front of his house where a small roof covered the beginnings of a porch. He motioned me to a chair and took another. To my surprise, he tipped his chair back to lean against the wall, a gesture seldom seen in Thailand. He noted my reaction and said, "Cowboys. They tipped their chairs in a movie I once saw in Chiang Mai. Long time ago." I tipped my chair back.

Even at their most voluble, rural Thais are economical speakers but the headman was downright parsimonious with his thoughts. He spoke as if he were removing each word from his pocket, examining it carefully, then handing it to me. Yet I felt comfortable. This was not the terse interrogation of the morning but the musings of a thoughtful man. We sat quietly for a long while; if we'd had pipes, we would have been smoking them. The full moon had not yet risen; wisps of cooking fire smoke hazed the housetops, blurring the crowns of the palm trees. Cricket drone was punctuated by an occasional dog yapping at the ghosts already creeping along the bamboo fences. Children's voices floated out of the houses as the village prepared for sleep. We seemed to be the only ones still out.

"What grains do you plant?" he ventured, breaking the silence.

"Wheat, oats, some rice. In California they plant rice by airplane."

He pondered for a long while, letting its import seep in before answering. "Airplanes," he said, at last. "Good idea. No bending over planting rice shoots. No back pains."

His frame of reference for nearly everything we discussed, was agricultural. He was a farmer, addressing his thoughts to soil, planting a few polished corn seeds per hill rather than broadcasting them, scattergun.

"No water buffalo?"

"No."

"So how do they plow?"

"Tractors."

He must have been storing up questions for some time, practical questions like: Do Americans live in bamboo houses? He was fascinated by the Japanese ability to grow square bamboo and had heard somewhere of their techniques for growing square watermelons. He seemed especially intrigued by the corporate farming practiced in the American Midwest but couldn't foresee it gaining a foothold in Thailand. "Wrong kind of land. Plots are too small, too many elevation changes, too many big stones in the fields."

Although he was one of the quietest men I would meet, his inquisitiveness seemed to embar rass him.

"Sorry I ask so many questions. You are the first foreigner that has ever come to this village," he said quietly. "I see them in the market in Chiang Mai but they don't speak Thai. I've never had anyone to answer my questions."

I assured him that I enjoyed talking with him, and asked him a few of my own. I learned that Baan Ba Jee had 260 "roofs", the traditional method for enumerating rural populations. Families grew beans, garlic, potatoes, and corn. The local school educated its pupils to grade six and the small wat had two monks. The village was three miles from the main road and the graveled track was a sign of its growing prosperity. "Five years ago, we didn't have a road. Now, we have a few pick-up trucks."

"How much land does a farmer need?"

He thought about it. "Eight, ten *rai* (three or four acres). Twice that if he has children. And that's just to get by."

The figure seemed high but all along the river, whenever I asked about the acreage needed to get by, I got a different number. I soon learned to use each number as a general indicator of soil fertility and village prosperity. Two or three acres to support a four-member family indicated very rich soil, usually in areas where forests had recently been felled. More than five acres suggested that farmers were struggling to get by, especially as sons grew to maturity and needed land of their own.

Thailand's crop yields were generally low. I'd been shocked to read that, despite its reputation as an Asian Rice Bowl, Thailand had one of the lowest rice yields in Asia, exceeding only Cambodia. The average Chinese farmer harvested three times as much grain per acre as a Thai farmer. However much it had distressed urban residents to see their populations burgeon, the cities and their factories had been godsends to farmers, providing off-season cash and employment for grown children who would otherwise have been asking their fathers for farm land.

Mr. Mun considered his village poor, yet by comparison with other regions, Baan Ba Jee was doing well. More encouraging, it seemed to have considerable potential, as if real affluence lay just around the corner.

To my surprise, Mun introduced me to his wife by name. "This is Saisawan," he said. Throughout our conversation, Saisawan sat to one side, listening and occasionally asking her own questions. Northern women were not shy about stating their opinions openly, and showed no dismay about talking with me, a trait I found refreshing. It contrasted with the reticence and subordination to husbands that I often found in Central Plains villages.

We continued to exchange thoughts for half an hour, talking farm talk about crops and harvesting methods. Mostly, we discussed the daily life of a farmer, the hard labor, the uncertain weather, the vagaries of the marketplace.

"All farmers have hard lives," he said. "Here, we say 'face to the earth, back to the sky, forever.' It must be the same in America." Thinking of the American farm failures of the 1980s and of farm families foreclosed on land they had tilled for generations, I could only agree. It occurred to me that when a nation on the road to industrialization plows small farmers under with big tractors and combines, it loses its soul. It was perhaps a simplistic view, but these people were clear-eyed realists, hard-working, open to new ideas, and in touch with their surroundings.

We sat in silence for a while and then, sensing the lateness of the hour, we tipped our chairs forward, stretched and got ready for bed. One by one, the children had sleepily stumbled home, leaving the map on the floor. I returned to measuring my distance. I had traveled 12 miles but what pleased me was that I now thought nothing of paddling all day. Perhaps, at last, my body was beginning to align with the river's rhythms.

Once again, dawn was announced by sound, rather than light. Cocks heralded the new day long before it arrived while ducks grumbled in protest at the early awakening. The cows lowed and rapped their hooves sharply on the hard ground, stamping impatiently in their confinement. Mynahs, crows, and coucals added their voices to the swelling choir, and dogs barked away the last of the night's phantoms. Buckets and farm implements clanged against one another, evidence that, as usual, nearly everyone but me was up.

I emerged into crisp air and a sallow sky. The low fog hanging over the fields muffled a similar cacophonous chorus echoing from an unseen village across the river. So much for the tranquil countryside.

My first step told me that I'd made a serious mistake in failing to treat my wounds the previous evening. My heel was cracked and infected; I winced when I put my full weight on it. My swollen hands burned and throbbed with a deep fire, and the rims of the cuts were an angry red. Had I changed the Band-Aids, the antiseptic cream could have healed through the night before everything was re-wetted the next day. I now put fresh cream on the cuts, knowing that while it would not repair the damage, it would halt the infection's advance.

I watched the cows being fed. Dirty gray and blown with chimney soot, their hip bones protruded and their ribs were latticework covered in a tissue hide. In temperament, they were the epitome of the contented cow; docile, Buddhist bovines that moved calmly through untroubled lives, taking little, giving little. As the bamboo poles penning them slid away, they flicked their tails and stepped jauntily to a day in the fields, driven there by boys one-half their height whacking their flanks with bamboo sticks. A creaking bullock cart burdened by a few sleepy farmers followed them.

I returned to the house to pack. From a nail on the living room wall hung a pair of handcuffs, symbol of the houseowner's authority. In one corner of the room, Mun was laying out a khaki uniform, attaching all the badges and symbols of his rank.

"Meeting in Mae Taeng," was all he said. At these weekly meetings, village leaders were told the government's latest development policy and were informed of new farm or marketing technology. They also gossiped and compared notes with headmen from other villages. When Mun asked me to write my name in Thai on a page torn from a school notebook, I knew I would be a topic of discussion. Good. It might smooth my entry into downstream villages. We said our good-byes and I pushed off.

It was another magical winter morning. The slow wave of the breeze through the tall riverbank grasses was interrupted by darting birds in search of insects. Below Baan Ba Jee, I slipped beneath a covered bridge, the first one I'd ever seen in Thailand. Painted white, it resembled the whitewashed, windowed bridges that spanned Vermont streams, an incongruity that could only be traced to a New England missionary long ago stationed in the North and pining for home.

More foreign objects appeared. Waterwheels, 20 feet tall and resembling the side-wheels on Mississippi riverboats, creaked as the current pressed against their blades. The wheel's iron pipe rims were fitted with bamboo tubes that dipped water from the river. As the wheel made its slow revolution, the brimming tubes were carried skyward where they spilled their burdens into a trough that guided the liquid into distant fields. The musical moans of the un-oiled wheel were counterpointed by the plink of water droplets falling to the Ping's steel drum surface.

I moved along an unhurried river with nowhere to go and all day to get there. The riverbanks drooped to reveal soybean fields and then rose to wall them off again. It was a strange sensation, as though the river itself was slowly undulating, escalating me upwards as an ocean swell carries a gull, then sliding me down to the trough again. Dotting the grasses was a green bush that bore delicately-scented flowers like baby's breath. Cows foraged unseen within the elephant grass, their neck gongs tuned in perfect fifths, their arrhythmic clanging assonant and soothing.

Riparian farmlands extended right to the water's edge. Undercut by the river, many had collapsed, laying bare the earth's bones. About five feet of dark brown loam rested atop a layer of large stones. In some places, erosion exposed entire grass plants in cutaway–as in a child's ant farm–revealing the grassroots I'd often read about.

As the morning warmed, the river came alive with fishermen. They dropped hooks in the water, set bamboo basket traps in its shallows, or cast nets to pinion unsuspecting fish. Boys wearing rude diving goggles and clutching pronged spears or homemade spear guns–a chunk of wood and an old bicycle innertube–inhaled with a gasp and plunged beneath the water along the river's edge. Their bodies were clearly visible just below the surface, their heads weaving back and forth in search of fish taking refuge in the reeds.

People smiled in delight and offered shy greetings when they saw me. At intervals, I passed families sitting 10 to 12 feet above the water on platforms made of saplings and bamboo.

"Where are you going?" they'd shout. I'd tell them.

"Where are you coming from?" I'd fill in the blanks.

"Isn't the water too deep?" No, I can swim, I'd tell them, paddling on.

From uninhabited sections came murmurs louder than those of the river or the wind through the grass. It may have been my active imagination but twice I heard what sounded like amorous couples hidden amidst them. With the lack of privacy in crowded family homes, the tall grass would provide the only seclusion a young couple might find in a village. The dark corners of Bangkok parks were notorious trysting places for couples who jokingly referred to the park's bushes and shrubs as *rongraem jingreed* or "cricket hotels."

Of course, pleasure is transitory; it is a free float only until the next obstacle appears. By the end of the morning I'd had to work my way down two more weirs. Several times the river split, sandwiching an island between twin channels. I could usually see where they rejoined downriver but twice I'd chosen the wrong branch and ground into a sandy shelf, and was forced to drag the heavy boat back upriver and into the correct waterway. "How will you know you that are going the right direction?" friends had asked. Early river explorers generally worked their way upriver from the sea. At each fork, they had to resolve which channel was the main stem and which was the tributary; and wasted considerable time paddling into dead ends. By comparison, I had it easy: if the water was coming towards me, I was going the wrong way. This flippant answer would serve me until I reached the Chao Phya where channels branching from the main stream often turned into entirely new rivers that entered the Gulf of Thailand through completely different mouths.

Soon, jungled walls pinched off the valley and I found myself in a long gorge. Partially forested, its steep rocky walls discouraged logger and farmer alike and thus was preserved from human harm. It was so beautiful that I lingered over lunch, sitting on a shady ledge above deep pools, the leaves set to whispering by a rumor wind, the deep red or dark blue dragonflies barely audible as they settled on my shirt or boat.

With great reluctance I peeled myself off the rock, unwrapped the chain from a shrub, and pushed into the current, not even bothering to pick up the paddle. Instead, I drifted, the boat bobbing among the rills and rocks as it found its way downstream. My reveries were interrupted by three of the largest weirs I'd yet encountered. I wrestled the boat down them but in the last, I slipped and fell into a pool. In an eddy, I stripped off and put on dry clothes, laying my wet sweatshirt on the locker lid to dry.

The narrowing river entered a valley hemmed by hills clad in the autumn reds and yellows. In the tropics, trees shed their leaves not to face the winter, but to endure the heat of the approaching hot season. Here, no cows grazed, the vegetation was uncut, and no paths led away from the river. I seemed to be in a forest preserve.

Suddenly, a gunshot reverberated off the hillside. I lifted my paddle from the water and let my boat drift. Other shots rang out nearer me. I floated, listening carefully, trying to pinpoint their source, distance, and heading. Two groups of hunters seemed to be moving independently. When, ten minutes later, the guns reported again, the shots were more muffled. They must have crossed the ridge and entered the next valley. I was safe.

"Maybe this is a good place to test my own gun," I thought. The left bank comprised rock walls, and the breaks in the vegetation allowed me to see anyone headed my way. Checking that the 13-bullet clip was full, I slid it home, surprised by the loud click as it seated itself. Standing in the boat, I aimed at a small tree and pulled the trigger. The pistol jerked in my hand, throwing me off balance and nearly pitching me into the water. "Wow, is it loud!" I thought as a dozen birds beat the air in panicked flight. I paddled over to my target; the tree was unmarked. Adjusting the sight did little to improve my aim. I fired half the clip with a noticeable lack of success. Concerned that I was attracting attention, I replaced the gun in the map box, musing that in my lack of expertise I had been environmentally responsible: although I'd winged a few branches, shattered a few leaves, the tree itself escaped unharmed.

For another hour I paddled. The trees leaned closer, dipping spindly fingers into the river. I reached behind me to see if the sweatshirt was dry... and touched wood. Wheeling around, I saw only a few water droplets dotting an empty locker lid. Damn. While my back was turned, the thieving trees had quietly lifted my only protection against the cold. I cursed them for conspiring with the river but they stood silent, their stillness betraying their guilt. I paddled on, despondent.

The Ping flattened and broadened, then deepened, and slowed. An hour later, no weir had appeared but I was paddling in a static river that was 60 feet wide. Then, banana trees appeared through a break in the jungle wall. I'd deduced by this point that the appearance of banana trees, palm trees, and dogs–none of them occurring naturally in the wild– suggested the presence of humans. Farther on, four wooden houses appeared on the right bank.

It was a tidy settlement, inviting enough, but something made my neck hair tingle. I considered it for several moments, drifting while my pounding brain sought to decipher the information it was receiving. Of course, it finally occurred to me, no blue smoke rose from roofs, there were no sounds, not even a dog. Why would people abandon a good house whose gardens were well tended? I pushed quietly up to the landing and stood atop the bank looking for movement.

The silence was eerie. I'd heard stories of Asian villages whose inhabitants had spotted an intruder before he was aware of their presence. When he came upon the houses, they were deserted, some with cooking fires still smoldering. What he couldn't know was that the villagers were hidden in the jungle, watching him carefully to see what he wanted. I could feel wary eyes peering from every black hole in the vegetation. If they had intended to spook me, they had succeeded. I stepped back in the boat and pushed off, moving to the middle of the river and watching to see if they would reveal themselves. Nothing moved. A ghost village.

A mile downstream, a small landing appeared on the left. On the bank above it was a roofed platform, a field hut built for shelter by farmers guarding their crops against birds and vermin. Far away, I heard shouts and the crackling of brush being burned. Smoke rose less than half a mile away. When no one came, I inspected the hut. A tattered plastic bag hanging from a beam nail held cooked rice but it was dry and hard. Another sack held moldy green beans. That meant the hut hadn't been occupied for some time. I partially unpacked but decided to wait until sundown before settling in completely.

The crickets were beginning their evening chirp when I heard voices. In the twilight, a boat was moving upstream along the opposite shore. One man was paddling, the other was casting a net. A rifle lay across the bow. I crouched frozen behind a screen of grass as I watched one of them scan along my shore, his eyes stopping at my boat. He called his partner's attention to it but they paddled on.

I didn't think they'd seen me but I couldn't take chances on their coming to investigate. Now what? If these were *jai dam*, they might return after dark when I was asleep. Already spooked by the deserted village, I grew paranoid. Any settlement was preferable to the potential dangers of sleeping in the open. Not bothering to tie anything down, I pushed off. Around a bend half a mile on, the river widened and the trees fell away. The horizon line told me I'd hit not a weir, but a broad concrete dam. Concrete houses were clustered on both shores; an official installation of some sort, I surmised. A man on the bank must have noticed my confusion because he called out that this was *cholaprathan*, a government barrage called Mae Faek.

"*Cholaprathan*" means "gift of water," in this instance, a gift from the government. Since its name signified charity, perhaps I would not be turned away as I had been at the army outpost. The jovial officer in charge told me there was a room on the opposite bank, and I was welcome to it. It contained a hard bed with a thin mattress but it would do. After a cold shower, I dined with several guards on curries they had prepared.

"What are those abandoned houses about a mile upstream?" I asked.

"Not abandoned, temporarily vacated," one said, to the others' laughter. "The merchants of Mae Taeng (a town a few miles away) are also farmers," he explained. "They keep gardens here and when they come out to tend them, they rest in the houses. You came late in the day, after they had returned to town." Such a simple explanation.

As I made my way back to the small house, a bright orange line worked its way slowly up the slopes, a fire loose among fallen leaves and underbrush. By burning dry debris while the trees were still moist from monsoon rains, the villagers kept it from becoming tinder that would ignite hot season forest fires.

For a change, it was the sun—not cock crows or farmyard sounds—that woke me. Wanting to refill my canteens, I crossed the dam crest and arrived at the opposite bank as a man hurtling down the hill reached me. "The chief wants to see you," he announced, breathlessly. I followed him up the hill to an impressive old house, the sort the teak *wallahs* of the last century had occupied. Solid, set on high stilts to discourage nocturnal prowlers, the upper story was surrounded on four sides by a wide verandah like a ranger's firewatch tower. The walls were screened and glassless, an airy aerie with a superb view of the dam, the valley, and the hills.

Through the open doorway, I could see that the living room walls were weighted in antlered trophies, no doubt shot during idle days between monsoon seasons when little water flowed down the river. After a few moments, the chief shuffled to the door and let me in. Chamlong was in his late fifties, slightly rotund, and unprepossessing to the point of melancholy. He motioned me to a rattan sofa with sagging cushions and then sat looking at me. His glasses might well have been mirrors, reflecting the world but revealing little of the owner's interior world.

When I realized he was not about to initiate the conversation, I outlined my travels to date. He listened politely but did not respond. I kept talking, hoping he would offer a comment. None came. Finally, I simply stopped and waited for him to reply. He seemed startled, struggling to say something but lapsed into silence. When I realized how uneasy he was, I began asking him questions. It was a meager harvest but I gleaned the fact that he was 59 and had been the dam's chief official for 20 years. After this comparative torrent of words, he lapsed into silence again. Searching for something to re-start him, my eyes moved upwards to the deer, sambar and other ungulents staring down at me. I asked about the animals in the area, and he stirred to life.

"Twenty years ago," he began, "the forest was filled with animals. You could stand here on the porch and see *chinee* (gibbons) and *keng* (barking deer). Right here on the lawn." He abruptly stood and walked out to the porch. I followed. His eyes dimmed behind the glasses, scanning the open area up to the tree line.

"Then, about ten years ago, all you could hear was bang, bang here, bang, bang there. Now there's no game at all."

Except for the chirps of tiny birds, the forest was silent. Chamlong folded into himself so completely that I refrained from asking where and how he had obtained the heads on the walls.

"Well," he said at last, "goodbye." I took my leave. At the bottom of the hill, I repacked the boat, then stood on the dam crest, paying out chain and letting the current carry the boat 30 feet down the stone face. The lower river was but a small rivulet. "*Nam haeng* (the stream's dry)", a voice above me said. I looked up, surprised to see Chamlong regarding me intently.

A thought occurred to him: "I'll contact Meng Ngat (a dam on another tributary). They can release more water so you travel easier. It'll take three or four hours to arrive. Don't be impatient." I lashed my gear to the deck but when I looked up to say goodbye, he was gone.

Angels on the Ceiling

(Plaa) Taay Naam Tuen
([A fish] dies in shallow water)
A smart person is flummoxed by a simple problem

Of course, no leave-taking would be complete without a spectacular blunder committed in full view of an audience.

Selecting the broader of two channels, I pushed boldly into a fast current, and looked up to see myself heading like a giant carp into a large-mesh fish net stretched across the waterway. Just before it trapped me, I grabbed the chain, jumped into the water, let the stern swing around. To the amusement of the men on the dam crest, I dragged the boat 200 feet back up the channel, turned and headed down the narrower passage, cursing the cosmos for tripping me up in public.

Backlit by the sun, the plumed elephant grasses were prayer flags, whispering their mantras in slithery sibilants to the skies. I was settling in to enjoy a carefree ride when, downriver, a new obstacle appeared. A palisade of bamboo stakes interrupted by a half dozen watchtowers stretched from bank to bank. Although mystified by its purpose I had little time to ruminate because I was about to be pinned against it. As a strong current carried me inexorably towards it, I paddled anxiously back and forth, looking for an opening. There was none. Fifty feet before I reached it, I pulled for shore and went to inspect.

A line of thumb-thick bamboo stakes with heads like chewed toothpicks had been sledged into the riverbed from one bank to the other. The three-walled watchtowers–the woven leaf roof set atop straw thatch walls–were perched on stout posts three feet above the water, the open side facing downriver. Each tower was protected by an upriver "V" made of sturdy logs, the "V" point aimed downstream. Sliding to one side, I could see that there were fewer stakes in the opening beneath the structure. If I could slip around one end of the "V" and beneath the tower, I might be able to squeeze through.

Easier said than done. Maneuvering around the "V", I wedged the boat into the space beneath the hut, grasping the floor beams to pull myself through. But then I got jammed. Tugging several bamboo stakes from their anchorages I managed to clear the structure. Paddling against the current, I returned to the fence, tied up, and drove the stakes in again.

The task allowed me to inspect the "watchtower" at close range. Its floor was strewn with straw. Stuck into the support posts were the bamboo spatulas fishermen use to mend nets. Nylon filament with barbed hooks hung on a rusted nail. So this was a fishing structure. The fence would block a fish's passage and the "V" would guide it to the net or hooked line dangled by a fisherman sitting in the hut above the opening. Fisherman ingenuity; simple but effective.

A mile downstream the next fish fence awaited me. And beyond it, another. My admiration for local initiative began to wear thin as I struggled to locate an opening, keep the boat from foundering against the fence, and move on without getting hung up. By the sixth one, I was beginning to regard them as nuisances, somewhat less picturesque than I had first thought them to be.

By noon, the fences had disappeared and I had a relatively easy hour or so before Chamlong's promise to release more water would result in a faster river. But then more fences appeared, this time at 100-yard intervals. By the eleventh fence, I was cursing, upset by my slow progress and by the sheer cussedness of their construction. I had to remind myself that the villagers had not erected the fences as barriers against boatmen; there were no other boatmen. I was the intruder and should respect their hegemony. Nonetheless, it was tempting to bull my way through and avoid the hard work of fighting back upstream to replace each stake, balancing precariously in a skittish boat. Just when my resolve was beginning to waver, the fences ceased and I had a long, uninterrupted run.

Rounding a bend, my eye caught a flash of movement far downstream on the left bank. A man appeared to be running away, head down and legs churning. Gliding closer, I could see he was on a bicycle but, despite his furiously rotating legs, the bicycle wasn't moving. As I watched, perplexed, a second man emerged from behind a waterborne log. In his hands were two wands which he swept slowly back and forth in the river. From time to time, the wader would pause, scoop up fish that appeared to be floating atop the water, dropping them into a basket hanging from a leather waist thong. Drawing even, I saw that the bicycle was propped up on blocks. The cyclist's frantic pedaling turned the headlamp generator, sending electric current through the wires to the wands to stun the fish. Intent on their task, the men looked up briefly, waved, and returned to zapping fish.

It was a hot afternoon. What would happen, I wondered, if I just let the boat drift, and let the river do all the work? I shipped the paddle and sat back to watch. Bad mistake. Leave a boat to its own devices and it will contrive to get you into trouble. It will spin, lodge on a sandbar, bang into a sunken log, collide with mimosa, or slip into an eddy and stop; anything but travel in a straight line. It was less work to paddle than constantly have to extricate myself from difficulties.

The waterwheels I encountered below Chiang Dao were the last I would see. Here, the silence was periodically broken by the soft, putt-putt of a diesel engine. A plastic hose snaking down the bank drew water from the Ping and the pump sent life-giving liquid to irrigate nearby fields. The pumps were indicative of the modernity now intruding into these villages, and the level of prosperity enjoyed by some farmers.

Once again, sundown brought with it the agonizing choice between paddling through the cool air and rich golden light and the need to find a village for the night. My prime criterion for choosing a village was that it have a landing; loose dirt banks were difficult to scale and they provided no anchorage for the boat. But if I failed to spot one from far upstream and immediately begin paddling towards it, I would miss it. With the river traveling at 3 mph and me paddling at 2 mph, it was futile to fight back upriver to reach it.

The landing at the village called Baan Don extended six feet into the river and, as usual, I made a grand entrance. Stepping off a sandbar, I sank into water up to my crotch. As I entered its streets, Baan Don's citizens were greeted by an apparition in sopping pants.

A quick glance told me Baan Don was on its last legs. When I asked the headman if I could stay the night, he scratched his head, then apologized. "I'm sorry but there's no space; I already have several visitors." One look at his tiny house told me his family alone would have filled it. "But I'll introduce you the *luang paw*," he offered. "You can sleep in the *viharn* (the monastery assembly hall)."

The walk through the village confirmed my initial impression. There was a lassitude to Baan Don exemplified by sagging houses, crumbling paths, and trash. What marks one village for success and another for bare subsistence? The date of its establishment, certainly. Those arriving after a valley is already settled have to take leftover, barren land, filled with rocks and with limited access to water. The tone of the village is also set by its headman. Without vibrant leadership, the village will spend an eternity treading water. Clean, thriving villages were generally guided by very sharp headmen, respected by their neighbors for their knowledge of agriculture, marketing, and bureaucracy.

The *viharn* looked as though it had been under construction for some time; rust rivers flowed down concrete surfaces where re-bar protruded. Seldom in a village was a monastery building erected at one go. Instead, the villagers took what money they had and laid the foundation. When they had more money, they built the walls, then the roof. It might take 10 years to complete. This one was little more than a roofed shell.

Like the poor everywhere whose chief concerns in life are monetary, Baan Don's lack of prosperity was apparent in the answers the headman gave when I asked about the new *viharn*.

"Will the gables be covered in glass mosaics?" I asked.

"200,000 *baht* (US$ 8,000)," he replied, without elaboration.

I tried again. "And will the doors be teak?"

"Also 200,000 *baht*," he said.

Similar questions evinced the same response until it became a game of "The Price is Right". I surmised that it was a language problem and that he simply wasn't understanding my questions.

"Is your house built of teak?"

"No, *mai takhien*."

O.K., so we were on the same wave length. I tried one last time. "How long will it take to complete the whole *viharn*?"

"1.5 million *baht* (US$ 60,000), including 70,000 *baht* (US$ 2,800), raised for the King's birthday." I gave up.

With the money, the village had hired outside artists to cover the interior walls in religious murals. While the spirit of the endeavor was intact, its execution somehow missed the point. In a normal *viharn*, the Tosachat (the final ten of the 550 incarnations through which the Buddha-to-be passed before he reached Enlightenment) appeared on the left wall and episodes from the life of Buddha were painted on the right wall. Here, the two stories were jumbled. Thus, the scene wherein Buddha leaves his palace, creeping past his sleeping wife and concubines (whose huge breasts had been lovingly rendered), was followed by the Tale of Punnakata, a previous incarnation of Buddha who clutches the tail of a flying horse ridden by a demon who is trying to dash him against the mountain peaks. The Maravijaya–when demons try to distract Buddha as he is meditating to reach Nirvana–normally appears on the back interior wall. Here, it appeared on the exterior wall just above the entrance doors. The haphazard arrangement mirrored the jumble evident in the rest of the village.

Genuine and unrestrained, however, was the hospitality of the monks. No sooner had I dropped my pack on a woven mat on the *viharn*'s concrete floor than a young *naen* (novice) arrived to announce that the abbot wanted to see me. I was tired but it would be unpardonable to ignore the summons. I walked across a trash-strewn compound and climbed the steps of his wooden house. The candlelight reflected off his pebble-lens glasses and highlighted the furrows in his face. He was beaming as he patted the mat next to him, inviting me to sit down.

"They tell me you came by boat. Is that true?" he asked quizzically, like an elderly grandfather. I assured him it was.

"Paddling?" he asked.

"Yes."

Then, to my surprise, he took my bicep in both his hands and squeezed.

"Um, um," he said approvingly as if to a grandson. "Strong. So where are we going?"

"We?"

"Yes. Down the river. Take me with you."

I was flummoxed. It would be difficult to imagine this frail man's surviving more than a day or two. He burst into laughter, pleased I had bitten.

"No, no. I'm too old," he chuckled. "Do you have maps?"

"Yes."

"Then take me down the maps."

I laid them out, each one a continuation of the one before, running perhaps eight feet across the floor, filling the tiny cell. Immediately the young monks were on their hands and knees, excitedly picking out the town names written in Thai, but disappointed not to find Baan Don. The old abbot made me take him down the entire length of the river. "Uh, uh," he would say approvingly as each town was named, clearly enjoying the ride. When we reached the sea and were safely home, he asked, "Have you eaten yet? No? Then you must go. Help him fold the maps, boys." Before I could stop them, the young monks began folding the nine maps every which way, handing me an origami menagerie.

In the *viharn*, the three artists were cooking dinner. When the abbot told them my plight, they immediately offered to share with me. To my surprise, they were cooking fluffy white rice rather than glutinous rice.

"Where are you from?" I asked.

"Phitsanulok," one said, a town 120 miles south of Chiang Mai. "Sticky rice is impossible to eat. Too heavy. Makes you sleepy."

I rummaged in my pack for a spoon and something bounced on the floor. One of the artists picked it up. Oh my god, my government nametag! I'd worn it as I'd traveled but generally put it in my pack when I had ascertained that a village was benign. He peered closely at it.

"Steve Van Beed," he said, reading it.

"No, Van Beek," I said.

"That's not what it says," he insisted, peering closely at the tiny Thai letters. I took a close look at it. Sure enough, my last name was misspelled. So much for deception.

"How can they misspell the name of a government official?" he asked incredulously.

"These things happen, you know," I replied nonchalantly, putting the pin in my bag where it would remain until the end of the trip.

As we ate a delicious curry of very gristly pork–most likely wild boar–several villagers were eavesdropping. One of them confirmed that the fences and huts were used for fishing.

"We build them at the end of the rainy season. After a few months, the river drops too low. No fish."

"How long do they last?"

"Until the next monsoon washes them away; then, we have to re-build everything. A lot of work for a few fish. I'd rather drop a grenade in the water and pick up whatever floats to the surface. Why spend all that time for so little?"

I was about to lecture him on environmental damage but it wouldn't have done any good. I was a foreigner with enough money to buy fish in the market; what did I know of the difficulties of scrounging for a daily living?

Once dinner was over, I was ready for bed. The artists were still talking quietly as I slipped into my sleeping bag, watched over by *apsaras* (angels) floating high on the dimly-lit walls in the flickering candlelight.

For 2,500 years, Buddhist monks have risen "at the hour when one can first see the lines on one's palms," wound saffron cloths about their bare bodies, and departed barefoot on *bintabaht* to collect alms. By tradition, what a monk wears and carries is fashioned from discards. In ancient times, he wore a dead man's shrouds hung on tree branches after the corpses were cremated. In commemoration, robes are still sewn from five pieces of cloth, although a single length would suffice.

Lining the chilly, pre-dawn roads, pious Buddhists stand beside tables laden with food. Each monk pauses and lifts the brass lid of his lacquered iron black bowl, also crafted from scrap. The villager places rice and curries in it, then kneels before him as he murmurs a blessing. No other words are exchanged, no thanks given. The monk owes him nothing. By receiving alms, he enables the donor to gain merit and ultimately escape the cycle of lives through which we must pass on the path to perfection.

By 6:30, the monks had returned to the monastery, burdened with food, some of it for monks too old or infirm to collect it themselves. For the next hour before breakfast, they swept the monastery yard. All bent low, one arm behind their backs as they wielded short, handleless bundles of bamboo bristles. Like specters, their orange robes disappeared into the thick fog, reappearing elsewhere against a backdrop of gauzy trees and white *chedi*s as the breeze shifted the mist. I found a broom and joined them. They didn't acknowledge my presence; I wasn't helping them, I was earning merit.

The yard clean, we ate and talked, and then I prepared to leave.

As I was rolling my sleeping bag, the headman appeared at the door, his manner hesitant as though something was bothering him.

"You're going to finish in Chiang Mai?" he asked.

"No, I'm going to the sea."

"Oh." He looked uncomfortable.

"Is there a problem?" I asked.

He paused. "The people here are good," he said.

"Yes," I said, "they have been very kind to me."

"But not below Chiang Mai."

I waited.

"Three days south of here, there are *jai dam*," he said, darkly. "You have to be careful."

"Really?" I replied.

"They steal, they are *jai lai* (evil-hearted), they..." He paused, leaving me to guess the rest. "Three days south."

My latent paranoia re-surfaced. I thought I had moved safely past the miscreants Jack Bain had warned me about. The headman thought otherwise.

"Do you have a gun?"

Remember, you don't have a permit. "No."

"Get one in Chiang Mai."

"Thank you, I'll see what I can do," I said. I continued packing but my mind was racing again. Had I just been lucky up to now? These people were clearly concerned about potential threats yet I, the neophyte outsider, was blissfully ignoring their warnings. They must have reasons for worrying; was I the only one not getting it? Perhaps I was shutting them out because adopting the same paranoia would make me wary of everyone I met. This journey would accomplish my objectives only if I embraced people.

The fog hanging above the fields had spilled over the banks to fill the river from bank to bank. The mist was so thick that by the time I was 50 feet from shore, I could still hear the eager "bye-byes" (in English) but no longer see anyone. It was eerie, the Ping defined only by the reeds along the banks, gauzy vertical wisps enveloped in gray. The river was invisible, muted; the land silent. The only sound was the steady splash of my paddle into the water and the tinkling cascade of droplets as it swung across the bow to plop on the opposite side.

I anticipated a relaxed paddle, reveling in the setting; but the river had other ideas. Looming out of the fog was another damned fishing fence. This time, the stakes were driven so deeply they would not budge. Since no one could see me, I removed my pants and slipped overboard to pull them up. The waist-deep water was icy cold and I was shivering when I re-entered the boat. Four more fences awaited me downstream, portending another endless day.

But by mid-morning, the fog had thinned. A couple sitting on the banks raised a glass of tea, inviting me to join them. Normally, I would have waved and moved on–if I responded to all the invitations I'd never make it to the sea–but I was cold and the tea would warm me. Moreover, I needed an answer to a nagging question.

The wife had taken a break from weaving cloth. Her husband, a shy man who sold the cloth in Chiang Mai's market, let her do most of the talking but as soon as I mentioned *jai lai*'s, he launched into a long, involved story about a foreigner who had been killed by thieves along the river below Tak. As usual with such stories, the details were hazy and there was no precise date attached to the attack. "*Lai pii, laew* (many years ago)," was the closest he could come.

I consoled myself with the knowledge that the portion between here and Chiang Mai would be trouble-free; until his wife interjected, "It is very risky traveling through Chiang Mai."

"Really?" I said, tensing.

"Oh yes. All those pretty young women working along the riverbanks will be accosting you, wanting you to take them with you. You'll never get out alive!" at which she began giggling, her sides shaking. Her reply was so unexpected that I burst out laughing, wagging a finger at her for her mischievousness, which increased her giggles until she was wiping tears from her eyes. I put back on the river in a cheerier frame of mind.

Late in the morning, the fog melted away, revealing a new, disturbing Thailand. On the left, a factory clad in rusted corrugated iron sheets thumped with activity. Moored mid-river were two rusting barges, whose powerful pumps noisily raised irrigation water to the fields beyond the high banks. Rounding a bend, I nearly collided with a group of men digging gravel from the river bottom for urban construction projects, the water silting where their *jop* (hodags) had cut. It was a jarring reminder that I had left the countryside behind and was entering the precincts of Chiang Mai.

More factories appeared, then modern concrete houses, eyesores with bay windows, balconies and dormers as only the nouveau riche can build them. Developers had replaced pristine forest and farmland with instant suburbs. Why the sub-division should have bothered me so, I don't know. It is endemic to any growing city, but it seemed out of harmony with the Thailand I had been experiencing. The princes of ancient Siam, the name by which Thailand was known until 1939, had tried to blend their homes into their surroundings. The new princes of commerce razed antique buildings or erected concrete sheaths to insulate themselves from the world.

In the early afternoon, my favorite Chiang Mai *chedi*–a humble lump of brick and stucco–appeared on the right, and moments later I passed beneath the Nakhon Ping Bridge and into the city's embrace. My impulse was to scoot past it and into the countryside again, but I had problems to resolve: a boat to modify, a camera to repair, and drown-proof food to locate.

After moving the boat to Moses' yard, the first priority on the repair list was me. My hands were a mass of blisters, abrasions, and smudge marks from old Band-Aid adhesive. In the cold shower at the Chumpol Guesthouse, I was alarmed by how red I was. Although the hat had shielded my head, my face had been burned by rays reflected off the water, giving me a "farmer's tan."

A small photo studio said the camera body was beyond repair but that it could clean the lenses. I telephoned Marshall, an Australian friend, in Bangkok and asked him to bring up a second camera body and extra lenses. After buying a box of luscious strawberries just coming into season, I headed for Bill Young's. Over coffee and berries, we discussed the trip so far and the long stretch ahead which would carry me south of Chiang Mai through valleys and into the long, winding gorge that lay behind a dam.

"What am I up against?" I asked.

"More of the same, I'm afraid. Except in the gorges there are no villages," he replied.

"So it's completely uninhabited?"

"No, there are fishermen and poachers, all of them outside the law and living off the land. You could be a target," Bill said.

"And the others," his wife interjected.

"Others?"

"The 50,000 convicts the King released. Many of them will be in the hills," she said.

"I'd forgotten about them. Great. A welcoming party," I said, morosely.

Bill regarded me silently, adding "below the gorge, you'll be O.K."

I looked at the map. "It could take me 15 days to reach the dam. That's a long time."

"You were looking for adventure, weren't you?"

"Yeah. Me and the elements, not me and the wackos."

He thought a moment. "I don't know what to advise you. You decided to do this and were warned of the dangers. It's just that now you are more of a believer than you were. It's your decision."

I left his house, despondent. In the late afternoon when I should have been in the market buying supplies, I slumped onto the river bank where I'd sat a week earlier. So much had happened in seven days. Now, at least, I had some solid experience on which to judge the wisdom of continuing the journey. I'd run into some questionable situations and people but in general I'd been well received. Again I asked myself if I'd just been lucky.

What did I know of the downriver terrain? The Ping's lower reaches would take me through a remote gorge, on a flat lake. Without a current to carry me, I'd have to paddle constantly. I needed to do some hard thinking. Maybe Marshall would have some ideas.

Over the next two days, I bought materials and modified the boat. As I added planks to the locker floor to raise my gear higher, I heard a familiar voice.

"So you made it this far. Good for you."

"Hi Jack. Yeah, it was very interesting."

"Had enough?"

"No. As soon as I get the boat repaired, I'm off again."

"Stubborn."

"Or possessed, I don't know which."

In the market, I looked for canned curries to replace the ruined dried foods. I would stash the empties on board and drop them at a town dump. I bought three dozen cans of curries as well as mixed fruit, pickled vegetables, more tea bags, sachets of sugar, and five pounds of oranges. I threw in half a dozen packs of UHT-treated malted chocolate for variety. I also bought new sandals and denim cut-offs. My legs would be exposed to thorns but the short pants would give me more mobility.

The following morning, I went to the photo studio. The owner's face fell as he saw me walk in.

"Lenses ready?" I asked.

"I've dried the lenses and they work o.k. Two of them," he said, laying them on the glass-topped counter.

"And the third?"

From beneath the counter he withdrew a box. Inside lay the barrel and prisms from my 35 mm lens. I looked at him, puzzled.

"Can't you reassemble it?"

"No. It requires nine prism elements."

"So?"

"One is broken."

"Broken? How?"

"It was an accident." He looked pained.

"I don't understand..."

"I'm sorry. I took the lens apart. I laid the prisms neatly on my workbench..."

I waited for the rest.

"I forgot about my cat. He jumped onto the workbench and knocked one of the prisms off. It shattered on the floor."

"Arghh." My favorite lens. And the most expensive, of course.

"I'll replace it," he said.

I looked at him in surprise. In all my dealings with Thai shop-keepers, never once had one offered to replace a damaged article, even when it was just out of the box and I was holding the receipt.

"You have a 35 mm, f/1.4 lens?" I asked.

"No, I have a 50 mm, f/2.0"

It was not what I needed but it would do. I thanked him, gathered up the pieces of the damaged 35 mm lens, paid and left, thinking I could buy a replacement for the broken prism. Later, after working my way through various dealers all the way back to Tokyo, I was told it would cost more to replace the prism than to buy a new lens, a contention that still baffles me.

At the guesthouse, Marshall handed me the back-up camera body. He had once lived in Bangkok and with great reluctance had returned to Melbourne to run a family business. He now jumped at every opportunity to return to Thailand, even for two weeks at a time.

In my room, I told him I was debating the wisdom of continuing the trip.

"What happened? You were so enthusiastic." he said.

I outlined what I had encountered and what I'd been told, especially the dangers which lay ahead.

"Doesn't sound good," he said. "But you've been talking about doing this for a long time. How would you feel about pulling out?"

"Bad. But continuing is just as unnerving. I'm not sure if it's a sincere desire to make the journey or stubbornness that drives me."

"Are the villagers' concerns justified?"

"So far, no. Villagers everywhere tend to distrust the outside world. They magnify a single bad instance into a general rule. I'm the outsider and as much as I think I know about Thailand my knowledge is essentially city-based. I have no yardstick to measure the truth of their concerns."

"Can anyone here offer a counter opinion?"

"I haven't found anyone. Worse yet, friends confirm what the villagers are saying."

"So it really means ignoring everyone's advice and hoping they are all wrong."

"I guess so. What bothers me is that I had more or less conquered my fears on the upper river. I thought that once I was past Chiang Mai I would have a clear run south, worrying only about physical obstacles. Instead, the journey is turning into a run through a shooting gallery."

"Can you shoot back?"

I hesitated. Should I tell him about the pistol? I was less concerned about the illegality of possessing it than about admitting that I had sold out to my fears. But not telling him would hamstring him in advising me.

I shut the door and shot the bolt. From my pack, I extracted the gun and clips.

"Jesus," he said.

The pistol's maker had intended it to do a deadly job and had expended little effort to make it beautiful. It was brushed in a matte black to cut reflections, an ominous hue that made it seem even more lethal. I jammed the clip into it, set the safety, and handed it to him.

He turned it this way and that. "This looks very nasty," he said quietly. He removed the clip and squinted at the dum-dum bullets. "Jesus," he said again, with more feeling. "These are meant for serious business. You can put a very large hole in someone."

Sighting down the barrel, he asked, "Is it reliable?"

I told him about testing it above Mae Faek. Any inaccuracy had been my own fault but I wasn't really worried because I hoped to use it only to scare off intruders. If I had to shoot someone, it would be at close range.

"Can you picture yourself actually shooting somebody?" he asked.

"Yeah, and it gives me the willies. It sounds easy in theory, but in a real situation, could I actually pull the trigger? I don't know."

"It may be more of a liability than a deterrent," Marshall said. "I've read that armed houseowners are more likely to be shot by burglars than those who are unarmed. The owner hesitates; the burglar has nothing to lose. The only way he is going to get away is to shoot and run."

"True, but that's the West," I said. "Here, I don't think people make such subtle distinctions. If they're determined to cover their tracks, they'll shoot whether or not I'm armed. With the gun, at least I'm giving myself a fighting chance. But that's not the point. I simply don't want to put myself in a situation where I have to make such a decision. Unfortunately, everyone is telling me that if I paddle south, it's less a matter of 'if' than of 'when'."

"Can I make a suggestion?"

"Sure..."

"I know you want to make this journey on your own, but can I go with you for a day and see what you're contending with under real circumstances? At the moment, I'm operating in a bit of a vacuum in trying to advise you."

His suggestion had merit but its prime appeal was that it let me delay deciding for a day or two. Sitting in a room far removed from the river was an exercise in spiraling anxiety. Let him taste what I've been experiencing to give him a context in which to help me reach a decision.

Into the Pig Realm

Pad Sawa Phaw Phon Naa Baan,
Pad Sawa Phaw Phon Tua
(To push away the water hyacinth from one's house,
to push the water hyacinth away from oneself)
To reject responsibility by pushing it on others

It was the kind of sunny morning that makes it difficult to shake off lethargy. But steaming glasses of thick Thai coffee, sipped on rickety stools in the riverside Ton Lamyai Market, quickly dissipated the brain fuzz. We dunked greasy *pathongkoh* pastries in the brew and thought ourselves in heaven.

While Marshall bought supplies, I assembled the urethaned pieces I'd spread out to dry in Moses' yard. I'd brushed so many layers on the hull that I'd nearly created a glass-bottomed boat. Perhaps the lacquer would armor my boat against rocks. The work went quickly and within two hours I was on the river again, this time with Marshall in the bow. We talked of past lives and directions as yet uncharted and the afternoon passed lazily. Marshall's weight so slowed our progress that by evening, we'd covered only five miles, half that of a normal day. Moreover, we were still in the Chiang Mai suburbs.

"Thinking of pulling in?" Marshall asked.

"Yeah, but I feel weird asking for accommodation."

"Why?"

"I don't know. It's too much like knocking on the door of a suburban house in the U.S. Can you imagine the reaction? 'Hi, my friend and

I were paddling down the river and we're really tired. May we stay the night?' Slam goes the door, out comes the shotgun."

"So you're saying it's easier to ask poor people."

"Oh god, you're right." But it was true that middle-class people everywhere were suspicious of anyone poorer than they. Poor people were quicker to share what little they had with strangers. But then, most middle-class Thai citizens had already met foreigners so found nothing exotic about them. Moreover, there were two of us, double the bother and threat.

"It sounds terrible but it is true," I said. "We're counting on villagers being awed by us. We're offering the novelty of our presence in exchange for food and a place to stay." I snorted with laughter at the thought. "It's as though we were monks giving the disenfranchised an opportunity to make merit. What an awful thought."

"And yet one which comforts most foreigners traveling in the Third World," Marshall said. "Can you imagine the ruckus we'd cause if we wandered into an American town and began hanging over fences, photographing people in their back yards while they were dressed in their faded work clothes, caught in unflattering poses by a couple of yabos dressed like hobos? We'd be turfed out in a flash. Yet, here we do it without thinking about it."

"And we think we're being so civilized," I snickered. "We're better than ordinary tourists because we've put colonial insensitivity behind us. We don't call people 'wogs' but we do expect deference based on the color of our skins. And the joke is: it still works. I think I'm being culturally sensitive to go out among these people on their terms and speak their language, and yet am I any different from a tourist?"

"Don't be so hard on yourself. You don't exploit them; you offer to pay but they refuse. It is they who make the decision to let you stay. I think they feel they are getting something back in being able to talk with people they've seen from a distance but have never had a chance to meet."

"I hope so." I replied. "Nonetheless, I don't want to knock on the door of a middle class house. It seems too much like begging."

Not that it was any longer an issue. In the time we had discussed it, we had entered the countryside. Tying the boat at a small landing, we climbed the bank and found ourselves overlooking a beautiful village filled with fruit trees. Several boys told us we were in Baan Hang Khwae and escorted us down a mango-shaded lane to the headman's house.

The headman was pleased to meet us but perplexed about where to put us. His wife suggested that we stay in a small house built–but not yet occupied–by their son. Set in a mango grove, its single room had a concrete floor and no furniture, but it would do. But then, the headman decided that the landing was not a secure shelter and insisted that I take a small boy to guide me to a safer spot just downriver. Once there, I padlocked the chain to a big tree. But the headman was still not satisfied.

"I think we should bring it into the village," he said.

Did he realize how much it weighed? Before I had a chance to protest, he deputized eight men to hoist it to their shoulders and carry it to the house.

"Hello?" said Marshall as we came up. "What's this? Valet parking?"

"What could I do? They insisted."

"I guess it gives the headman peace of mind," he said.

"And if everyone hasn't scattered to the fields when we're ready to leave tomorrow morning..." I reminded him.

"Ow. That could be difficult."

It is odd to exchange thoughts before a crowd that has no idea what you're saying. Almost impolite. We switched to Thai.

Baan Hang Khwae was doing well and there was a genuine affection for the headman who, no doubt, had been instrumental in introducing new ideas and securing government financing. The village had electricity and, of course, the first thing a family buys after a fan and a refrigerator is a television. We were invited to watch the 9 o'clock news at a neighboring house. Reception was poor, and picture was black-and-white but the TV brought news from the outside world. In the middle of an otherwise peaceful valley, it seemed odd to watch Lebanese slaughter each other in Beirut streets and then to watch Dutchmen build a wonderful structure of 137,000 dominoes which, when knocked down, revealed the "Mona Lisa" and "The Night Watch." Our hosts then insisted we watch an inane Chinese television drama based on "Miami Vice," endless gangland mayhem whose first 15 minutes included a firefight that lasted a full five minutes. Given the farmers' gentleness, their receptiveness to gun-fighting was puzzling. The liberal arguments that televised violence incited viewers to replicate it seemed wide of the mark. Yet, we both found the firefights unsettling and eventually excused ourselves and went to bed, gunshots reverberating through the village for the next hour.

I awoke at dawn to what sounded like a harmonica playing the notes A, C, and E over and over. I traced the song down the lane to the open area beneath a house where, in a cage, a hill mynah was singing to itself; A, C, E. His silky ebon body shuddered slightly with the effort, yet the notes poured effortlessly from his amber beak. When I echoed him, he paused, twisting his head so he was looking at me upside down from near the level of his feet, a bright orange-yellow line across his cheeks framing his gleaming eyes. Again and again, he would sing his notes then dip his head upside down to listen to my response. We played this game for several moments until he became bored and plunged into a ripe papaya left by the small boy who owned him.

When Marshall was up, we wandered among the houses in their tidy houseyards. At one, a middle-aged couple, and his mother, enjoying the early morning air on their stairs, invited us to talk. Through circumstances he declined to describe, Thongchai told us his farmer father had lost his land, salvaging only the small plot on which his son's house stood. Thongchai was 48 and drove a *songtaew* in Chiang Mai. His much-younger wife, whose sweet disposition seemed to mask a hardy interior, sold vegetables in the market. As he talked, the man smoked a hand-rolled green leaf cheroot, cheerfully sharing it with his wife and his mother, a crone in her 70's who was bundled in a thick brown sweater yet was shivering in the morning cold. When Marshall handed him a Davidoff cigar he puffed it appraisingly for a few moments, then passed it to his wife who drew on it, made a face, and gave it back.

Just then, the headman arrived and offered to take us on a tour of the village. Shaded by dozens of fruit trees, each wooden plank house was raised on head-high pillars. The open area beneath the house was generally occupied by a loom which sat on a hard dirt floor. In the corner of each yard was a similarly-raised rice barn, a well, a concrete outhouse, a small garden, and a pig sty. Instead of the usual bamboo fences, families had planted red and yellow cannae lilies, as well as bright magenta, white, and orange bougainvillea. There was even a semblance of lawn with short green grass instead of the normal baked dirt where hens and their broods scratched for grains and grubs. There was an air of peace to the setting that rubbed off on the people who quietly greeted us, contented smiles on their faces.

At his house–the only one with glass panes in the latticed windows–the headman offered us scented drinking water. He proudly showed us the government certificate declaring Baan Hang Khwae to be a model village. We then leafed through a photo album of visiting dignitaries, all of them wearing uniforms and sober expressions conveying their devotion to their jobs. These photos always struck me as anomalies, the subjects' solemnity so at variance with their natural cheerfulness. The headman then produced a guest book with entries from Senegalese, Korean, and other delegations that had visited.

When we finally got underway around noon, I was feeling unbalanced, perhaps as a result of eating richer food in Chiang Mai or having taken a few days off. Whatever it was, I was not feeling in a groove as I had on the upper river. The day passed slowly and I became more aware of the boat's weight. The burning sun glared off the still water with enervating fierceness.

Soon, the river became turbid, sure sign of a dam ahead. In the upper river, it had been satisfying to glance back and see that landmarks I had just passed were 100-200 yards astern. But here, hard paddling in dead water brought little progress. After flailing the water courageously, my shirt damp with sweat, I would turn to find the landmark only a stone's throw behind me. It didn't help that the Ping was fouled by bloated, stinking animals, rusty cans, garbage, and bits of Styrofoam, gifts from its upstream neighbors. Overhead, hundreds of dirty tattered plastic bags lifted by flood waters festooned the tree branches, urban prayer flags.

When, three hours later, the Lamphun dam appeared before us, I pulled to the riverbank to inspect it. Its face sloped gently and on those areas not covered in ropy algae, there were good footholds; I would have little problem negotiating it. When Marshall announced he wanted to return to Chiang Mai the following morning, I decided to call it a day.

A dam official offered us a single-room house with a concrete floor strewn with thin straw mats where the guards normally slept. On a table sat a hot plate corroded with the remains of past meals. Three walls were latticed; the fourth was decorated with a provocative poster of Farah Fawcett. Since the lattice would admit mosquitoes, our first task was to find mosquito coils. The deputy administrator was driving to the Saraphi market a few miles away and offered to take us. There, we bought sticky rice and several curries which the vendors poured into plastic bags. We returned in the back of a pick-up that lurched over a bumpy dirt road, passing other rickety trucks loaded to twice their height with rice straw, teetering and tipping in the ruts and potholes, threatening at any moment to topple on to their sides.

At the dam, we sat on the riverbank and talked, watching the orange sun and its reflection in the Ping. We discussed the wisdom of my continuing, but somewhere deep in my mind, almost without knowing it, I'd already decided. Sheer obtuseness, stupidity, I didn't know what. I would push forward until something pushed back.

After wolfing down the curries and encircling ourselves with mosquito coils, Marshall and I listened to the crickets and stared like moths at the candle flame. Vague fears flitted across my brain but I brushed them away like the mosquitoes that braved our smoky ring.

I awakened to the acrid odor of burning straw and walked out to find the night guard, Chalerm, warming his hands by a fire.

"Not having an early morning cigarette?" I asked.

"No, I don't smoke," he replied matter-of-factly. "The smoke goes in, the smoke comes out, to no purpose."

"Tell me about your life," I said.

"Not much of a life to talk about," he replied. "I'm 30. I've been working the night shift here for three years, riding my motorcycle to and from Doi Saket (a town 18 miles away) each day."

"Are you afraid of ghosts?" I asked, knowing that they terrify most Thais.

"No," he replied. "From the age of 12 to 19, I was a *naen* (novice monk) at a monastery in Doi Saket." It was a somewhat incongruous explanation but it seemed to work for him. His courage was probably the reason he worked the night shift; no one else wanted it.

"And after the monastery?" I urged him.

"For a few years, I was a soldier near Chiang Mai. I quit to become a policeman. But when I applied, they told me I didn't have enough education. I'd only had a chance to study through third grade," he said ruefully.

I waited for him to continue.

"I thought I might study for the examination but my father died. I had to arrange the funeral so I wasn't able to apply again. I had nothing else to do so I stayed home in the village for three years. I wanted to go back in the army–I loved the camaraderie among the soldiers–but my mother cried because I was her only son. So I got this job."

"And you like it?"

"It's o.k. I only make 1,300 *baht* (US$ 50) a month. It supports me and my family...I have a wife and a four-year-old daughter. My wife tends a garden and sells the produce and my mother helps her. We get by."

As he related his story in a resigned tone, I watched his face. His eyes flicked back and forth as he talked. He smiled but there was a sense of desperation, of dashed hopes, of being trapped and desiring something better.

"Can you find other work?"

"I look for work in the daytime after I've finished the night shift but I can't find anything steady. I studied at a Christian school for a while and learned some English. I'm sorry I never used it because it would be useful. By now I've forgotten most of it."

His reverie ended, he suddenly became self-conscious, embarrassed that he had burdened the listener with his problems.

"It's getting late," he said, rising from a squat. "I have to get home." He *waiied* me before striding off. A few dozen yards away, he turned and called, "Good luck on getting down the river."

I sat a while longer by the fire, thinking about lives cast in concrete. What I was doing was a luxury that few Thais could afford. I would try to savor every moment, recognizing what a gift I had been given.

Marshall and I finished the remaining curries. A pick-up truck would take him to Saraphi to catch a bus to Chiang Mai. We had already talked our fill; there was nothing more to say. We hugged and, with a wave, he set off. I unlocked the boat, noting its lightness. With minimal maneuvering, I got it down the dam face and pulled it to shore to load it. The water below the dam was shallow but at least it was moving. I stuck the paddle into the river and pulled it towards me, looking downstream at the distant hole between the hills where the river disappeared.

Sapped of substance by the dam and its diversion canals, the Ping braided listlessly through a series of stagnant pools, winding among willows and rocks as it struggled to regain strength and momentum. For four miles, my boat stumbled along, caught and held time and again by shoals and shallows, yet I was appalled less about my lack of progress than with the enervation of my companion that had flowed so confidently in its upper reaches.

Eventually, with contributions from tiny side streams, it regained some of its fullness as I entered a lovely vale. Its steep banks were covered by flowering bamboo that hung far over the Ping and coated its surface with dun-colored bamboo pollen. The occasional raintree spread thick branches over the river, its small bottle-brush blossoms appearing like pink stars against its dark foliage. Exposed by the river's constant abrading, the raintrees' massive gnarled root systems resembled knotted tangles of dendrites.

At intervals, 20-foot-long wooden ferries would silently cross my bow, oarsmen pushing long poles against the river bottom or pulling themselves and their boats hand over hand along a rope strung between the banks. Barely clearing the water, they carried motorcycles and baskets of produce; each passenger paid one *baht* (four cents) regardless of his of her cargo.

Little by little the tall banks sank to water level and I was back amidst tall grasses. Just downriver, I saw my first water buffaloes since Baan Don. The great gray beasts lolled placidly in the river, only their massive, crescent-horned heads visible above the surface. They would casually watch my approach, snorting water from their nostrils, snuffling to catch my scent. Not until I was well past, however, would they react. Then, in a blind panic, they would explode from the river and scramble in a frenzy up the banks. At the crest, they would pause and gaze over their backs at me, their eyes wide with alarm until I had moved far down the river. With such slow wits, how had they survived for so long?

The afternoon passed peacefully, the mesmerizing sun filtering through knife-blade bamboo leaves. Several times, I was disturbed by young men sitting along the riverbanks with long rifles. "Hunting fish," they said but it seemed like an excuse to lounge rather than a plausible pursuit. Young men with nothing to do made me wary. Older, married farmers had a stake in the community they were unwilling to jeopardize by rash actions.

The warm sun impelled me to continue paddling until the hour it faded from the sky. I was still technically in "black hearts" territory, and while I hadn't met anyone answering to the description, sleeping in the open seemed inadvisable. Until I could ascertain who could be trusted and who couldn't, spending the night in a village was the only practical course. Almost on cue, a village appeared. On the sandy shore a cadaverous man watched my approach.

"Where is the headman's house?" I asked.

"Why?" he replied.

"I need a place for the night."

"Its about 500 yards farther on. But why go there? Stay here," he suggested.

While I considered the offer, a young boy ran down to the shore. The moment I beached the boat he climbed in and seated himself on the locker. He grabbed the paddle and would have set off down the river if his embarrassed father had not told him to put it down and get out. Undaunted, the boy grabbed my hand and began pulling me towards the house, asking me questions about the boat and the river: "Can it go really fast? Are their ghosts in the river? Can I go down the river with you? My name is Jek; what's yours?" Once he'd leeched onto me it was difficult to get away. His father kept shushing him but he paid no attention. "He's nine and very curious," he said. I didn't really mind; he was cheerful and his questions were intriguing.

Tha Na village ran along either side of a raised dirt road that served as a levee. Protected by the dike were fields of rice, garlic, mung beans, and *lamyai* (longan). Chao, 51, his wife, in her 20s or 30s (it is difficult to tell with Northern women), and their three children lived in a wood slat house high on stilts atop the embankment. In the yard were several sheds and the first hand pump I'd seen. But when Mrs. Chao handed me a glass of water, I hesitated. "It's clean. Not like the river," she said. When I still hesitated, she added, "We have a sand filter," pointing to a clay pot sheltered beneath the house. Pump water poured into the pot filtered through several layers of stones and sand to clean it. I drained my glass.

At dinner, Jek pelted me with questions. "Uncle," he asked, using a familiar term for an older man, "how much does a house cost in America? Uncle, do dogs like snow?" Although he tried to hush him, his father listened attentively to my answers. When Jek paused for breath, I asked his 13-year-old sister what grade she was in and she shyly replied, "I stay home to help mother." She was bright and it seemed unfair that she should be denied schooling while her brothers were encouraged to go as far as they could.

Jek asked me again whether I'd take him for a ride.

"What time do you leave for school?"

"Six-thirty."

"Oh my god. Way too early."

"I don't go until 8:30," his younger brother piped up eagerly, to everyone's laughter. But Jek had such a long face that I told him I'd get up early just for him.

At this point, the headman arrived. His was farmer's talk of crops and markets but it was apparent that change was already coming to Tha Na.

"We no longer use water buffaloes," he said in response to my question. "There are only four or five left in the village because most people can afford to use rototillers. We only raise buffaloes for meat; a two-year-old brings 4,000 *baht*!" I recalled Sin's concern about thieves stealing his valuable buffalo.

The concept of what constituted "big money" was quickly changing, as urban investors bought farm land. For the farmers, it meant instant wealth.

"A foreign company is building a fruit-processing factory on the other side of the river and is planting *lamyai* orchards," he said. "They bought seven *rai* of land (just under three acres) for 3.7 million *baht* (US$ 150,000). That's a lot of money," he said, aghast.

"What will the farmers do after selling their land?"

He looked at me incredulously. "They won't have to do anything."

A development fever was raging through Thailand. To the farmers, the lump sum they received from city speculators–who then re-sold the land to developers for ten times the price–looked enormous. Villagers rushed to buy pick-up trucks, appliances, and other luxuries which ate up most of the bonanza. Only then did they sit down to figure out what to do next. Without land to farm, most would be forced to migrate to the cities to labor in factories. It was boom time for the rich, most of it at the expense of the poor, and the government–comprising the rich, or soon-to-be rich–did little to curb the madness. Cities would pay the price later when the number of landless exceeded factory labor requirements, straining urban resources and infrastructures. Meanwhile, everyone was so mesmerized by the instant riches, they failed to notice the dark clouds gathering on the horizon.

Other than asking the question, however, I did not pursue the matter. It was clear from the gleam in their eyes that no one would listen. On this sobering thought, I went to bed.

Dressed in his pink sweatshirt, Jek was waiting at the bottom of the stairs at first light, the paddle laid across his shoulders. I hurried to shave remembering how impatient I was at that age when a neighboring farmer had promised me a ride on plow horse and then had dawdled for half a day. I asked Jek's shy sister if she wanted to come along, thinking she'd jump at the chance, but she shook her head. When I pressed her, she said she had to finish sweeping the leaves out of the yard. I said I'd wait and noticed a stricken look on Jek's face. She still said no. She spent her days helping her mother and seemed to know no other world.

Mist clung to the river's surface as Jek flailed away with the paddle, splashing as much water into the boat as he put behind us, jabbering excitedly all the time. Finally sated, he let me guide us to shore where he hopped off and ran to tell his sleepy-eyed younger brother all about it. I prepared to leave. As I was loading the boat, Chao took me aside and whispered conspiratorially, "Be careful. The people in this village are good, but those south of Chom Thong, three days from here, are *jai lai*. They can't be trusted."

I almost burst out laughing. This was deja vu with a vengeance, the second time in six days I'd been warned. Why was it always three days down the river? It would seem more logical to revile upriver folks since they could block the stream's flow and deprive a downstream village of water. Or flood them with debris and feces to pollute the village water supply. But no, the threat was perceived as coming from downriver people who would have great difficulty paddling against the current to cause a problem. What was it that made them so fearful?

"They used to come up to steal buffalo to sell in downriver towns," Chao explained ominously.

"But no one has any buffalo."

"They'll find something. It's in their nature to steal," Chao said, repeating in essence the suspicions I'd heard voiced before.

"Would you be surprised if I told you that the people three days upriver told me that your village was evil?"

He seemed genuinely shocked. "You've seen the people here. They are good people."

It seemed futile to pursue it further. "I'll be careful," I promised.

Jek had gotten me up so early that I was able to get away while the sun was still low in the sky. Soon I was gliding along a flat river with gently sloping shores planted in corn. Fishermen were out and my education of the various ways to catch fish gained another few dimensions. Near the shore, bamboo stakes had been driven into the soft bottom to create a circle 25 feet in diameter. The interior had been filled with broken branches to create what appeared to be a leafy island. Lured by a false sense of security, fish took refuge in it while the fishermen waited outside with baited lines. Other circles of tightly-bound bamboo slats covered in fish nets served as holding ponds for the live fish they'd caught, keeping them fresh for later collection.

As the day was ending, I arrived at Hua Kuang. The landing was at the base of a steep bank and I had to paddle into a backwater to reach it. A strange scent hung in the air. I tied up and scrambled to the top of the bank, where, I discovered to my disgust that I had moored below an enormous pig sty. I hastened down to re-tie the boat farther upstream. Perhaps I should find another village.

Except that I'd been heard. When I looked up, a host of murmuring people were standing on the bluff above me, staring down. Among them was a man with a perpetual smile, his short bristly hair suggesting constant surprise. His smile quickly warmed my mood.

"Where can I find the headman?" I asked, as I topped the bank.

They all pointed to smiley who identified himself as "Yen" before picking up one of my bags and leading me into the house that stood next to the pig sty. It wasn't often that I stumbled onto the precise house I needed to find. Yen's wife was a quieter version of her husband and despite her wry smile she matched him in warmth. They put my bag on a table and one of the men in the crowd immediately opened it and began pawing through it, commenting to those around him. Not a good sign. Pretending I needed something from the bag, I removed a notebook, and then placed the bag in a far corner of the room away from curious hands.

Hua Kuang's human population was outnumbered three-fold by the pigs it raised. These were not the black, nasty-tempered, sway-backed wild boar that snuffled through most villages but pink giants bred from superior stock and raised by farmers to marketable weight. I had arrived at swine supper time and we could barely hear ourselves above the squeals and grunts of pigs jostling for position at the feed troughs.

After a dinner of vegetables and–no surprise–pork, we talked briefly about how a traditional village had become incorporated into a city-based market economy, devoting its primary energies to raising pigs. For Thailand, this was a new approach to agriculture, one that had worked well for the villagers, who seemed better off than their upriver neighbors.

Ultimately we ran out of things to talk about. The questions raised in Chiang Mai were still churning in my brain and at a lull in the conversation, I asked about distances to and through the gorge. To my dismay, the talk quickly turned to the outlaws who prowled the shore areas.

"They are men without homes," Yen said quietly. "They look for any chance to make some money. Some fish, others hunt for deer."

"And you're going to be their deer," said one lanky man. His neighbors pushed at him, admonishing him with exasperated "Aohs," the closest Thais come to showing open disapproval of a friend. The ensuing moment of silence suggested that while they disapproved of the statement, it echoed their sentiments. "You'll just have to be careful," Yen finally said. "Trust no one, and stay out of sight. Once you get into the lake, it will be a long while before you see a village again."

I'd worked out the distance through the gorges at 80 miles but I'd be paddling without the aid of a current; that would add several days. I was watching my time schedule reach farther into the future. The 30 days I'd initially envisioned it would take to reach the sea had stretched to 40 days. Maybe more.

The conversation flowed but by the dinner's end, I was so tired that I was beginning to slur. Yen's wife sensed that I was rapidly slipping from consciousness and put me to bed on a back room floor. Several times during the night, I was jolted to wakefulness certain that someone was being stabbed. It took me a moment to realize it was only a pig having a nightmare.

The Cowboys of Tha Sala

Naam Lod, Tor Phud
(When the water recedes, the stumps show)
When artifice is stripped away,
one sees things as they really are

In the morning, Yen's house filled with farmers and naturally, the talk was of pigs, mash, and market prices. They shouted to make themselves heard above pig conversations devoted, no doubt, to the qualities of one farmer over another in his care and feed choice. After breakfast–more pork–I wandered deeper into the village.

The sun-suffused fog boiled off the river like sulfurous vapor, pouring across the road where children in blue and white tunics skipped and reeled on their way to school. I followed them until I came to a small hut with bamboo slats for walls. Inside, a wooden table was flanked by benches; on the opposite wall a rack held tattered newspapers and a few tatty books. It seemed to be a news vendor's stall but the newspapers were several weeks old.

"How do you like our reading room?" said a voice behind me.

"Oh, is that what it is. But aren't the newspapers a bit old?"

"Doesn't matter; we get our news from the radio. This room lets the children read something besides their schoolbooks." From his gently paternalistic tone, I guessed him to be the school teacher.

"Lived here long?"

"Oh, I stay in Chiang Mai. I travel here by bus every day."

"Why don't you live in the village?"

"All the houses are occupied." He noted my puzzled look. "In the city, people build hostels and apartments for other people to rent. Village people build homes to raise their families. There are no houses to rent."

That made sense.

"And besides," he added. "If I lived here, I'd never be able to find a wife."

"Why not?"

"These are village women," he said airily. "I want a wife with as much education as me. I also want my own life. Here, everyone knows what everyone else is doing. And they talk. In the city, no one asks me questions."

"So you lead two lives."

"I suppose so. When I come here in the morning, I am a teacher. When I get on the bus, I leave this life behind and go to my other life." He glanced at his watch. "Excuse me, I have to begin my village life." He hurried away.

In a sense, he was right. There *are* no secrets in a village. And it would be hard to court a woman, every move silently watched by all. I love rural life but I like solitude and I love anonymity. Asia prizes the community, not the individual, and its antennae are constantly attuned to others' responses to their actions. Even if solitude had been acceptable within the culture, it would have been impossible for me to maintain. My skin color mitigated against my blending in and I had too many edges sticking out to make a snug fit.

So why had I chosen to live among people who scrutinized and commented upon my every move? And why had I set out on a river trip that made me the center of attention for weeks on end? So intent was I upon embarking on my journey that this factor had not occurred to me. And I had expected to find more forest and fewer people. Once I realized that moments alone would be rare, I accepted it as the downside.

But I hadn't really accepted it. It wasn't that I chaffed at being public property, it was the discomfort of having people stand before me and comment on my appearance and my motivations, as though I were unable to understand what they were saying: "Look, he's reaching into his bag. Look at the hair on his arm" (which they'd then pull). At first it was amusing but I soon tired of being treated as a thing, not a person. In my Nepalese village I had called it my "zoo complex"; I was an oddity to be prodded and poked like an animal in a cage.

While most of the attention was positive–and although I was accepted much better than I would be by many cultures–it put a spotlight on me that I did not want and was powerless to discourage. I felt that a certain decorum was expected of me, that I was an ambassador for my nation, required to be on my best behavior lest people think unfavorably of "my people," whoever they were. Maybe it had been instilled when I was a Peace Corps Volunteer, perhaps it was something of my own invention, as bound up in my being as a DNA helical. Yet, I really didn't want the responsibility. In the gorges, I would be exposed to danger. On the other hand, I would be on by own, united with my surroundings.

I'd hoped to leave Hua Kuang early but Yen invited me to help him feed the pigs. I knew the habits of the wild boar with their rod-like bristles exploding from their black bodies, but I was unfamiliar with these fat, fleshy damsels of the porcine world. Not that their manners were any better. We poured steaming gourmet feed into their troughs and jumped back as they jabbed snouts between fellow diners to get at it, snapping with sharp teeth at any competitor, huge ears flapping as they noisily masticated their mash. Squeals echoed through the village as other farmers fed their charges.

"This used to be a quiet village," said Yen, grinning, as he snatched the bucket away from a pair of pigs trying to clamber over the barrier to reach it.

"Where do you get the piglets?" I asked.

"Chiang Mai. We buy them when they're a couple of months old. We fatten them up, then the traders come to buy them."

"Is it a good living?"

"My daughter graduated from university because of these pigs," he replied. "She's a nurse."

"What do you think would happen if you fell in the pen?"

Yen looked at the maddened pigs for a moment. "If they'd already been fed, they'd probably be more startled than I. Right now...I don't think they could tell the difference between me and mash."

"Has it ever happened?"

"A few months ago. A boy down the road got a little too adventurous and climbed over the wall. Luckily someone heard the pigs squeal and grabbed him just as he was about to drop into the pen. I don't know what would have happened if he'd gotten inside. Maybe nothing. But then again..."

"Was the boy punished?"

Yen looked at me with wide eyes. "Punished? Why would he be punished? He's just a boy. He doesn't know anything."

Thais seldom swatted a child. A quiet word and an explanation of possible consequences sufficed. Moreover, the weight of disapproval by the parent or the village would have been sufficient to stay a reprimanding hand.

The sun was well on its way to the zenith when we completed our chores. Yen and his wife accompanied me to the riverbank where, suddenly solemn, he handed me a scrap of paper. On it was scrawled his address. "Write us when you arrive in Bangkok because we will worry about you," he said, his face reflecting concern. I felt something poke me in the side and, behind her husband's back, Yen's smiling wife passed me a leaf-wrapped lunch of roasted pork and rice.

Relieved that the boat wasn't covered in pig droppings, I pushed out of the slough into a fast-running river. My speed was probably no more than three miles per hour but I seemed to fly. Proximity to a riverbank is deceiving in the same way that one seems to move faster through a narrow alley than along a broad boulevard.

Around a bend, a hill with a lovely white *chedi* came into view and followed me most of the morning. Standing stark white against the thick vegetation, the *chedi* put a Thai stamp on undifferentiated jungle. Although alien to the environment, it rose from it organically, mimicking a pale conifer.

By noon, sluggish water said "dam ahead." This one was concrete and its steep face dropped 15 feet. I paddled to one side where a groove between face and embankment channeled the water downwards. Someone had lashed a framed net in the channel to catch fish trying to move upstream. Downstream, several fisher families were camped on a gravel bar. When I shouted down to ask if I could remove the net for a moment three young men rushed up, grabbed the chain, and pulled me out of the boat.

"What are you doing?" I shouted above the din of rushing water.

"It's too dangerous for you," one said. "We'll do it for you."

One stood in the rushing water on the dam crest and edged the boat over. Once in the groove, it shot down the face, lodged at the bottom and began filling with water. As I ran to it, it suddenly broke free and began floating away, heading toward open water and the strong current. Not again, I thought. One man ran full tilt down the steep face in his sandaled feet. With a prodigious leap, he sailed across the open gap and landed in the boat. What balls! I couldn't help applauding as did everyone else. He grandstanded, paddling to the gravel bar where we joined him.

"Why did you stop me?" I asked the group.

"We thought you were going to ride the boat over the dam," said one.

"Oh my god, no! I was trying to do the same thing you did, except you did it better."

We drained the boat and, leaving it to dry, moved into the shade to sit around a small fire. On a grill, several silvery fish–most no longer than a finger–popped and hissed. And then the questions began. Their frame of reference extended only to Chiang Mai; north of it was terra incognito. They wanted to know what it was like. Where there still tigers? What about the outlaws? Was I armed? I sensed that by talking with me, they felt they were participating in the journey and I was happy to oblige them.

The sky was a shade of blue seldom seen in Bangkok; a few cotton ball clouds hovered as if spray-painted. A half-dozen families were camped here, the elders and the children sheltering beneath a bamboo-frame canopy covered in elephant grass. Nets slung between poles dried in the hot sun. A few men and women sat before heaps of netting, searching intently for tears which they repaired with cord threaded through bamboo needles. Extra needles were stuck in the men's floppy straw hats.

They lived in a nearby village. With the rice season over they spent the afternoons fishing. The dam blocked the passage of migrating fish which were trapped when they tried to leap the dam, or in the shallows where they lay, too exhausted to continue.

A woman gave me sticky rice on banana leaves and a few small fish while Hero showed me how I could dig a shallow cavity in the gravel about two feet from the river's edge. Because the hole's bottom was beneath the level of the river, capillary action pulled groundwater into it, filling the hole from the bottom up. When the sediment settled, I'd have filtered water to drink, a bit of rural technology that would later serve me well.

Back on the river, I spent a lazy afternoon, the Ping slowing as I moved toward the end of Chiang Mai Valley. To the south, the mountains converged, a sign that I'd soon be in their embrace. I thrilled at the prospect. It must have been the way American pioneers felt after crossing the Great Plains and seeing the Rockies loom on the horizon.

But then, a cold wind pulled a cloud tarpaulin over the valley and frigid air blew up the river. Where the next village should have been, a herd of Lampang white cows stood placidly chewing their cuds. Nobody on the banks knew how far it was to Tha Sala so, as usual, I resorted to asking at intervals and drawing my own conclusions. Sunset was half-an-hour away when I spotted the orange roof of a *wat* amidst the tall trees on the right bank. Not seeing a landing, I hopped to the bank and tied the boat to a tree.

The *wat* was as peaceful as the large trees clustered around it; how had the villagers kept the loggers at bay? The 30-ish abbot appeared at a window, an orange apparition in a black velvet ground framed by a vermilion frame. With a warm smile, he said, "If there's anything I can do to help you, just ask." I told him I was looking for the *phu yai baan*'s house and he summoned a *dek wat* (temple boy) to escort me there.

We walked nearly a mile on a cathedral road with arching bamboo forming a leafy corridor before entering a cluster of buildings composed primarily of large, brick barns. Their presence was perplexing since cows normally slept in the fields or in pens like Sin's buffaloes. The buildings were empty, not even the fragrance of manure to indicate recent occupation. Just beyond them lay Tha Sala itself. Unlike previous habitations, these houses were stark, no-nonsense shelters against the elements, wooden boxes with shuttered holes set atop gray concrete piles, the kind of houses men build when there are no women around. I soon saw that the spartan village reflected the cut-to-the-bone lives of its inhabitants, both sexes rough-looking, dressed in denim jackets, and brown porkpie hats. With their swarthy Mongoloid features, they resembled cowboys, or American Indians burned by a desert sun. These were not ordinary Thais.

As I passed one barn, I spotted a man who, from the way the workmen crowded around him, could only have been the headman. When I greeted him, he started. Frowning, he peered around the door frame to see if anyone was with me, then he just looked at me. The air became taut and I sensed that I needed to explain myself, and fast. My story always sounded suspicious but this headman scrutinized me closely as I talked. When I finished, he remained tensed for a moment and then relaxed, apparently deciding I was harmless. What was going on here that made him so suspicious of me?

"You can stay at my house," he said, brusquely. After ordering a stable hand to retrieve my bags from the boat, he ignored me, returning to his conversation, this time in lower tones. Something was not right but this was not the time to pursue it.

While walking, I asked the man what was kept in the barns.

"Cows."

"Where are they?"

"Coming."

Coming? A light gleamed. The outskirts of Chiang Mai held several cattle markets. Although they functioned in the open, they were, in essence, gray markets. The cows were driven over the border from Burma, given bogus medical certificates declaring them anthrax-free, and trucked to holding pens like these. From here, they would be transported to the markets where they would be purchased by agents working for Bangkok's abattoirs. That explained why the men looked so rough and spoke a gritty Thai. Although Thai citizens, they were Shans, regarded as predecessors to the Thais. They roamed back and forth across the border to pursue business in northern Burma. I thought of the government I.D. pin buried in my pack and was glad I wasn't wearing it.

"When are the cattle coming in?" I asked innocently.

He regarded me with squinting eyes. "Tonight."

The headman was back at the house when I returned, and his first word was "Dinner." As on a ranch, we all ate together, but in a tented pavilion rather than a prairie kitchen. The men dove into plates of sticky rice and *laab*: minced, barely-cooked spiced meats. They ate in silence, directing their full attention to the meal before them.

"Well, let's find you a place to sleep," said the headman. I followed him to a windowless concrete block outbuilding that, when he switched on the bare light bulb, I saw was a storage shed. In the middle was a single bed with springs but no mattress. I showered in the yard and returned to find several men sitting or standing around the room. They watched as I dressed, making no comments, not even talking among themselves, an eerie silence.

More men entered, and then some children, and a bit later, several women. On the rare occasions that they spoke, it was in hushed tones. It took me a moment to realize that they were just shy and didn't know what to say. They were ticketholders waiting for me to entertain them, to pull a rabbit out of a hat, or dance. Instead of a rabbit, I produced a map. That galvanized them. The men pored over it, laying it atop the springs, while the kids wriggled between them for a look.

The tiny room filled and emptied, again and again, so that no sooner had I answered one question that I'd be asked the same question again by a new arrival. Some questions I answered five or six times. Gradually, people began leaving, until there were only a handful. Without all the bodies, I was able to examine the room for the first time. It was nothing fancy. The walls had once been painted a pale blue but most of it had flaked away. The bottom two feet of the wall was a silty brown.

"What happened here?"

"Flood."

"Flood?" We were a half mile from the river.

"Four years ago. The banks are 11 feet high. Came right over them. Into the fields. Killed all the gardens. The chickens slept in the trees and the pigs came into the houses. Rats, too. But it only lasted a week."

It was then that I noticed the fine white powder scattered around the floor, spillage from sacks of some kind. Oh, my god, it couldn't be... The headman's brother followed my eyes.

"Insecticide. We used to store it here."

I had no time to digest this piece of news because someone appeared at the door to announce that the headman wanted to see us all at the sala (pavilion). A sizeable crowd had gathered in the sala and a village meeting was in progress. The headman beckoned me to sit beside him on a wooden bench.

The main item on the agenda was the inauguration of a new school. The headman had just begun to talk when he stopped, and turned to look at me. He then began explaining to the crowd who I was and what I was doing there. He got no further than a few words and then began guffawing uncontrollably. Others shifted uneasily. He began again, only to interrupt himself again with laughter. After several false starts, he finally got through it while I sat, baffled by his mirth. This routine was repeated after the meeting and the next morning when new people arrived in the village. He would begin to explain what I was doing and then, halfway through, would begin chuckling. It was difficult to tell whether he was bowled over by the magnitude of my venture or thought it was the barmiest thing he'd ever heard. When I asked him what was so amusing, he shook his head and laughed even harder.

After regaining his composure, he returned to the main topic. Three months earlier, the *sao ek* (first pillar) for the new school had been erected, an act which, like the laying a cornerstone, signifies the start of construction. Elaborate rituals had been conducted to propitiate the naga or serpent that protected the land and, by extension, the school. Although the school was now ready to receive students, its official opening would not take place until February 14. Invited dignitaries would have to be entertained in regal fashion and for this reason tonight's meeting had been called. Eight thousand *baht* had been allocated for the festivities, not a small amount for a village of Tha Sala's size. In addition, school furnishings like blackboards had to be purchased. For this and other expenses, the headman was asking a cess of 30 *baht* from each of the village's 169 "roofs". The villagers readily consented.

I thought it intriguing that such a labor of love should be celebrated on February 14, a holiday they'd likely never heard about. Until, that is, the schoolmaster stood up to say, "Since February 14 is Valentine's Day, each person should bring a red rose."

When the conversation veered into Shan my attention wandered. Behind the *sala*, a bar of green light burned brightly about 12 feet above the ground. A white neon tube rose from the ground to form a "T" with the green tube; behind them, a white polyethylene fertilizer bag served as a reflector. At the base of the upright was a white enamel pan filled with water and the inert bodies of hundreds of flying insects. Drawn by the green light, the beasts had dive-bombed the white light, stunning themselves and dropping into the pan where they drowned. The ingenious bug zapper ensured everyone an insect-free evening.

Eventually the meeting drew to a close. A moon sliver smiled high in the sky as I trekked back to my gas chamber. Unsure whether the insecticide had retained its potency, I left the door open and, spreading a sleeping bag over the springs, I sank into squeaky sleep.

Cicadas had lulled me to sleep, and cows lowed me awake. The barnyard was awash in cattle, mooing their fright and disorientation as they milled in the barns. Men shouted to each other, and occasionally a truck revved its engine.

The bedsprings protested when I swung my legs over the side, and my feet echoed their agony as they hit the floor. With the constant wetting and drying, my soles had dried again. I rubbed ointment into the cracks before hobbling into the bright sunlight where two herders blocked the paths to keep the cattle from straying.

"How long you been bringing in the cows?"

He looked at me quizzically. "Since midnight. You didn't hear them?"

"I must have slept through it."

The cows were big white Brahmans, a breed popular in India. From the side, their blocky bodies–narrow to the point of toppling when viewed from the front–were set atop spindly, knock-kneed legs, and surmounted by the Brahman's distinctive hump. Their long floppy ears hung along their faces like muttonchop whiskers. Soft, luminous black eyes were enhanced by the short, dirty gray fur that covered the bodies right down to the whitish tuft at tail tip. The headman insisted that they were Burmese, a breed I'd never encountered.

"Is it difficult getting them into Thailand?," I asked.

"There's a stiff border tax," he said enigmatically. The other man laughed.

"How much does one bring in the markets?"

"5,000 *baht* (US$ 200)," said the foreman, "if it's large."

Given the sad state of the Burmese economy, the Shans probably bought it for 2,000 *baht* at the border, not a bad profit for a night's work, a few liters of diesel, and payments for official co-operation. Concern about public health was an urban issue. That was driven home the day I caught several men pouring pesticide into a stream to poison the fish. Weren't they concerned about their health? "Oh no," they replied, "we aren't going to eat them. We'll sell them in the market." Their responsibility ended the moment they unloaded them on the wholesaler; even if the wholesaler knew how the fish had been killed, he would sell them to the retailer and say nothing. The chance that someone might actually be jailed for inadvertently poisoning people was as remote as flying to the moon. Life was a crapshoot and fate dictated its course. If you were meant to die, you were meant to die and it didn't matter how.

Risk in the cattle business was of a personal nature. A year later, while working my way back up the chain to find Shan cowboys herding the cattle across the border, I visited the Tha Sala headman and found the barns empty and derelict. The ranch hands were gone. The headman was evasive. "There was a business conflict," was all he said.

After a breakfast of chicken, bamboo shoots, and sticky rice, I thanked the headman and set off. A short way down the river, my attention was caught by a dozen boats arrayed in a wide circle, their bows pointing like spokes towards an invisible hub. On each prow a man peered into the water. Other men sat amidships, and in the stern, an oarsman sculled, holding the boat in position against the current. As I drew nearer, I saw nets wrapped around the prowmen's arms. Something was up, but I couldn't figure out what.

Suddenly, the water erupted. At a shout, the oarsmen began paddling furiously towards the hub. The men seated amidships smacked the water with paddles and flat sticks. At a second shout, those on the bows flung their white nets simultaneously, canopies unfurling gracefully in wide domes to trap fish beneath their mesh. Judging from the sunlit silver flashes in nets slowly drawn from the water, the communal effort had been successful. The fish hadn't stood a chance.

It turned out to be a fish-filled morning. Downstream, I encountered a fish fence more firmly set into the riverbed that those upstream, one that required 20 minutes of hard work to get past. Congratulating myself on having negotiated it without destroying it, I rounded a bend to find seven more blocking my passage. Two hours of tedious pulling and replacing stakes passed before I moved into open water.

Of course, there had to be a weir just to keep the day interesting. Observed objectively, this one was magnificent; thousands of stakes driven so tightly together that I could walk down their crowns to the river 150 feet below. It must have taken hundreds of man-hours and half a forest to build it. Large channels reached to both sides for several miles to irrigate hundreds of acres.

But after a day of delays, my admiration for rural craftsmanship was evaporating as I contemplated maneuvering down its steep face through a welter of sharp stakes. Then I saw–half hidden at one side–

water rushing down a long chute. Its lower end was blocked by an elaborate barrier of bamboo sticks. While I was gingerly tugging at the lower structure to see if it might be temporarily removed, a man appeared at the dam crest. Recalling the punishments meted out for destroying weirs, I took great care to show him that I was respecting village property. For several long moments, he watched me struggle, Then, he worked his way down to where I stood and, to my surprise, pushed me aside. With one quick motion he ripped the entire structure out of the weir and tossed it away.

"Now it won't block your way," he said, emphatically. Shocked by the swiftness and completeness of the motion, I began cackling. He looked at me, clearly wondering if I was mad. Shaking my head and waving to dissolve his concern, I walked to the boat. He reached it before I did and set it so the bow pointed down the chute.

"No, no," I protested, "it has to go down stern first."

He looked down the chute. "Why?"

Why, indeed. What the heck, why not try it head-first? I got in but before I could settle properly, he gave the boat a hard shove and I nearly fell out. Clutching the gunwales and squatting amidships, I shot down the channel, landing with a whump in the quiet water below. I let out a holler. He laughed, waved, and walked off.

I gave myself lots of time to reach Baan Huai Muay, my nighttime stop. When I neared it, however, I was told that it lacked a *phu yai baan*. "Push on for Mae Soi," a fisherman said, "they have a *kamnan* (leader of several villages)." I did, but he was away. The sun was dropping quickly and I had no choice but to paddle hard for Loong Wua, several miles downriver. I had resigned myself to camping on the riverbank, when I spotted bathers on the left, evidence of a nearby village. Exhausted, I relaxed and coasted to shore.

The dying sun warmed the bathers who were immersed to their knees in a flat sheet of green tinged with peach reflected from a cloud-ceilinged sky. The wide beach rose gently to a village set back some distance from the river, its wooden buildings resembling an Old West fortress. It was the children who saw me first, running into the water, windmilling their arms and shouting joyously. The adults, more reserved, greeted me shyly. It was amusing to see the ripple effect as, one after the other, each woman raised her arms to loosen the *pasin*'s (female sarong) upper hem, and retie it higher above her breasts, thereby preserving modesty.

I walked to the village, following the dust clouds kicked up by cows on their homeward journey. I was directed to the home of the assistant *kamnan*, a solid, amiable man named Thong-in who immediately decided that I would spend the night at his house. He took me on a roundabout tour of the village to get my gear from the boat.

Loong Wua seemed in stasis, as if it had developed to a certain point and no further. There was a dust-blown feel to it, a bit like a farm town during the American Depression. The arrangement of its 310 "roofs" was haphazard with no street running true for more than a few yards; I never knew what I was going to find around the next curve. No roads were paved, and although the village had been electrified for three years, villagers used it only to light their homes and power fans and a few refrigerators and television sets. Thong-in told me the land was dry and would support only cattle, chilies, beans, and a bit of rice.

"We've been having a problem with water," he explained.

"A drought?"

"Not really. This is a dry region even at normal times."

"You don't have irrigation?"

"No. The system silted up some time ago and we've not been able to fix it. Everyone bathes and washes clothes in the river. Like the old days. We have a few wells with pumps and pipes to ensure everyone has enough drinking water, but we rely on the skies to irrigate our crops." It seemed incongruous that we were only a few miles north of the country's largest reservoir and yet these people were limited to growing dryland vegetables.

Depositing my gear on his porch, I slung my *pakoma* over my shoulder and walked with Thong-in to the river. Through the dust pall hanging over the distant fields, the sun was a ball of red; fleecy clouds dotted a blue and orange sky. Unlike upriver areas, the land around Loong Wua held few trees, and almost none near the riverbanks; the scenery felt parched. Thong-in and I bathed silently, nearly the last ones in the river. I took my time, chilled by the water but luxuriating in its softness. For the past few days, my hands had been stiff when I awoke and stayed that way for several hours until paddling loosened them up. Now, sharp pains shot through them when I tried to wring out my wet *pakoma*. Each morning, I flexed them by playing an imaginary piano. Perhaps I should do the same before retiring each night.

As we ate sticky rice and vegetables, farmers crowded the porch, listening to us talk. All during dinner, Thong-in, tipsy from rice whiskey, barked orders to his wife: "Get me my cigarettes. Bring a lighter. An ashtray. Go get the *farang* some sweets. No, don't send your daughter; get them yourself." This seemed to be typical behavior for Loong Wua and I watched to see how the woman responded. We were only a few miles downstream from the independent women of the north yet these women seemed subdued, scurrying about to please their master and their exotic guest. Yet their unsmiling faces were as impassive as the masks worn by Thai dancers. I felt uneasy about not protesting Thong-in's sharpness; it was as if I were condoning his behavior. I desisted, telling myself that I was there for only a short time and could not effect a change. Unless there was outright abuse, my criticism of my host would be treated as a breach of etiquette. Or so I tried to convince myself.

Morning brought thick fog. Villagers were wrapped in tattered sweaters and scarves. In one yard, a small boy in a hooded shirt squatted by a straw fire, thrusting his hands towards the flames. Snuggled up against him was an enormous but utterly benign dog, soaking up the warmth from the fire and from his small master. In another yard, a woman squatted by a wooden contraption comprising an upright board with a fist-sized hole through it. With one hand, she fed green tobacco leaves through the hole and slid a cleaver up and down the opposite side, guillotining the leaves into coleslaw strips. Dried and wrapped in corn leaves, it would be smoked by men and women alike.

Crackling fires, shouts from impatient mothers prodding sleepy children towards school, and the hiss of brooms sweeping hard-packed houseyards were the only sounds. I liked Loong Wua. It had a quiet resilience as it struggled through hard times, each member helping the others, hopeful of movement towards better things.

The rapidity of change meant the villagers had visible landmarks of their progress, improvements they could see in their own lifetimes. Electric lights illuminated nights that only a few short years before had been lit by the moon and stars. Health had improved, pipes had been installed to bring fresh water, diets had become more varied and nutritious. Unlike their parents, children were receiving an education.

As everywhere, however, the benefits of development were accompanied by other, more insidious, changes that threatened the cohesiveness that had enabled Loong Wua to prosper. A few televisions had brought the world crashing into their small enclaves, weakening the comforting fetters of tradition. The lure of money had loosened communal bonds, had brought strangers to the village, had taken children to distant cities in search of employment. Some children would send back money to free their parents from dependence on unreliable Nature. Others would be broken by the city and return diseased, or as prostitutes or drug addicts. Some would simply disappear, swallowed up in the urban maelstrom, maintaining ever more tenuous links to their family lands.

Although machinery liberated villagers from drudgery, and gave them goods that their elders had not even known existed, it also brought pollution, ugliness, noise, and a dependence on the outside world that undermined the self-sufficiency that was their strength. While reluctant to deny them the benefits of progress, I hated to see their way of life disappear. Perhaps I was being selfish. Perhaps I could see, as they could not, Bangkok's slums, the filth, the crowding, the de-humanization that pitted one person against another, and the lack of a social support system to ensure justice and succor in times of trouble. It seemed to me that the losses were greater than the gains.

They constantly apologized shyly to me, dismissing their own accomplishments with the words: "we're *baan nawk*" (backwards)." I wanted to shout, "Yes, and thank god for it!" I desisted because they could not know what I was talking about. Instead, I protested that I enjoyed being among them, living as they did because they had things to teach me, and I was grateful for their kindness. They begged my forgiveness for the poor quality and variety of their food. The sight of so much conspicuous wealth on television had become the measurements of a person's worth, had given them a sense of inferiority and robbed them of pride in their self-sufficiency.

As I wandered and mused, Thong-in appeared at my side, walking unsteadily, recovering from a hangover, no doubt. As we reached the market, a tall woman in makeup and dress much too elaborate for a village, sidled up to me and whispered huskily, "Where did you sleep last night?" It was so unexpected that I nearly jumped. Everyone was watching me expectantly. Something flashed and I took a long, hard look at the woman. The Adam's apple and hands were a bit too large. My smile and raised eyebrows set off howls of laughter which pleased the "lady" for having gotten a rise out of me.

"Isn't it hard to be a *katoey* (transvestite) in a small village?" I asked.

"Nobody minds," he simpered. "I was one in Bangkok too but I didn't like it."

"Because?..."

"Too many of them. Here, I'm the only one. I'm unique," he squealed, smiling brightly, raising his arms like a diva at the end of a performance.

I didn't doubt it. He sashayed about freely, knowing no one would harm him. It was hard to imagine his receiving the same welcome in a rural town in the U.S.

Watchers

Naam Maa Plaa Kin Mod, Naam Lod Mod Kin Plaa
(When the river rises, the fish eats the ants;
when the river falls, the ants eat the fish)
The wheel of fortune turns

For the entire morning, I was embraced by gorgeous hills thatched in bamboo the color of flax, their hot season hue. Falling away at their feet, the lower slopes were clad in Lincoln green trees and the shore was carpeted in lush gardens that extended into the water. Villages had thinned to small clumps of houses separated by broad bands of vegetation. I reveled in the thought that I had it all to myself.

Or so I imagined. Ranged along the shore were a new set of watchers, vastly different from the hunters of the previous day. Zombie-like, they sat behind bushes or perched on tree branches. I'd think I was alone, and then glance up to see a silhouette, or hear a cough. No fishing lines hung from their hands, no activity animated them. They just sat, looking at the river...and me. It was disconcerting to ask a question of a man visible on the bank and hear a reply from a nearby bush. Equally unnerving were the people who walked along the banks muttering to themselves and gesticulating like crazies on a New York street. Add to this the frequent gunshots where there was nothing to shoot, and I was on edge whenever I neared shore.

In this state of mind, I reached the Kong Hin Bridge and climbed to the highway linking the small towns of Hot and Li. The road was virtually deserted, only an occasional truck whooshing past, whining into the distance. It seemed a perfect place for lunch. I opened the still-warm packet Thong-in's wife had given me and the aroma of roast chicken assailed my nostrils. Next to it was a wad of sticky rice. I sat on the parapet, enjoying the quiet of a beautiful winter day, and breathing the faint scent of *mai daeng* wood smoke that wafted across the river from a whiskey still hidden somewhere in the brush.

The sparkling waters of the Ping flowed quietly far below my feet. What better place to meditate on a mellow afternoon? But it was not to be. For the next half hour, young men with the wind blowing through their long hair hurtled by in pick-up trucks, shouting nonsense at me. I tried to close them off and let my mind float downstream, but behind me, a motorcycle crossed the bridge, slowed, turned around, and muttered to a stop. Damn.

A lanky young man, short and muscular, strode comfortably at a diagonal across the two lanes, making a slow beeline for me. Tight black pants and no shirt, his rubber boots scuffed the asphalt as he walked.

"*Sawasdee, khrap*," he said without slowing.

"*Sawasdee*," I replied, "*pen yunggai* (how are you)?"

"*Ah, phuut Thai dai*, (You can speak Thai)," he said

I wondered if he would go away if I feigned incomprehension. Perhaps a bit sooner, but not much. He'd likely hang around just watching me doing nothing and just as abruptly as he'd arrived, he'd wave and walk off.

I wasn't sure why I was being so unsociable. Perhaps because I'd been bending myself into a pretzel to deal with strangers and I needed a break. A Westerner doesn't realize how much solitude he requires until he is denied it; and then he discovers he needs a lot. This need to be alone is inconceivable to a Thai. Tell someone you are going up-country alone and he is appalled. "*Khon diew* (one person)," he says "*mai sanuk, mai sanuk thaorai* (not fun, not fun at all)." A Thai's idea of up-country fun is to travel with a mob of friends or relatives, a radio, and all the accouterments of city life. Thais just feel more comfortable in packs, be it a group of city Thais heading into the countryside or a group of villagers visiting the city. It underscores another aspect of the gap between West and East.

Or does it? Would I respond negatively to someone's approaching me were I sitting on a bridge in, say, rural England? Probably not. So what was different? Perhaps it was the work involved in conversing. No matter how fluent one is in a foreign language, it is laborious to speak it all the time, especially when one is repeating conversation he has had a thousand times, as if from a prepared script. And I was the intruder in their realm; didn't I owe it to them to take time to make a connection? Didn't I have an obligation to be friendly? Yes, and yes, but at that moment I wanted to be by myself.

Of course, these thoughts didn't go through my head until later. For the moment, I embarked on a course I'd often adopted in such situations: inventing a persona for myself. It is childish but it keeps the fun in what can often be a grueling half-hour of rote answers to a litany of questions I've heard ten thousand times.

And so it began.

"Where are you going?"

"Here. There," I said, continuing to chew my roast chicken.

"What is your name?"

"Bill."

"Bill. Bill," he said, trying it out for the sound of it. He paused. "Do you want to buy a *lamyai* (longan) farm?"

I stopped in mid-bite. "A what?"

"A *lamyai* farm. It's a good one."

I'd been offered many things before but never a farm and never while sitting on a bridge in the middle of nowhere chewing sticky rice, and certainly not an offer filled with trees bearing the luscious tan fruit I loved to eat.

I looked at him and he stared back from small eyes and a slightly askew grin. It occurred to me he was serious.

"Tell me more," I said, at a loss for anything else to say.

"It belongs to an old man. He's had it all his life, but his children have gone to the town to work. He's got no one to farm it for him."

"Why don't you buy it?"

"No money."

He wasn't really pushing the sale, just musing in a more or less conversational tone.

"What's your name?" I asked. Would he would play the same game with me?

"Pa Sut," he said with a broader smile, leaning forward, confident we were now engaged in more than a tentative conversation.

Pivoting on the parapet so my back was now to the river, I offered him some sticky rice. He took a step back, shaking his head and rubbing his stomach. *"Im laew (already full)."*

"How big is this farm?" I continued.

"Seven *rai* (2.5 acres). The trees are all young, only three years old."

"How much?"

"300,000 *baht* ($12,000). No bargaining," he said and then added hastily, "I'm not making any money on it. This is for my friend."

"What else is on the property?"

"Nothing, just *lamyai*."

"Nothing?"

"Well, a hand pump to bring the water from the irrigation ditch."

"Anything else?"

"Yeah," he said, thinking hard, "a shed for farm implements."

"That's it?"

"Well, and it has a house. Two stories."

This guy had to be on the level. Any real salesman would have mentioned the house straight off. I soon discovered, however, that he had a fixation about *lamyai* which blinkered his vision to anything else.

"Hmmm," I said, for want of anything more intelligent to say. "I'll think about it."

"Ummm," he replied.

I liked him. He wasn't terribly complex, just a friendly guy leaning against a bridge railing. He seemed to have nothing else to do on this lazy afternoon which seemed ideally suited to...well...leaning against bridge railings. Occasionally, he would break off the conversation to flag down a passing pick-up truck or a tractor and engage in serious conversation with the driver. Although he could not have been more than 30, it was obvious he was a person of some consequence in the area.

We said nothing for a few moments. Then, abruptly, he asked "What is the Malay word for *"khap khun maak* (thank you)?" Without waiting for a reply, he began trying to sort it out himself. This conversation just wasn't going according to the script. He finally shook his head in disgust with himself for his faulty memory.

"Do you speak Malay?" I asked.

"A little," he replied. "I got a job in Malaysia a few years ago. In a factory. I learned a bit of Malay."

"Where were you in Malaysia?"

He paused, surprised by the question. "I don't know." And then he brightened. "It was a good job. Paid 100 *baht* a day. Here you can only make 50 *baht* a day. I was there 12 days."

"Only 12 days? Why?"

"Oh, I had a 15-day visa but they couldn't make it for longer and anyway, I wanted to come home."

"Did you ever think of going to *Sa-oo*?" I asked, using the Thai truncation of Saudi Arabia where many village men made good money as construction workers.

"I didn't want to. I was gone to Malay for only 12 days and I missed my *lamyai* orchard," he said. He paused a moment before adding, almost as an afterthought, "and my wife and child. That was only 12 days; how could I go away for a year?" he snorted in disbelief.

Another moment of silence passed and suddenly he said "*Serima Kasi*. That's it. *Serima kasi*." His brows furrowed. "Or something like that. That's the Malay word for 'thank you'."

Now I remembered. "*Terima kasi*," I thought, not wanting to correct him.

"How do you say '*sawasdee*' (the Thai greeting) in English?" he asked.

"Hello," I replied.

"Oh yes," he said, brightening. "Hello, Hello. One, Two, Three, Four. Hello, Hello," he said, holding an imaginary microphone to his mouth as he'd undoubtedly seen a technician do with a public address. system.

"I have cows. A lot of them. Do you have cows?" he asked.

"I don't, but my family did when I was a boy."

"Are the cows the same as here?"

"Pretty much the same. Bigger and heavier, though."

"Like you," he said, flashing a mischievous smile and then chuckling to himself.

"I like my wife," he volunteered. "Didn't like the first one, though. Bossy. I have a 13-year-old son by her. He is a novice in a *wat* in Chiang Mai. My new wife. I really love her. We have two children, one eight and one six. I miss her right now and I saw her just this morning," he said in wonderment.

The pangs of separation must have begun tugging at him because he stood for a moment more, then began shifting his feet. He unbent his body, nodded to me and began walking across the bridge. He swung a leg over his ancient headlight-less motorcycle with electrical wiring snaking out from half a dozen ports. It took several kicks to stir it to life. He turned, waved to me, said "hello" and rode away.

It was then that I remembered that in Thai "*sawasdee*" means both hello and goodbye.

The afternoon put me down a corridor with dun sandstone cliffs rising 100 feet above me. Sculpted by wind and water, they resembled organ pipes, but the only sound was the breeze whispering in the crevices. As though weary of transporting it, the slowing river dropped the sand load that, prior to the dam's construction, it would have carried to the sea. The sand had formed into low islands separated by shallow channels. For the next hour, I worked my way among the channels, misjudging most of them, a rasping crunch announcing a meeting with the riverbed. At first, I tried bulling my way through, paddling hard to get unstuck. I discovered that if I just sat, the flowing water would shift the sand and free me, a little like standing in the surf as the sea removed sand from beneath my feet. It took more time but was less exhausting.

High, fleecy clouds followed me like parasols. Snowy egrets walked delicately on spindly legs through tall green grass, and the breeze created a snowstorm of cotton-like flowers that floated gently to the water, covering it in white fuzz. On one island, two short-haired, reddish-brown puppies, all legs and floppy ears, chased each other around and around, splashing in and out of the shallows. At least someone was enjoying the sandbars.

Humans had added color accents to the landscape. Near the shore, an orange and blue boat–the first painted boat I'd come across–floated quietly among the dark green reeds. Along the opposite shore, a small dugout in pink and robin's egg blue was moving towards a distant hut. It announced itself, not by the sound of paddle strokes, but by bright flashes of sunlight reflecting off the blade as it was lifted for a stroke, quicksilver tears dripping into the river. Farther on, a young man clad only in a *pakoma* splashed in the shallows, lost to the world, singing a lilting country song to himself.

My reveries were shattered by the approach of a motorboat, also the first I had seen. Clamped to the right gunwale was a small two-stroke engine with a long drive-shaft ending in a propeller. Producing more sound than power, it seemed to be straining, as though to climb a hill. When it came into sight, I saw the analogy was apt; passengers and cargo combined to depress the craft nearly to the gunwales. The annoying engine was the prelude to a long evening of paddling. It began when I hailed a farmer.

"What's the next village?"

"Ho Ngam." I ran a finger over the map. No village by that name.

"How far away is it?"

Long pause while he looked up in the sky, and upriver and downriver. "Two miles." This should have set off alarms but I failed to hear them until too late. Distances in Asia are normally given in multiples of two. How far is the next town? "Two miles." How far is the market? "Two blocks." How far is the noodle shop? "Two doors down." What it generally means is that the director has no more idea how far it is than the directee.

"Thanks."

"Think nothing of it."

A mile down river, I met a fisherman.

"How far to Ho Ngam?"

"Ehhh? Never heard of it?"

"So how far to the next village?"

"Two miles."

I paddled approximately two miles but no houses appeared. I sat in the middle of nowhere for half-an-hour before a herder wandered by.

"I was told there is a village here."

"There is."

"Where? I don't see anything."

"Oh, it's over there, over the hill," he said, pointing into the distance directly away from the riverbank.

"How far?"

"Um. About two miles."

There were no boat guardians nor secluded coves in which to tie up for the night. I wasn't about to haul the craft over the hill, especially since I had no idea what I might find when I got there. Best to push on.

The herder had stopped to watch me while his cows meandered into the distance without him.

"Is there another village farther downriver?"

"Yes."

"How far?"

"Oh, *mai klai thaorai* (not far at all)."

Reckoned on a scale of the distance between here and Mars, it was probably "not far at all," but in river terms, it could be infinite.

"Thanks," I said. "Where are your cows?"

The cows had become dots disappearing over the horizon. The herder whirled around to look, then turned back to shoot me a chagrined smile before trotting after his charges. I paddled on.

A few miles later, a small village appeared on the right. The map said that I was looking at Pa Teen. A group of people watched me from a tall bluff.

"Where is the headman's house?" I shouted.

"Back two miles."

Oof.

One man sensed what I was looking for. "You can stay in the next village."

"How far away is that?"

"Two miles."

I began paddling hard. It was at that point that the river–robbed of a current by the approaching lake–decided to turn to Jell-O and my boat into a pig. Time and again, I misjudged and lodged on a shoal. It didn't help that the low sun shone directly into my eyes so I couldn't see the sandbars or fishing nets until I was trapped in them. Cursing the river, the people, the boat, and every animate and inanimate object, I thrashed my way down the river until, finally, a village appeared. Between me and it waited one last sandbar and a shallow channel. Watched by everyone, I made an ignominious entrance, forced to exit twice to push the boat over a shelf.

My legs aching after a day of shoving the heavy boat off islands, I climbed a long concrete stairway to find Baan Phae Din Daeng village straddling a dead-end road. Among those greeting me was the *kamnan* who said "Welcome, welcome," with a wide smile and sad eyes.

The walls of his wooden home were painted pale yellow, the first painted house I'd seen since Chiang Mai. They were a cheery contrast to the four, sullen teenagers who stood at the open doors of a pickup truck, bathed in the blare of its radio. They regarded me with hostile indifference, a scene reminiscent of some inner-city ghetto. After days among gentler people, it was a jarring encounter.

The *kamnan* was as innocuous as his wife was loquacious. In her mid-50s, distracted and scatty, she immediately launched into a complex story, her wild eyes never meeting mine. The first of her two children, a son, had died of internal problems at the age of five months. Her surviving child, a daughter, had recently undergone an operation for ovarian cancer and died at 35. The poor woman was living in a haunted house, and her husband had to endure her bitterness as well as his own sadness. My troubles with a recalcitrant river suddenly seemed petty.

Dinner was meager, comprising but two dishes: fish and an omelet. The *kamnan* insisted on serving me polished white rice rather than the sticky variety. "It is better for you," he insisted. I didn't argue. The *kamnan*'s mother, a stooped woman in her 70s, joined us, sighing deeply as she sank painfully onto the mat that served as table and tablecloth. I soon saw that her calm demeanor masked an alertness and perceptiveness not shared by the other family members, who were wrapped in their own problems. When she saw I was tired, she told her son to fix my bed. Her son told his wife to fix my bed. Within moments, I was stretched out on the floor on a pad about a foot too short, but I was too tired to care. My roommate was a small clock that struck the hour and the half hour. All night. Too sleepy to silence it, I suffered its rudeness until 4 a.m. when I muffled its bleats beneath my pack.

I woke at first light to a silent house; a family of late sleepers, apparently, which suggested that they earned their living not from farming but from services of some sort. I pulled out my journal and began writing. Aside from yesterday's difficulties, I was now beginning to flow according to the river's rhythm. I'd learned to control my strokes, pulling just enough to keep the boat moving in a straight line. I'd also learned to read the river. Weeks of watching it had attuned me to its mindset, taught me how to cope with its pettish moods. It was powerful, ever-changing. I now knew that even when its surface was placid, currents surged deep within it, ropes of water caressing the banks and bottom, like a large cat rubbing against passing objects.

What else had I learned? That a river preferred to flow in a straight line, heading towards the opposite bank rather than around a bend. I'd learned to flow with those currents, discovering that the boat often knew where it was going; usually not, but occasionally. I now knew that rivers start and stop as they work their way across plateaus and down slopes. They follow where the land leads them, snakes slithering across the landscape without any purpose or destination.

As I wrote, I heard footsteps and remembered the clock still under the pack. Leaping for it, I replaced it on the table just as the *kamnan* came through the door.

"Breakfast," he said.

The *kamnan*'s wife had gone to visit a neighbor so we dined in peace, attended by his mother who listened attentively but said nothing. Dishes of curry, and others of broth with fatty pork and vegetables, were placed on the mat. A dainty gray Burmese cat tentatively prowled along the mat's edge, wary of a swat if she ventured too close. I motioned to the cat and asked if it had a name, expecting that, as in most households, it would simply be called *maew*, literally "cat." "*Mawk*," (fog) said Grandmother, as the fog crept in on tiny cat's feet, retreating when a hand was waved in her direction.

Sanit Puengtham was 59 and had been kamnan for several years. With 247 "roofs", the village was large enough to be divided into five "*moo*" or "wards" to facilitate administration. Sanit was responsible for all five moo, a large task for an unprepossessing man. I suspected that, despite his tragedies, much of his mother's strength flowed through his veins; how else could he oversee such a large village and still pursue his own business? For his government services, he received 1,000 *baht* a month for expenses. Although it was 400-600 *baht* a month more than a headman received, it couldn't have covered a fraction of the costs of administering his office.

There were almost no old houses in Phae Din Daeng (Red Earth Landing), a surprise since it takes the tropics little time to devour buildings. Paint a building white and after a year, black fungus has attacked it and it looks antique. Everything here looked new, too new.

"How old is the village?" I asked.

"Twenty-three, 24 years," Sanit replied.

Twenty-three, 24? Strange. Then it flashed. "The Dam?"

"Yes. We once lived farther down the river but when they built the dam, we had to move up here."

"For the better?"

He paused, rubbing his hands together. "Better. And worse. The land there was better but it doesn't flood here."

But the bad soil was killing the village.

"It is hard to make a living," he said, echoing Thong-in's comments about Loong Wua. Our children go elsewhere to work." He looked uncomfortable; the exodus clearly bothered him.

"Where do they go?"

"Bangkok, Chiang Mai, Lampang. A lot of the men go to Chonburi to work on the trawlers, catching fish in the sea. They have to catch fish there because they can't catch enough here." He smiled. "At least the fish there are already salted. It saves time."

But his little joke was a desperate attempt to cover a grave concern.

"Do they come back?"

"Nothing to come back to. No work. They only come back to visit."

"What would bring them back to live?"

"Jobs, better land, anything. Most of them would rather be in the village than in the city. Here, they are part of something. In the city, they are country bumpkins, and laughed at. It's unfair. The city could not grow without them. But they'll never get rich there; they aren't *phu dii* (the elite). They have dark skins, they speak with country accents, they don't know anybody important." I'd seldom heard a farmer describe the lot of his fellow villagers in such harsh terms. Yet, his eyes betrayed no rancor; this was the life lived by most Thais, and there wasn't much they could do to change it.

With these sobering thoughts, I took my leave, feeling more like the privileged class–and therefore an intruder–than I ever did in Bangkok. It was a miracle that they welcomed me instead of reviling me for my urbaneness.

The *kamnan* followed me down the stairway to the landing, and silently watched me load my gear. I pushed off and stood in the boat to *wai* him. With a rueful smile, he *waiied* back and waved one or two mournful wags. "See, even you are leaving," he said, and laughed at his joke.

"I'll be back," I lied as I pushed into the main current. Somewhere along the cliffs, a young boy was playing a flute, the dulcet tones ringing through the air. I rounded a bend and it was lost.

As the current slowed, the landscape changed. The bamboo was replaced by my old nemesis, the giant mimosa. The dam-dulled river had deposited its sand cargo in huge islands that were covered in mimosa so thick and extending so far in the water that at times it was difficult to know where the land ended and the lake began.

This time I had allies. From the thickets came the arrhythmic thock, thock of wooden clappers against wooden gongs hung from the necks of wandering cows. Like slow-moving threshers, they chomped their way through the infant mimosa, cropping it before it could mature and reproduce. I applauded their poor taste; would that a thousand of them could be loosed amidst the thickets, devouring it as they went. Although I couldn't see them, their clappers followed me all afternoon.

Where the shore was not hummocked by mimosa, flashes of metallic blue wings announced the passage of kingfishers darting along the banks. High overhead, fishhawks wheeled lazily. At intervals they plummeted towards and then peeled away from the water, silver flashes in their beaks.

When I was leaving Loong Wua, Thong-in had told me that the area at the head of the Thale Sap (lake) was populated by fishermen and hunters. "Once you are in the gorges, most villages are a mile or two from the river. There are very few families; most of the fishermen are drifters, bachelors living in tents or on unregistered rafthouses. Be careful of their nets because they can be nasty if you damage them. The fact that you speak Thai will help." I had dismissed it as another *jai lai* story. Was the absence of villages or social organization bad? Could these be the equivalent of mountain men, honest but preferring the solitude of nature to the tumult of humans? Like me?

The river widened into a lake. It became sullen. I peered closely at a mimosa clump to discern the current's movement but there were no telltale "V"s. The river had stopped dead. It didn't take long to realize that the boat that had proved itself to be unstable and tippable, now, in unmoving water, had became a blunt instrument, snowplowing its way through a glassy lake. I was in for a long hard slog.

I'd been told of a floating village at Doi Tao at the head of the gorge. It was described as a market and provisioner for fishermen and the last village I'd see for many days. After two tough hours, it became apparent I was not going to make it by nightfall. Another half hour of paddling revealed no shoreline nor solid ground on which to camp. Then, from far in the distance, a low, steady drone became a dot, became a boat. It rapidly closed the gap between us; I waved and he slowed.

"Is there a village nearby?"

"No, none."

"What about rafthouses?"

"Around the next bend."

"Around the next bend" turned out to be a 45-minute paddle. As the light was fading, I pulled in at a cluster of six rafthouses all, except one, deserted. Several men were stowing gear in a motorboat as my bow bumped the landing.

"Nobody else here?" I asked a stocky man with a thick shock of hair.

"No one."

"Are you staying for the night?"

"No, we're going up to Hot for supplies. We'll sleep there. You want to spend the night?" I nodded. "Go ahead," he said.

I pulled out the chain and the lock.

"You don't have to lock up," one said. "There are no thieves here."

I paused.

"Look at the other boats," he said. "They're not locked."

He was right. I wrapped the chain around a post.

The motorboat coughed to life and pulled away. I watched it round the bend and heard the mimosa muffle the exhaust. I was left in silence to inspect my home for the evening.

The rafthouses were crude; rough, raw wood, single-room shells that opened onto verandahs; simple shelter from the rain. I sat cross-legged before the open wall framing a mirror sea rippled by passing gusts, its salmon surface reflecting a twilight sky. As I ate the rest of the sticky rice, a pale orange sliver of first-quarter moon paralleled by two stars sank behind the ridge, the moon's horns the last to go. Only after the day had faded to black, did I begin preparing for bed. In one rafthouse, I found a pile of roof thatching and spread my sleeping bag over it. I lay on this soft cushion, the brittle leaves crackling under my weight.

The night was peaceful but it held too many bumps for comfort. From the mimosa came the sharp cries of night birds. The bamboo floats beneath the rafts creaked loudly as swells from god-knows-what source occasionally lifted them. Rats skittered and scritched across the floor. Crickets, frogs, and mosquitoes droned an incessant chorus and two mysterious orange "eyes" glowed on a northern hill. The sounds unnerved me and no logic would dispel them. After locking the boat, I removed the pistol from its bag, cocked and safetyed it and slipped it beneath my pack next to my head. I reasoned that one loud bang would balance all the sounds the night could produce.

The River at Rest

Sorn Jalakhae Hai Wai Naam
(Teach a crocodile to swim)
Don't try to teach an expert

The sense of vulnerability that solitariness had imparted the previous evening evaporated at dawn, the night taking with it all the unsettling sounds that had inhabited it. The cold air was utterly still as a flock of birds beat silently across the mauve sky, their image twinned in the water below. Eighty yards from shore, a fisherman set his hooks, his movements mimicked by an upside down fisherman beneath him.

Even when the monochromes turned to Kodachromes I lingered, mesmerized by the morning's beauty, unwilling to enter the day. Each dawn, I'd had to delay my departure to satisfy my hosts, even when the light was beckoning. This was the first morning that belonged to me alone.

Eventually, the sun warmed me to action. I didn't bother eating, just packed and pushed off. The air's stillness was matched by the water; I paddled through malachite. Beneath the surface, pale green tendrils undulated as though animated by a sub-aquatic wind.

Every stroke reaffirmed how ill-designed the boat was for these waters, or any waters, for that matter. A few miles on, a fisherman asked me why I was paddling a *rua hang yao* (long-tailed boat). He was right, I had a motorboat without a motor. What I needed was a canoe. A long-tail passed and the driver picked up a rope and pointed to his transom. I was sweating and his offer to tow me was tempting, but I was determined to make it on my own. The hours dragged on and I got no closer to Doi Tao.

It was odd that a current of even half a mile had not only increased my speed, but the illusion of movement. Here, I constantly struggled to overcome inertia. The moment I stopped, the boat stopped, not even coasting for a moment.

As my fatigue increased, I began thinking about how to increase my speed. Perhaps I could shift my paddling position. I sat on the bow, one leg hanging port, the other starboard, but I couldn't gain leverage for a solid stroke. And my weight lifted the stern causing it to slide back and forth. I sat on the back locker but the bow wandered from side to side. I still had the reserve paddle; maybe I could rig the two as oars and row the boat. I tied each oar to the gunwales but without oarlocks, the oars wobbled and rolled and I got nowhere. What to do? Sink the boat and start all over? Tempting, but impractical. I was only going to get downriver if I paddled so instead of dreaming up elaborate schemes to increase my speed, I paddled.

Ten a.m. became 11 a.m. and began creeping towards noon. Finally, I rounded a bend and saw before me a cluster of rafthouses. This had to be Doi Tao. A dozen boats were tied to the landings and people were moving about.

As I pulled for the dock, I heard "plick, plick, plick" to my left. An elderly woman in a tiny boat glided across my bow and on towards the other side of the lake. In her hands was a double-bladed paddle like that for a kayak. "Plick, plick, plick," it went as first the left blade dipped into the water, and then lifted as the other blade dropped in briefly. I was now even with her stern and the sight was mesmerizing, like watching a goose flapping its wings to move from waterborne to airborne. This was exactly the paddle I needed.

I tied up and went exploring. The dozen rafthouses were connected by plank gangways, a small community with its own streets. There was a general store, a gas pump, a barber shop, a hardware store, all floating on bamboo pontoons, all rising and falling in a low-amplitude sine wave as a motorboat arrived or departed. In the general store, I asked the shopkeeper about the paddle. A clutch of men listened to our exchange.

"Yeah, we use them here, but we don't sell them."

"Where could I get one?"

"I don't know. Everybody carves his own."

"Know anyone who could carve one for me?"

They pondered the question. "Me," said a voice. A tall man detached himself from the huddle.

"How would you make it?"

He looked at my boat. Then, he stood beside me to measure my height against his. He lifted my arm and measured from shoulder to fingertips. Stepping back, he looked at the boat again, looked at me, and said "six *sawk*," a *sawk* being the distance from elbow to the fingertips. So I'd need a nine-foot paddle.

"Seems a bit long," I ventured.

"No, your gunwales are high so you need the extra length to clear them." He was right, and he was the right man to carve it.

"How much?"

He thought a moment. "70 *baht*." 70 *baht*? That was under three dollars. I tried not to betray my surprise.

"How long to carve it."

"I have to find the wood. *Maruni*." (the day after tomorrow)

I peeled the bills from my packet. "9 a.m., day after tomorrow?"

"Can."

Doi Tao was a working town and I liked working towns. The interior and exterior walls of the hardware store were festooned with the utensils of the fisherman's trade. Nylon filament nets, knives, baskets, brightly-colored plastic buckets, motor oil, propellers, nylon mooring ropes, and fish hooks hung from the walls or were arrayed on the floor. I looked at water containers but couldn't make up my mind whether to buy the large one and carry all my drinking and rice cooking water, or to purify lake water and carry only a small container for emergencies. Filled, the large tank would weigh perhaps 80 pounds, a liability in still water. The smaller one would keep my weight down but if the lake water wasn't drinkable, I risked falling ill, a dangerous condition in the remote gorges. Unable to decide, I went to find a cup of coffee.

On a charcoal stove in the noodle shop next door, vapor rose from a silver canister and the aroma of thick Thai coffee percolated through the air. The owner strained the coffee through a cloth bag and into a scorching glass which burned my fingers as I made my way to a table where three sun-blackened fishermen silently sipped their own coffee. Although they had been watching me move towards them, they seemed shocked when I asked to join them, hurriedly sliding empty noodle bowls and condiments out of my way. I pumped them for information about the lake. They were a bit hazy on distances, so I pulled out the map. At first, they looked at it out of politeness. As I talked, they gradually began to realize that it bore some relation to the lake they fished every day. Their stubby, water-dried fingers with broken nails began stabbing along the shore, identifying nameless contours as if discovering them for the first time.

The lake zigged and zagged for 120 miles through deep gorges. After running south for 20 miles, it jagged to the right through a narrow passage before resuming its southerly direction through a canyon that once held the river's most ferocious rapids. Just below them was a key juncture where a gap opened to the left. If I missed it, I would paddle south for two days into a cul-de-sac. If I hit the gap correctly, I would curve to the northeast and then south into the largest portion of the lake, again having to look for a narrow passage that would carry me to the dam.

The men offered the usual warnings about watching out for *jai dams*. I changed the subject.

"What is the fishing like?" I asked, thinking I might use the gear I'd packed.

They leaned back, sighing. "Not good. Too little rain."

"But last year was worse," another added.

"What happened last year?"

"The fish died."

"Died?"

"Thousands. We went out one day and they were floating on the surface."

"What happened?"

"They said it was a heavy rain up north. Washed pesticide out of the fields. It all came down here and the fish died. It was many weeks before new fish came in."

That settled it. Finishing my coffee, I returned to the hardware store and bought a large water tank. Weight or no weight, I would carry all my drinking water. I didn't relish floating belly up, preserved by pesticides.

"Is there somewhere to spend the night?" I asked the shopkeeper.

He pointed to the middle of the lake where a long raft bearing several orange-roofed buildings was moored.

"What is it?"

"It's a hotel. Without guests. You'll have no problem finding a room."

It took 20 minutes' paddling to reach it. The closer I got, the more bizarre it looked. Resting on bamboo pontoons were several single-story buildings constructed of smoothed planks. The windows were nothing more than shuttered openings. A water tank on a tall platform was surrounded by multi-hued geometric structures. Several saronged young women silently watched my approach.

"Good morning. Do you have a room for rent?" I asked. There was an explosion of movement. *"Mae, mae* (mother, mother), he speaks Thai," they shouted. One grabbed the chain and wrapped it around a post, another began unlashing the bag, while a third darted into the kitchen to return with a glass of water. I was so thirsty that I didn't bother asking the source.

Calling itself Tan Thong, the "resort "had been designed as a poor man's Coney Island. The geometric shapes turned out to be crude diving platforms arrayed around a rectangle of lake that served as a swimming pool. Cages held rabbits and cooing doves. Gazebos, a restaurant, and outbuildings were connected by boardwalks. Some surfaces had been painted in bright colors that myriad suns and rains had faded and flaked, yet it had a certain rough charm. Apparently it was too rough for jaded cosmopolites, because the resort was patronized by winds and shadows.

"Too far away from big towns," said the rotund manager, mother of the girls. She ferried passengers in a small motorboat welded together from 50-gallon oil drums. In the winters, university students took it over on weekends, drinking, playing guitars, and singing *luuk thung* (songs of the field) until dawn. I decided it was a perfect place to write, jettison some gear, and read.

Two rows of rooms either side of a long, dark corridor framed the bright lake at the far end. Half carrying, half dragging my bags, two diminutive, giggling girls led me to a corner room, far from the conversations and kitchen noise. Calling the room Spartan would be stretching the description. There were no interior walls, only the unpainted backsides of the outer cladding. A plank bed and a small desk bearing candles and matches sat on a bare wooden floor. But when a girl slid open the window shutter, the sunshine flooding in made it a cozy den. The window on the adjacent wall opened onto the distant ridge crowned by a gleaming white *chedi*. When I returned with the rest of the bags a scrawny cat was sleeping in a rectangle of sunlight on the floor. For the remainder of my stay, he treated with calm tolerance my presence in his room.

Inspired by the cat, I fell asleep, the soft breeze currying me. When I awoke two hours later, the sundial cat had followed the patch of sunlight across the floor. At the end of the platform, I washed clothes, dipping them in the lake to rinse them. Fat brown fish swam lazily near the platform. Later, on completing a visit to the squat toilet, I poured water in the bowl, heard thrashing beneath the floor and understood why the fish were so large.

I began writing, summing up what I'd learned, and noting my physical changes. My body had slimmed and hardened, my abdomen and back were now a solid band of muscle. My hands, however, were cramping and my feet were cracking again; putting weight upon them was painful. With the deep water, I'd be stepping out of the boat less often; giving them a chance to heal.

I noted that my reaction time had slowed, due perhaps to fitful sleep, or the food. The nutrients seemed insufficient for paddling six hours a day, yet farmers worked even longer days and seemed none the worse for it. It was apparent, however, that my concentration levels were down. I was making more errors, misjudging angles and currents, failing to maneuver intelligently through fish fences, or to spot sandbars or anticipate cross-currents in time. I'd become impatient, substituting brawn for finesse, pushing my way past an obstacle rather than thinking out a solution. It was a dangerous state because I was causing problems for myself at a time I needed to be clear-headed. The gorges would not forgive errors. I needed a lot more sleep.

After a plate of fried rice, I cleaned the boat and then sat in the shade to read old books about the North, books I hadn't touched since the headwaters. It was a pleasant afternoon of doing nothing.

A rising breeze broke my concentration. Looking up from the pages, I was momentarily disoriented. The late afternoon sun was streaming through the same window through which the morning sun had previously pored. It took a moment to realize that the wind had nudged the rafthouses around 180 degrees so I now faced west.

As the sun was setting behind a hill, I pushed aside my journal and wandered down to the restaurant. The menu advertised fresh fish.

"Fresh fish? From Doi Tao market?"

"No, from here," said the proprietress. Recalling the earlier tumult beneath the bathroom, I ordered chicken.

After dinner, I sat on the edge of the raft, watching the stars. The wind was still blowing steadily across the lake, following a distant sun that had slipped over the horizon, sliding downhill toward another's day.

The night had been long and I awoke well before dawn. The stars reflecting off the water were almost as bright as those in the sky, making a limitless firmament that embraced the heavens and the earth. There is a warm, muzzy feeling to the early morning when the brain registers nothing but sensation. I made no effort to break its embrace. Eventually, a streaky orange flame-like light licked across the far range and the wind rushed to greet it.

With the dawn came a muted roar from far down the lake. Sound materialized into shape as an armored boat with four men cut its engine to coast the final yards to the dock. They wore green flak jackets and carried repeater shotguns. Rangers, I deduced. Their bellicose equipment was unsettling. What was out there that required heavy armaments, protective clothing, and a very fast and very well-sheathed boat?

The leader, a solid, scholarly-looking man with horn-rimmed glasses introduced himself as Sunthorn and asked about my "mission". After satisfying him, I asked similar questions and learned that they were based at the dam and patrolled the lake area, which the government regarded as a protected forest. They said they were on the lookout for poachers and I mentioned the prisoners who had been freed on the king's birthday.

"Yes, the hills are more populated than they were a month ago. They keep a low profile. Plus the boat engine is so loud that they are well out of our way before we reach them."

"How often do you come through the area?"

"Every four days."

This wasn't reassuring. "What game are the poachers looking for?" I asked.

"Anything that will get them through another few days. They don't have money when they are released and many don't have homes to go to. They come up here to forage for anything they can find."

And a foreigner with a boat load of gear would be an excellent find, I surmised. Christ, Buddha and other wise men were right: goods encumbered one. Concern about the potential loss of possessions had created an entire class of neurotics who bought insurance, locked all the doors, and struggled to stack the odds against mishap. Yet, here I was being as neurotic as the worst of them. But would living off the land–an option I'd considered and rejected–have been feasible? Perhaps, but I was already dealing with enough imponderables. Was my journey worth any less because it depended on support systems? Deep in my heart, I knew that it was, that such endeavors of the purity I desired occurred only when they pitted one against the odds with wits the only weapon.

But while I might feel compelled to rely on possessions it didn't prevent me from lightening my load.

"Would you mind carrying some things to the dam for me?" I asked.

"Sure. We have to go to Doi Tao first but we'll be back in an hour," said Sunthorn.

In my room, I went on a manic binge, seeking every way possible to reduce my weight. I culled books and gear I wouldn't need until I reached the lower river. After a half-hour's work, the bag weighed 10 pounds, not a lot, but it would help. After handing it to Sunthorn, I reduced my load still further. Salt, pepper, and mosquito coils I donated to the kitchen. I sawed two feet from the anchor chain, giving it to a fisherman to weight his line.

When there was nothing more to toss, I relaxed and spent a peaceful afternoon that recalled other rare moments of peace and oneness with the world: a balmy day in the Turkish port town of Marmaris, an evening on a barren hill outside of the desert town of Farahrod in southwestern Afghanistan, a morning on the Barkhor pilgrim circuit in Lhasa, and nearly every morning during an August in Paris. I read Christopher Isherwood's translation of the *Bhagavad Gita* until evening descended. White birds flew through a blue sky over the brilliant green of the mimosa marshes. Moments later, a sleek black crow followed them towards the *chedi*-crowned hill. The sky hues changed almost imperceptibly to orange. I monitored the lengthening of my shadow, watching myself disappear as the sun slipped behind a distant range.

It was the new moon and without electric lamps to dilute the light, the stars sparkled against an ebon sky. I tried to visualize "The Horse," as the Thais call it, but all I could see was a big dipper. Given the small size of the cluster we know as the "Pleiades," the Thai constellation "Chickens" made sense. Others were as obscure as their English counterparts: "Deer Head," "Cotton Wool," "Monkey," "Crow," "Crocodile's Eye," and the enigmatically named "Man Observing the Precepts." There were no words to describe the night's beauty. The stay had done me good. I was knitted together, well-rested, and eager to set forth again.

When I rose to watch the sunrise the night-long hard wind had hushed to a whisper along the eaves. Before the day fully dawned, I had packed my gear, and sat blowing on a glass of hot coffee, warming my hands on its sides. I then began paddling to Doi Tao. At intervals, bubbles burst on the surface. I slipped my fingers into the water. It was warm. I paddled a bit farther and this time my hand entered cold water. Then, in and out of the warm bubbles until I reached the general store. Where were they coming from?

It was market day and the shoreline was filled with blue plastic awnings. Beneath them, buyers scrutinized trays of large silvery fish still flopping in a thin film of water as they hyperventilated from an excess of O and a dearth of H. Blued by other awnings were clothing, soap detergent, and urban goods through which fisher families pawed. I wandered, marveling at the size of the fish, some nearly three feet long. Tangerines were in season and selling for 20 cents a pound; I bought four pounds. I also bought dried fish and beef jerky. Extra water would be required in order to chew and swallow them, but they would add variety to my diet.

My fishermen friends were sipping *oliang* (iced black coffee).

"Still paddling to Bangkok?"

"Still fishing?"

They laughed. "Yeah. We're heading down the river a bit, like a tow?"

"No, thanks. Why downriver?"

"Away from the *ai nam* (steam)."

"The bubbles? I saw those. What are they?"

"Underwater hot springs. They were buried when the dam waters rose. Fish don't like them; I think there's something, a chemical, in them they don't like. Smells like rotten eggs."

"What kind of water do the fish like?"

"Cold."

"Near the dam?"

"No, just south of here, in the upper third of the lake. In the lower two-thirds, the water is lifeless. Too many chemicals, not enough air. The fish can't breathe."

Pollution and sediment, no doubt, a water that moved too slowly beneath a sun that turned it into primordial soup ideal for growing algae and everything else that would rob the water of oxygen and drive the fish away.

"Do you think the lake will rise again?"

They considered this a moment. "*Mai nae* (not sure)," one said. He searched the banks inland from Doi Tao. "You see where the vegetation ends and the yellower bushes begin?" he said, nodding towards an area 100 feet from the water's edge and a 4-5 feet higher than the lake. "That's where the water was last year. It just keeps dropping."

Their discouragement was palpable. They depended on this lake and it was shrinking. In 20 years, the amount of water running through the river system had fallen from 28.7 million cubic yards to 20.9 million cubic yards. Experts claimed that reduced rainfall was responsible yet rainfall records showed that not only had there been a minimal decrease—two inches down from an average of 47 inches a year—in some areas, rainfall was actually higher than it had been in 30 years. The real problem lay in government programs to increase agricultural output in the North, and its insistence that farmers plant water-intensive crops. The water was being leached from the river faster than the northern streams could replenish it.

Three years later, I would recall the fishermen's disconsolate expressions. Doi Tao would be gone, a few decrepit rafthouses stranded on dry land 1,500 yards from the new river banks. The vast lake, two miles across, would have shrunk to a river flowing between its original banks. Similarly beached, the broken resort would be abandoned. In 1994, I would find only a few herders, their belled charges wandering among the giant mimosa which had flowed in like a tidal wave to cover with green what had formerly been blue-black water.

After the fishermen left, I went to the hardware store. Waiting for me was the carver and leaning against the wall was my new paddle. The wood was old, the color of dock planks, and the thickness of a boat oar. I hefted it. It was heavy, but if it provided additional propulsion it would be worth the extra weight. I thanked the craftsman and paid him.

After filling the water tank with rainwater, I shoved off. I gripped the paddle, seeking its mid-point. The carver had balanced it properly but it was very heavy and my first strokes were clumsy. I dug in with one blade but when I dipped the opposite blade, the water from the wetted blade ran to the paddle center and down my arms. Within minutes, my shirt was soaked. Across the lake, I heard idlers at the general store guffawing at my awkward efforts. Just get out of range, I thought, and then work on the strokes.

At one point, I thrust my hand along the hull. It emerged wet to the base of my thumb; I was riding two inches lower in the water. The water tank had undone my efforts to reduce my weight. It would be a long, tiring struggle to reach the dam. But sitting here wasn't going to accomplish it. I dipped the blade into the water and pulled, shoveling a little more water behind me.

The Phantom Woodmen

Khwaa Naam Leew
(To grab water)
Try to grab a swimming fish
and all you'll get is a wet hand

My clumsy, soggy progress continued far down the lake. The challenge was to overcome inertia and my initial response was to dig deeply with one blade and then with the other. It took a while before I realized that the old woman's "plick, plick, plick" was the proper technique, barely dipping into the water on one side and then dipping briefly on the other. I was surprised how quickly I built up momentum. And how quickly my shoulders tired. Weeks of paddling had toned me but had not conditioned a single muscle to wield this new paddle. I had to start all over.

Gradually, the paddle and I began to function as a team and by early afternoon, I was out of the upper lake and into the gorge proper. Trees in autumnal colors glowed on the hillsides and were reflected in the calm lake that also reflected a thick slice of cobalt sky. Soon, the sun slipped behind the rock walls, plunging the river banks into darkness. With no rafthouses in sight, I decided to camp. On a gentle incline rising to the tree line I saw an inlet where I could hide the boat among the mimosa. Getting to it was another matter, requiring that I paddle through 90 feet of cat claws. By the time the bow bumped the muddy bank, my arms were bloody.

On shore, I became aware of a low hum that seemed to come from everywhere at once. Bees, thousands of them, were feasting on pink mimosa blossoms. I waited, thinking that nightfall might drive them home but darkness descended and well past their bedtime they continued to flit from flower to flower. I elected to ignore them and hoped they would ignore me.

Thinking that the trees higher up the slope might provide shelter and a vantage point from which to watch passing boats I began hacking a path through the mimosa. But the longknife was dull and a half-hour of chopping cleared a path only 40 feet long. Moreover, I found myself in a copse which seemed to hold the main body of bees. Their buzzing crescendoed as they shifted their attention from the flowers to me, smacking into my head and body with increasing ferocity. Certain that I was about to be attacked in force, I fled downhill, crashing through mimosa, slashing my legs in my panic to reach the water. But I was too slow. The bees caught up, crawling all over me as I slapped frantically at their tiny bodies. After long minutes of brushing them off my hair and clothes, however, I realized I'd not been stung. They must be stingless!

By now my hair was gooey with mooshed bees, and I was sweaty and tired. To hell with finding a vantage point. I dumped my gear on a semi-level spot a few yards from the water, screened from the lake by mimosa. It wasn't perfect but it would do. All I wanted to do was clean up and settle in.

I had just stripped to my underwear when a boat silently entered the inlet. Absorbed in setting a net across the cove entrance, its fisherman owner failed to see me. His progress was an exasperatingly slow, as he paid out a long tennis-like net into the water, its lower edge weighted with stones, its upper rim buoyed by plastic motor oil containers. I crouched motionless, waiting for him to leave, shivering in a cold breeze, nearly nude and targeted by mosquitoes, bees still crawling through my hair. I was reluctant to reveal my presence, concerned that he might bumble into my boat, and apprehensive that he might return later in the night. He worked in the dark, however, and couldn't see beyond his net.

After what seemed like an eternity, I heard him cough in the next inlet. When I was certain he was gone, I slipped into soft water that had retained the sun's warmth. I emerged, clean and refreshed, and climbed into the boat to dry myself. It was now too dark to light my stove so I ate the last of the fried rice that had been my lunch. Grabbing a few essentials, I made my way up the slope and after wrapping my sleeping bag in a plastic sheet, I lay back to watch the thousands of stars orphaned by the sun's departure.

Several times during the night, boats eased into the inlet in search of fish, their motors wakening me to alertness. Hunters' searchlights swept the slopes hoping to freeze a deer in their powerful beams. The deer apparently stayed close to the tree line because most of the lights moved slowly back and forth across it, right where I would have been had I been able to hack a path to it. It was frightening to lie in the underbrush like a prison escapee, wondering when the penetrating beam would fix on me. How would the hunters react if they found me?

When the night wasn't rent by engines, it was filled with bug songs and bird calls. Owls hooted. Nightjars twanged like taut wires struck by mallets. Other birds mimicked rusty door hinges. Frogs sang one-note love ballads.

My sound-riven sleep had taken its toll and I awoke groggy and slow-witted. Everything not covered by plastic sheets was soaked with dew. For the first time, I lit the small alcohol stove I'd bought in Paris on a whim years before, and watched the blue flame massage the underside of the pan. Water boiled, rice bubbled, curry cans were opened. Reluctant to move in such a beautiful morning, I indulged in a cup of tea. Before it was even in the cup, I heard a boat engine laboring to turn a tiny propeller and saw the fisherman from the previous evening coming to check his nets. I had heard fish splashing all night, so he would likely be pleased. Crouching and sipping my tea, I watched him work. He killed the engine and pulled himself along by the net, singing quietly. Minuscule fish were tossed into the bilge where they flipped and flopped. Occasionally, one would lash its tail with sufficient force to clear the gunwales and continue living.

I'd heard fishermen complain that the fish were smaller than those in the old days and now I understood why. With so many fishermen competing for dwindling supplies, the fish were caught before they had a chance to mature. "They think only of today," Sunthorn had said. But when the water level is dropping, the time to strike is today. By tomorrow, someone else may have cleared the lake.

By the time I pushed off, the sun was illuminating the lake but the shore was still in darkness. Paddling to the sunlit middle was like walking through a door from the cold into a warm interior. Dragonflies darted in to inspect me, hovering, zigging, zagging, and occasionally resting on the boat, calm yet coiled like watch springs, poised to zip away at the slightest disturbance. Each iridescent body gleamed a different color: blue, green, yellow, orange, red, my own private rainbow lined up on the gunwales.

Rummaging the front locker for a rope, I surprised several stow-aways: spiders, water bugs, a potato bug, and a big-eyed albino frog, un-doubtedly a cousin of the white and brown-striped one I'd found in my shoe the previous morning. I tapped him lightly, but when he refused to hop overboard, I returned to paddling. An hour later, as the sun blazed down, he sprang to life, plopping into the water, his long legs scissoring powerfully.

Shortly after noon, the Day of the Phantom Woodsmen began. The gorge walls had moved closer. Above me, thickets of bamboo wore leaves the yellow of corn shocks. Somewhere on the hill to my right, some-one was chopping a bamboo tree. He would take a single stroke, pause, then stroke again. It was an odd sound, like two rocks struck together underwater. He seemed to be high on the slope but though I peered hard I couldn't locate him.

Then, the same sound came from high on the left slope. Once again, I was unable to locate the source. Confusing me was the long inter-val between strokes. Was the woodsman so tired that he could not man-age more than a stroke at a time? I'd seldom seen Thai axes tempered to Toledo edges capable of slicing arm-thick trees in a single stroke but per-haps they existed.

As I considered it, chopping began coming from all directions, loud and sharp, dozens of woodsmen at work. But still I couldn't see them. For two miles I paddled, the sound never diminishing, the men never re-vealing themselves. They apparently didn't talk because the gorge was otherwise silent and I never heard a word exchanged. It was spooky and I was spooked. I concluded that as long as I could hear chopping, I was safe. When it ceased, it would mean they had spotted me. It didn't stop. I paddled on until I was once more in green forest, perplexed by the non-encounter.

The day proved to be extremely long, the new paddle straining muscles as yet undeveloped. Even 15 minutes of paddling shot spasms of pain through my lower back. I calculated that I was making eight miles a day. At that rate, it would take nine days to reach the dam. Would my body hold up?

By mid-afternoon, the sun had disappeared from the river but shone with such intensity on the hills that its brilliance reflected on the water long afterwards, lighting my way. An hour later, however, even that light was fading and when I saw a rafthouse at the end of the gorge where the river turned right, I headed for it.

Gojasan sat at the mouth of an inlet leading to Baan Ko Chok. It was uninhabited except for a government bungalow on the hill and two rafthouses, one of them occupied by a fishing family. The other was deserted, intended, they told me, as a rustic resort that had never opened. The family caught and dried fish but apparently made little money from it. They told the same story of water levels dropping and fish disappearing. Everyone wore soiled and tattered clothes and the men smoked cigarettes made from local, very rough tobacco rolled in scraps of old newspaper. Such a beautiful setting for poverty.

The family put me in the empty rafthouse which had wide openings for doors and windows. I spread my sleeping bag in the middle of the room but the space was so vast that I felt like a tiny island in an empty sea. I moved closer to the wall.

The family offered to prepare dinner which, no surprise, was fish followed by more fish. While waiting in the semi-darkness for it to cook, I talked with the couple's children, a 19-year-old boy, Pradej, and his 17-year sister, Somjai. She spoke quietly with the trapped, distracted air of one who disliked being where she was but fear going elsewhere.

"How long have you been here?" I asked her, the more verbal of the two.

"We were born here. My father came here 20 years ago. From Tak."

"Have you been outside?"

"Once to Tak. And another time to Lamphun."

"Do you want to go anywhere else?"

"Father won't let me," she said shyly.

"And if he did, where would you go?"

She became animated. "Oh, Chiang Mai. Even Bangkok. We have relatives both places. But he says no." She deflated again. "He says there are bad people there."

Their *jai dam*, I mused.

She perked up again. "But I listen to the radio. At night I can pick up Bangkok, Korat. Even Khon Kaen."

"And what do you hear?"

"Pop music. City people talking. It sounds exciting."

If she could go to the city, she enthused, she could study. Her education had ended at grade six and listening to her, I could feel her conflict. She was bright, with a nice, uncomplicated view of the world that stopped short of being naive. Her brother had no ambitions whatever and seemed incapable of thinking past today. Yet it was fun watching them talk together, wrapped in blankets, listening to each other with respect, joshing each other, genuinely enjoying each others' company. I wondered which of them was luckier, the one with dreams or the one with none.

Dinner finished, I went to my rafthouse and lit a candle, intending to write my journal. Weariness weighed on me before the wick had burned a quarter inch so I snuffed the candle and dropped into a tortured sleep filled with the sounds of chopping, unnerving even while in my unconscious state.

Sometime after midnight, I was awakened by a dull thud which my brain translated as a log banging into my rafthouse. In the bright starlight I saw that the wind had propelled the house into the dead tree to which it was moored. The tree, killed by the rising lake decades before, stood in 15 feet of water. In the pale light it resembled a spindly, disembodied hand reaching from the bottom of the lake, protesting its drowning to an unhearing sky.

As sleep dissolved, I became aware of dew plopping heavy and slow on the corrugated iron roof, as though the sky were about to unleash a torrential storm. In the distance, a nightjar twang echoed off the limestone cliffs. Nocturnal animal sounds were short and sharp, perhaps to communicate with mates but deny predators a fix on their position. Perhaps Marshall had been right; I should have left the camera home and carried a tape recorder instead.

Water softly lapped at the raft's bamboo pontoons until dawn. Without my glasses, everything was hazy but even after putting them on, the view through the wide door was of another wall, this one gray. Through the opposite doorway, the cliffs were partially obscured by thick patches of fog, giving them the look of a fjord. The effect was heightened by the absence of any sound but the dew's steady beat on the timpani roof and the lapping waves. A silent bird soared across the cliffs, in and out of the fog patches. Nothing else moved.

Just as the sky began to pinken, a heavy mist rolled like a great crashing breaker off the land, enveloping me in gray. I was socked in so completely that I could only see a few skeletal, pleading trees rising from the water. With the fog came a sharp drop in temperature and one by one I drew on a long-sleeved shirt, a sweater, windbreaker, and a balaclava.

Breakfast was fish drowned in a broth. The daughter who the previous evening had shared her dreams with me was engrossed in scraping fish scales off the drying frames. Her eyes no longer looked into the distance but were intent on the brush she scraped stroke by stroke across the hissing mesh.

The fog hung like cotton wool as I pushed away from the landing. Within a few strokes, the houseboat disappeared. It was exhilarating to have no idea where I was headed. I paddled for a long while, each moment expecting the cliff to loom up before me. I slapped the paddle blade flat on the surface hoping to be guided by its echo off the walls. No sound returned. Somewhere far behind, a motorboat approached, and my attention shifted to staying out of his way. His passing would give me a line on the passage through the channel which the map told me led into the next lake. He passed a dozen yards to my left, neither of us visible to the other but his ripples plashing against my hull indicated the angle I should take. I paddled towards the receding sound.

Half an hour later, a pale disk appeared in the gray wall, like a welder's torch trying to cut through steel. I had enjoyed my childish game, closing my eyes and pretending to be blind. But as a child's excitement is soon replaced by a gnawing concern that he is about to collide with something–a branch at eye level, a hole, or some other danger–the suspicion that something was wrong began to form deep in my brain. The child slows and slides a foot gingerly forward, putting up an arm to ward off imagined obstacles. Finally, unable to endure it, he squints, admitting a tiny sliver of light. The moment he ascertains his position, there is no longer a point to the game.

Ahead, the tip of the torch continued to burn through the gray. But...shouldn't the sun be ahead, not behind, me? I stopped paddling, waited, listened. Water was dripping from a great height to my left. From somewhere to my right came a faint rasping on mesh.

The sun's blurred edges hardened. The veil began to part, layer by layer, then in patches. Damn. I was facing the upper portion of the lake, the rafthouse far to my right. Like a hunter lost in the forest, I had circled. The boat I had followed was headed up the lake, not down. Next time I'd wait for the fog to lift before setting out.

No I wouldn't. It had been fun, a bit of a mind jolt, the kind I get when I fall asleep on a bus and awaken without a clue where I am. Digging deep with the left blade, I spun the boat and set off again.

The moment I entered the "fjord," the sun disappeared behind the cliffs and the air cooled. No more than 150 feet across, the fjord cliffs rose 200-300 feet out of the water. Farther on, they alternately constricted, then broadened to create a series of rooms. Approaching each one was like reaching a doorway; I did not know what lay beyond until I had paddled through it to discover a room different from its predecessors. Again, I sensed I was not alone. I paused. On the opposite bank, the tree canopies were shaking and I could hear growling. Peering intently, I could make out a family of foraging macaque monkeys. Unaware of my presence, they squabbled and dined, leaping from branch to branch.

Another growling reached my ears, this from a boat behind me moving through the watery "rooms" towards me. The trees ceased shaking as I paddled into the shadows to let the boat pass. Low in the water, it held two men, roughly-dressed as though they'd been out here a while. They sat expectantly, eyes scanning the hillsides, rifles raised in anticipation. In the bow, three lean hounds keened into the wind. They were obviously hunters, although Thais don't normally hunt with dogs. I pushed backwards, concealing myself even more. Blinded by the sunlight, the duo didn't see me but one of the dogs spotted me and began barking. To my relief, neither man paid attention to it. They passed and I heard them pull to shore in the next chamber, cutting their engines.

Something about their dress and manner told me to keep my distance. Cautiously, I paddled through the doorway. The hounds were racing up a slope in hot pursuit of something, perhaps a deer, the men crashing through the underbrush after them, before disappearing into the trees. The slope ended at a cliff and they seemed to have their quarry pinned against it. The beasts were baying maniacally and the men were yelling to each other. One shouted that "it" had found a slit between the rocks. "Shoot it before it escapes!" Feet scrambled on scree and then a shot rang out. A dog howled in pain, and a man swore. I was now even with the boat they had wedged into the bank, too hurried to tie up. I moved past and into the next room. The confused tumult faded; with another shot and a sharp yip, it ceased altogether. The encounter was unsettling, my sympathies laying with the quarry and the dead dog. These men fit the description of the *jai dam* against whom I'd been warned. I paddled hard, until my lower back ached and my shoulders were in flames.

After an hour, I left the final cliff-walled room and entered the next major section of the lake. The new gorge was wider than the passage but not as wide as the upper lake. Lying back, exhausted, I drank an entire canteen.

It was a long, pleasant afternoon. This gorge was greener and cleaner than those before. With the altered landscape came new perspectives. For reasons I couldn't explain, my memory was sharper than it had been in years; long-forgotten childhood events appeared with great clarity. Names of sites which normally slipped from memory the moment I folded the map now stuck for hours without my writing them down.

I struggled to find an explanation. It was tempting to believe that I was in an enchanted realm where the normal rules didn't apply, but there must be a more rational explanation. Perhaps by reducing my life to simplicities, I had opened up more room for memories. City dwellers are inundated with so much information, they simply push out details the moment they receive them to leave room for the next batch of data. For me, paddling was mentally undemanding, a repetitive action that, like a physical mantra, centered and calmed me, creating a vast sea in which thought could cavort. Maybe it was nothing more than the mere perception that I was doing something purposeful: moving forward a clock tick at a time–and leaving my mind free to wander.

The hills were pale orange when I spotted a small knoll on the left. The view improved with each stroke; it would be a perfect place to spend the night. I was searching for a path through the mimosa when I heard a boat engine just upriver, apparently emerging from a creek I'd missed. "Go on by," I whispered. Of the dozens of bays they could have entered, they chose mine. A man, his wife and two children were so intent on the red line running along the fish nets' upper rim, they were on me before they saw me. I nodded to them and they backed out. I let them move on, and then pulled into the next inlet. Almost immediately they pulled in behind me, again surprised to see me. Another red line lay beneath the surface, and in the next inlet, still another. Was there an unfished cove anywhere along this shore?

The sun was going and once again I had no resting spot. The riverbank was so steep that I'd have to tie my sleeping bag to a tree to avoid rolling into the lake. I poked into one inlet after another, looking for telltale red cords. When I finally found one without a fishing net, it was nearly dark. Mimosa blocked the approach to the land, invading the water for a dozen yards. I pushed the boat into the mimosa until it was hidden, and prepared for bed.

I had designed the boat so I could sleep on deck, but that was before I extended the back locker into the deck area. Could I still fit? I lay down and found the soles of my feet flat against the locker and my head jammed painfully against the front locker, about one inch too short for comfort. I'd just have to fold myself. It would be messy to prepare a meal on deck, so I devoured a can of curry.

For several hours, I tossed and turned, aware of the deck's hardness. Of all the eventualities I'd anticipated, boredom and endless nights had not been among them. A person lives an entire life between dinner and bedtime. Here, I couldn't read, I couldn't walk. I could only talk to myself or listen to the frogs serenading each other, fingers strumming comb tines. This was what life was like before electricity.

I hovered in a no-zone between sleep and wakefulness; too tired to stay awake, too uncomfortable to sleep. It would be an eternity until dawn and there wasn't anything I could do about it.

Hunted

Plaa Maw Tai Phraw Paak
(The Maw fish dies because it opens its mouth-releasing
bubbles the fisherman can see)
Don't seal your doom by making noise

Seldom have I yearned for a night to end. I awakened a dozen
times, hoping my eyes would be flooded with sunlight. Instead, I'd slip
from consciousness for brief moments, then, cramped by the hard boat,
become aware of the moon's pallid beams prizing open my eyes.

After eons, pale fire licked along the tall ridge beneath the indigo
sky. Fish splashed and fat bugs blundered noisily by, a perfect morning
heralding a gorgeous day. From my sleeping bag, I lit the stove and brewed
tea. Long before the sun topped the ridge, I was dipping a blade into the
silent lake. For two hours, I paddled quietly, watching the sky paint the
right bank in rich greens and yellows that melted like butter down the
slopes and into the lake. I lazed, fascinated by the mini tornadoes my
paddle blades stirred up just below the surface. I watched meteor craters
dimple the surface when droplets fell from my paddle. It was a day to
meld with my surroundings and I indulged to the fullest.

In the afternoon, as though grown restive of the serenity, the land
changed. The sun still burnt in a clear sky, but something far across the
lake was moving towards me, creping the water as it came. It advanced at
glacial speed but when it slammed into me, it rocked the boat and the
water's surface erupted in whitecaps. The gale-force wind was so strong
that if I stopped paddling for a moment, I was shoved backwards; I was

soon paddling hard just to maintain my position. When the air began howling I headed for shore.

In a small cove protected from the wind, I considered calling it a day but the steep slope was littered with rocks and vegetation and I didn't relish sleeping in the boat again. When I climbed the slope to get my bearings, the wind blew my hair straight back. A half mile across the lake, a lone white spire glowed atop a green knoll; perhaps I'd find refuge there. I waited half an hour for the wind to drop, but when it didn't, I pushed off anyway.

As I moved from the cove's polished surface to the corduroy lake, the gale struck with undiminished force, obliterating all sound with its manic shriek. To gain headway, I needed to cut diagonally across the lake, pointing the boat directly into the wind. I began paddling, constantly correcting as the gale caught first one side and the other side of the hull, rotating the boat.

After half an hour, I'd progressed only a few hundred feet. I changed course to paddle straight across, ignoring the fact that I was being blown upstream. After an hour, I glided into an inlet and found myself a half-mile north of the *chedi*. I now began to work my way downstream from bay to bay. I'd paddle across the mouth of the cove, staying in the lee just inside a line of ruffled water. After a moment's rest, I would power my way around the point and straight into the gale, paddling hard until I dropped into the next bay. After an hour, I reached the shore below the *chedi*, and for long moments lay in the boat, exhausted.

The sun had left the knoll but the light reflected from the ridge east of the lake was bright enough to illuminate the area. The hill was an inspired choice for a *chedi* site. Some 250 feet above the lake, it commanded a spectacular view of the entire valley. In the 13th century, the gorge had been a strategic conduit for goods and armies. Whoever ruled it controlled movement between northern and central Thailand. A sentinel city had been built on both banks and by the 14th century, had become wealthy enough to erect 99 temples and *chedis*. Since there were few tracts of fertile land to farm–and because the steep walls blocked the sunlight needed to grow crops–it survived by exacting tribute from passing convoys and caravans.

With the growth of north-south commerce in the 19th century, the river became an important transportation route. Below me lay what had once been the Gaeng Soy rapids, the most treacherous on any Thai river, and the most dangerous obstacles on the six-week journey between Bangkok and Chiang Mai. Had I stood here 60 years before, I would have seen large boats inching their way upriver, serfs walking along the gunwales, pushing against the river bottom with long bamboo poles. In photos from the 1940s, long *maeng pong* (scorpion tail) cargo boats, their tall sterns curving over the boat's back, were pulled by men in loincloths and harnessed in ropes and bent almost parallel to the ground as they tugged the boats step by step up the river. The return trip would have been a toboggan ride, roaring through the boulder-strewn chute to the valleys below. Doubtless, among the splinters of shattered boats were the broken bones of sailors smashed between hulls and rocks.

Construction of the Bhumibol Dam in 1964 silenced the rapids and buried 98 of the monuments. The gorge walls no longer reverberated with the din of water, commerce, or war. Shouts once muffled by the roar of rapids were now smothered by a bed of water, men calling from beneath a pane of glass.

The orphaned *chedi* had recently been restored, its ancient bricks stuccoed, whitewashed, and trimmed in yellow. Its shape was Burmese, odd since the Burmese, constant enemies of the Thais, would have been alien to the 14th century landscape. Just below the *chedi* was a small kuti (meditation hut). On a tall bamboo pole a yellow Buddhist flag snapped in the wind; a bronze bell hung from a nearby tree branch. Behind it, a shed sheltered a stucco statue of an elephant offering water–and a monkey offering a honeycomb–to a roughly-molded meditating Buddha.

Trash lay everywhere, probably left by villagers restoring the *chedi*. The debris was an insult to the setting; how could people sully such a beautiful spot? After cleaning it up, I scrounged around the shed until I found an unburned incense stick and several candle stubs. In the lee of the *chedi*, I lit them and prayed for safe passage to the dam, as the wind howled around me.

Three things are better enjoyed in the cold than in the heat: soup, wine, and pipe tobacco. Lacking soup and wine, I settled for a pipe. Hand cupped over the bowl to keep the wind from sucking out the embers, I puffed contentedly, watching the soft sun climb the hills opposite me.

Beneath the light of a moon sliver, I dined on sardines and rice and then prepared for bed. I considered sleeping outside but the cold wind was picking up. Finding the *kuti* unlocked, I pushed open the door, it's rusty hinges protesting. Rats' feet scratched furiously on the dirt floor, legs fleeing the unexpected intrusion. Both sounds suggested that no one had been here in a while and I could sleep unmolested.

The *kuti* was sparsely decorated, as a meditation cell should be. A few faded photos of antique abbots hung from nails, their faces springing to life in the beam of my flashlight. In a small back room I placed my camera, food, and other valuables. In the absence of a bed I unrolled by sleeping bag on the floor and climbed in. I placed a candle on the door sill and, lying on my stomach, I wrote of the day while I listened to the wind and watched the lake below me.

A low murmur on the far shore set my nerves twanging. I quickly blew out the candle and lay quietly as a disk of light began sweeping back and forth across the far hill, pausing occasionally like a sniffer dog. The powerful beam of kleig-light intensity allowed me even from this distance to pick out trees and boulders. These hunters might spare other expenses–even hunt with antiquated rifles–but they treated themselves to the biggest searchlights they could buy.

As I watched, the beam suddenly swept off the slope and across the water towards me. Oh, oh, I thought. It scanned the slope below and began working its way up the hill. Too late, it occurred to me that the *kuti*'s open door would suggest occupation but the beam was approaching too rapidly for me to spring from the bag and shut it. It flowed across the front wall just above my head while I pressed myself into the floor until not an atom separated it from my body. Almost immediately, the light returned to rest on the *kuti*, bathing it in near daylight. Jeez, let's hope he has weak eyes, I thought. After an eternity the beam moved up the hill and I began breathing again. I'd slipped the beam's noose and the hunter's bead.

Wary that he might return later in the night, I slipped the gun from its bag, cocked it, checked that the safety was on, and laid it on the floor. It was probably a sin of unimaginable magnitude to desecrate the *kuti* with a weapon of violence. I would pay heavily in the afterlife but I preferred to extend my present lifespan and delay punishment as long as possible. As I settled in for the night, the Buddhist flag was flapping and popping.

The clink of a boat chain instantly awakened me. I listened carefully for a repeat, or for any other sound to orient me. Nothing came except a high keening in ears so long battered by city traffic din that they were unused to silence. The setting moon had taken the wind with it. For some reason, fear centered me. What if I were to find someone rifling the boat? I would face the choice of letting him go or confronting him. Pointing the gun at him would start a new chapter in my life. Either he'd be innocent and would talk to someone and word would get to the police. Or he (or they) would be armed and I'd be forced to a new decision: shoot or not. If I killed him, I would open a world of personal pain. If I wounded him, he, or others, would come back for me. It didn't occur to me until later that he might get the drop on me. Thoughts, propelled by cold terror, whirled in my sleep-hazed brain. The other alternative was to go back to bed, trust to fate. If the boat was gone, I'd hike out and begin again. Very Buddhist.

Very impractical. "This is nuts," I thought. "I'm blunting my effectiveness by succumbing to paranoia." I took a few breaths to clear my head and, clutching the pistol and a flashlight, slipped out of the hut. I was assailed by a strange sensation as I picked my way down the hillside: I couldn't find my balance. In the dark, the visual cues were gone as were my instincts. Sound was of little help in orienting myself. In the distance a flock of birds cried like cats meowing.

I descended the path, step, pause, step, hoping the earth would muffle my steps. I was aware of each sound and to my dismay found that I was making most of them. The more stealthily I tried to creep, the more noise I made. Objects seemed to rush from nowhere and place themselves beneath my feet: dry leaves, a twig, sliding pebbles, a kickable rock. I would make a wretched guerrilla, unable even to sneak up on a tree stump. It was so ridiculous that I began chuckling, probably a case of taut nerves seeking release. A foreign man dressed in a sarong, bent over to conceal himself, lifting his feet high in the air, setting a foot on what might as well have been a claxon horn, a pistol in one hand, a flashlight in the other, tottering off-balance as if walking a railway track; it was all too absurd. In this manner, it took me 10 minutes to cover 100 yards.

I slipped behind a bush and scanned the foreshore, flashlight ready but not on. If I had to use it, I would finally be able to employ the Dick Tracy "Crimebusters" tip I'd seen in the comics as a boy: hold the flashlight at arm's length to one side. The gunman would shoot at the light and miss me. The opportunity failed to present itself. My eyes adjusted to the starlight to see that the boat was firmly on shore and the locks were untouched. What had I heard? It was definitely a chain but where?

The wind was rising again. I climbed the hill and stood listening to a distant owl, and heard a fish flop in the lake below. It was a gorgeous night and I might have stood there until sunrise, but my limbs were growing heavy and demanding that they be laid on a mat. I entered the *kuti* to sleep.

But I had other visitors. Feet were scraping and plastic bags were crinkling. Damn, the rats were in my food! Pushing the door, I beamed the flashlight on a large rat atop my bag which I had suspended from a nail. He scampered down the wall, his claws digging all the way. So much for my premise that caching food guaranteed security from scavengers. I placed the bag next to me, thrust my legs into the sleeping bag and passed out.

At first light, I emerged from the hut to brew tea, burn the trash I had collected, and eat the remains of the previous night's meal. Lighting my last incense stick and clasping it in my hands, I walked three times around the *chedi* barefoot, thanking Buddha for the beauty of the gorges, the pungent incense perfuming a morning air largely devoid of scents. When the sunlight flowing down the hills behind me illuminated the tip of the *chedi* spire, I struck the bell once and listened to its reverberations from the distant hill, mingling with the bright songs of the morning's first birds. With the sun, a gentle breeze shook the leaves and thrilled across my bare chest.

The morning took me among walls of limestone, shale, and slate flecked with mica. The stone layers were tilted between 45 and 60 degrees, loose rock that broke easily in my hands. Reddish outcrops high on the ridges resembled badly weathered battlements. The scene echoed the American West; from a distance, even the yellow bamboo looked like sagebrush.

Once again, I encountered another inexplicable phenomenon in a gorge that seemed filled with weirdness. As I paddled down the middle of the lake, I collided with single filaments of spider webs strung across the sky, as if suspended between the heavens and the water. Where could these single filaments be coming from and where were they going?

By mid-morning, I was approaching The Gap. The map noted a huai (stream) on the right. One mile past it would be a narrow "door" in the left bank that should lead me east into another section of the lake. If I missed the "door", I would find myself in a 20-mile-long "appendix" from which it would take two days to extricate myself. With only enough food and water to last me the remaining four days to the dam, a miscalculation would put me in trouble.

Where the map indicated it should be, a small ravine appeared on the right. In the rainy season, it would have been filled with water; it was undoubtedly the *huai*. The outlet should appear on the left in another mile. I began to enjoy the scenery but then caught myself. Too many times while walking down a street, I'd zoned out and not bothered to look for a sign or a shop because I figured I was still a long way from it. Of course, I usually passed it and had to backtrack. Looking down the lake, I gauged where a mile should be and mentally marked one tree.

In the past few days, I'd become aware of my heightened senses in the silent air. I could now hear a boat engine several miles away, and within seconds I could tell if it was coming towards me or moving away. Even 60 feet from shore, I could hear the drone of bees as they worked among the mimosa blossoms. I could also read distances. New reckoning skills were allowing me to gauge them to within a hundred yards, and water speeds to within a half-mile an hour. As I paddled towards the tree, I could see an opening just beyond it. I relaxed, pleased that I was about to thread the needle.

As I moved past the tree, I began angling into the gap. Turning the corner, I found myself looking at a wall of rushes. Perplexed, I pulled the map from the locker. I had mentally noted the position of the huai as I passed it. Peering upriver, I could see the spot. My eye also told me I had traveled a mile. Could the map be wrong? I'd already found several gross errors; it was possible this was another one. I glanced at the date printed on it: 1974. A lot could happen in 14 years, but still... Perhaps I had marked an incorrect position for the previous night's stay at the *chedi*.

Cautiously, I began paddling south again, but instead of holding to the middle of the lake, I hugged the left bank, nerves taut with concentration. Another mile. And then another went by. No opening appeared.

The banks were tall enough to conceal anything beyond them but some sort of opening should have been evident to suggest a body of water or a wide space between the mountains that could be occupied by a lake. Nothing.

Yet another mile. Still nothing. How could I have missed it? An hour later, I was four miles past where the passage should have lain. The lake was narrower here; was I now in the cul-de-sac? Should I turn back? I continued to paddle, watching, watching, looking downriver, looking upriver. No hints. Each time, my heart jumped when I saw an opening, and sank just as quickly when it revealed itself to be a cove. I was approaching the fifth mile and the coves were not even inciting anticipation any more. Then, I rounded a point, and there it lay before me. I glanced upstream at the right bank but there was no huai. The map had failed me but I was too relieved to care. Pointing the bow southeast, I set a blade in the lake and shoved water behind me.

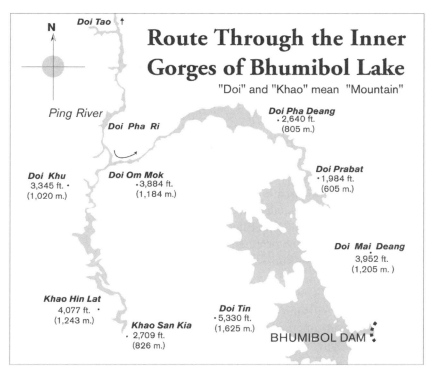

N

Doi Tao

Route Through the Inner Gorges of Bhumibol Lake

"Doi" and "Khao" mean "Mountain"

Ping River

Doi Pha Ri

Doi Pha Deang
. 2,640 ft.
(805 m.)

Doi Khu
3,345 ft. ·
(1,020 m.)

Doi Om Mok
·3,884 ft.
(1,184 m.)

Doi Prabat
·1,984 ft.
(605 m.)

Doi Mai Deang
3,952 ft.
(1,205 m.)

Khao Hin Lat
4,077 ft. ·
(1,243 m.)

Khao San Kia
· 2,709 ft.
(826 m.)

Doi Tin
·5,330 ft.
(1,625 m.)

BHUMIBOL DAM

Somewhere mid-afternoon, my eye awakened to a bit of flotsam, colorful enough that I stopped and backtracked. Barely touching the water was a single iridescent feather, half dark blue and half light blue, likely that of a kingfisher. I lay it on the boat, marveling at how beautifully its hues contrasted with the wood grain. A few strokes on, I encountered a second one and saved it too, delighted that the bird had been so accommodating. But then, a dozen feet later, small clumps of downy feathers appeared. Obviously, the bird hadn't been that obliging, it had been shot and plucked. It seemed such a waste; a kingfisher offered so little meat. That it was being shot suggested the paucity of game in these hills. I realized with a moment's panic that the sheen of the feathers meant it had been killed recently. The hunter must be nearby.

I didn't have to look to find him. He found me.

He rounded a bend a half-mile away, wielding a double-bladed paddle as he moved upriver. Spotting me, he turned towards me, slowly reducing the distance between us.

He was one of the wildest looking men I've ever seen, short, all bone and sun-browned muscle; his tangled black hair made it look like his head was exploding. His face was contorted in pain and as he got to me, he reached out to clutch my gunwale, a gesture I normally regarded as threatening. He had closed his eyes against the sun's glare. A rifle lay in the boat. Next to it lay a small, de-feathered bird.

"*Mii Buat Hai mai*?" he asked, his voice strained.

Buat Hai was an all-purpose snake oil remedy that enjoyed great favor in areas without doctors. The packet was designed for those unable to read. Against a dark green background, a man grimaced, his head elongated to thrice normal volume, his hand clenching his jaw. The picture said it all: an analgesic for headache, toothache, ear ache, and every other ache that might afflict one's body.

"No. What's the problem, headache?"

He nodded without opening his eyes. So his head was exploding.

"I have aspirin. Do you want that?"

He nodded.

I extracted some capsules and handed them to him. He opened his eyes, focused, and popped them in his mouth. He released his grip to reach into the lake, cupping his hand to bring water to his lips. A couple of scoops and swallows and he grasped the boat again.

"*Raw diew* (I'll wait a moment)."

"What are you hunting?"

"*Kwang, keng* (deer, barking deer)."

It was illegal but I didn't think he knew the meaning of the word, so I said nothing. He hung on a moment longer and then pushed away.

"*Pai.*" (Leaving).

He didn't look back and, if asked, I doubt he'd be able to describe me. "Plick, plick, plick" and that was the last I saw of him.

As evening came, I began looking for shelter. Moments later, I passed a small lagoon-like cove. It looked perfect. Too perfect. I paddled in cautiously but something seemed wrong. Along the foreshore, some-one had driven a fence of wooden stakes and behind them was what looked like pale green water hyacinth. Someone was raising or storing fish in it. Beyond it lay a rafthouse with a motorless boat tied up before it.

I returned to the lake. In the distance, a boat was moving along the opposite shore. As I watched, it turned abruptly and headed towards me. The effect was like that of standing in a street and watching a huge truck bearing down. Go left, go right, do what? As it closed, I saw two rough-looking men with unkempt hair and soiled clothes. One wore the kind of toothy, ingratiating smile that invites suspicion about his/her motive. My anxiety level shot up the moment he grabbed my boat. Shutting off the engine would mean they planned to stay a while. They shut off the engine. I was being unsociable but these two were not eliciting my confidence.

"*Sawasdee, khrap. Pai nai,*" their lips said while their eyes pulled aside the protective cloth, unzipped the pockets, and untied the pack top. In the middle of the boat lay two large silver fish and next to it, an enormous shotgun.

I had three modes of defense in uncertain territory: "I'm survey-ing; I'm an official; and there's another boat behind me." I used all three.

They pounced on the third. "Where's the other boat?"

"Just up the lake."

"Same as you?"

"Different."

"How?"

"They have an inboard engine."

The only boats in the gorges with inboard engines were those driven by the dam guards. They looked at each other. I could see them mentally calculating when the next patrol should be through.

"*Chok dii,*" (good luck) they said, remembering an appointment elsewhere. The engine rattled to life and they headed towards the opposite shore, occasionally turning to look back at me.

Honest people don't flee.

No villages had appeared since Loong Wua, and the rafthouses were thinning to one every two or three hours. By late afternoon of the following day, I'd not seen another human being or heard a boat engine all day, and I reveled in serenity. As the sun illuminated golden bands of bamboo pressed between the azure sky and the green river, I paddled lazily, trying to stretch the afternoon to eternity.

Suddenly, like a rifleshot, a single "yip" echoed off the hills. Other than the family of macaques, and the hunting hounds, I'd seen nothing but birds. I ceased paddling and listened, keening to pinpoint its source. Then it came, full-throated: the bark of a large dog. In the wilds, three sounds indicated human presence: cow bells, cock's crow, and a dog's bark. I was not alone.

The cry came from the right, perhaps 100 yards inland. The banks were broken by coves and as I moved past the mouth of one, I saw at the far end a rafthouse glowering in the late afternoon shadows. Smoke rose a fire blazing on the bank. Once past the entrance, I heard no more so forgot about it and returned to enjoying the scenery.

Half-an-hour later, I heard what sounded like a muffled bandsaw. Since it was far behind me I kept paddling. When the volume leapt up, I realized without looking that a boat had emerged from the cove. I glanced back. The sun, low behind me, gleamed off the starboard side of a motorboat. Still half a mile upstream, it was beelining towards me. I continued paddling but listened for changes in engine pitch that might reveal his intentions.

I recognized it as a Rotax two-stroke engine that creates more noise than motion, so it took him a while to catch up. Instead of passing me, however, he slowed to match my speed, paralleling me about 20 yards to my left. He stared at me, his features immobile. I said "*sawasdee*". No response. "*Pai nai* (where are you going)?" I asked. No answer. Dark, and in his late 20s, he wore shaggy, disheveled hair pinioned by a dirty, billed cap. His clothes were grimed with oil and dirt. I tried to engage him in conversation but still he said nothing. Instead, his eyes swept between me and my boat's visible cargo. I did the same, and saw the dark blue of a rifle barrel on his deck. Still without a word, he veered left in a wide circle, accelerated, and roared back up the lake. Strange behavior, I thought.

Something told me I'd not seen the last of him. I moved a bit closer to shore and increased my pace. The silent mountains watched impassively, their dark beauty suddenly ominous. Ten minutes passed before I heard the low drone again. There was something different this time. The pitch was broader suggesting a heavier load the engine was straining to propel. But then the amplitude split and in a flash I understood; there were now two boats.

I looked back. They were about 800 yards behind and moving steadily towards me, a man in each boat. I looked down the lake to see where they might be going, and saw nothing but barren shore. The terrors instilled by Jack Bain and others began to grip me. Was my imagination working overtime? I looked back again and saw they were now 600 yards astern and still heading directly for me. As I watched, the one on the right began to edge towards the bank. If he kept the same course, he would be between me and the shore when he reached me. The other boat held its course.

I dug the paddle deep and began angling the boat gently towards the bank, trying to calculate vectors so I would reach it before they reached me. I kept the angle shallow to avoid alerting them that I was fleeing although that is exactly what I was doing, my adrenaline level climbing. I still was not sure of their motive but I'd rather deal with them on the riverbank than in the middle of the lake. They were now 400 yards behind me.

Remembering the gleaming rifle barrel, I stopped paddling long enough to pull out my gun, cock it, and conceal it beneath a bag. The action took only a moment, but when I looked back, they had gained on me. I sharpened my angle and heard their engine pitch climb as if they anticipated what I was trying to do and were trying to cut me off. That told me what I needed to know. I abandoned all calm and began paddling furiously straight towards the bank. A welter of thoughts ran through my mind. Uppermost was the thought that once I hit the shore, I would grab the gun and the food pack and head as far up the hill as I could. If robbery was their motive, let them take everything. I could hike out in three or four days and find a village.

With the boats now 200 yards behind me, it was now a question of who reached shore first. I paddled and they accelerated, the engines' high screams alternating with my furious splashing, my shoulders aching. Blood filled my ears with hissing sounds, and a faint buzzing.

It took me a moment to realize that the buzzing was only in my left ear. Could it be coming from another source? Down the lake, a dot slowly moved towards me. I squinted. Behind the dot was the low white rooster tail from a propeller. At nearly the same moment, the upriver boats decelerated slightly, suggesting they'd seen the apparition too. The dot grew steadily larger, as did the engine volume, that of the upriver boats dropping in direct correlation. I allowed myself to glance upstream. I could see the faces clearly but I was now just a foreground object; their eyes were looking downstream. One shouted "*pai* (go)" to the other and both began cutting left, inscribing wide arcs as they moved back upriver. The downstream dot became the three smiling faces of a fisherman, his wife, and their child. I waved and we all nodded happily over the engine racket. They moved by and their wake gently washed my boat.

Silence returned to the lake, and I resumed normal breathing. Had I imagined their intent? The air was so calm that the latent violence of the previous 10 minutes seemed far removed. Glancing down, I could see the butt of the gun poking from beneath my bag. I shuddered to think that I might have had to use it, firing blindly to erase the anxiety pressing on me, furious at the men for having put me in a position where normal responses were blurred, replaced by primitive reaction to a perceived threat.

Something in me refused to believe they meant me harm. I searched for another reason they might have been headed towards me. I've never been the victim of a violent crime. My house has been burgled while I slept, and I could recall the blind anger I felt at being violated, that something that was mine–objects, space, the security of my home–had been invaded. But that I should be the target of an attack by these two boatmen seemed incomprehensible.

On the other hand, the evidence seemed too blatant. How else to explain why two men with an entire lake to cover had headed straight for me? Or that the first boatman had failed to return my greeting; a breach of Thai etiquette? Or why when they encountered another boat, they broke with their original plan and returned to their base? If I was their prey, I made an ideal target. I was moving slowly and whatever I was carrying would certainly be of value; after all, every Thai knew that *farangs* were rich. And they would never be caught. I could be buried and the boat burned for firewood. Who would know? I couldn't even pinpoint my location; how would a search party–assuming there was one–ever find me? Yet despite the logic, my mind still wanted to believe that I'd misread the situation.

What now? The lake was now dark and a gray band was creeping up the far hillsides. I needed to find shelter. If I really was the quarry, they'd be back once the sun was gone.

I searched for a cove in which to hide but all were devoid of cover. I paddled past stands of reeds that grew on the riverbanks and extended 50 feet into the lake. The next cove was little more than an indentation in the hill. I pushed on past more reeds but the next opening offered no protection either.

As I paddled, I noticed how effectively the reeds walled off the bank. Standing nearly four feet above the water, they looked like a solid, dark brown band. Wait. If they walled off the bank they would also wall off the river if someone, like me, slipped behind them.

No more droning echoed down the lake. I looked for an entry point but the reeds were so tightly packed that I would have to push my way through them, crushing a yard-wide swath, a highway anyone could follow. I backed out and paddled on, looking for a break. It lay about 30 yards downriver, a thinning that ran to the bank. I headed in. At the bank, I turned right and paddled upstream, parallel with the shore. From the lake, no break was visible. I bulled my way into the middle and nudged the nose into the soft mud.

While it was still light, I prepared dinner, setting the stove on the back locker. While the rice water heated, I tried to tidy the boat and was appalled by my inability to do anything quietly. I'd forget that I had put something down and then in the dim light would bang into it. Then, the stove burned too high and the rice boiled over. In the process of re-filling the pan to cook the remaining rice, I nearly knocked the stove overboard. Even in opening a can of sardines, I managed to make a racket.

As I ate, I felt short, sharp pains on my arms and legs. Lured by the food, thousands of fire ants had climbed aboard for their share. For the rest of the meal, I alternately fed myself and crushed ants when they stung me, the only way I could locate them in the dark.

I went ashore to find a place to lay my sleeping bag. Something crumbled beneath my foot; my nose informed me that I'd stepped on an old cow pie. In the dim light, trampled plants betrayed the presence of cows. A ten-minute search for a path by which the herder might return revealed nothing; the site apparently having been abandoned for a while. I was unrolling the sleeping bag when I felt more sharp stabs. Thinking I might have brought them from the boat, I sat and waited, mashing one after another, hoping they would go away. But the numbers didn't diminish. They were everywhere and I would spend a sleepless night if I remained here.

I prepared to leave when it occurred to me that simply by backing into deeper water I would put a liquid barrier between me and the ants. But more ants had climbed aboard and for an hour, I watched the stars and killed ants, consoling myself with the thought that being devoured by ants beat being hunted by humans. When the bites ceased, I placed the gun where I could reach it, and bedded down in the boat. The occasional survivor would sink its mandibles into my flesh but it was minor payment for the security I enjoyed. Finally, I nodded off.

I was roused by a light which my fogged brain interpreted as the moon. I looked up, but aside from winking stars, the sky was empty. I was awake in an instant.

A boat was moving back and forth just beyond the outer boundary of the reeds. One voice paddled while another shone a light into the reeds, some of it filtering through. I was concerned by their presence but reasoned that if I couldn't see them, then they couldn't see me. Their voices came from no more than 20 feet from my head.

"*Mun pai nai* (where did it go)?"

Hunters. Or fishermen. Good. They weren't looking for me. Besides, my hunters' boat had an engine. They'd soon pass.

"*Mun mai dai maa thung nii*" (It didn't come down this far).

Eh? Before it hit me, the other voice said.

"*Mun pai thung thii nai dai* " (Where else could it have gone)?"

Then I remembered. *Mun* (it) refers to things, animals, and foreigners. They were looking for me. But they couldn't have paddled all the way here.

The boat moved past and I could see the light shining into the indentation. "Move on, move on," I whispered.

"*An nun alai* (What's that)?"

There was a long pause as the light settled on something near the shore.

"*Thawn mai.*" (Just a log)

They moved down the lake but were clearly audible. I heard the paddle lifted from the water, heard the droplets strike the surface. The boat moved towards the next clump of reeds.

"*Mai mii alai luay.* (There's nothing)"

"*Pai laew!* (Let's go)", a disgusted voice hissed.

Something wooden rapped their boat deck. I realized that he was shipping his paddle. Why? Did "*pai laew*" mean they were entering the opening? I strained to hear. Nothing. Then, a click, a whirr and a moment later, an engine roared to life, a frightening sound so close to my head. My breath caught in my throat, my chest paralyzed. Then, the boat began to move away, the sound gradually ebbing as they headed back up the lake. Jeez. They must have motored to within a short distance of me, then, thinking they might alert me, had killed the engine and paddled. I hadn't heard a thing.

In a newborn silence broken only by the chirping of frogs, I slumped back in the boat, breathing heavily. In my shirt pocket lay the tiny Buddha amulet the *luang paw* in Chiang Dao had given me. I removed it, laying it in the palm of my hand. It was superstition, I thought, an archaic belief that a piece of clay could protect one from harm. And yet...

I lay back but sleep was a long time coming.

Sanctuary

Plaa Kradii Dai Naam
(The dying fish is revived by the rain)
Being back in familiar surroundings rejuvenates one

The sun stuttered through the Venetian blinds formed by the reeds. Birds sang on the hillside but I was oblivious to their song. Instead, I keened for human sounds, something that would reveal my pursuers' presence. They'd come twice, there was nothing to prevent their coming a third time. On an uninhabited lake, it didn't matter if they struck in the daytime or the night; I had no protection except concealment.

I delayed taking a look. Instead, camouflaged like a grebe in the rushes, I shaved, using the dark lake as my mirror. Nearing the final strokes, a water bug skittered across the surface and my face shattered into a dozen concentric circles. Then, I unhinged my body, rising slowly until I could see through the reed slats to the lake. A flock of birds floated lazily across the wide sky. I stood to full height, looked far up the lake and slowly scanned south to its lower end. Nothing. I had it to myself.

"*Nai* (Mister)?"

I jumped, tipping the boat and nearly pitching into the lake.

"*Mong alai* (What are you looking at)?" the voice behind me demanded.

I turned to see a boy observing me from the river bank, a bag on his shoulder, a bamboo staff polished by long use in his left hand. I was so stunned that he had snuck up behind me that it took a moment to form a coherent thought. He was obviously a herder.

"Where are your cows?" I asked, my composure returning.

He pointed over the hill with his staff.

"Aren't you afraid they will stray."

"Nowhere to go. The hills are too steep."

If they were too steep for cows, they would have been too steep for me to climb the previous evening. So much for my escape plan.

He sank to his haunches, still watching me. In his mid-teens, spindly and knock-kneed, he was dressed in a T-shirt and shorts the color of dust, and likely permeated by it. I offered him water but he waved his hand in front of his face and pointed at the lake. Brave lad.

"So if the cows can't climb the hills, how did you get in here?"

"Stayed along the shore."

"But this is a forest preserve. Isn't grazing illegal?"

He shrugged as if to say "who's going to stop me?"

I joined him on the bank. I was in no hurry to take off and was glad of his company. His village lay up one of the valleys. He stayed out for as long as his food lasted–a few days, at most–then went home to get more, leaving the cows to fend for themselves. He sensed where they would go and that they would be so busy eating that they wouldn't wander far.

"Have you ever lost them?" I asked.

"Never."

As we talked, wooden clappers drew nearer. Moments later, horns, then heads appeared on the ridge, followed by swishing tails, hocks, and hooves. How handy; a herd that followed the herder.

The clappers jogged my memory and I asked him about the mysterious wood choppers. He looked puzzled until I added more details.

"Ah," he said, with a smile. "Bamboo."

"Yes, people chopping bamboo."

"No, the bamboo chopping itself." I frowned, perplexed.

"The bamboo sections fill with water. Sometimes, the sun heats the water. It expands and the bamboo explodes. Like *khao lam*."

To make *khao lam*, one filled a section of bamboo with glutinous rice, red beans, and coconut milk and plugged it with a folded banana leaf. Rows of these tubes were staked along a shallow trench filled with embers which boiled the coconut milk, cooking the rice and beans. When the pressure built, the leaf stoppers popped like champagne corks to announce that one of Thailand's most succulent desserts was ready to eat. A similar principle had been at work on the day of my mysterious choppers.

Abruptly and without a word, the herder stood up and strolled over the hill. He paid no attention to his charges but they changed direction without missing a bite, the Pied Piper of Cows. I packed and set off.

The morning was made long by the static water, and longer by my lack of sleep. At least the wind blew downstream, cooling my perspiring back and clinging shirt. The afternoon was a repeat of the morning, the paddling made more difficult by the millstone of the sun pressing down on me. Loquacious birds provided counterpoint to the tedium of a plunging, dripping paddle. From the cliff tops came the bark of numerous *keng*, although the deer calls sounded more like dry coughing.

But in the heat, other, more disturbing, forces began to manifest themselves. My mind seemed to meld with the monotony of paddling, but instead of the expanded memory I'd previously experienced, they manifested themselves in a monomania that I would come to call "The Furies", like those that assailed Oedipus after he slew his father. Frightening to experience, they seemed to arise from my narrowed focus on the mind-numbing task of paddling. I'd later discuss the phenomenon with other adventurers–sailors, paddlers, desert trekkers, long-distance swimmers– and find that it was common among solo travelers. For walkers in a bland landscape, it was daylong footfalls that didn't seem to reduce distances. For long-journey paddlers, it was the hypnotism induced by endless up-down stroke of the blade. It was abetted by heat, a sense of isolation and vulnerability, and the low-level fear that had become a constant since I'd entered the lake and found myself questioning everyone's motives, the product of functioning in an alien environment over which I had no control.

It differed from the "voices" of schizophrenia because its chief component was rage. Old grudges welled up, unresolved disputes: a former friend who had selfishly pulled out of our company and stranded the partners, a tyrannical boss who had caused a Thai friend's mental breakdown, a pair of scoundrels who had violated my copyright by publishing on their own a book I had written. Psychic garbage that had never been fully expelled was now laid out in painful detail. Hurts and betrayals were hashed and rehashed, assuming an intensity they'd never had in real life. Dreadful and inescapable, it was no doubt the transference of the anger I was feeling at the strangers I was meeting, but it was irrational and misdirected, and all the more disturbing for it.

"Snap out of it, stand up, stretch, look at the mountains," I'd command myself. It would work for a moment but once I'd resumed my steady beating of the water, the black thoughts would flood back in. Seeking respite, I sat for long moments nearly catatonic, relishing the relief from the monotony that precipitated the anger. I realized that I had to make a choice. If I sat here, I would make no headway on my journey. Or, I could step outside of the Furies, realizing them for what they were and enduring them as though they were happening to another "me". To my surprise, it worked. For the rest of the day, someone else, not the real me, dealt with them. The "Furies" would plague me all the way to the dam and then cease once I was among people again.

In the evening, I had grand plans to bathe, dine, and then climb a hill to sleep on its summit, high above the lake. I moved the boat behind a large, flat, vertical rock that walled me off from the world. After a swim, I made a tasty dinner of rice and a *Kaeng Musselman Kai* (Muslim chicken curry) before shouldering my pack to climb the hill. Covered in loose stones, the slope wasn't unduly steep but, to my surprise, my legs wouldn't work. I shambled like a drunk, unable to make headway, every step leaving me breathless. So little used in the past week, my legs seemed ignorant of how to function. After a 10-minute struggle, I gave up, frustrated. Sipping orange juice and munching peanuts, I sat on a rock and gazed at the sky until sunset. Still stumbling, I descended to the boat, realizing that with no flat ground near me, it would be my bed again.

It was another unsettling night of light and sound. I had no sooner slipped into my sleeping bag than I heard engines. Two boats went by, then a third with a powerful light. The last one stopped nearby and idled, his popping engine ricocheting off the cliffs. The racket seemed obscene, a violation of tranquility, the intrusion of the 20th century into the timeless. When he didn't move for five minutes, I peered over the rock to see what he was doing.

Anchored to the opposite shore, he appeared to be fishing, working a crevice in the rock wall. From the way he swept his parallel arms back and forth, I assumed he was electrocuting the fish. I snuggled into the cramped boat to wait him out but was immediately beset by small, sharp pains on my head. Running a hand through my hair, I dislodged insects so tiny that when I crushed them there was almost nothing left. When the motorboat moved downriver to search another fissure, I turned on my flashlight to see hundreds of stowaway ants, but this time they were black. Realizing they must have come aboard on the dry weeds brushing the bow, I paid out more anchor chain, letting it droop into the water to deny them a gangway. Then, as on the previous night, I mashed the bugs, dozens at a time. An hour later, the numbers began to thin and I slept. Badly.

At dawn I awoke groggy and stiff from being accordianed by the boat. Once again, my hands were throbbing; clubs that would not grip objects without pain. Only after wrapping them around the shaft and paddling for half an hour did they regain flexibility. The paddle was obviously too heavy but I couldn't trim it without reducing its strength. Since the pain subsided once I got underway, it was easier to ignore it.

Brewing a cup of tea, I sat in the warm sunshine to write, using my left hand to wrap the aching fingers of my right around the pen. A month had passed since I had picked up the boat in Baan Tak and now I was four days north of it. So much had happened. I marveled at how clumsy I'd been, barely able to maneuver the boat. Terrors that had assailed me had been replaced by others but I'd learned to devise strategies to deal with most of them.

I'd become better at recognizing whom to trust and whom to avoid. In general, people had been kind, although it would only take one person to kill me, as I had learned two nights previously. Figuring out which was which was the challenge. Within my own culture, I could sense from a distance who was ill-intentioned. Here, despite my 20-year residence, most of the subtle signs that any Thai would immediately spot, flew by me unrecognized.

The really smarmy people were easy; their false smiles seemed too fixed, their voices too ingratiating, their friendliness too friendly for someone I'd just met. The ones who concealed shadiness beneath sunny dispositions were more difficult to read. A person could be smiling and jovial as he closed the distance between us, never setting off the alarm bells until he was on top of me. I was learning to trust nobody until they proved trustworthy. I hated to relate to people this way but imprudence had been the undoing of many strangers and it was wise to adopt the same smiling-almost phony-gaiety with potential miscreants that they did with me. At least we both knew ourselves to be false, which put us on equal ground.

As I wrote, I was draped over the back locker, using it for a desk, pausing every so often to enjoy the pristine scenery. I was engrossed in putting thoughts on paper when the water two feet from my head erupted. An enormous fish, fully three feet long, broke the surface, gasping loudly like a sleeper waking from a bad dream. His hiss was so loud and so unexpected that I dropped my pen overboard. My shirt and journal were soaked and the ink ran. Nature in the flesh had spoken to me.

Daubing the page with my shirt tail, I set the book to dry in the sun and retrieved another pen from my pack. Peering into the dark green water, I saw him far below me. As I watched, he changed shape from oblong to oval and rapidly grew larger. I reared back just as he broke the surface, again with another loud gasp. This time I had longer to observe him. The scars on his back attested to numerous skirmishes with fishermen. Perhaps he was aiming for me, avenging ancient slights.

The sudden appearance of the huge *Plaa Cha-do* (Snakehead) fish stirred memories of other conversations. Upriver villagers had asked if I was afraid when the water was deep. The question was asked so many times that I began to suspect they weren't simply asking if I could swim. There was something down there and it frightened them. When I probed deeper, I learned that there were many "somethings" down there, spirits that lay in wait for the unwary. Belief in the *nguak*, a water spirit, was so pervasive that a cult propitiating it had appeared in northern Thailand in the 12th century. In northern Burma, the *nguak* was believed to be the spirit of a drowned person. To the Lao, northern Thais, and Khmers it was a serpent deity worshiped for its magical powers. It inhabited rivers, lakes and even wells, especially the portions shaded by trees.

The *nguak* that terrified the villagers was *Phi Phrai*, thought to be the restless spirit of a stillborn child or a drowned adult. In the North, this female ghost was considered malevolent, killing people who threatened her underwater realm. On the weekly holy day, *wan phra*, and at the Songkran water festival, she snatched the non-vigilant and carried them to her watery home. In the Northeast, boatman would curry favor with *Phi Phrai* by tossing cigarettes and pouring whiskey into each whirlpool they passed.

In parts of the Central Plains, the long-tressed *Phi Phrai* was regarded as murderous but ignorant of the effects of her misdeeds. She dwelt at the river bottom, usually beneath an overhanging bough. Fond of gold combs and accessories, this spirit magpie would wander through the night, wailing as she entered houses to take whatever she found. More frightening, she watched waders and bathers from below, and pulled them under. She was not considered malicious because she only wanted to take the humans home to show them her gold and did not realize that they could not breathe underwater.

A logical explanation for the supposed touch of a *Phi Phrai* on submerged flesh could be fish, eels, entangling weeds, or other marine debris common in Thai waterways. Or even a sudden cramp. The belief does, however, provide a cogent explanation for accidental drowning, the disappearance of objects, and how gold of the type for which prospectors pan first appeared in streams.

At one time, I would have dismissed the *Phi Phrai* as a fiction, but one day my maid told me that her mother, then 93, had encountered a *Phi Phrai* three decades earlier. "She was bathing in a canal when a *Phi Phrai* clutched her leg," she recounted. "She grabbed the landing stairway and held on, screaming until her relatives ran to pull her free." I was prepared to nod wisely and dismiss the incident as rural fantasy when she added, "she's been lame in that leg ever since." It gave me pause for thought.

The fear of watery depths is universal. In nightmares, we struggle to the surface to escape a phantom pursuer, waking with the sensation of suffocating. For no reason, we panic while swimming in a lake, convinced that something is waiting down there to grab us. At my high school lakeside graduation party I swam after a departing rowboat, realized I couldn't reach it, and found myself a half-mile from shore. I turned back but soon tired. When my legs became entangled in weeds, my fear turned to terror as unseen coils shackled me to the lake bottom. When at last, I broke loose and heaved myself ashore, thoughts of death from a marine assailant curdled in my young mind. Perhaps death was in the air that day. Two hours earlier, the radio had announced that police had found Marilyn Monroe dead in her apartment.

But the *nguak* was a Thai concept and for once I was glad to be outside the pale, immune to the karmic vicissitudes Thais regarded as part of life. To me, the fish was a fish, however much he might startle me.

More disturbing to me was the weirdness I'd encountered since entering the gorges, sounds I found baffling and inexplicable.

Just past noon I rounded a bend and entered the *talay sap* (inland sea) where the lake widened so much that I could barely see the opposite shore. After the comparative intimacy of the gorges it was like emerging from a cozy den into the bright outdoors. Distances were attenuated. A half-hour's paddling seemed to get me nowhere. The sun blazed and the sky was no longer blue but hazed, hot-season yellow. Thai winters are as short as English summers but surely it couldn't be over already. Sheltering clouds seethed along the southern horizon but where I was, it was an oven.

It was then that I heard voices behind me, men talking. I turned, expecting to see fishermen, or someone playing a radio but...nothing. I sought an explanation in the following wind but even that didn't explain it fully. Was this another hallucination? After resting beneath a tree, I put out on the lake again and, moments later, the voices returned. These were not the voices of the "Furies." These seemed disembodied, hanging in the air nearby and always slightly indistinct so that I could never make out their meaning, or even their language. It was yet one more emanation of the spirits that seemed to infest this strange realm, and for this one, there would be no explanation, then or later, other than surmising that they arose from jangled nerves and lack of sleep. Near dawn, they would fade away with the dying wind.

For the moment, however, and as if in emulation of my mental turbulence, the earth externalized the forces that simmered within it. The entire lake was raging. The burgeoning wind began piling up the waves, spume blowing off the crests like banners off snowy peaks. Huge waves splashed over my gunwales, the waves the fishermen at Doi Tao had warned me about. I battled them for a while but they ultimately pushed me backwards onto a beach that reached 100 feet back to the treeline. Jamming the paddle into the sand, I rigged the ground cloth to shade me and waited for the wind to die. But when, after an hour, the wind blew undiminished and the waves began to break like ocean rollers I realized I was finished for the day.

As the sun was setting far across the inland sea, I found a site where hunters had leveled two bed-sized spaces. I would sleep here. I considered dragging the boat the 200 feet to my camp but since I'd not seen anyone all day, I decided to leave it where it was. Threading the chain through the holes in a porous, cabinet-sized boulder that resembled a meteorite, I locked up to one of my sturdiest anchorages yet.

In unloading the boat, I hefted the water tank and to my surprise found it nearly weightless. The previous day, I had noticed its water level dropping but not paid much attention to it, thinking I had ample supplies. But in the day's unrelenting heat, I had drained all my canteens. Now, I was alarmed to find I could fill only one of them. I still had a day's paddling to reach the dam and tonight I needed the remaining water to cook my dinner. I couldn't travel with empty canteens and the "sea" was too impure to drink. I sat for a long while, wondering what to do.

Then, I recalled the fishermen who had created a sand filter on the riverbank. Dropping to my knees, I scraped a deep hole in the sand, six feet from the water lapping the shore. As I watched, the crater began to fill from below, slowly but steadily. After dinner I was delighted to find the hole contained nearly two canteens worth of clear water; two more canteens would filter overnight. I uttered a silent prayer of thanks to the fishermen.

As I unrolled my sleeping bag, a nightjar began to sing. His cry was different from those farther up the lake. Here, instead of falling onto a single "thunk," his voice trilled the final note until it faded to silence. The moon fell on sand white as snow.

Sometime after midnight, I was awakened by the distant screech of shearing metal somewhere across the moon-drenched sea. I listened intently but when it did not repeat, I lay back, unable to sleep. It was an unearthly night, filled with alien sound. Overhead an angry sky hissed and crackled like a radio telescope tuned to an ancient star furious in its death throes. High overhead, billowy clouds drifted towards shore. As they crossed the line between lake and land, they were rent by stratospheric winds. Writhing as they approached the implacable moon, they died tortured deaths, tea kettle vapor evaporating to nothingness as it struck cool air. The sea roared as though assaulted by a raging storm but no rain came. Restless spirits were abroad, rasping their wrath. Too tired to contend with them, and realizing there was nothing I could do anyway, I dropped off to sleep.

I awoke to the sound of a motor. It stopped half a mile away and searchlights scanned the shore. I fought sleep but must have nodded off because a moment later, I sprang to wakefulness at a loud roar in my ears. It was now within 100 yards and its searchlight was moving steadily along the shore. They could only be hunters.

It was too late to flee; if I ran inland, I would be caught in the beam. I had to conceal that I was a *farang*. I had just wrapped the plastic groundsheet over my head when the full glare of the light hit me. Almost immediately, a second one locked on, the brilliant light poring through the blue plastic. I briefly considered popping out to shout my irritation at being disturbed. Even in my addled brain, I sensed that this would be the wrong move. So I stayed put while they discussed the situation, enduring long, agonizing moments as I strained to hear their conversation above the engine.

One lamp nailed me to the ground while the other ran up and down shore, probably to see if I was alone. After long moments, the first light moved away and the engine volume increased as they moved up the lake. I prayed they wouldn't see the boat which was partially hidden by the boulder, but they did, and commented on it, although their engine muffled their words. Eventually, they moved on, but it was some time before I dozed again. It would be wonderful to sleep at the dam and not tense every time I heard a motor rev or a twig crackle.

The sun brightened the horizon and warmed the air. To the west, Orion had sunk into the sea. Since I wasn't going to get any more sleep, I began packing. Only six miles to the dam.

A scuffling froze me in my steps. I turned to see three furry animals scrambling down the cliff face and onto the beach. Three feet long–half of it, bushy black tails–they wore long reddish fur, pale throats, and black feet, ears, and masks. Absorbed in play, they did not see me as they bounced from rock to rock, working their way toward the water. Quietly sliding my camera from my pack, I fired off several shots before one spotted me and barked sharply. The others whirled to look at me and, without further pause, turned and bounded across the rocks, up the cliff face and disappeared into the trees. The photos would identify them as Yellow-throated Martens, members of the weasel family.

Two hours of paddling in the shade of the looming cliffs brought me to a small island with a Chinese-style pavilion marking the channel leading to the dam. At last. Rounding the final promontory, I saw the dam's massive wall. Some 200 yards from its rear, I tied up at the foot of a steep dirt road running to the dam crest. Drenched in sweat, I poured one of the canteens over my head in celebration and began the long hike to the dam rim.

It had been comforting to know that if I failed to show up within a few days, the security guards I had met at Doi Tao would eventually have come looking for me. I approached the guard booth and identified myself.

"I'm looking for Sunthorn, the chief security guard on the lake."

Blank stares.

"There are many Sunthorns," one said, eager to help. "Do you know his last name?" I'd written his full name in my journal. Another guard searched the duty roster, his long finger finally stabbing at the name. He looked at me.

"Day off."

I recalled that there had been a Chom with Sunthorn. They couldn't locate him. And Prasert.

"Many Praserts, too."

"Yes, but he must be listed as part of Sunthorn's unit."

The finger moved again, tapping on a likely Prasert.

"He's below the dam," he said, reaching for a telephone. Hearing confusion on the other end of the line, I motioned the guard to give me the receiver. I explained who I was and Prasert finally said, "I'll come up to get you". As I waited, I soberly realized that had I disappeared, no one would have come looking for me.

A pick-up completed the climb up the dam face and out jumped Prasert, his relieved smile acknowledging that he recognized me. "Let's load your boat on my truck," he offered.

After dropping the boat in the river a half-mile below the dam, Prasert left to arrange a room for me, and to retrieve my gear from the security storeroom. Leisurely, I tied up the boat, marveling at the suddenly rejuvenated river. It was the first moving water I'd seen in nearly two weeks and the sound alone was exhilarating. About 100 feet wide, the Ping, dark and clean, flowed rapidly through a series of cataracts. After being pent up by the dam for so long, it had burst free and was running for its life. How nice it would be to have some help getting downstream.

Prasert was trying to tell the bungalow staff that I'd paddled all the way from Chiang Mai but they were busy gossiping among themselves about the world they inhabited. If he had told them I'd just flown in from the moon, they would probably have exhibited the same disinterest. Prasert left with vague plans to get together later and, in my room, I washed and sorted gear, then went to find lunch.

Wedged in a gorge, its broad 400-foot-tall back arched to stay the river, Bhumibol Dam, on its completion in 1964, had been Asia's largest concrete structure. Its construction and maintenance had created a community of 10,000 engineers and their families who worked for the Electricity Generating Authority of Thailand which had built houses, schools, clinics, parks, and stores in a former wilderness.

The staff restaurant was a slab of concrete covered by a high roof and open to the breezes. It was probably as much my weird attire–I was dressed like a farmer in short pants–as the fact that I was a foreigner that attracted the curious stares and whispered exchanges. I smiled and tucked into a plate of green curry and rice. A few people drifted over, asked me questions, then wandered away.

While spooning a small eggplant onto my rice, someone dropped into the chair opposite me. I looked up and into lovely almond eyes set in a gorgeous face. The eyes locked on mine, an uncommon boldness for a Thai woman. With a teasing smile, she said "*samphat khun* (I'm going to interview you)." And she did, asking me questions far more penetrating than those posed by her workmates: "How did villagers react to you, what were the headwaters like, what kinds of people were the most helpful?"

She was a delight and I immediately tumbled to her. In her twenties, Sasithorn worked in the accounting office and to my immense disappointment had a husband and two children. This information was tacked onto the earnestly-posed question, "Do you want an extra passenger?"

"What is missing in your life that you want to go down a river?" I asked.

"Nothing," then, "everything" and "I don't know". She paused, then looked down at the table. "I have a husband and two children," she repeated, but it was couched so vaguely that it was unclear whether it was a comfort or a complaint.

"What do you want? In life."

"To build a house. In Lampang. Wood, not concrete," suggesting she had modest ambitions. "Or maybe in Chiang Mai."

"What do you love to do?"

"Study English," she said without hesitation, her eyes back on mine.

"So let's talk in English," I said in English.

"Oh no," she said. "My English very bad" and immediately switched back to Thai.

"Hmmm. What do you do best?" The interviewee had become the interviewer.

"Type. I type fast but I don't know anything."

It soon became clear that her sense of entrapment stemmed from a belief that she could never survive in a wider world. It was also based, once again, on the enticement/fear of Bangkok. Unlike other rural women I'd met, however, I felt she could really make it but with a husband and children, I hesitated to suggest it.

We talked at length of our lives as she wavered over this new alternative to what she felt was a humdrum existence. The conversation was in danger of exposing deep seams of dissatisfaction. She must have sensed it too because she suddenly glanced at the clock and leapt from the chair. "I have to pick up my son from school," she said, having decided that, deep down, she knew where her destiny lay.

I spent the afternoon thinking about what had happened in the gorges and found myself ambivalent about the experience. Like Sasithorn, I was torn between the excitement of the unknown and the comfort of the knowable. While I had been mesmerized by its beauty and solitude, I had been unnerved by encounters with iffy people and weird, unnatural sensations: the mysterious woodchoppers, the Furies, the voices, and the hunters. Only in hindsight did I question whether my imagination had run rampant; at the time, the causes of my fears had seemed very real and undeniable.

What had I learned? I had wanted to challenge all my senses, to test my survival skills. In general, I had done well but I was concerned that I had yielded to my fears and been unable to separate them from those implanted by others. Giving in to one's own fears is one thing; giving in to others' fears is inexcusable. It would take months to digest entirely what I had seen but for the moment, I was happy I no longer had to contend with them. Below the dam, I would enjoy smooth sailing all the way to the sea.

After buying supplies, I had my first cup of coffee in many days. With the caffeine singing in my veins, I wandered across a suspension bridge to survey the rapids. Beginning high upstream, my eye slid down white foam channels, jigged and jogged between the rocks, hugged the bank, and then shot into a "V" between two boulders, sliding out to pass beneath the bridge. Crossing to the bridge's downstream side, I continued the journey. Seldom had I anticipated with such joy the coming day.

Back at the landing, I tugged gently on the chain and, like an obedient dog, the lightened boat glided across to me, a delightful contrast to the dead weight of the previous days. With three feet of water beneath the hull, there would still be sufficient clearance to give me a clean getaway.

For the rest of the day, I lay beneath a tree and read, dozing until awakened by bugs curious to know what lay beneath my shirt.

Prasert appeared at 6 p.m.

"*Pai tiew* (let's party)."

"Where?"

"Nightclub," he said in English.

Oh no, I'd been in too many of these. Pitch black clubs, tables overflowing with men bleary with drink. It was never a matter of popping in for an hour or so but a marathon to see who'd close the place.

"Prasert, thank you very much but I'm exhausted from the paddling."

"*Mai pen rai*," he said, disappointed. I hated these moments when, having said what I really felt, I ended up feeling guilty. I usually gave in and had a miserable time and was disgusted with myself for being so pliable. This time, however, I was tottering from fatigue and Prasert could see it.

"Maybe next time," he said.

I went to my room, turned off the light, and a second later tuned out the world.

Murder Suspect

Tid Raang Hae
(Caught in the back of the net)
To find oneself in the wrong place at the wrong time

The previous afternoon as I was mooring the boat, Prasert had said, "Tie it the full length of the chain." It seemed odd advice but I took it anyway, locking the final links around the iron stanchion. This morning, I looked out the window to see rocks sticking high out of the water. Wondering where they could have come from, I slipped out for a look.

Instead of a thick knotted river, a rivulet one-third yesterday's width was trickling between tan rocks. The boat had pulled the chain to full length and was sitting on dry land 20 feet from the water's edge. Had I tied it short, it would have been hanging vertically from the landing. What had happened to my lovely rushing Ping?

"*Nam haeng* (the water's dry)," a workman explained.

"I can see that. But why?"

"There's less demand for hydroelectric power during day so they shut down the dam. Saves water."

"When do they turn it on again?"

"10 a.m.," he replied, negating any hope I had of getting away early.

"Do they turn it on gradually?" I pictured myself sitting patiently in a loaded boat looking up to see a tidal wave bearing down on me.

"Slowly, slowly."

At 10 a.m., the flow increased infinitesimally. Blame it on my impatience to be underway, but the river seemed to take ages to gain steam. At 10:30 there was barely enough water to float the boat. To my relief, by 11 it had become the thundering torrent I'd seen the previous day. Once launched, I zipped along, threading a path among the rocks. Just below the bridge, with the strong current shoving me towards a breakwater, I angled left, aiming for a gap between two boulders. As I was lining up, something rope-like caught my eye. Swimming at right-angles towards the same opening was a five-foot cobra. Realizing that we were on a collision course, I tried to backpaddle but the river was too powerful. We reached the gap simultaneously and I plowed over him. He came up with his mouth open just as I was digging deep with my right blade. I quickly snatched my hand away and the river carried me past him and into quieter water.

The calm lasted only a moment. Then, the river picked me up and skimmed me along at the fastest speed yet. It was the first time I'd used the kayak paddle in whitewater and I was delighted with the maneuverability it gave me. For mile after mile, I searched out the swiftest water I could find, exultant after days on the dead lake. I shot past a cowherd who shouted something but I only caught the word *jalakhae*. "Crocodiles?" Impossible! Nonetheless, for the next hour, I scanned the shallows and reeds for glassy eyes, then decided that *jalakhae* must be a euphemism for the sunken logs littering the water course. But then, while passing a stilt house, a young woman rushed out yelling "*rawang jalakhae* (beware the crocodiles)."

Crocodiles had once been the scourge of the waterways. They lazed on the banks and, during floods, swam into villages to dine on chickens and puppies. Their fierceness had inspired numerous folk tales. Downriver near Nakhon Sawan, villagers believed that an enormous crocodile named Ta Khe Chao labored as the servant of the *Phra Phrom* (God of the Land).

In the lower Valley, the *nguak* had metamorphosed into a crocodile king named Chalawan, ruler of Muang Badan, a fabled river-bottom city made of gold and gems. According to the tale, Chalawan ventured onto land and was so smitten by a merchant's beautiful daughter, that he carried her to his underwater realm in his powerful jaws. A poor farmer named Kraithong dove deep beneath the surface and, Beowulf-like, killed him and rescued the beauty. Her delighted father gave him wealth and his daughter's hand. But Chalawan was a myth, and crocodiles had been wiped out by hunters in the 1960s, their hides commanding high prices from leather goods manufacturers. What could the villagers have meant by their warnings?

I continued to hurtle downstream, the stone-strewn riverbed flying by. From dry cattle country, I slid through lush corn fields and banana plantations. Elephant ear plants replaced the mimosa, vegetation became more varied. Then, all too soon, the rapids ceased and the valley widened. The sky hazed to the slate-gray peculiar to the Central Plains, a harsh light that bleaches and flattens all objects.

Within an hour, the breeze engraved the sky's gray canvas with wispy lines, and gently ruffled the river's wooly surface. Cumulus clouds billowed and the sky blackened, a single ray of sun turning the river to quicksilver. Gibraltar thunderheads hovered a thousand feet above the ground, lit internally by veins of russet lightning, their flat bases trailing mist. Although they blustered, they dropped no rain and soon they slid north, grumbling as they went.

In the afternoon, the sky cleared, the water became glassy. The mountains stepped back even farther as if to receive a visitor, and the Ping responded like an impolite guest, broadening to occupy all the space allotted it. As the riverbed rose to the surface, sandbars and mudflats appeared, the flowing water braiding between them. From the morning's joy of unhindered movement, paddling became hard work, the boat often lodging on a sandbar.

The settlements, too, changed. Houses were shabby, the untrimmed plank ends extending far beyond the house corners. The boards were not even properly affixed but seemed tacked on with gaping spaces between them. The scene revived a long-dormant memory. In 1969, I'd found work at the *Bangkok World* re-writing Thai reporters' stories. Among them were several accounts of illegal logging in the north. The law forbade the felling and transport of trees without a permit but there was a loophole. If a house were dismantled, the lumber could be carried to Bangkok and sold. To get around the logging ban, illegal loggers felled trees and sawed them into rough planks which were then half-nailed onto a crude frame. Once an obliging forestry official had certified that the planks were from a house, the loggers dismantled the "house" and trucked the boards to Bangkok lumber yards. Legally. More than once I'd bought lumber marred by small nail holes. Could loggers be following the same practice 20 years later?

When the river slowed, I spread my map and was surprised to find I'd passed Sam Ngao. That meant I had covered 22 miles, the longest one-day distance yet! Revived, I pushed off and was soon rewarded by the sight of the Wang River entering from the left, raising the Ping's level and submerging the sandbars. I was now within reach of Baan Tak where my boat had been born.

Mile after mile, the Ping expanded until it was 450 yards from bank to bank–the greatest width of its entire course–and no more than four feet deep. Along its margins, it broke into a dozen streams, each no wider than 10 feet, flowing around lush islands topped by five-foot swordgrass. The waterway seldom opened into a bay or straight stretch, so I had no idea of where I was in the twisting maze, nor of what lay ahead. The thrill of being lost in a dream world excited me. Occasionally, I'd pass a man staring placidly at the river, waving lazily to me. It was as though I'd entered a realm of lotus eaters.

An hour later, a late afternoon glow settled over the land, softening the watery labyrinth. Children's laughter filtered through the grassy walls. I moved channel by channel until at last I broke into the open, surprising a gaggle of naked boys and girls splashing in the shallow water. Recovering from their shock, they included me in the fun, jabbering excitedly, grabbing the boat to keep me from floating away. One began cartwheeling and the others followed, each trying to see who could make the biggest splash. Little girls giddily pranced with tiny steps and hugged themselves with glee as they watched the bigger children's antics. As if in a fairy tale, I moved through the scene and into farther waterways which swallowed up their laughter.

Twenty minutes later I again broke free to find myself at the T-junction of Baan Tak's narrow frontage road and the byway leading to the main highway. Motorbikes sped noisily down the street, a radio blared, a rickety bus farted black smoke, and my only thought was to get back to the world I'd just left. But I'd been recognized and the townspeople quickly enveloped me, patting me on the back and shouting greetings. I locked the boat and went to find Sirichai, my boat builder.

A man offered to take me there on his tiny, ancient motorcycle, and off we crawled. In the last century when the potential for motorized travel was first discussed, someone recalled that the Greeks thought that a man traveling more than 12 miles per hour would disintegrate from friction with the air. I was hardly in danger of atomizing on this rackety motorbike. I'd probably have made better time trotting alongside him.

It quickly became apparent that my coachman had no idea where to point his steed. "Sirichai...Sirichai," he muttered, probing a cobwebbed brain. As we approached the main road, coordinates for mind maps began forming, and I directed him: "Turn left, now right, now straight." Finally, the house appeared before us. In the front yard, wielding a long bamboo pole to knock coconuts from a tree was diminutive Mrs. Sirichai with several of her eight children. On sighting her, I felt my chauffeur's body relax. "Ah, Somporn, my student," he said and she beamed. Several years before, he had been a sewing instructor and Mrs. Sirichai had been his star pupil. Accepting 20 *baht* for his services, he climbed on his chainsaw and roared off.

"Sirichai is away," she said. "You can stay at my mother's house." On her motorcycle, we made our way back through Baan Tak, the towns-people waving as we passed. With growing alarm, I realized that her mother lived a long, long way down the river, two miles at least, giving me a long paddle to reach it. With the sun dangerously close to the horizon, and concerned that I wouldn't find my way through the liquid labyrinth in the dark, I hung my hat on a riverbank post as a marker. Somporn left one son on the riverbank to watch for me and drove me back to my boat.

The sun was now among the trees and I figured there was no use in pushing myself, it would be night when I arrived anyway. Relaxing, I slipped into a side passage and was again engulfed in a beautiful, magical world, alive with people and small boats. Trees rose above some islands; on others, small huts served as fishing perches. On one island, someone had built a lovely pavilion reached by a bridge. On another, a table and chairs faced the sunset. A lone singer serenaded a hidden inamorata with a plaintive *luuk thung* song. "*Luuk thung*" generally identified the singer as a lonely country boy far from home. This lonely boy was from Mukdahan, a Mekong River town and his song gave pleasure to himself, me, and his secret, pined-for lover. Eventually, I heard a child softly calling "*Khun, khun*" (sir, sir) and in the dim light I paddled towards my beacon hat.

Dinner was delicious roasted pork, fish in a clear broth, chicken in a piquant gravy...and the inevitable omelet. As I was readying for bed, Mrs. Sirichai decided it was story time, and I didn't like the subject. When I had talked of the journey in December, she had subjected me to a litany of plaints about the influx of bad people into the area.

"They've been coming here from *E-sarn* (Thailand's poor northeastern region) looking for work," she had told me, her face solemn. "Of course, there is no work but instead of going back home, they stay. We used to have good people here. We could walk into the market wearing a Buddha amulet on a golden necklace. Now, you don't dare because it will be snatched by some thief," she had said, agitated. This evening's conversation turned out to be a continuation of the earlier one.

"You have to be really careful between here and Paknampoh (Nakhon Sawan). There are *jai lai* all the way, not good people like in the North."

Damn. I thought I had gotten through the worst of it and could enjoy a smooth journey. Instead, according to Somporn, even worse perils awaited me. Her face reflected concern but I was straining to dismiss the warnings as more of the same I had heard so many times.

"What should I do?" I asked.

"Leave the boat."

"Where?"

"Here. We'll look after it."

"Then?"

"Take the bus to Bangkok."

"What? And the rest of the journey?"

"Forget it. You've seen enough already."

My face must have conveyed my rejection of such a daft option because she immediately leapt in with: "Then take a friend."

For a brief moment, I thought she was referring to my gun, but she couldn't have known about it.

"What friend?"

"Any friend. You must have lots of friends."

"They think I'm crazy."

She paused a moment too long to consider this, then raced on, undaunted.

"Start very early each morning."

"How early?"

"One or two a.m. Paddle all night. No one will see you."

"And I won't see anything I came to see. And what happens during the day?"

"You sleep."

"No, not possible," I insisted but my resistance failed to deter her.

"Then disguise yourself."

"As?"

As if on cue, one child sped into the next room and another rummaged in a cabinet. The first returned with a conical peasant's hat, the other dragging an old sarong and blouse.

"They'll watch a *farang*, but ignore a Thai woman."

"You really think anyone is going to mistake me for a Thai woman?" I asked, laughing.

She looked at the blouse, about five sizes too small and then at me. "We could let it out a bit," she said, thoughtfully.

The image of me squeezed into a blouse and sarong and trying to paddle a boat was too ridiculous to contemplate. I shook my head and Mrs. Sirichai slumped back resigned.

"I want to continue as I have begun," I said. "If there is danger, I'll deal with it. This part of the Ping is more populated than the upper river. If I survived that I can survive this."

She was unconvinced. "Well, think about it," she said.

I spent an uncomfortable night on a thin mattress on the wooden floor, and awoke to find that Mrs. Sirichai had been up formulating new stratagems.

"Take a gun," she whispered.

"Now where would I find a gun?"

She looked at me, incredulous. "Anywhere. Just ask."

"Except I'd probably end up shooting the wrong person," I jested.

"True," she said, indifferent to the affront to my vanity, then "O.K.," in English, consigning me to my fate.

"Are there other dangers out there?" I asked.

"Like what?"

"Crocodiles?"

She scoffed. "Crocodiles? Gone. Completely gone."

"So why was I being warned about them yesterday?"

She looked puzzled. "What did they say?"

"*Rawang jalakhae.*"

She burst into laughter, clapping her hands in glee.

"Years ago there were crocodiles in the river. Thousands. When a guest left your house, you said '*rawang jalakhae*' to him. It was like 'good luck'."

"So why were they saying it to me?"

"They were just teasing you. Weren't they laughing?"

"Yeah."

"See?" Her spirits had revived and she scurried about gathering provisions. I marveled again at her energy, undiminished after eight children.

The river had risen and the boat was pulling at its chain like a tethered cow eager to graze an open field. As I loaded, Somporn admired the paddle, discussing its construction with her younger children. Then she stood it on end and measured herself against it; she barely reached its midpoint. Saying our goodbyes I pushed off, little knowing how soon I'd see her again.

Half a mile downstream, a concrete bridge spanned the Ping. The thin pilings were spaced five feet apart, a forest of concrete posts to support a two-lane road. The current was strong and I realized I would have to line up on an opening well upstream to avoid last-minute scrambling. As I approached, I noticed that bamboo poles and tree branches were trapped against the pilings, jamming all the openings for about 50 feet from the left bank. I moved to the right, calmly searching for a clear passage as the current swept me closer. Selecting one, I lined up. But, 15 feet from it, the boat suddenly veered to the right. Blocked by the debris, the current was rushing parallel to the bridge, like me, seeking a clear opening and shoving me sideways. To late to change course, I realized that I was going to slam into the bridge.

I braced myself. In raising my arms to fend off a pillar, the paddle caught between it and the boat, snapping in two like a toothpick. The shorter section dropped into the water, leaving me with a single blade ending in a jagged point that, fortunately, did not impale me. Banging and bouncing off pilings, I pinballed through to the downstream side.

"*Nai, nai!* Over here."

It was my guardian angel Somporn. Her 17-year-old son, Prawat was already racing across the bridge to shinny down the piling and grab the paddle piece which, luckily, had been trapped by the debris. Still dazed from the collision, I used the longer piece to paddle to where his mother stood. Prawat trotted up, shaking his head in amazement at my close call.

The paddle had broken into three pieces; a short piece bridging the other two, each with too little surface area to bolt them together securely. If I couldn't find someone to carve me another, I'd have to switch to the single-blade spare paddle.

But Mrs. Sirichai had other ideas.

"Wait," she said, brightening. "I know a man who can carve a new one."

"Really?" I replied, but she was already climbing on to her huge motorcycle. Balancing the long portion of the paddle on her shoulder and tucking it under her chin, she took off. Fifteen minutes later, she was back. Her carpenter friend was away and his apprentice couldn't find a board six sawk long. Even if he could, it would take two days to craft.

"I have another idea," said Mrs. Sirichai, who was seldom short of them. "What if we fashion a sleeve and fit the pieces into it?"

"Might work."

"Is there a machine shop around here?" she asked Prawat.

"What about the iron monger out on the secondary road?" he suggested.

"Go!" she said to me, herding me towards the motorcycle.

The ironmonger fitted the pieces together and then began rummaging in his scrap heap. Metal clattered and clanked as he tossed aside anything that wouldn't work. At last, he extracted a square pipe about eight inches long and measured it against the broken parts. "*Dai* (can)," he said with the smug confidence with which one says "piece of cake".

Within 20 minutes, the paddle was back in one piece, looking a bit odd with its metal, rust-flecked collar screwed into the paddle's weather-bleached shaft. Hefting it, I found that it now weighed about six pounds. And it was off-balance. I laid it on an extended finger to center it; the left blade dropped immediately and the paddle slid off my finger. Because the iron monger had shaved six inches from it, I would have to reach farther over the gunwales to grab water. But I'd get used to it. At least I was mobile again.

Heat, heat, and more heat. And no shelter from it. To make matters worse, the sandbars had returned. My temper was frayed by the impossibility of reading them, even when I was standing up. I'd slip by one, thinking I was in a clear channel, and find myself in a dead end. I'd slog up the channel, knee-deep in muck, the sun beating down on me and reflecting off the water into my eyes. At the head of the channel, I'd launch down another branch, not knowing if it would actually move me downriver. In my irritation, I childishly smacked the Ping with the paddle, punishing it for toying with me. I'd been reading the "*Mahabharata*" and Krishna's soothing counsel to Arjuna: "Avoid frustration caused by thinking of results." It was no solace. Time for a new approach.

The broad river continued to unravel into a dozen strands but instead of cursing it, I looked for ways to make it work for me. My eyes told me that the deep, dark-green water lay at the edges, not the middle. Surface ripples and undulating submarine plants told me which direction the current was flowing. Too often, it proved to be a longer route and I was tempted to cut across the neck in hopes of finding deeper water. The price for my impatience and lack of faith was the scrape of hull against sand. But even then, the river provided clues to extricating myself. Its bottom was scalloped into ridges and valleys; if high-centered on a ridge, I could dig a paddle into a valley and the river would pull me into dark green water. Soon, I was making slow but steady pace.

Sooner than I expected, the orange "Golden Gate" bridge at Tak appeared. Above the left bank, the town's low buildings rose like tire studs. For the first time in days, I was approaching a real town but, having forgotten the fear inspired by being on my own in the gorges, I felt little elation at being surrounded by people.

Suppressing my misgivings about lawmen, I decided to leave the boat at a riverside police booth near the market. When I got there, however, I found the windows open, the lights on, but the booth deserted. From time to time, a shortwave radio cleared its throat but seldom spoke. Thinking they had strolled into the market for a bite, I waited. After 45 minutes, I gave up, locked the boat and headed for the Ping Hotel where I took a 60-*baht* ($2.40) room.

As in most small towns, the shopfront shutters banged down when the sky darkened, but I found an open food stall and enjoyed a good meal.

I walked deserted streets back to the hotel, detouring to check on the boat. The police booth was still unmanned, the radio still squawking. But the boat was fine so I went to bed.

The market below my window began stirring long before dawn. I tried to grab extra sleep but when the sky lightened, I gave up and opened the window for a breath of air. The small roof below it was strewn with used condoms, emblematic of creative energy spinning its wheels. In the market, I slurped a bowl of noodles, then headed for the river.

Twice during the night, I had risen and slipped out to check the boat. The police booth was deserted; doors wide open, log book on the desk, insistent radio, nobody home. This morning, it was still empty but the boat had not been touched. It probably had less to do with the police booth than the presence of a maggoty dog, days dead and lodged between the bow chain and the bank. With the paddle, I lifted the chain and pushed it free. It bobbed down the river, taking its overpowering stench with it. When it was well out of range, I set off.

Hugging the eastern bank, I worked my way through a grassy maze past tall *Hang Nok Yung* (Flame of the Forest) trees. Although bare of leaves, their branches were cloaked in red blossoms, heralding the approach of the hot season. The gray branches of kapok trees were hung with bat-like pods that would soon explode and waft mattress stuffing across the countryside.

People with seemingly nothing to do picnicked on the islands, inviting me to raise a glass. The narrow canals' myriad bends hid surprises: a woman quietly washing clothes until she looked up, startled, to see me before her; a saronged couple caught in mid-dalliance, scrambling out of the water, all of us embarrassed by our encounter. Two puppies chased each other through the water, their splashing muffling my approach so that they stopped in shock on seeing me, then turned tail and zipped up a side channel where, behind a tall grass screen, they yipped and yapped at me. The grass also hid snakes, their presence revealed only by the croak of the frogs they were ingesting. Tall herons blended into the underbrush, frozen. I would have passed without seeing them but at the last minute, virtually under my nose, they would explode in a flurry of wings and cries, scaring the hell out of me. As they lifted, they cawed like crows, a rough cry incongruous with their sleek grace.

People clung to the rivers margins but seldom ventured into the mainstream. Kids splashed in the shallows. Goggled youths wielded spear guns made of wood and old surgical tubing. Stilted houses faced the road and hung their backsides over the river, mimicking the occasional bare bottom that used the river as a toilet.

It was nearly sunset when I reached Ma Dua Chumporn. I climbed the high bank and into the path of a heavyset man pedaling lazily down the road towards me. He was so lost in thought that when I materialized before him, he slammed on the brakes and his bicycle fell over. He looked down the road behind me, then turned and looked behind him.

"Where did you come from?" he asked.

"The river."

"The what?"

"River. In a boat." I said, echoing my encounter with Sin.

He walked to a wide opening between the buildings where he could see the boat below, gently tugging at its chain. Convinced, he decided we were the best of friends. I asked about the *phu yai baan*.

"*Kamnam*. You want to meet him?"

"Sure."

He turned his bike around and patted the flat rack over the back wheel. I got on and off we went.

"Oof. *Farangs* are heavy," he said, laughing, his stout legs straining against the pedals. As we rode the half-mile to the *kamnan*'s house, Prachuab told me he'd been a cook and driven a truck in Bangkok. He'd just come back and was happy to be home. All the while he pointed the bike towards a scrawny man standing in the middle of the road, one hand under his ma hom scratching his chest and regarding me speculatively. I would note that he always scratched or rubbed his chest as he talked.

"*Wai* him, he's the *kamnan*," Prachuab prompted me in a whisper.

I did and, half-heartedly, he *waiied* me back.

"Do you have any I.D.?" he asked curtly. Like an official, he looked either side of me but not directly at me, refusing to commit himself to making a connection. His question caught me off-guard; I'd never been asked for identification in a village.

"Passport?" I asked, reaching into my bag.

Apparently satisfied that I had some piece of official paper, he waved it away without examining it. He seemed pre-occupied and when he next looked at me, it was to ask what I wanted. I told him.

"You can stay in my son's house."

Raised knee-high off the ground, the small house doubled as a general store. The son, Nikom, dusted off a mat and tossed it on the floor where it raised more dust, a fine ash blown in from the dirt road inches from the open-front shop. Leaving my pack behind a rack of fish sauce bottles, I rejoined the *kamnan*.

When Prachuab told him I'd photographed him, the *kamnan* asked me to take some shots of the school. The request was in the form of an order. Something was clearly bothering him. As we walked towards a battered pick-up truck, he kept turning to look at me. The vehicle was a mess, with broken taillights and patches of touch-up paint that didn't match. When it wouldn't turn over, we push-started it.

We drove down a river of dust, our bow wakes washing the roadsides. As we passed the last house, another pick-up truck pulled up, blocking our way; out stepped a brown-uniformed provincial policeman. The *kamnan* braked and walked to him and the two stood talking inaudibly 30 feet away, the *kamnan* glancing back over his shoulder and the policemen ducking his head past him to observe me. I was obviously the subject of conversation. "Oh, just business," said Prachuab, when I asked him about it. The policeman walked to his truck and made a radio call. After talking a few more minutes, the cop drove off and the *kamnan* strode back to us.

"O.K., what's going on?" I asked.

The *kamnan* was not used to being addressed so directly and it took him a moment to react.

"Why do you think something is going on?"

"You have acted as though I was a *jai lai* from the moment I set foot in the village. Have I done something wrong?"

He stared through the grimy windshield, tight-lipped. "We had an... *incident* last night."

I waited.

"An old man, a fisherman, went to the market to sell his catch. He was walking home with his grandson shortly after dark. Someone, we don't know who, walked up to him and shot him in the head."

"Jeez."

"It was dark and the grandson didn't get a look at the murderer."

"He's dead?"

"Dead."

"What's this got to do with me?"

"You're our only suspect."

Hell! But before I could protest my innocence, he added, "I just had the policeman radio to Tak where you told Prachuab you stayed last night. You're clear."

I exhaled in relief, mystified who could have confirmed my presence since the guard booth was never occupied. Someone must have told him about my moored boat and he'd covered his tail by claiming I was there. A quick thinker. Lucky for me. And him.

I photographed the school in dusk light, then changed into a *pakoma* and wandered to the river to bathe. It occurred to me that my pack would be searched while I was absent but there was nothing of value in it and I had secured the gun in the back locker. When I returned to the house, I found the *kamnan* hefting my belt bag. "It would be just right for a pistol," he said.

Dinner entertainment was provided by Prachuab who sang a bawdy song about a *farang* woman who sunbathed nude. The key line was "*hoi thit hin*" ("her vagina"–literally, her 'mussel'–"touched a rock"), at which he would laugh hysterically. It was funny the first time. After a dozen repetitions, it began to pall.

After dinner, the *kamnan* invited me to the old fisherman's funeral. It was being held in the next ward which lay beyond rice and sugar cane fields. As we piled into the truck, I noticed that one man carried a battered carbine that looked like it had barely survived World War One–in which the Thais had fought for the Allies in France. He saw me looking at it.

"Nobody pays attention when you talk to them. They listen when you have a gun," he confided.

Apparently it didn't occur to him that driving down a one-lane dirt road at night between 10-foot-tall stands of sugar cane made us easy targets. Anyone concealed in the cane could open fire at point-blank range and we'd all be dead.

Inside the victim's single-story wooden house, a dim fluorescent tube illuminated an open coffin covered with a saffron cloth, one corner folded back to reveal the unmarked half of his face. A white string tied to the deceased's hands ran along one wall to four seated monks who concealed their faces behind *talabats* (sacred fans). Two limp bedspreads, one blue, red, and purple with a fringed pink hem, and the other, an orange and yellow floral print, had been nailed to the wall to provide a backdrop.

The monks chanted sonorously while the mourners chatted, ignoring the monks and the proceedings. The men's rugged faces were striking; weathered, solid, with big smiles and big, sound teeth like shelves of Chicklets, faces not Thai but those of yak herders on a windswept Mongolian plain. I assumed they were Shans like the Tha Sala cattle smugglers.

As usual, the men, their hands clasped in prayer, sat on the right side of the hard wooden floor, the women and children on the left. The atmosphere was that of a shambling Saturday night hoe-down. Occasionally, someone would lay a finger aside his nose and blow snot through the floorboard cracks. One grizzled man opened bottles of orange soda with his teeth before handing them to the monks. Plates of *miang* (fermented tea leaves) with big crystals of rock salt at the side, were passed around, each person stuffing a wad into his or her mouth.

The funeral was not solemnly celebrated in the West, but more like a wake, a social gathering to farewell a friend as you might send him off at a bus station. The family would grieve in private but here, they worked to ensure that their neighbors enjoyed themselves. What impressed me was how they welcomed me as if I were a distant relative, making sure I had enough to drink and eat. Grandmothers would fuss over me. "Oh, this floor is so hard; aren't you cramped?" they'd ask.

When the chants ended, a full dinner was served. Afterwards, Prachuab invited me to the porch to watch a game of "halo" (high-low) played under a bare light bulb. An oil cloth hand-painted with a roulette wheel was ringed by a half dozen players who set coins or bills on squares. On the floor before the dealer was an ordinary dinner plate with a small basket as a lid. When all bets had been placed, he clasped plate and lid in both hands and shook them several times. All eyes were riveted on the plate as he dramatically removed the basket to reveal three dice. It was a 2:1 payoff for a single-number winner. The game apparently had been organized by an outsider because the *kamnan* appeared on the porch to demand that he pay the deceased's son 100 *baht* to cover electricity. He did so without protest.

At last, the *kamnan* and his passengers squeezed into the truck. This time I squatted in the back. Although we took a different route back, I have seldom felt so exposed as we threaded another sugar cane corridor back to the village to prepare for bed.

Nikom, his wife and son slept at the back of the shop. I lay across the entrance, just inside the rough, removable vertical boards which served as the front wall during the night. My body was apparently the first line of defense against intruders, a disquieting thought. Nevertheless, I slept soundly, the sleep of a man innocent of murder.

Ancient Kingdoms

Jab Plaa Song Muu
(Try to catch a fish in each hand)
Try to accomplish two things at once,
and you risk losing both

The calm that had descended over the village at bedtime proved illusory. In the middle of the night, a fist pounded on the door and a drunken voice bellowed "*Lao!*" (whiskey). Nikom drowsily told him that he had none but the drunk was not convinced. "*Lao!*" he shouted repeatedly at the plank wall, inches from my ear. Just as I was on the point of shouting back, one of his friends hollered from down the road that he'd found some whiskey at his house. Our friend grunted and stumbled off.

Sometime before dawn, the planks were again rattled, this time by a woman needing fish sauce. Next door, a woman began pounding spices in a pestle, its dull thumping impossible to ignore. Sleep was over for the night. I stretched my stiff limbs, rolled up my sleeping bag, and watched as Nikom removed the dozen boards, one by one, allowing the cold and the customers to push into the shop. I retreated behind a rack and wrote my journal.

Today marked a full month since I'd set the boat in the water. We were nearly one by now, the boat and I, synched with the Ping's moods and rhythms. I could also read the river well enough to ensure I would eventually reach the ocean in one piece.

Yet, something had changed since I'd passed the dam; I was becoming impatient to complete the journey, sensing deep down that the adventure was over. The sparkle of newness was gone and I wasn't exploring with the same intensity. I missed the mountains' embrace, the bucolic beauty of northern villages, the cerulean sky, the clear river. Ahead lay dun flatlands, slate skies, a sluggish river. I sensed that no more surprises awaited me and that from here on, I'd be digging water until I arrived at the sea, a plow mule intent on reaching the end of a row, shaving away a field one plowshare-width at a time.

What was at work in my brain's back rooms to interfere with the joy of the journey? Fatigue played a major role. In 31 days, I had rarely slept on the same floor or ground twice. Each night, exhaustion sedated me but I tossed and turned. Neither could the heat be discounted. Temperatures in the 90s were sapping my strength, the hammer sun beating down on me from above, and the Ping's surface reflecting it into my face. Heat has always made me irritable. Even in my teens, I instinctively understood why Camus' stranger acted as he had. I, too, had been riled by petty annoyances which would not have fazed me on a cool day.

I now found myself less enthusiastic about meeting new people. At the end of a tiring day, all I wanted to do was collapse and collect my thoughts. Perhaps I'd been spoiled by the solitude of the lake but I was weary of pulling in to face the same routine: charm, win confidence, secure accommodations. The gains of one day were erased the next, each evening having to begin anew what I had done the previous night. The ritual–my regarding it as such was indicative of my changing mood–was obscuring my appreciation of the people themselves.

My behavior puzzled me. I had always enjoyed delving into foreign cultures, taking people on their own terms. For 12 years, I had lived in a remote Bangkok neighborhood with no foreigners within a mile radius, and few Thais who spoke English. Not for me a life spent in *farang* districts, shopping at supermarkets, socializing with other foreigners. During my first 15 years in Asia, I'd lived with the basics, showering by pouring cold water over myself from a Shanghai jar, eating market food, riding buses, living in a wooden house with furniture I'd built myself or bought in the bazaar. I felt my life was richer for it. I was rewarded by a tacit recognition that by learning to speak Thai, I was validating their culture, and Thais responded warmly to that, treating me as one of them. Why was I pushing now them away?

It didn't help that latent security concerns were back again, triggered by the unexplained death of the old fisherman, and Mrs. Sirichai's ploys for protecting myself. In one sense, I was more annoyed with Mrs. Sirichai and other supposed guardians for disturbing my peace, than with the miscreants who might harm me. I was running the fear gauntlet again and it was a negative way to travel. I needed to change my attitude, to adopt a fatalistic approach: if something was going to happen, it would happen, but meanwhile I'd concentrate on experiencing my surroundings. Since the dam, I'd met delightful people. It was they on whom I would focus, not on the *jai lai* and the boors.

Prachuab had volunteered to ferry the boat downriver to Nikom's shop, but 20 minutes later, the boat had not arrived. I saw him down the road casually chatting with someone. When I raised my arms to ask, "What's the problem?" he shouted, "I can't paddle."

"Can anyone else?"

He began walking towards me, scratching his head. "No. Nobody has ever had a boat."

"No problem. I'll carry my gear to the boat. There's not much," I said.

Prachuab accompanied me while I considered the implications of his confession. In 1898, Ernest Young had observed that "The water is the true home of the Siamese, and it is on this, their native element, that their real character and genius are best exhibited." Others had noted that boats outnumbered the people and that everyone, even small children, could paddle them. Yet, since the dam, I'd seen only small sampans hugging the shore. It was apparent that a people who had once depended on the river for transportation and sustenance had turned their backs on it and lost their ability to utilize it. It was a sobering thought, as though in settling for land transport, they had sacrificed some of their self-reliance. More important, they had lost a vital component of their character.

By mid-morning, my new resolve had evaporated, replaced by exhaustion so complete it was frightening. An egg yolk sun burned in an oatmeal sky, the banks shimmered as though aflame, the heat waves distorting the landscape. The heat, the sameness of the scenery, and the return of the sandbanks, knocked the center out of me. Everything dragged: time, my paddle through the water, the boat, the river. Two hours into the day, I just let the boat drift, lay back, and listened for it to crunch into a shoal. To my surprise, it behaved itself and for the next hour I glided back and forth across the river on the currents, never touching the banks. After two miles it was time to take charge but the stifling heat discouraged even the slightest effort. I could only paddle a dozen strokes before I'd have to rest.

When a vendor hailed me from the right bank, I pulled beneath the shade of an overhanging tree. "You look so hot out there," she said. "Do you want some *moh gaeng*?" (a delicious custard of eggs, coconut milk, and palm sugar). I wolfed one down to the delight of an elderly woman with a betel-red smile and her spindly, comical-looking husband. The toothless husband attached his broken spectacles to his ears by rubber bands and wore baggy black shorts beneath an oversized khaki shirt that fell to his knees.

Other villagers wandered up to ask the usual questions and the wife hung on every word, her head wagging from speaker to speaker and then back to me, eager to hear my reply. To each answer, the husband would append a comment that teetered between profound and wholly inane, initially addressing his coda to me and then, halfway through, to the group. "The ocean isn't like the river," he'd intone. "The tail of the river is a long way from here," he observed. "So's the head, like a snake slithering to the sea," he added as an afterthought. "Boats go downstream. Like the river," he'd say solemnly, nodding to himself, amazed by the mystery of it all.

For their part, the spectators ignored him so that inevitably his eyes would land on his wife who'd grin goofily at him. Or, since she never stopped smiling, his face would pass within the beam of her unremitting good cheer.

One woman, of indeterminate middle age, won my heart. Every few minutes, she would leave the shade of the tree and walk to the river to run her hand over my boat. Catching me watching her, she said: "It's so beautiful!" To the others, an older woman wrapped in a faded sarong said, "*Farang*s are *geng* (clever or able). Thais would be afraid to travel like this."

I'd heard similar sentiments many times. They emanated from kindness and were intended as flattery rather than envy. Yet, although they might not have admitted it, it was also a statement of economic distress, a lack of money and leisure to pursue such an adventure. Even if he were moderately wealthy, a Thai would not have had two months to paddle down a river. I was fortunate to own the biggest luxury of all: time to do what I wanted to do.

I also knew their reception in a strange village would be quite different from mine. Thais perceived another brown-skinned stranger as a threat until he could establish a link to someone in the village. As Marshall and I had noted, white skin enjoyed privilege. Villagers could not conceive that a foreigner might do something dishonest. I could almost see their thoughts: I spoke Thai so I had probably been in Thailand for a while which meant that I was approved by the Thai government which meant I was probably o.k. Sigh of relief; I was safe. It didn't always work, but the odds were better than average that if I talked long enough, I'd be welcomed.

For the next hour, I soldiered on, intent on paddling, barely looking at the riverbank. Until, that is, at an opening in the reeds, I surprised a woman bathing bare-breasted, who immediately hoisted up her sarong. Nineteenth-century chroniclers had solemnly noted that Thai women invariably appeared in public bare-breasted–a predilection they ascribed to primitive, uncivilized Thai ways. Thereupon, the West introduced a sense of shame about nudity and Thai women, eager to be regarded as modern, covered themselves from nape to ankle. Today, only elderly village women still bathed bare-breasted; a behavior accepted because their bodies were unlikely to inspire desire. It was easy to imagine Thai consternation when Western women reversed course, appearing topless on Thai beaches and wearing little more than a patch on their pubis.

By contrast, men bathed in bikini briefs, ignoring nearby women bathers. There was no machismo in the men's attire and no leering at the women. Indeed, Thai men seldom gawked at women; it was me who swung around, tongue hanging, to ogle a passing beauty, my Thai friends perplexed that I should find pleasure in it.

I'd hardly recovered from my sighting when I rounded a grassy island and surprised a father, a young son, and his 30ish, somewhat plump mother perched on a small landing, her upper torso bare. She didn't miss a beat, however. Scowling, she covered herself with a gray wash tub. Perhaps the scowl was meant for her husband because he broke into uproarious laughter, his young son aping him. As I moved away, I heard her hissing displeasure at him, which only inspired him to laugh louder.

Soon, the villages began to crowd together and I found myself in the ancient city of Kampaeng Phet. When I could find no place to tie up along the seawall, a man grasping a fishing line suggested I paddle to a mid-river island. There, I would find another fisherman who might let me moor next to his hut for the night. I paddled across to find Pun, a swarthy, bare-chested man in a black and white checked *pakoma* standing on the shore watching me. He reached for the chain and seemed not at all surprised by my presence or my request. For 50 *baht* a day, he'd look after the boat and ferry me to the shore. "When you want to come back, just shout 'Pun'"; a rustic valet service.

Situated on a dogleg of the Ping, Kampaeng Phet in the 13th century was a southern gateway to Sukhothai. As Sukhothai's political influence ebbed, so too did Kampaeng Phet's, its economic decline coeval with the cessation of riverine trade. Today, little distinguished it from its sister provincial towns; three-story shophouses–their flaking paint corroded by black fungus–crowded each other along narrow streets. I chose my back street hotel less for its ambiance than its tranquility. The grime encrusting it suggested it dated from the Sukhothai period but was probably not more than a dozen years old.

As I had entered the city, I'd passed an old two-tier riverboat moored at the bank. I'd assumed it was a derelict until someone called to me from the upper deck. I looked over to see half a dozen young people hanging over the railing, laughing and hollering, "*Sawasdee*," (hello), "*Pai nai?*" (where are you going?) and other pleasantries. They told me it was a floating restaurant and invited me to come back for lunch when I had settled in. I now walked along quiet streets and up the gangway linking the restaurant with the land.

While the restaurant did a very credible business in the evenings, it was moribund at noon with twice as many waiters as patrons. A waiter recognized me and, with his mates, ran to the gangplank, bowing low and pantomiming exaggerated welcomes. After a pleasant lunch, Chokchai, the restaurant's late 20ish owner, suggested that we tour the city's ruins.

Kampaeng Phet provided another example of the Ping's declining importance. In the 13th-century, this minor kingdom had grown rich after a 42-mile canal known as the Phra Ruang Road was dug to link it with Sukhothai and, from there, another 34 miles to Si Satchanalai on the Ping

River. It was a gargantuan task given the period's small labor pool but it gave Sukhothai irrigation water for its crops. To all three cities, it gave a transportation channel to ship goods to distant points, and a military route to move troops quickly to defend its borders.

Kampaeng Phet's resultant wealth financed the construction of dozens of beautiful temples on the hills ringing the city. On Chokchai's small motorcycle, we toured them, crunching through fallen teak leaves two feet long, marveling at the carvings and the pleasant settings amidst the trees. We then visited the collapsed walls of the former royal city, at whose gates the Phra Ruang Road had began. With the decline of Sukhothai in the 14th-century, the Road had silted up and Kampaeng Phet reverted to a sleepy riverine town, the laterite ruins the only testament to its former prominence.

We returned to town at dusk. Chokchai returned to his restaurant and I went to a traditional massage parlor to remove the kinks from my back. The masseuse had little concept of her art, her technique consisting of prodding my body as a baker kneads dough. Not that she was particularly interested since it interfered with gossiping with her friend. Nonetheless, I fell into a blissful semi-doze, the first relaxation my knotted body had enjoyed in weeks. After too few brief moments I was jolted awake, writhing in agony. I had asked her to go easy on my hands which were daily becoming more cramped. Her response was to bend my fingers backwards like a Thai dancer's. The pain was so excruciating that it took me several moments to recover. She apologized but moments later did the same thing to my other hand. My yelps shocked her into paying attention but my pleasure had been blunted and I was happy when the session ended.

Shaking my hands to relieve the pain, I wandered into the street. From somewhere across the river a sound system was blaring *luuk thung* music.

"What's going I on?" I asked a fruit seller, nodding towards the sound.

"Temple fair," he said, the words slipping around a toothpick that bobbed as he spoke. I caught a trishaw and headed across the river.

Designed to raise funds for repairs, temple fairs were much like county fairs everywhere: product demonstrations, craft exhibits, carnival rides, and a games arcade. Farm families, many of them in town for the evening, smiled happily as they wandered amidst the wonder of twinkling lights and grand exhibits, waves of deafening sound washing over them. The racket was provided by p.a. systems touting the advantages of farm products and carny offerings. Weighing in from the sidelines was the horrifically amplified soundtracks for an outdoor movie, a Thai-dubbed copy of "Runaway Train" with Jon Voight. Bangkok dubbers had added interesting twists to the dialogue, especially helpful in scenes so far removed from a Thai's experience they would have taken hours to explain.

At the *viharn*, orange-robed monks sat behind a table piled high with tan, glazed roof tiles. For ten *baht*, a monk would paint the donor's name on the back of a tile which would later be installed on the leaky roof, proof of the contributor's generosity. I bought three tiles, an act which gave me a great deal of satisfaction as well as considerable merit. Perhaps I wouldn't return in a future life as a cockroach. The jolly monks insisted that instead of transliterating my name into Thai, that they should try out their English by painting my name in Roman letters. It took them three tiles to get it right but I'm sure the heavens understood.

In the amusement arcade, under the harsh light of fluorescent tubes, boys shot pop guns at wooden figures on shelves, collecting packets of dried noodles as prizes for their marksmanship. Instead of corks, their "bullets" were the red plastic caps normally found on fish sauce bottles, a clever bit of rustic recycling. Crude ring tosses, balloons and darts, wheels of fortune, and other games of chance blended into amusement park rides that included a toy train that chugged around the perimeter of the compound, and bumper cars powered by bolts of electricity that popped blue light as the metal contacts brushed against the chicken-wire roof.

Near the Ferris wheel, I stumbled across a lively *likay* performance. *Likay* is street theater, a bawdy adaptation of the lakhon dance/drama formerly performed for princes in their palaces. Where the former danced silently while off-stage singers sang the lyrics, *likay* actors sang their own lines. And what lines. *Likay* had evolved its own repertoire which included bawdy, rapid-fire repartee between the male and female actors, humorous exchanges which generally had the audience in stitches.

The evening's troupe, from Bangkok, performed on a wooden stage set atop oil drums and lit with bare 100-watt bulbs. Rouged actors garbed in tawdry costumes spangled with tiny mirrors and sequins strutted and posed against a backdrop depicting a 19th-century palace hall as imagined by rural folk who associated garish colors and geegaws with luxurious living. They saw no incongruity in the television set painted in one corner or an electric fan in another. Nor in the sound system feeding every voice through an echo-chamber that so distorted the voices that it obscured many of the lyrics.

Thais love extemporaneous speech and honor quick-witted actors able to banter at high speed. They applauded wildly as male actors engaged in no-holds-barred, risqué exchanges with acid-tongued women more than their equal in declamation. Some performers were in their 70s, their sprightliness belying their ages.

On an adjoining stage, folksingers crooned tales of country boys lost in big cities, "Country & Eastern" music, as it were. They were backed by a chorus line of teen-age beauties with tentative smiles, oblivious to everything but getting their steps right and staying in synch, and ignoring the flirtatious comments from the farm boys who leaned on the apron. In many small towns, unscrupulous promoters lured the swains to crowd the stage front by placing mirrors on the floor and passing the word that the girls were not wearing underwear. Things were more sedate here, the boys gawking shyly at the heavily made-up girls.

On yet another stage, older men bought tickets to dance the *ramwong*–a traditional no-touch dance–with girls who earned their living like the taxi dancers of the American 1930s. I was usually leery of these gatherings because fights over girls were not uncommon. It was not unknown for a spurned man–often a soldier and usually drunk–to stagger back to his barracks and return with a hand grenade which he would toss onto the dance floor, killing and maiming indiscriminately.

A noodle vendor's cart was bathed in the cold light of a single fluorescent tube powered by bare wires leading to the overhead mains. I ordered a couple of bowls of *Ba Mii Haeng*; egg noodles topped by fish balls, beef slices, chopped shallots, and coriander, and flavored with fish sauce and a pinch of dried chili flakes. I was so hungry, I added a *khanom buang*, a wafer-thin egg crepe stuffed with minced pork, sprouts, and other savories. Then, with throngs of weary fairgoers, I rode a *songtaew* back to town.

Before the morning sky had sloughed off its nighttime hue, I was packed and striding towards the river. When I hollered "Pun," a hand fluttered flag-like above the tall grass, followed by a head. A *pakoma*-ed body trotted to a dugout, paddled across, and ferried me back to his island. Cleverly concealed by overhanging reeds, my boat bobbed in the shallows. Paying him for guard duty, I readied the boat. But when I turned to say goodbye, he was gone, swallowed up by foliage.

A breeze whispering up the lazy river rippled its surface. The paddle dipped and rose, concentric circles exploding from the blade. A thousand strokes later, a great fulmination alerted me to an ostrich plume of inky smoke smudging the sky, so large it suggested a gigantic fire. The grassy banks slid away to reveal a sprawling sugar mill belching sooty smoke from five chimneys. It was less the noxious smoke than the cloying sweetness of raw molasses that weighed on my nostrils. Mountains of black ash caked the bank or spilled into the river like icebergs breaking from an ebon glacier; varnishing the river with an oily sheen. Rancid water gushed from a nearby pipe onto a river coated with yellow dust like dissolved feces. The stench from the riverbank was more noxious than that rising from the chimneys. Sugar mill pollution killed fish by the thousands and had prompted the usual government prohibition and lax enforcement. It wasn't as though the mill were operating secretly.

The pounding, crashing mill was still audible as I began to bail out foul water. As I worked, a fuzzy black caterpillar inched its way across the back hatch. Like a good Buddhist, I picked it up, planning to fling it to freedom in the bushes. Instantly, searing pain burned my fingers. Dozens of black bristles were embedded in my fingers, and the pain was excruciating. Scraping them with my knife only drove them deeper. The butterfly-to-be continued his leisurely crawl across the hatch. I was tempted to smack him with the paddle but he was only doing what evolution had taught him. Instead, I placed the paddle blade in his path and when he was aboard, I swept it in a wide arc, shooting him bankward. The rest of the morning, the slightest pressure on the paddle reminded me of my error in assuming the beast's benign nature.

The afternoon passed slowly. Smoke rose from cane fields, the ash falling like snow, coating me, the boat, and the water. When the landscape did not accord with my map I asked directions from each person I met and each one gave me conflicting information. One man told me Baan Mae Fai was straight ahead when my map indicated I had already passed it. A woman claimed that the village the previous informant had told me was Baan Mae Fai, was, in fact, Baan Khon Thi, meaning I was farther downstream than I'd thought. I gave up trying to follow the map. It was so late in the day that I'd have to take whatever accommodations I could find.

A few miles later, a landing appeared and a bather told me the headman's house was a short way inland. Chaining the boat I walked a winding road through tall trees and fresh green banana trees that ended at the village of Baan Pruk Makrut. The headman's house was evident by the gas pump–a glass cylinder atop a pipe stuck into a 50-gallon barrel–and the small general store on the ground floor. One look at the men told me I'd erred in my choice. Most had shaved heads meaning someone had died. I prayed the deceased wasn't from the headman's house but luck was against me. The headman's elder sister had passed away two days before. While I'd been busy at the funeral at Ma Dua Chumporn, she had been busy dying.

Dinner was Lao food–*laab* (minced meat), *plaa raa* (raw, fermented fish)–and most of the conversation was in the Lao language.

"Why is everyone speaking Lao?" I asked.

"War captives."

"War? When?"

"Phra Buddha Yod Fah."

In an 18th-century campaign against Laos the Thais, under the leadership of Phra Buddha Yod Fah (King Rama the First), had removed the Emerald Buddha from Vientiane, and installed it in Bangkok's Wat Phra Kaew. The army had also returned with Laotian prisoners of war who were forced to constructed Bangkok's city walls and moats, and various projects in the countryside. But that was over 200 years ago. Many had remained and apparently they still spoke Lao. Some traditions died hard.

Somthawin, the headman's soft-spoken 30ish son plied me with questions, offering insights into the village's workings. The villagers grew bananas and rice but made their biggest money from sugar cane that a Chinese towkay (middleman) bought for 440 *baht* (US$ 18) per ton, a pittance considering its re-sale value. The cane had once been transported by barge but today, it was large trunks that hauled it to the refineries.

After dinner, I went outside to breathe air perfumed by the delicate scent of the *Dok Ratri* (Lady of the Night) flower. As I had feared, the headman emerged from the house to invite me to the funeral. Before departing, he insisted that I put my belongings in a side room where they would be safe.

"We can't trust the neighbors," he said within earshot of the neighbors, none of whom seemed the slightest bit offended.

Few things happen on schedule in rural Thailand and of course the dead have all the time in the world. After bustling in preparation, the household calmed as if someone had pushed a "pause" button. I settled back to wait.

But my catapillared hands were still burning.

"What happened?" asked Somthawin as I peered closely at my fingers. When I told him, he chuckled in sympathy.

"Ah, *maeng boong*. A lot of poison in such a small body," he said, rising to his feet. From a shelf, he took down a candle, and lit the wick. He balled a bit of softened wax and blotted it over my finger, withdrawing a couple dozen embedded bristles. The pain did not entirely subside, but diminished considerably; another bit of village ingenuity.

The headman's rusted pick-up truck squeaked with every jounce on the rutted road to the monastery in a neighboring village. The third and final night of mourning seemed more of a party than a ritual of grieving. Most of the men were drunk and the women were chatting, sitting on mats beneath a ceiling strung with the inevitable twinkling Christmas lights. An ornate coffin stood on a flower-covered dais. To one side the occupant's portrait, a severe-looking woman of 57, glared at the gathering.

I sat on the floor and the men crowded around me, blowing alcohol fumes in my face. To punctuate his pronouncements, one would slap me on the knee and hold two fingers before his leering face. Had I been Italian I might have slugged him but I couldn't figure out what he meant and he was so near to passing out that I wasn't likely to get an explanation. Another bulky man, also seriously inebriated, rocked like a knock-over balloon figure as he talked in a booming voice. He spoke in this volume only to me and at one point, his friend said, "He's not stupid. He understands everything you say. You don't have to shout." The big man considered this for a moment. Turning to me, the friend said, "*Geng, geng*, you speak Thai so well." In true Thai fashion, he had shifted the spotlight to me, thereby deflecting criticism of his friend to avoid embarrassing him.

The big man beamed. In a softer voice he asked, "Do you want some *matum* (bael fruit) juice?"

I accepted and the big man yelled, "Get some matum for the *farang!*" This time his friend's impatience overrode his manners. "He isn't hard of hearing either. But if you keep it up we'll all be deaf." The others laughed. Chastened, his friend seemed to fold into himself, but only for a moment, his joy at my presence overwhelming his chagrin.

He quieted when four monks, concealed behind their *talabaht* (fans), began chanting the Buddha's teachings in the ancient Pali language. Two young monks, barely more than boys, peeked at me. When the abbot barked at them, the fans snapped back into place and the droning intensified.

I was offered a glass of *lao khao* (white whiskey) which I refused, smiling and patting my stomach. More sticky juice was brought. I imagined a smile of approval on the black and white photo that until then had shown only stern rebuke for the gossip and laughter nearly drowning out the monks' chants.

I seemed to be alone among the congregation in trying to maintain decorum but I couldn't figure out why. If it wasn't important to them, why was it important to me? She was gone, and I didn't even know her. The monks shambled through their chants, stumbling from time to time as if aware that few people were listening to them. But at least one was. I was shocked to hear an older woman call out to the concealing fans, "*Mai suat dii kwa*" (it's better that you don't pray). The others laughed, at which the sagging fans straightened and the enunciation and rhythm improved dramatically. I'd never heard a monk censured in that manner but obviously these had a history.

The reputation of a hallowed institution had been in decline for some time. There were frequent newspaper stories of monks fathering children, or pulling guns on fellow monks; or of theft, fraud, and the breaking of one of the 227 rules by which they were supposed to live. It wasn't surprising. After all, most were laymen in orange robes, not gods. With nearly 200,000 of them, it was not inconceivable that a few would step out of line from time to time.

Eventually, the murmurs ceased and the monks returned to their *wat*. We rose and left for home. Only the chief guest stayed behind. Later that night, the elaborate casket would be opened and her plain wooden coffin would be removed to a roofed concrete platform. On its far end, an oven was already turning firewood to embers. Soon, smoke would rise from the tall, narrow chimney. In the morning, the cooled bones and ashes would be placed in an urn. If the headman had enough money, they would be cemented into a small *stupa* in the monastery courtyard, her photograph sealed into the concrete.

Halfway home, the headman stopped and stepped out, giving Somthawin the wheel before disappearing into the darkness. "He's spending the night at his other wife's house," Somthawin explained.

The night had been warm. Twice, when sweating profusely, I turned back the sleeping bag and the mosquitoes found me. By contrast, the morning was cool. When the headman failed to return, Somthawin prepared breakfast. He confessed that although the headman referred to him as *luuk* (son), he was actually the son-in-law, born in a village to the south. I liked him. He was gentle and when someone spoke he looked directly into their eyes, listening intently to every word.

Several times our meal was interrupted by vehicles clamoring for gasoline. I felt transported to boyhood trips into the countryside. The motorist would tell Somthawin how many liters of petrol he wanted. Somthawin would then wind the crank to draw the requisite amount from the barrel to fill a glass cylinder etched at five levels corresponding to five liters. At the correct level, he would flip a lever and the cylinder would empty, the gas flowing down a hose and into the vehicle's tank.

"Would you like to see the cane harvest?" he asked as he strolled back into the house. "I want to see if the cutters need anything." In my Nepalese village, cane had been my salvation during bouts of dysentery. With no toilets, the villagers had squatted near a distant irrigation canal. When diarrhea struck, the canal was too far away so I'd duck into the nearby cane fields, ignoring the rats and the cobras that hunted them. I recalled the panic I felt the day they harvested the fields.

The sun burned through the banana leaves, the heat evaporating the night's dew and thickening the air with a tropical fragrance. A quarter mile later, we arrived at a school just as a tinny national anthem began blaring from a loudspeaker on a high pole. With the assembled students, we stood attention while a boy and girl hoisted the red, white, and blue striped flag skywards, a squeaky pulley providing accompaniment. Arranged in platoons, the students were dressed in identical white shirts or blouses and blue shorts or skirts, many of them obvious hand-me-downs from older siblings. Some students wore brown tennis shoes but most were shod in rubber sandals. The identical scene was being enacted at the same moment in tens of thousands of schoolyards reached by Radio Thailand.

When the broadcast faded away, teachers marched their charges to the classrooms in crooked columns. While the intent was militaristic, the effect was Christopher Robinish, shambling Pooh and the others bringing up the rear.

"I have to talk with someone. Do you mind waiting at the school?" Somthawin asked and walked to the opposite side of the soccer field.

Like Buddhist monasteries, Thai schools are built to a universal template. They almost always comprise a single long, two-story building with ground floor classrooms opening onto a wide concrete stoop, and upper floors onto a wide balcony. They are stained reddish-brown or painted light green and are covered in gray asbestos tiles. This primary school (first to sixth grades) was attended by 65 children, divided equally between the sexes. Good family planning programs had resulted in declining birth rates. The benefit, one teacher told me, was that students received more individual attention. Students normally provided their own meals but on Tuesdays and Thursdays, the teachers cooked government-subsidized lunches.

The school was impressive less for its facilities than for the enthusiasm displayed by its five teachers who compensated for the lack of amenities with creative thinking. The curriculum emphasized not only the basics but subjects as practical as how to address a parcel to ensure proper postal delivery.

A harrumphing beside me alerted me to the presence of the headmaster, a somber little man who invited me to his office. There, he assumed the role of Grand Inquisitor. His range of knowledge would have been quite impressive were it not for the strange slant he put on everything. Most of his questions were so abstruse that they have blurred in memory but a few remain:

"What is the political and social significance of your journey," he asked as we sat in his office. His hands were folded over a round little belly set atop stout legs. Eyes regarded me intently through pebble glasses, a countenance so solemn that I struggled, first to decipher the question, and then to formulate some sort of intelligent answer.

"In a larger, global sense," I began uncertainly, "not a lot."

"Umm, umm," he hummed, deep in thought.

"In a smaller one, it is a meeting of cultures, a blending of thoughts of people whose societies differ in many respects..." I stumbled on, having no idea what I was saying.

He drank it all in, nodding sagely as I spoke, ignoring the sweat on my brow as I negotiated, a step at a time, the conversational path, as though hopping from slippery stone to unsteady rock across a rushing stream. When I paused, he posed another question:

"What is the moral objective of your journey?"

I stumbled my way through this one as well, with something along the lines of my hopes that I might influence others to protect the river.

"What will be the end result of your journey?" he asked.

"For me, or for society in general?" I asked.

"Yes," he elucidated.

"A book," was all I could think to say, but this apparently was the correct answer. I felt like an eight-year-old standing before the school principal. He paused, only to launch into another series of baffling questions-how would the journey benefit those who had financed it (who???), didn't I think that the world's nations needed to understand each other better (uh, yes), what advice would I have for Thais to ensure that the world had a better image of them? The questions arose from no coherent philosophy and seemed fore-doomed to reach no destination. My answer was not acknowledged, responded to, or even regarded as fodder for the subsequent question. Instead, each new question would arrive from a distant planet in a small envelope which he would open (I could almost hear him clearing his throat as he did) and ask.

I was perplexed until I realized that there was no point to the conversation. This was social talk. In formulating his questions, he was winging it as much as I was in answering them. It didn't matter what answer I gave. The only rule was that I should give replies long enough to allow him time to think up another question. Once I settled into the rhythm, the conversation proceeded smoothly. We were present merely to pass the same gift back and forth to each other; what the box contained was unimportant.

As I was wearying of the ordeal, he invited me to the schoolyard to view his artistic masterpiece: a concrete waterfall. A hose led water to its six-foot summit where it tumbled down the sides of something resembling a volcano, before cascading into a pond surrounded by flocks of herons and deer, apparently the only beasts for which statues were available. Besides the incongruity of the animals crowding the perimeter, the symmetry was severely disturbed by proportion problems; here, a deer standing knee-high to a heron; there, a tiny heron nose to nose with a deer.

But it wasn't my duty to judge but to "ooh" and "ahh" at the appropriate places. The headmaster beamed as though he'd created the Parthenon, explaining that this was a replica of Deer Park in India's Saranath town where the Buddha had preached. He'd created it, of course, not for personal reasons but "for the children's education." It would take a lot of signage for a child to draw meaning from this menagerie beneath the mini-mountain. I was about to point out that there are no hills near Saranath but as verisimilitude was not the point of the exercise, I dutifully photographed it from a number of angles.

I was lining up another shot when I heard someone say, "Why are you photographing a volcano?" I turned to see Somthawin; to my surprise, the headmaster was gone. As I explained the sculpture's symbolism and features, Somthawin regarded it pensively, then said, "I've always wondered what it was," and, abruptly, "Well, let's head for the fields before the day heats up."

The sun's heat was exacerbated by the fires set to burn away dry cane leaves before harvest. Most of the harvesting work fell to the women, and despite the sun's intense glare, their faces were scarved, their eyes visible as slits beneath broad straw hats. They were dressed in long-sleeved blouses and they had wrapped their arms with thick cloths. One gloved hand grasped a cane stalk and the other, a nasty-looking knife with a beaked blade. After chopping the stalk below the ground line, they lopped off the crown, ran the knife along the stalk to remove burnt leaves, then tossed it behind them for another woman to stack.

Wanting to see how difficult harvesting was, I asked to join them. They handed me a knife and I waded in. Like bamboo, sugar cane is a grass and I felt like a Lilliputian laboring in someone's lawn, the flowery heads towering three feet above my head as I hacked away. After 10 minutes, I understood why the women were bundled up; my arms were scored with bloody lines where the razor-sharp grass had sliced them. Like the caterpillar, the leaves were covered in fine hairs that embedded in my skin, a burning rash made worse by rubbing. That set most of the women to clucking, the ones that weren't laughing in amusement, that is.

"You shouldn't try it without covering up first," said one young woman. She began looking for cloth to wrap my arms but an older woman laid a gentle hand on her shoulder and shook her head, suggesting that the foreigner should be allowed to retire from the scene before he made an even bigger fool of himself. The young woman then poured water over my burning arms, murmuring sympathy, as she did. If nothing else, I'd savor the sweetness of the sugar I spooned into my next cup of coffee.

Back at the boat, I thanked Somthawin and pushed off on yet another day. Contrary to my expectations, the riverbanks hadn't run out of surprises.

Rivers are metaphors for life, flowing from birth to death, purposeful in intent, single-minded in their surge to the sea... Where had I read that? And how familiar was the writer with a river's true nature? It is my guess that the author scrawled the lines while sprawled on a riverbank, far from the surging currents.

Poets often sing of rivers as embodiments of purposefulness, serenely following destinies dictated by river DNA. In truth, a river's course–like that of even the best-planned human life–is decreed by random events. A fallen tree, gravity's betrayal in a shallow valley, obdurate rocks it cannot wear away, a collapsing bank undercut by a flash flood, or human intervention, can alter its course.

Within the confines of its banks, a river is a metaphor for a personality disorder. It wanders a dozen directions at once, its uncertainty displayed in surface currents that run at angles to each other. Plunge into its depths and discover a half dozen layers moving, not in concert with each other, but in contradiction. Deep currents slide downstream faster than, and at angles to, the surface flow. Dead leaves swirl along the bottom, swiftly slipping past twigs floating lazily along the surface, as though the undercurrents are pulling a resisting surface faster than it wants to go.

All morning, I played with currents–like fishing, an excuse for doing nothing. The river flowed powerfully as the little-hand sun passed zenith and began falling towards evening. As I drifted south, the breeze rose and the sky hazed, smothering the sun and its burning rays. The clouds piled higher and higher, becoming a mountain range behind which the sun set an hour before normal. The promised rain did not fall.

A long seawall appeared on the left. The water's surface began to wrinkle, straining towards the wall as if drawn by a magnet, pulling me along with increasing force. A water gate, I thought, and worth investigating.

Not that I had a choice. Round the wall's end, I was sucked into a concrete canyon ending in an three iron gates, under which the water flowed. The suction was so great that it slammed me into the far wall. Above me, two men whirled around at the sound. Thinking I'd been trapped, they rushed down the sloping rampart to grab and hold my boat.

"Where were you trying to go?" the big one asked.

"Talat Sanjao Mae."

"Why?" the thin one asked.

"To find a place to stay for the night."

"Stay here," the first one said. "We've got an extra room."

"What is this?" I asked.

"A *cholaprathan* (irrigation dam). We're the gatekeepers," he said proudly.

Securing the boat, I climbed the wall. Behind the gates, a broad canal ran die-straight for 50 miles, disappearing into the dust-hazed sky. River water coursed down it to irrigate miles of fields on either side. The huge gates were raised and lowered by capstans whose worm gears were turned by a large hand crank. A third man was winding down a gate to reduce water flow during the coming night.

Excavated by the government 20 years before, the waterway was part of an immense canal system the Thais had begun constructing in the 15th century. Despite minimal gravity, water had been made to flow into remote regions, turning them into vast seas of green rice.

Water distribution was governed by the Royal Irrigation Department (RID), the "royal" in the agency's title indicative of its importance. For a thousand years, monarchs had provided their subjects with life-giving water. Some historians have suggested that kings derived their power from their ability to control water distribution. These three technicians were RID employees, tethered to their headquarters in Kampaeng Phet by a short-wave radio. Daily directives dictated how many hours the gates would remain open.

On a nearby knoll, a single raintree sheltered a two-story house reminiscent of a farm home on a wind-swept prairie. Here, the trio and their wives lived. I'd always been amazed how easily Thai strangers thrown together by work became a close-knit family, co-operating with minimal bickering or territoriality. These five–two couples and an older man, ranging in age from 25 to 50–were bright, articulate, and fun. They shared space, teased each other, and talked with the ease of childhood friends.

In part, their relationship was founded on mutual respect. Nilaphan, in his 20s, deferred to Banjerd, a jovial 40-year-old, listening attentively to everything he said. Part of Banjerd's appeal derived from the gypsy life he had led as a young traveling salesman in northern villages. He often crossed into Burma where basic commodities were in such short supply that half the goods sold in towns like Mandalay bore brand names in Thai script. This black market thrived under the noses of socialist government officials who themselves shopped there. Banjerd had a wealth of stories about paying off Burmese officials to slip in goods duty-free. He had nothing but scorn for life in Burma.

"We have corruption here but at least we get something for our money. Even if you pay the officials there, your life is still bad. *Oeuy! Phama yae* (Burma is awful)", he said, clearly relieved to be living on this side of the border.

Nilaphan had never traveled. For him, Banjerd was Marco Polo returned from fabulous expeditions to exotic lands. He was a bit of a naïf, and was probably saved from misadventure by his wife Vilai. Tall and rangy for a Thai woman, she had few illusions. She laughed easily but her smiling face masked a steely resolve. She was loyal and supportive of her husband but was not above huffing impatiently whenever he gushed his admiration of someone or something. I suspected she'd pulled him back from the brink of foolishness more than once but she was warmly affectionate towards him. Thai couples often treated each other as sister and brother, even addressing each other as *phi* (elder) and *nong* (younger). Like many Thai marriages, it was less a passionate than a symbiotic relationship founded on the premise that they would survive life only by cooperating. Unlike many Thai husbands, Nilaphan didn't seem the type to stray; that would be a large plus in the eyes of a Thai woman familiar with male philandering.

Like her husband Banjerd, Somsri verged on roly-poly. She found everything her husband said amusing and seemed pleased that others sought his advice. While shy, she was hospitable; I was touched by her efforts to make me feel comfortable and her apologies for her spartan home. She put me in a side room bare of furniture or decoration, laying a thin mattress on the floor, stacking two blankets atop it, and placing an electric fan in one corner.

In the bathroom, a Shanghai water jar brimmed with water and mosquito larva. As I scooped a pan of it to sluice my body, a small frog lurking in the dark interior popped out. It took refuge on the floor between the jar and a hole that led waste water to the ground below. After a day of heat, I luxuriated in the water's refreshing coolness, slowly pouring several pans over me before soaping up my hair, and rinsing. Changing to fresh clothes and combing my hair, I joined the others in the living room.

"*Oii, law laew*," (so handsome) Vilai teased, her eyes twinkling. The others chimed in with similar compliments. This response was not unusual; I generally looked disheveled when I stepped from the boat, my hair sweat-plastered to my head, my *moh hom* sopping, my legs dirty and scratched. Barefooted and dressed in shorts, I must have been frightening, making the welcome I received all the more remarkable. But then came "The Transformation" and I looked almost human again, quelling any lingering doubts about my being a deranged convict on the lam.

We moved to the yard, an expanse of hard dirt. Beneath the raintree whose leaves were coated in dust, we sat at a teak slab table sheltered by a thatch canopy, enjoying a commanding view of the river, orange in the setting sun. There were no sounds, not even a bird or a cicada, just the quiet shivering of leaves in an evening breeze. While I was in the shower, friends had dropped by the house with snacks–dried beef, popped corn, fresh pineapple, and nuts. On the table sat a small dish filled with salt and bits of red and green *prik khii nuu* (rat dropping) chilies, the fiercest. We talked, dipping nuts and pineapple chunks into the fiery mixture, sucking air to cool our mouths. To the men's cheers, Banjerd produced a bottle of orange soda, that looked suspiciously pale. "Orange soda whiskey," he laughed.

When I demurred, Nilaphan said, "Government issue for special guests so it's o.k." Normally I would have refused but it was such a congenial group and the evening was so pleasant that I let them fill a small glass. We were joined by the third man, a quiet official in his late 40s. He lived and worked here, far from his home village, seeing his wife and children only once a year. "I can't afford to see them more often," he said, without complaint.

In my youth, I had read Chinese poems in which the author, generally a minor government official, lamented that his wife was 10,000 *li* (3,500 miles) away and he hadn't seen her in three years. I'd thought it odd that a man and his wife had to live so far apart. I soon learned that in Asia it was normal for a government official to be stationed in a distant town. Too poor to support his family at his post, he sent part of his meager pay home each month, and visited them once a year. His family would work the farmlands and his wife would supplement their income by selling sweets at the school or the weekly fresh market. Had the other two couples had children, they might have been forced to do the same.

Outsiders who criticized local Thai officials for seeming disinterest in their work had to consider that there was little motivation to exert themselves or perform well. They were stuck there and weren't going anywhere unless they ingratiated themselves to a superior. There was but one way to do that and few could afford it. The two couples did their best to make the older man's life comfortable. To them, he was "*Loong*" (uncle), and they took care of him as though he were family. He responded avuncularly, quietly accepting what he had, overlooking what he lacked.

Somsri and Vilai had retired to the kitchen and now re-appeared carrying bowls loaded with wondrous curries wafting mouth-watering aromas. We tucked into the delicious fare as details of private lives were revealed. Banjerd and Somsri's single child, an 18-year-old daughter, was studying in Kampaeng Phet. Nilaphan and Vilai had no children.

"Do you plan to start a family soon?" I asked.

Nilaphan flushed and mumbled something. The others looked at him sympathetically and I hastily switched the subject, asking them how they normally enjoyed themselves.

"We drink," said Nilaphan with eyes glazed. "Until we get drunk," he said happily as if boasting of a major accomplishment. "Last night I was so drunk, I drove my motorcycle off the road into a sugarcane field."

"Were you hurt?"

"Nah," he said; the brave were impervious to harm. Vilai was not amused.

"You weren't injured, but the motorcycle was," she said.

"That wasn't my fault," he protested.

Seeing my puzzled look Banjerd said, "This morning when we went to get it, the battery was missing. Stolen." Batteries were expensive, especially for those with low incomes. But this little cloud soon passed. Somsri ladled out more food and the conversation picked up. Nilaphan poured himself another drink.

An interesting dynamic was at work. The men were getting progressively drunker, genial drunks but slurring their words and making little sense. Yet, although they didn't touch a drop, the wives accepted it all, not minding in the least what would have irritated non-drinking wives in the West. Somsri's only complaint was about Banjerd's smoking.

"He coughs in the morning," was all she said, concerned more about its effect on him than about the harsh cigarette smoke blowing in her face.

Night was descending and so were the mosquitoes. The women shooed us indoors to watch the 8 p.m. news on television while they worked in the kitchen. Television programs beamed to upcountry audiences were different from those viewed in Bangkok. Rural families avidly watched programs on sanitation, cultivation techniques, conservation, child care, agricultural extension, and public health. At 9 p.m. the news ended and "kung fu" and urban soap operas came on. But they held little appeal for farm families. When the news credits rolled, the family turned off the TV and went to bed.

We talked a while longer but weariness overwhelmed us and we headed to our respective rooms. The crickets had begun chirping as night descended and were now in full chorus. In the bathroom, the small frog croaked in unison. I fell asleep to their songs.

It wasn't the night chill that woke me but Banjerd's hacking cough. Dawn was breaking and I walked outside to look at the sky, clear except for a few, high, wispy clouds.

"It's going to rain," said Loong, emerging from the house. The sky betrayed no hint of rain. I'd learned not to challenge the locals' reading of the sky but this prediction seemed a bit off.

Loong led me to the gazebo and a few moments later, Somsri appeared with glasses of Thai coffee. Banjerd and Nilaphan stumbled out to join us, looking not too bad for all the damage they'd done to themselves the previous evening. A few sips of syrupy coffee cleared the fog and moments later they were ready to face the day.

Banjerd leaned back to look up at the sky above the raintree.

"It's going to be a beautiful day," he said. "Looks like the radio was wrong," Banjerd said to Loong.

After a leisurely breakfast of papaya and fried eggs, Banjerd asked me if I wanted to accompany him up the canal. The trio patrolled the waterway every few days, looking for obstructions. Today, it was his turn.

"How far are we going" I asked.

"Just to a sugar mill a few miles away. Farmers have been complaining that foul water has been leaking into the canal and killing the fish."

We set off on a motorcycle displeased by all the weight bearing down on it. Soon, the breeze blew the sticky sweet scent of molasses to our nostrils and as cloying as it was, it was a welcome contrast to the choking dust. The mill was a nightmare. Ancient machinery-little more than cogs and crushers-hugged cane stalks between iron rollers, squeezing out their juice. The workers were from the Northeast and from their ragged clothes it was obvious they were paid a pittance. The owner greeted us with the unctuous smile reserved for officials who might give him trouble and must be placated. While Banjerd talked with him, I wandered through the factory.

From the crusher, the juice flowed along a channel dug in the dirt floor leading to the boiling vats. The spent cane, bagasse, fueled a furnace made of clay-covered bricks lashed together with bamboo strips. It evaporated the juice leaving raw sugar resembling red soil which men shoveled into cooling pans: packed earth hemmed by rough boards. A rototiller roamed back and forth over the steaming sugar, stirring it. It was a crude process with little concern about workers or consumers' health. It was as though I was peering into a 19th-century sweatshop where life meant little, profits everything.

Back at the house, Nilaphan had moved the boat to the near bank. Banjerd glanced at the sky, squinting. Suddenly animated, he turned to me.

"Do you have a *pakoma* [sarong]?"

"Two."

"Get them out," he ordered. He hurried to the top of the slope, calling back, "Nilaphan, find me some bamboo poles," before disappearing into the house. Something was up.

Banjerd emerged with a broad cleaver. Nilaphan appeared with two, arm-thick poles. When people pitch in to do something, it is best to back off and watch. Using the chopper like a wedge, Banjerd neatly split the bamboo into long, inch-wide strips. Carrying two eight-foot lengths, he bounced nimbly down the bank, his excitement overcoming his bulk. He bent one into an upside down "u" whose ends he lodged between the floor boards and gunwales near the bow. He inserted the second length near the stern. The other slats he used as spacers, lashing them to the front and back upside-down "u"s with plastic string. The *pakoma*s were laid on the resultant trellis, their corners tied to the uprights.

Then he stepped back, pleased with his invention. My boat now looked like the shikara sampans that ply Dal lake in Kashmir or the floating brothels once moored under Bangkok's Pratunam bridge. Still, it would shield me from an intense sun. I applauded their handiwork but it was the cheers from the women atop the banks that caused them to glow with pride.

The morning had slipped away and Somsri was now preparing lunch. I had been looking for an excuse to loiter and this was as good as any. It was early afternoon before I left, and not without regrets.

Jamrat and the "Boom Boom" Girl

Tam Namprik Lalaai Menam
(To make chili paste and dissolve it in the river)
A big investment for a small return

While the sunshade provided welcome shelter, the struts barked my knuckles on every stroke. Each time the wind gusted, the *pakoma*s pulled loose. I was reluctant to discard the system after all their good-hearted effort, but it simply didn't work. After two days of struggles, I would leave the framework at a village and return the *pakomas* to the storage bin.

My late start and the sunshade difficulties slowed me and, once again, I got caught between villages as the sun was setting. I was pulling hard for Khanoralakburi when a flatbed ferry boat burdened by cars, motorcycles, and passengers lumbered across my bow. I paused to watch. Once again, I was witnessing a bit of history verging on extinction. Its replacement lay just downriver: a new concrete bridge a month from completion. With the bridge's inauguration, the ferry operation would move upstream, retreating to smaller and smaller towns as each new bridge stapled the banks together. Finally, in a river too narrow, it would be retired from service, a rich aspect of the river's heritage abandoned to rust and rot.

But I couldn't linger. When Khanoralakburi proved to be too large I continued paddling, and a mile downstream, arrived at a town. Or sort of a town. The map identified it as Baan Kaew. It sat on an outside bend and the ramshackle houses on its high banks seemed poised to topple into the river. On its upstream edge, I passed a trim concrete house with a large, neat garden. A well-built, smooth-skinned man in his 30s was carrying two buckets of water on either end of a bamboo staff laid across his shoulder; his short, shuffling steps kept the water from sloshing out. His appearance was an anachronism, as though he'd stepped out of a 19th century Chinese village. He wore a loose blue blouse and baggy pants; his hair beneath a conical Chinese hat was braided in a long queue. Odder still was that he spoke excellent English.

"The *kamnan*'s house is beyond the market about half a mile from the river," he said in precise, rounded tones.

"Who lives here?" I asked, indicating the house behind him.

"A Chinese merchant. The rice mill owner." I had more questions but couldn't ask them. Like an impatient child pulling his mother down the street, away from the conversation she is conducting, the river tugged at my boat, and in a moment he was out of earshot.

The *kamnan*'s house was too far way and Baan Kaew looked so decrepit I doubted that it would offer any lodgings. Just downstream, however, the 200-foot-long tan wall of a Buddhist monastery paralleled the riverbank. Like most towns in this stretch, it was shaded by huge raintrees but no bushes or grass appeared on its adobe soil. Tying up at the landing, I climbed a steep, 15-foot embankment, crossed a dirt road, and found myself at a monastery gate guarded by two lions slathered in brown house paint.

The monastery forecourt was the size of a soccer field. Beyond it were dozens of two- and three-story buildings, tightly-packed and placed haphazardly. They were distinguished by no singular architectural style, indeed, no sense of style whatever. Near the belltower stood an asbestos-tiled primary school with a dozen classrooms. It seemed abandoned, its flaking, fungused paint suggesting it had seen better days. Despite the number of empty buildings, new ones were under construction. Or had been, since construction work seemed to have halted. Re-bar leaked red oxide onto the rough foundations; their bricks wore dusty coats.

Several children spotted me and ran to the back of the compound. Figuring they must be heading for the abbot's quarters to report my arrival, I followed them. Turning a corner, I came to a single-story faded-yellow concrete house. As I stepped onto the porch, one of the girls opened the door.

The interior was a hodge-podge of mismatched furniture, glass cabinets filled with souvenirs of a lifetime, photos taped to the cement walls, and books and papers stacked waist high. Lounging on the floor, his back against a cushionless wooden divan, was the abbot, a scrawny, bald man wearing an inane smile. Another man glided noiselessly through the room, gathering papers, fetching water glasses, and demonstrating by his movements that he was an aide of some sort. Seated cross-legged before the abbot was a broad-shouldered, burly man. His back was to me and he was in deep conversation, his booming voice so loud that he was unaware of my entry until he realized that the abbot was no longer listening to him. He swung around and sprang to his feet. The moment I set eyes on him, I knew he was trouble.

"What do you want?" the abbot asked me.

"I need a place to store my boat for the night," I replied. Before I could say more, the stocky man began rubbing his hands together, saying, "Today's my lucky star," a phrase he would repeat several times in the next few hours.

"Jamrat will help you," the abbot said and Jamrat leapt into action, initiating one of the stranger evenings of my journey.

The contrast between the two men was startling. The abbot, a giggling, tiny, frail man in his 60s, seemed on the verge of expiration. I would soon learn that despite his impious behavior, he was held in high repute in the town. Jamrat, on the other hand, was powerful looking, full of energy and obscenities, a gross loudmouth one heard long before he came into view. He saw nothing wrong with talking about his love of "boom boom" with whores in front of the *luang paw* or the children, the abbot exploding in high-pitched cackles at everything he said.

Having been appointed my guardian, Jamrat brushed past me and out the door. "Where's the boat?" he shouted, and without answering, headed for the landing. "Come on, follow me," he said to the posse of preteen boys. He was halfway across the compound before I caught up to him. In mid-stride, he turned and demanded 13 *baht*.

"For what?" I asked, breathlessly.

"A packet of cigarettes. Can't have fire without smoke," he said, then leered at me, "some fires make a lot of smoke," he laughed lasciviously.

At the dock, he took one look at the boat, said "no problem," stripped to his shorts and jumped into the water, shouting to the children "the *farang* will pay each of you one *baht* to carry the boat to the monastery." The kids cheered lustily.

"No, leave it here," I said, dreading the thought of lugging it so far.

"If you leave it here," said the abbot's aide, "the children will play with it"–a euphemism for stealing or damaging it. I preferred to lock up everything but it was now Jamrat's show and he was in full tilt.

I cautioned him that the fully-loaded boat was heavy but he waved me away. Standing waist-deep in the water, he set his feet and positioned his body. Repeating, "No problem," he hefted the stern. I was surprised he got it as high as he did but in the end, he dropped it. "Oof! It's really heavy," he grunted. "What's in the back, heroin?" he shouted, laughing uproariously. The children who a moment before had been eager to carry the boat, watched his struggles, and became silent. Several drifted away and were not seen again.

Only momentarily subdued, Jamrat was determined to try it again. Before he could do himself serious damage, I unloaded some of the bags. Tugging together, we hoisted it onto the dock. Once again, I tried to dissuade them from moving it away from the river.

"We'll just lock it up here," I said. "I'm sure it will be all right."

But Jamrat was already marshaling the remaining kids and shanghaiing passersby to carry it up the steep bank and across the road. Even without gear, it weighed a ton. Of course, when Jamrat asked the aide where we should put it, he suggested the building at the very back of the compound, a back-breaking walk of 100 yards. But Jamrat was already moving and the boat, sprouting two dozen legs, moved like a bulky centipede across the dusty courtyard. Even with a second man, Jamrat, the 10 boys and me, it was a very long trek. After a few steps banter was replaced by huffing and puffing. As my back, already strained by paddling, screamed in protest, I thought "how in hell are we going to get it back to the river in the morning?"

When we were about to drop, we arrived at the pavilion. It was locked. A boy was sent for the key and returned 10 minutes later. "He couldn't find it on his key chain," he explained.

The pavilion was filthy. Dust covered everything and ancient cobwebs hung like shrouds from corners, ceiling, rotting cabinets, and ancient effluvia that covered the floor. Already, the mosquitoes were humming in the shadows. We cleared a place and set down the boat.

I then discovered I was out of one-*baht* coins. I pulled 10-*baht* from a roll of bills and asked a boy to split it with the others. Before I could consider my next move, Jamrat shouted, "20 *baht* for the grown-ups!" and grabbed the wad from my hand, peeling off 20 *baht* for himself and 20 for the other man. He thrust the remainder my direction and strode back to the abbot's quarters. We locked the pavilion and followed him.

The abbot asked me what I was doing on the river. I told him, with Jamrat impetuously inserting comments or questions, seldom waiting for an answer before plunging on to the next. It was impossible to converse with him around but the abbot seemed unperturbed. At last, we came to the question of where I would spend the night.

"Are you afraid of ghosts," the abbot asked.

"No," I replied.

"Then you can sleep with the boat." He laughed uproariously at his own cleverness. "And the mosquitoes and dust," I thought. At least it was shelter.

I bathed at a well before an audience of children and adults. As I poured buckets of water over myself, I listened to Jamrat tell everyone he was taking me to dinner, he, the man who had just borrowed 13 *baht* for cigarettes and shown me an empty wallet. Since it might turn out to be an interesting evening, I said nothing. The moment I was dressed, Jamrat grabbed my arm and propelled me towards the front gate, half dragging me across the yard.

The first stars were beginning to appear as we headed for the bright lights of Baan Kaew. Jamrat insisted on walking down the center of the dirt road, forcing the bicycles and motorcycles to swerve around us. His idea of humor was to shout insults at everyone, and then laugh raucously. He tried to flag down a couple of motorcyclists, hollering "hey, give us a ride" but they knew him and drove by without even a dignifying glance.

"First we eat and then 'boom, boom,' a nice 17-year-old," he announced as we entered Baan Kaew's darkened streets. Voices from the shadows invited us to join them to smoke ganja but Jamrat didn't pause. "Nah," he said, "we have business in town."

And a dead-end town it was. From snatched conversations, I

learned that Baan Kaew had once been a thriving port. Boats had lined the waterfront, three-deep, loading rice for downstream markets. Then the government built the Paholyothin Highway, six miles west, and the smart money moved there. Left behind was a two-lane dirt track that followed the river's turnings, meandering between sagging wooden shophouses.

The street was unlit but rectangles of yellow light from unglazed windows fell across the road. In and out of them, like figures momentarily caught in strobes, passed a motley collection of men, many of them thick-set like Jamrat. They labored in the rice mill, the town's only industry. The women were short and dumpy or tall and rake-thin. The children were of normal proportions, so must have been imported.

Jamrat was a bus driver and as a sideline, he ran a lottery scheme. He bought tickets in Nakhon Sawan 50 miles downriver, and resold them to the locals. They grumbled that he never bought winners. Jamrat brushed by, waving several people away and then, in mid-stride, abruptly turned and strode into a general store/barbershop/restaurant nearly bowling me over. He walked to a wall mirror to comb his hair, blocking the barber's view of his customer's head. "Any food?" he demanded. "None," the proprietress replied.

"No?" he shouted, somewhat pained. With a pause, he strode out, bumping into me on my way in. He pushed past and down the street. "I'm taking the *farang* to dinner," he announced. Nobody paid any attention to him.

I struggled to keep up as he careered along, bee-lining for an unrevealed destination. Again, he turned abruptly and bounded into a rude restaurant run by a man Jamrat kept summoning as "*Jek*," a pejorative term for Chinese.

"*Jek*, three fried rice and a beer," he hollered.

Before I could ask 'why three orders?' he said, conspiratorially, "The third fried rice is for the other man who helped us." He also ordered *khai pulao* (boiled egg in a sweet soy sauce) and a concoction he said would "give us 'boom boom' strength." Ever the gracious host, he asked me to join him but I declined. We watched as the shopkeeper poured a Sprite and two raw eggs into a glass. With great gusto, Jamrat downed the revolting mixture, smacking his lips and slapping his stomach. He spent the next few minutes bantering loudly with diners at the next table.

When the food arrived, he dove in. But he couldn't sit still. Center of the world, he would take a bite, jump up to confer with someone, then rush back to the table for another bite before heading off to another rendezvous. The purpose of all these mysterious conferences was unclear but appeared to be concerned with money and lottery tickets. As a result, it took him 45 minutes to finish the meal.

Finally, he shouted for the bill. When it arrived, he leapt up and moved away to talk with someone outside. The owner stood by the table holding the bill, uncertain what to do with it. When it became apparent that my "host" had deserted me, I reached for my money. As the owner handed me the change, Jamrat returned. "Oh, you paid? O.K., then, let's go," he said, grabbing the plastic bag of fried rice and heading for the street. By now, I knew that I had to stick with him or be left in his dust. As he reached the door, however, he whipped around, banging into me and shouting, "Hey, I promised my friend a Krating Daeng (Red Bull, a caffeine-laden restorative invented by the Thais and favored by long-distance truck drivers). Give the Jek ten more *baht*."

Back in the road, I stutter-stepped in his wake as he barged into one shop and then immediately out again, colliding with me each time until I learned to wait outside until he'd made up his mind. Near the edge of town, the shops melded into homes; Jamrat strode into and out of one after another until we arrived at his parked bus where friends were gathered. Leaving me in their care, he walked into the night, intent on god knows what mission.

Among the raffish men was a broad-faced, grinning, gap-toothed man who leered at two teenaged girls across the street. Turning to me, he asked "What does 'I love you' mean?" Seeing what he was planning, I looked at him knowingly and with a smile, warned him, "Be careful". Without pausing to hear the translation, he shuffled across the street and, to the two shocked girls, said in English, "I love you." Seeing them befuddled, he leaned into them and said in Thai, "It means 'be careful'." They were. They turned and ran. He looked at me in consternation and accusation for steering him wrong.

Before I had a chance to clarify matters, Jamrat was audible somewhere up the dark street and heading our way. Without braking, he grabbed my arm, towing me along at high speed to the house of an elderly, rather distinguished-looking man who was as surprised by the intrusion as I was to be there. Jamrat introduced me, sat me down to converse, jumped up, disappeared out the door. I had just ascertained that the man was a retired school teacher when Jamrat rushed back in the door, said, "Let's go", and we went.

I had no idea where we were heading and Jamrat wasn't one for explanations. He tried twice to hitch rides with motorcyclists but they gave him wide berth. He cursed at their fading taillights but they just laughed. I suggested that we walk since we seemed to be heading for the monastery. Out of the dark appeared the third man. Jamrat tossed him the bag of fried rice as we sped by. Another motorcyclist passed and when Jamrat shouted at him to stop, he did. Without a backward look, Jamrat climbed on and chugged off into the night, presumably in search of the 17-year-old "boom boom" girl, leaving me to find my way back to the monastery.

The abbot was still up when I got back. "Where's Jamrat?" he asked. When I told him he'd gone to see a friend, the abbot apparently guessed the nature of the mission because he said, "well, we won't see him again tonight" and we didn't.

I bade the abbot good night and asked him for the key to the pavilion.

"No, no. You sleep here," he said.

His aide sidled up to whisper, "He was just joking, before." As he laid a thin reed mat on the floor, the aide revealed that he was the abbot's nephew. A large man in his 50s, with the physique of a 40-year-old, he dyed his hair black as most Thais did when the gray began to show. The practice distinguished ethnic Thais from the Chinese-Thais who didn't bother to counter nature, that and the fact that only the Chinese went bald when they aged.

"I look after the *luang paw* because he is getting old," he said.

"How old?"

Nephew turned to his uncle and they did some quick calculations.

"Seventy-six," the abbot announced.

I liked Nephew. Although he had a family down the road, he was devoted to his uncle. He hovered in the background, keenly aware of everything going on around him. Among his tasks, the abbot listened to villagers' problems and counseled them, but he did it with half an ear. His nephew would have done a better job because he had a reassuring manner, concerned without being solicitous. Usurping his uncle's authority would never have crossed his mind, of course. His earthly job was to look after his uncle and his family. Period.

As Nephew labored to string up a mosquito net and lay two bricklike pillows on the mat, he listened to our conversation, never interrupting or even offering a comment. At several points, I would have appreciated his input but protocol forbade my addressing comments to him. The abbot ignored him. Half an hour into a conversation on the impiety of city people, the abbot uncrossed his legs and struggled to his feet. Rushing to support his elbow, Nephew steered him towards bed. The day was over.

Making sure I was settled in, the abbot turned out the light. As I was beginning to doze, his voice floated out of the darkness.

"One more question."

"Yes?"

"How much did the boat cost?"

It had cost 5,500 *baht* ($220) and, although remarkably low considering the materials and workmanship, villagers thought it exorbitantly expensive. Thais are not shy about asking an object's price nor voicing thoughts about how much it should cost. As I descended the Ping, I kept lowering the price and still they said, "Too much. You were cheated." By this point, it had dropped to less than half its original price, which seemed to satisfy most interrogators.

"2,500 *baht*," I replied, and braced myself.

"Too much," said the voice. Reassured, I dropped into a deep sleep.

Dawn seeped into the room about 6 a.m. Something large loomed in the shadows high above the entry door. I am quite near-sighted without my glasses but I knew it was an animal of some sort. I donned my glasses and saw what appeared to be large lizard clinging to the wall.

A three-foot-long monitor lizard had once found its way into my river house. It hid under my bed and for four nights, its sharp claws rasping on the wooden floor woke me. There was enough clutter stored beneath the bed that even with a flashlight, I saw nothing. It was not until he spotted the open front door one afternoon and made a dash for it that I realized what it was. Unfortunately, he was a country monitor and knew nothing of screen doors until he discovered that it wasn't his poor vision that was hazing the garden but a mesh barrier. After one bounce, and seeing me come towards him, he hurled himself at the screen, punched through, and was gone. Hearing the tumult, my landlady's gardeners rushed over to corner and eventually trap it. Since they were from the Northeast, they were accustomed to diets that included grubs, larvae, and reptiles. No doubt my lizard became the main course that evening.

But this beast, barely discernible in the dim light, was even larger. Perhaps five feet long and 18 inches wide, it was definitely a reptile. I lay very still, trying to read its species from its dim contours. My nerves were so taut that I thought I heard it hiss. Listening intently, I traced the sound to Nephew hissing at me from his bed along the wall. He must have been watching me for some time because he said, "Crocodile" and chuckled softly.

Crocodile? How could a crocodile cling to a wall? Just as I understood the foolish tricks the light and my mind had been playing on me, Nephew said, "Dead," and laughed even harder.

Stupid ass, of course-it was stuffed. Shadows can animate any object, but how had I missed it the previous night? And what was it doing here?

"A villager gave it to the previous abbot," Nephew explained. "He caught it in the river. Skinned and ate it. Stuffed the hide."

"Strange gift," I said.

"Yeah, they usually brought them alive and put them in the pond out back."

"I thought it was alive."

"It's o.k., some nights I wake up and forget it's there. Scary. Want some coffee?"

Nephew and I were chatting about his family when the abbot stumbled in, yawning. Nephew told him the story of my fright and the abbot laughed his high-pitched giggles.

"Until 10 years ago there were crocodiles but they were in the marshes away from the banks. Deer, too, and gibbons, everything. When I was a boy and had to walk somewhere in the morning...if we saw piles of elephant dung, we touched them with our feet before moving on."

"Why?"

"Safety. If the dung was cold, we kept walking. If it was warm, we stayed put until we were sure the elephant was gone. They look so big and slow but they can run down a man after a few yards. It's best to be cautious." His expression suggested that the memory of such fearful times was still fresh.

Breakfast arrived. As we were balling rice and dipping it into the various sauces, Nephew said, "We want to take you on a tour." A day with what I took to be a giggling fool did not appeal.

Sensing my hesitation, Nephew said: "We can show you things you've probably not seen before." I piled my gear in a corner and as the abbot adjusted his robe, we walked into the morning light.

Once outside the gate, we turned right down a dirt road. The road became hard and oily black as we entered a small settlement. It also felt tacky, my sandals sticking to it. I bent to inspect it and a faint, somewhat putrid odor struck my nostrils.

"Molasses," said the abbot, chuckling. "Never seen it before?"

"Not on a road."

"Keeps the dust down. The sugar mills just throw it away but it makes a good road surface." More local ingenuity.

Just down the yellow molasses road was a Mercedes-Benz, a strange sight so far from a city. It was over 20 years old and country roads had taken their toll on it. Nephew noted my surprise when he slipped a key into the lock.

"A Bangkok patron gave it to *Luang Paw* to travel around in." Chariots and sedan chairs had once transported abbots; the Benz was a natural extension. It ran counter to my concept of a simple, monastic life but few Thais regarded it as contradictory. Whatever served the abbot, served religion. Despite vows of austerity, many abbots were far richer than their parishioners. Gifts of new BMWs and Benzes were frequently reported in the newspapers, the gift bestowing merit on the donor. It's not my country, I reminded myself.

Several miles down the road, we pulled onto the north-south Paholyothin Highway that had robbed Baan Kaew of its prosperity. It ran dead level through flatlands, all the way to the horizon. To one side, sawtooth limestone ridges rose high in the sky, stegosaurus plates on a dusty plain. As we approached, the abbot said, "That's where we're going: Khao Naw."

Three outcrops thrust 600 vertical feet into the air. One was blasted and pitted, "by a quarry company owned by an influential local man," said the abbot. Quarrying was illegal but it took local authorities three years to get the Mineral Resources Department in Bangkok to shut down his operation. By that time, he had destroyed most of the mountain. He simply moved his machinery to another province whose authorities were more pliable. Exploitation of natural resources for personal gain was widespread in a country where opposition could be bought or silenced. It was a wonder that Thailand had any resources left at all. When we got out to look at the damage, I discovered that the abbot was a bit more complicated than I'd thought.

"Bad, bad," he said picking up a shard, and shaking his head. "How can people do this to a beautiful mountain. What a shame." I was moved by his distress. It was rare to hear someone express concern about environmental damage in Thailand's pell-mell, environment-be-damned race towards economic development. But then, the abbot voiced the reason for his concern.

"This mountain used to be filled with caves," he said, "in constant use as monks' meditation cells." Concern about nature as nature was a Western concept, I mused. In Asia, it was necessary that nature serve man; materially, metaphorically, spiritually. There was no concept of a finite earth, even as it disappeared before their eyes.

After gathering a few stones, we moved on. The two mountains that had escaped the quarrymen's whittling were spectacular. The far slope held a *wat* in whose trees monkeys scampered. Monkeys often inhabited *wat*s but unlike the pious monkeys of Buddhist tales, these were nasty tyrants, not above snatching food from a child's hands and biting anyone who intervened.

"Naughty animals," Nephew said.

"What do they do?"

"Tear the aerials off cars so city people don't come here. That's why the *wat* is so poor. No donors."

"Can't anything be done?"

"No, they're sacred. And to make it worse, the abbot is obliged to feed them, the animals who are breaking his alms bowl."

The *wat*'s abbot hardly looked as if he were suffering. He was extremely fat and perspired heavily as he anointed two motorcycles while their owners stood proudly by. Lost in chanting, he dipped a stubby finger into a sandalwood paste and wrote cabalistic signs and the letters of Buddhism's Pali alphabet on the motorcycles' fenders. When finished, he greeted our abbot and they began a pleasant, casual conversation, their hands folded across their stomachs. Nephew drew me aside.

"They have a nice garden here." I followed him into a grove of trees gnarled by age and coated with limestone dust, souvenirs of the quarry operations. It must have been impossible to breathe while the quarrying was underway, and we were a good 100 yards from the blast site.

A path wound through the garden past statues of modern Thailand's founder King Chulalongkorn, another of a huge crocodile, and one of a grotesque horse. The area around one tree had been penned by a low cement wall but it seemed empty. Then, out of the corner of my eye, I saw the tree bark move. A eight-inch-long mahogany-colored turtle was making his way up the trunk towards the upper branches. His head was an inch-and-a-half across, his sharp beak was curved like a pruning hook; his tail was thick and nearly as long as he. I'd never seen anything like it.

"What is it?" I asked Nephew.

"*Tao Pulu* (Big-headed Turtle)."

"What's it doing on the tree?"

"It climbs them. And it eats animals."

"You mean meat?"

"No, live animals. It isn't a vegetarian like most turtles. It normally lives high in the mountains and hunts shrimp, cockles, and crabs in the streams." A later check of a zoology book bore him out and revealed the species to be one of the oldest reptiles on earth, just one of many oddities resident in a seemingly ordinary *wat*.

The abbots were just finishing their talk when we returned. The fat abbot glanced at his watch, saw that it was not yet noon (after which monks were forbidden to eat) and invited us to have a bite. During lunch, he jocularly teased the skinny abbot about eating so little. Our abbot just giggled. Then the fat abbot turned to me:

"Why don't you take the *Luang Paw* to America with you."

"I'm not sure I could afford it."

"No problem. He can pay for the trip himself."

"How am I going to do that?" our abbot retorted, surprised.

"Sell your *kuti* (meditation cell)," he whooped. The thought of selling something so sacred and of such small value struck everyone as uproariously funny. Thus began a jolly discussion of how much money the abbot might realize from such a sale, everyone knowing that if he even contemplated it he would be disrobed and ejected from the monkhood. Nothing was sacred to these two, however, especially if it made the time pass pleasantly.

After lunch, a young monk suggested that our abbot, his nephew, and I climb the smaller of the two hills. I was feeling the heat and rubber sandals were not the best footwear for ascending a hill. I was hoping the others might decline but Nephew became animated.

"I've not done that since I was a boy!" he enthused. So off we went.

Stairs reached up a few dozen feet but from there on, it was a steep climb on large, loose stones that rolled under our feet. I seemed to be the only one having trouble with sandals. Several times, one would slip off, the toe-thong holding it firmly to the side of my foot and hobbling me until I could remove it, straighten it and put it back on. The Thais seemed to have no problem with their footing. I suspect they glued the sandals to their feet when I wasn't looking.

The final ascent up a sheer face with footholds and handholds left us breathless, but at the summit we were rewarded with a brisk breeze that fluttered the yellow Buddhist flag with its red wheel of law. We'd been there only moments when the abbot's face appeared over the edge and a moment later the rest of his body bounced into view. Not bad for 76 years old. My respect for the man was growing.

We surveyed the landscape. The monsoons and floods which had freshened the plain only two months before seemed like a vague memory. The land was parched, dust devils skittered across bare pastures. One field appeared to shimmer until we spotted a man with a long tree branch, a plastic bag tied to its end. This he flapped at an army of 300 ducks to herd them towards a muddy pond that had somehow survived the scorching sun.

On our descent, the abbot counted the steps and inspected the trees, displaying a child-like but discerning interest in everything he saw. Near the bottom, we turned off the path and walked a narrow ledge to a wide cave mouth. I've never understood the Thai fascination with caves. They're dark, hot, humid, devoid of any natural beauty, and stink of bat shit. Was it a Freudian trip back to the womb? Whatever it was, we ventured inside. A natural stone shelf along the back wall served as an altar; the dim recesses held several tarnished Buddha images. We knelt, lit candles and incense and prayed. The abbot busied himself with repairing a broken poor box. Nephew sat in a perfect lotus before the Buddha images, oblivious to our presence.

In the afternoon, we returned to Khanoralakburi to a *wat* where the abbot had several friends. I commented on the beautifully-decorated crematorium. "It cost two million *baht* ($80,000)," the abbot told me, "all from donations." In a country whose per capita income was low, it seemed far more was being spent on the dead than on the living. But I was carping again.

"Let me show you something," our abbot said. He led me out of the *wat*, down to a landing, and onto a ferry boat. Nephew was nowhere in sight and the abbot didn't seem worried about leaving him behind. A n orange sun, low in the sky, was turning the Ping to molten gold as the ferry chugged across the river, its nose pointing upstream into the current, its diesel engine straining. The ferry was little more than a flat barge without railings. At this hour, it was crowded with students and workers hurrying home. Passengers *waiied* the abbot; he responded with abbotic indifference. At a *wat* near the opposite landing, an obese abbot sat on a wooden porch surrounded by a dozen meowing cats. Seeming not to have a care in the world, he was jolly and his humor was self-deprecating.

"I'm a bad monk," confessed the fat abbot.

"Bad?"

"Yes. I don't go to Bangkok like the rest of them to convince rich patrons to contribute to constructing more wat buildings. Bad monk, bad monk. This is a good monk," he said, pointing to our abbot. I'd just heard a similar conversation at the cross-river *wat*. Like politicians dipping pork from the barrel for local constituents, abbots were considered effective if they could persuade Bangkok patrons to add new buildings to the wat; crematoria, funeral pavilions, *kuti*, ordination halls, libraries, meeting rooms, schools, belltowers, many serving no purpose whatever. The fat monk's courtyard was dotted with half-completed structures. Down the road, another *wat* was filled with the same skeletal buildings, and another beyond that. It seemed so extravagant but was justified as "making merit for the donor" and was condoned. Little merit was to be accrued from public welfare or education projects. It seemed a corruption of Buddhism's basic values, promoted by the abbots and blindly adhered to by the laity.

Nephew had driven over a distant bridge and was waiting at the ferry slip when we banged into the landing. By the time we arrived home, it was too late to leave so I settled in for the evening. Nephew had put some of the morning's alms in one of the many half-dozen donated refrigerators that hummed along one wall. While the abbot read, we ate, then turned in. I slept to the sounds of Nephew's snores and the abbot's labored breathing.

The crocodile regarded me balefully through yellow slit eyes. I was eager to get away but Nephew was already preparing coffee.

"*Luang paw* wants to take you on a tour," said Nephew.

Oh-oh. Yesterday had been fun but I was already mentally setting paddle in water, synching with the current. Still, I didn't want to insult a man about whom my feelings had substantially changed as I had gotten to know him. My face must have betrayed conflicting emotions.

"Just around the wat," Nephew said. "He wants to show you the buildings."

"Oh, fine. Where is he?"

As if on cue, the abbot appeared, yawning. He said little as he ate but perked up when Nephew reminded him of the tour.

"Oh, good, good," he said, and without finishing his breakfast, headed for the door. As he passed a table, he picked up a massive bunch of keys, scores of them clinking dully. No wonder the boy sent to fetch a key had taken so long; there were enough for a small town.

Once we began our tour, I understood why: the *wat* was a small town. We walked by building after building, each standing empty. The commentary was hardly spiritual.

"Look at the dragons and Chinese motifs on this shrine," he said.

The craftsmanship was excellent and I told him so.

"The artist wanted 35,000 *baht* for the job. I knocked him down to 30,000 *baht*," he said proudly.

"See this crematorium," he said as we rounded a corner. "Did you see one at yesterday's wats that can compete with it?"

With each structure, the emphasis was not on its beauty or utility but its role in some sort of weird contest with other abbots, the size or elaborateness of a building signifying one's favor with rich patrons. Buddha would have wept to see it. My recently-gained respect for the man was now rapidly eroding. In the main hall holding an enormous bronze Buddha, I noted the irony of a locked iron strongbox with a slot in the top through which parishioners could drop coins. It stood inside a cage of iron bars bound with four locks to deter thieves.

But the tour was far from over. The abbot opened the door of every building and every room including the closets. At one bathroom he proudly flushed each of the six toilets. I thought the trip would never end. What he thought he was showing me was a lifetime of achievement. What I saw was room after empty room strewn with cobwebs and dust.

One large building was used to house visitors who came for an annual gathering at the *wat*.

"How long are they here," I asked.

"About three weeks."

"And how is the building used the rest of the year?"

"It isn't."

I knew I was being judgmental but it all seemed such a waste of money. I kept thinking of the ramshackle buildings in the town and of how donor money could have built a recreation hall for the children, a reading room, a subscription to a daily newspaper which all could read.

Along the compound's eastern wall, a large two-story building was under construction. An enormous hall occupied the ground floor with perhaps a dozen rooms upstairs.

"This is going to be a school for monks," he said, beaming.

"How many monks do you have?"

"Five."

It was an evil thought but I couldn't resist.

"Why couldn't you teach the monks in the empty building that is only used three weeks a year. It would save having to construct another building."

His eyes challenged my rationality. It was clear that my question had no meaning for him.

"But...a monks' school is a monks' school. A meeting hall is a meeting hall. No, no, not possible." Case closed. I changed the subject.

"How many monks used to live here?" I asked.

He became solemn.

"Lots. Twenty. There were 30 when I ordained."

"What happened to them all?"

"They died. Or moved to other wats."

He walked to a window and struggled with a rusted latch before the shutters flew open to reveal a splendid view of the rooftops, town, and river.

"This used to be a rich town," he said, his voice strangely quiet. "Twenty years ago, the river was so full of boats, you wouldn't have been able to paddle in a straight line through them."

"What happened?"

"Everybody left," he said, as if 20 years later, it still hadn't sunk in that the small town had been abandoned. "The government built the highway and people with money moved to live there. It was the poor people who stayed behind because they couldn't afford to move."

"So the town was no longer big enough to feed the monks?"

"Yes. This used to be an important *wat*. When I was young, eminent abbots came from Bangkok to speak. People came from all around to hear them. When the town died, so did the wat. That's why I have to get money from people in Bangkok who still remember Wat Baan Kaew. There isn't enough local money to build even a *kuti*."

So all the construction was to preserve an illusion. Like a monarch in an enormous castle surveying a ruined realm emptied of its subjects by more affluent kingdoms, the abbot sought to maintain a semblance of the old days. It was a *wat* filled with ghosts and presided over by a dotty old man trying to revivify it. The buildings were birdhouses. Build enough of them and the birds would come. But history, like the river, had bypassed Baan Kaew, ignoring it on its journey elsewhere. Like the molasses-coated road, it was stuck in place forever, or until it crumbled away and fell into the river. The abbot was making the last stand against its demise. It still seemed a waste but now it made better sense to me.

Inelegant Behavior

Chak Mae Naam Thang Haa
(Draw water from five rivers)
Attempt to convince someone
by overwhelming them with data

The leisurely morning was marked by striking changes in the land-scape. Tall bamboo shaded the banks, palm trees marched in orderly rows, and perfume burst from velvety white flowers dotting thick green bushes. Even the kingfisher had changed. In the Golden Triangle, blue was his dominant color but as I moved south, his feathers had darkened until here, 500 miles from the headwaters, he wore an indigo coat, an orange belly, white wingtips and a red beak–gorgeous, metallic hues that flashed as he darted across the sunlit river or perched on logs amidst magenta water lilies.

In the shallows, women pushed wicker baskets, bulldozer blades whose toothed edges dislodged tiny cockles. Individually, the shellfish were too small to bother about but the river provided them in sufficient volume to feed a family. It was a quiet reminder of the lengths to which poor farmers would go to gain a day's meal. I silently rejoiced that I would never know that degree of hunger.

For two days, red shrines had begun appearing along the banks, indicating the presence of Chinese-Thai villagers. Near one, I tied the boat to a landing, climbed the stairs and found myself in a virtual replica of settlements I'd seen in China. Facing the river was a two-story wooden building, its ground floor serving as a general store. The shopkeeper poured me a glass of green tea and explained how his grandfather had founded the store.

"Seventy years ago, Chinese merchants in Bangkok began looking upcountry for new markets. Since there were few roads into the interior, the easiest way into the provinces was by boat. They stocked two-tier 'storeboats' with foods and sundries and sent them upriver to sell door-to-door."

These floating stores kept to a strict schedule so customers knew which day they would call. Small boats traveled for 10 days before returning to their home base to replenish stocks. Larger boats could cruise for 30 days.

"My grandfather started out as a storeboat owner but when villagers demanded more frequent access to goods, he built this shop. Until they disappeared, the storeboats supplied him with items."

"What happened to them?"

"Trucks moved faster than boats. By the 1970s, the storeboats were gone. Too bad; I miss them. Their arrival days were almost like festivals. We'd hear the horn far down river and the town would come to life for a few hours. It kept us in touch with the outside world."

In the 1970s, I'd watched the double-decker boats pass my riverside porch, and had even ridden one 90 miles upriver to Ang Thong. Until he mentioned it, I'd not even noticed they were gone, one more casualty of the thirst for speed and convenience. I'd been lucky to arrive in Thailand before an era ended. When he was called away by a customer, I took my leave, musing that much of what I was seeing would also soon be gone.

The river broadened, the sandbars reappeared. On one, schoolboys kicked a soccer ball between two goals marked by their piled shirts. There were few arguments about out-of-bounds balls: if the ball was wet, it had gone out of bounds. From time to time, a boy would break from the field, leap into the water and swim for a while before returning to his position. Often, the entire team would call a time-out to turn cartwheels in the shallows.

I was tempted to join them but dead dogs were appearing off my bow again and their stench hinted of vermin and contagions. In the 1860s, King Mongkut had issued an edict titled (in his typically whimsical fashion), "On the Inelegant Practice of Throwing Dead Animals into the Rivers and Waterways." It outlined in considerable detail why the practice was unsanitary and stated that henceforth, anyone caught doing it would be paraded through the streets as a public nuisance. Nearly 130 years later, dead animals were still thrown into rivers and canals, polluting them and detracting from their charm. The soccer players seemed healthy but I put it down to resilient youth.

I had hoped to hit Khao Liao by nightfall. That would leave me half a day to reach Nakhon Sawan where the waters of the Ping and Nan co-mingled to form the Chao Phya which would carry me to the sea. When, by late afternoon, it was clear I wouldn't make it I began looking for shelter. Sprawled along the left bank was a pretty village. I hailed a man setting a fish trap.

"Excuse me. Can you direct me to the headman's house?"

"Why?" he asked.

I explained the journey and my need for a place to stay.

"Stay with me. I'm the assistant headman."

On the way home, Sanae, 31, talked enthusiastically about his family and when I stepped across the threshold, I saw why. He and his very pretty wife, Duangporn, were the parents of two lively children, and the family's warmth and hospitality permeated their small house. "You stay here," he said, spreading his arms wide and adding, "everything's free," a phrase he would repeat several times.

The single room was part of a long, two-story clapboard rowhouse, mirrored by a twin across the town's dusty main street. Sanae's pride was a hyperactive five-year-old son, Chai, who lived with relatives in Nakhon Sawan five days a week while he attended kindergarten. His two-year-old daughter, Prinya, was a pair of bright eyes peering through a mop of unruly hair. Willful and moody, she never got over her fear of me, despite my best efforts. Even my handing her a balloon sent her panicking into her laughing mother's arms.

I wanted to write my journals but Chai had a thousand questions and a predilection to paw through everything I owned. Only stern rebukes from his mother dissuaded him and, even then, only temporarily. His sister used him as a proxy. "What's that?" she'd ask him quietly from her corner refuge. He'd plunge into my bag and detail everything he encountered. I was having fun and wanted nothing more than to sit and savor it, but it was not to be.

Among the many visitors was an older man named Sathit. Slender, bespectacled, and intense, his smarmy smile and oleaginous manner suggested trouble.

"I'm the town doctor," he announced, "for all these people," he added, his arm sweeping proprietarily over the assemblage peering through the doorway. I felt I was being asked to applaud, so I did.

"Good for you," I said. "Where did you study?"

"Oh, not one of those doctors," he replied. "No, no, not them."

"There's another kind?" I asked, perplexed.

"Yes," he said, brightly. "Can you guess what kind?"

Duangporn eavesdropped as she worked. Her knitted brows and pursed mouth suggested that the "doctor" didn't enjoy universal acclaim.

"No," I said blandly. "What kind of doctor are you?"

"I'm like the barefoot doctors in China," he said proudly. "I cure people with herbal remedies." It sounded laudable enough.

"Do you want to see my office?" he asked.

I demurred but he was insistent. "It will only take a few minutes," he said. Sanae had gone out on business and Duangporn said that it would be an hour until dinner so I accompanied him down the street. It was an odd procession, the doctor leading me like a prize stallion for all to admire.

At the top of a long flight of stairs was a small wooden consultation room. The only furniture was a desk; behind it, a window opened onto the river. The room lacked interior walls so one saw the building's 2x4 framing and the backsides of the vertical boards covering the exterior. The 2x4s along one wall served as shelves for bottles of odd concoctions that didn't resemble anything compounded by an apothecary or even an herbal doctor'. They bore labels for patent medicines with strange titles and even stranger illustrations.

It was the other three walls that were disconcerting. Here and there, medical posters issued by the district health officer, stressed the importance of prenatal care, warned against drinking unsafe water, detailed with graphic illustrations the perils of untreated venereal diseases, and explained the benefits of sound nutrition. They were far outnumbered, however, by dozens of large pin-ups of naked women, *farang* and Thai, in suggestive poses. They were obviously not intended as aids to anatomical study, and formed a gallery so erotic it was hard to imagine a female patient feeling comfortable.

But he hadn't brought me here to comment on his professional decorum or decor. Leading me through a doorway into pitch blackness, he walked to the opposite wall and threw open the shutters to reveal a large room bare except for a folding chair and a mattress.

"Big, yes?" he asked.

"Yes, big."

"Bigger than where you are now," he said. "A lot bigger."

"I suppose so."

"And look here," he said, leading me to the window and pointing down at the water. "See, the river flows right by the house."

"Yes, I can see that."

"It's easy to watch a moored boat from here," he said.

"Yessss, it is," I said, sensing where the conversation was leading.

"And I could watch it for you."

To my surprise, he bounded across the room towards the door.

"You stay here and I'll bring your belongings back."

"Wait, I'm happy at Sanae's house."

"But I have so much more room."

"Yes, but he asked me first and I accepted."

"I'll explain it to him," he said, and started down the stairs.

I was right behind him as we emerged onto the street. "There's nothing to explain," I said firmly. "I appreciate your hospitality but I'm staying where I am."

He stared at me with wild eyes.

"Why don't I come back later to talk with you?" I offered, but he didn't reply. This was getting creepy, and I wondered briefly if he was "on" one of his own medications. It was useless to argue with him–my causing him to lose face would be a greater affront than his pushiness–so I set off for Sanae's house. Glancing back, I saw him in the middle of the street, crestfallen. Another situation I couldn't win. With relief I re-entered Sanae's home to find a smiling Duangporn.

"Did you enjoy your talk with the doctor?" She asked it sweetly but muted malice infused her words.

"It was very...interesting," I replied. I wanted to ask her how he was regarded in the village but putting her on the spot would have been a breach of etiquette. Instead, I asked her about her family's farm, although it was a question one would normally direct to a husband.

"He has 47 *rai* (19 acres), 20 *rai* in rice and 27 in sugar cane," she said. It was a lot of land for a small family and apparently it provided them a good living. Although the revenues would be utilized by the entire family, she was careful to say it was her husband's land. Only recently had the laws been changed to allow married women to own property. In the past, single women had been legally entitled to conduct business, and buy and sell property but once they married, they ceded these rights to their husbands. They could not even sign a document without his counter signature. I had friends in Bangkok who had divorced so the wives could do business. They continued to live together and raise their children but officially they were no longer married. In rural areas, such an arrangement would have been unthinkable.

On Sanae's return we dined on fish curry, greens, eggs, and rice. Prinya alternated between silence and temper tantrums while Chai leapt up between bites to race in and out of the house on his bicycle, a Jamrat in the making.

After dinner, we sat at a low table in front of the house, enjoying the night air. Like Baan Kaew, time had bypassed Hua Dong but rather than killing it, it had bestowed upon it a pleasant sleepiness. Families strolled, exchanging pleasantries with their neighbors while the crickets chirped in the trees.

The couple demonstrated a sophistication that suggested familiarity with a wider world. In every village, there were always a few men whose gaze seemed directed towards a more distant horizon. Something about the gravity of their bearing told me they had worked in the Middle East, usually in construction.

"Have you been abroad?" I asked Sanae.

"*Sa-oo* (Saudi Arabia)," he replied. "Two years. Good money."

"And your wife?"

"No," he laughed, but Duangporn immediately jumped in.

"I know about the United States because I have relatives living there. I have more there and in Bangkok than in Hua Dong." she said.

Duangporn was pretty and I was willing to bet that some of her American relatives had arrived in the U.S. as wives of GIs or workers. Village women normally did not meet Americans except around U.S. military bases or in Bangkok. There, they met and married, and when the man's tour of duty ended, they accompanied him back to America. Once the language and cultural differences had been ironed out, the marriages were generally successful. Most wives were family-oriented and hard-working, qualities which endeared them to American in-laws who might have had some initial reservations about their son's marrying an exotic jungle flower from the back pages of the atlas.

As we talked, promenaders stopped to talk. One woman offered me som-tam the fiery Northeastern salad made with slivers of raw papaya, dried shrimp, tomatoes, marinated waterbugs, and chilies. It was very spicy and I was pleased to see others sucking in their cheeks, waving a hand before their faces, laughing, and wiping tears from their eyes. Another woman offered to make me a non-spicy version but I waved her away with, "If it isn't spicy, it isn't *som-tam*," to which everyone agreed although my mouth was aflame.

The evening's entertainment was a *likay* performance at yet another funeral, a woman well-respected in the village. Sanae put me on his small motorbike and then loaded Chai onto my lap and Prinya on his, and we chugged off to the *wat*. It was a lovely setting, the *wat* bathed in half-moon light that, poring through the tall palm trees cast fern-like shadows on the hard earth.

While the *likay* performers in their spangled costumes danced and sang, Sanae's small son performed his own dance, humming to himself, oblivious to all. As he twirled, he was watched closely by an adoring five-year-old girl sitting ahead of him. The first time she turned around to look at him, I nearly gasped. With her shining black hair cropped in bangs and her luminous eyes and tiny features set in a pale complexion, she was stunning. But she had eyes only for Chai, turning around frequently to bathe him in her luminous gaze. Absorbed in his own antics, he didn't at first notice her. When he did, the effect was electric. He stopped in mid-note and a look of utter panic crossed his face. He snuggled into his father's arms, squirming and insisting that they go home. Sanae was concentrating on the stage and couldn't understand why his son wanted to leave. It wasn't until the little girl's mother, also unaware of what was happening, pulled her away, that Chai calmed down. He regained his exuberance when his 13-year-old cousin appeared with delicious crispy rice cakes. Normally a hands-width in diameter, these were the circumference of a basketball–the largest I'd ever seen–and were still warm from roasting.

When Prinya began to nod Sanae suggested that we head home. I had no objection since my eardrums were beginning to disintegrate from the amplified din. At home, Duangporn had hung a mosquito net over the floor pad and placed an electric fan nearby, a welcome respite on a stifling night. Once again, I marveled at the hospitality of people who had few possessions but were willing to share them with a stranger.

In the morning, Duangporn took her son on his weekly 12-mile rickety *songtaew* ride to Nakhon Sawan. Sanae had left at dawn for his fields so when Duangporn's *songtaew* pulled away, I readied the boat and set off. It was a chilly but magical morning with a light following wind fluttering the bamboo leaves. Despite all my years in the tropics, I was still an Oregon boy in heart and thermostat, thriving on cold weather and wilting in heat.

At noon, I dined on pickled cabbage, jerky, and lychee and prepared to leave the Ping and paddle triumphantly into the Chao Phya at Nakhon Sawan. But I must have misread the map because the afternoon crawled on and I seemed nowhere near it.

Finally, as the sun was dropping, I rounded a bend and the land–like a Japanese *shoji* wall–slid sideways to reveal an ocean: the Chao Phya! Energized, I pushed on, anticipation rising with each stroke. But as I neared it, my heart sank. Instead of a shining city, I was greeted by an eyesore of major proportions. Concrete slabs walled off the river from the city and a good thing too; had citizens ventured beyond it they would have seen what I saw: raw sewage pouring through concrete culverts onto banks strewn with rubbish. Perhaps my expectations were high, maybe I'd been in rural areas too long, but my return to a large metropolis revulsed me.

The Dynastic Chronicles for A.D. 1788 had described a Thai victory here, adding that "the slain Burmese were so thick in the river that for days afterward, the water was undrinkable." Dead Burmese had been replaced by rotting dogs and the effluvia of an uncaring city. I took the pollution as a personal affront, illogically, of course. Thais have always regarded rivers as garbage disposals. Such was tolerable as long as populations were small, but towns had grown and their biodegradable waste had been replaced by synthetic materials which resisted decomposition. I had grown weary of rationalizing this type of behavior; it was filthy and piggish, whichever way you looked at it. I pulled for shore. Even King

Mongkut would have gagged.

As I tied up and picked my way gingerly through the trash to the base of the seawall, louts leaning on the parapet, conferred derisively with each other. I caught drifts of *"farang mai luu luang"* (*farangs* don't know anything) and the usual *"farang khii nok"* (foreign bird shit, a vulgar play on the Thai word for a variety of guava) but when I addressed them quietly in Thai, they became flustered. Suddenly eager to answer my questions, they told me a hotel lay three stairways farther down. While part of me wanted to bypass the town altogether and find a downstream village I needed supplies. I paddled father on and tied up next to a long boat shaded by a canopy.

"Where are you going?" a wheezy voice asked.

I traced it to a skeletal man lounging in the boat, clad only in a *pakoma*.

"I'm looking for a place to leave the boat for the night."

A lazy arm pointed back upriver.

"See that barge. The one with the Thai flag?"

"Yeah."

"Leave it there. They'll look after it."

"Thanks."

Five minutes of paddling against the current put me at the barge's foredeck where an elderly woman was washing clothes. She was startled to see me inches from her face and immediately called to her husband who shuffled up from the depths of the hull, a big smile wreathing his face.

"Look, mother, a *farang* has come to visit us,"

I told them what I wanted and assured them that I would pay.

"Sure, sure," said the old man. "Tie it up to the stern. We'll watch it. Don't worry about paying. We're not going anywhere. Tell us where you've been." And so we sat as they asked me intelligent questions that suggested long association with the river. They seemed pleased to find a foreigner who shared their love. As we sat cross-legged on the front deck, the old man would occasionally reach over to pat me on the thigh, saying "good, good."

I revered old people. Schooled in pragmatism, they knew how to do things. This couple had earned their livelihoods when the river was still the center of commerce. Like the river, they had been left behind.

"We used to carry supplies up the Nan River and rice back down," he said. "That was a long time ago. I finally paid for this boat when I was 30. That was..." He ran his fingers through his hair, trying to recall what year it might have been. He looked imploringly at his wife but she was wringing out clothes with barely any life in them "...a long time ago," he concluded.

"So you've lived on this boat all the time?"

"We raised our family here," his wife said.

"Where are they now?"

"Bangkok," the old man said. "There was nothing for them here so they left to find work in the city."

"What do you do now?"

"Not much," he replied. "The boat's old and falling apart. So are we," he chuckled, his wife's merry laughter echoing his. "Nobody wants us any more. There's no work for us."

"So how do you support yourselves?"

"She makes *khanoms* (sweets) and sells them in the market."

The wife pointed to a charcoal stove at the far side of the deck. The aroma of roasted coconut drifted across.

"I catch fish," the man said. "There's a lot of garbage but a few fish still come to visit, and I invite them to stay," he chortled. "We get by." I'd always been amazed by how little it took for people to survive. A roof for the night, a few clothes, and a few *baht* each day seemed to keep them going. Many had no ambitions and the few *baht* they accumulated they donated to the *wat*.

Talking with them cheered me considerably but I couldn't spend the night on the barge so I set off to find the hotel and buy supplies. I bounced as I walked the narrow, trampoline plank connecting the barge with the shore and slogged across the beach to the stairway.

The interface between land and water reveals much about the way Thais view their river. In upcountry areas, bamboo or single-plank landings set at water level suggest intimate attachment to the river, that humans actually descend into it and mingle with its waters. Larger rural towns generally have a wooden ramp leading from the shore to a floating platform. The platform's wooden deck sits two feet above water and rests atop bundles of bamboo that fishermen use as perches and children employ as diving platforms.

In large, downriver towns, the wooden decks are replaced by concrete platforms resting on steel tank pontoons and standing three feet above the water. On them, produce is unloaded from boats, passengers board ferries. By raising one so high above the water, the platform essentially cuts one off from all contact with the river. Here, in Nakhon Sawan, the Chao Phya had been walled off entirely. Anyone walking the quay street would not have known that a river lay beyond the high concrete parapet.

The river's exclusion from city life became apparent when I stepped into the street and entered a world utterly unrelated to the one I had just left. Goods that were once delivered by boats were now unloaded from ten-wheeled trucks belching clouds of filthy diesel fumes; young men ran the goods to shops on clattering trolleys. Ironically, although Nakhon Sawan originally owed its prosperity to the river, even the fish sold in its markets were trucked in from elsewhere. I walked a corridor of large umbrellas beneath which vendors sold live fish thrashing in wide metal pans, tropical fruits, plastic buckets in garish oranges and blues, and scores of other products. It was less the romantic bazaar of yesteryear than a cauldron of chaos. Fish scent hung in the air, vendors barked their wares, cleavers chopped, trucks farted, handcarts clanged in collision. Grime adhesed to every surface, water blended with discarded vegetable waste to coat the sidewalk in a slimy paste.

The biggest shock came when I stepped out of the market and into the city itself. It was singularly ugly, a mass of flat, featureless, three-story shophouses, their windows covered in iron grills to deter burglars, a concrete prison block whose severe geometry of grids and cubes was at variance with Nature's soft curves and hues. Apparently I wasn't the only one affected by its ugliness because everyone I met wore sour expressions. I wanted to flee the moment my business was done.

It was cheering to recall that while the Chao Phya's relegation to inferiority seemed complete, each September and October, the river reasserted its ancient supremacy, teaming with the monsoon rains to inundate the streets and bring traffic to a standstill. In bad flood years, citizens abandoned their cars and dusted off their boats, paddling through the streets on their daily rounds. The river would rule for two months until it was betrayed by the skies. As the annual rains ceased, the floodwaters would retreat, receding street by street, slinking over the seawall to the bottom of the stairways, then shrinking past the foreshore to its original channel to remain quiescent and orderly until the following year.

I slipped and slid along the quay street, stopping to check several waterfront hotels, all of which proved to be grotty and cockroach-infested. At the end of the wharf was the Wang Mai (New Palace) Hotel neither new nor palatial, but passable. The reception desk sat behind the food-cluttered tables of a busy restaurant. Open to the street, it was inhabited by loiterers with nothing better to do than comment sourly on the passing scene and their lousy lot in life. Upstairs wasn't much better.

The hallway was barren, its walls covered in a thin coat of moldy paint. A lazy fan panted on a cobwebbed ceiling and the terrazzo floor was begrimed by years of sandaled feet dragging in the street dirt, squashed cigarette butts, and bloody blotches of betel juice which had missed the spittoons. Many rooms seemed permanently inhabited by older men. They huddled under the fans in their shorts and sleeveless undershirts or bare chests and little pot bellies, haranguing each other in loud voices or listening to loud radios. I retreated to the streets, eventually coming across a post office.

The boat had begun to feel heavy again and I felt impelled to discard non-essentials. The definition of "essentials" changes depending on how far the traveler is into his journey. I usually began a trip by trying to carry the entire city, ready for any contingency. By stages, I'd pare away gear until I could experience my environment directly, un-insulated from it. The postmaster told me it would cost three *baht* (12 cents) per pound to send items to Bangkok. At the hotel, I sorted gear until I had a pile 18 pounds high.

After packing and posting it, I paused for coffee at a stall overlooking a foreshore running 40 yards to the river. From there, it was 100 yards across the Ping to a piece of land shaved to a pencil-point by the conjoining of the Ping and Nan. Six years later, almost to the day, I would return here and find the river so depleted of water that I would trudge 120 yards across the beach before reaching the Ping, 50 yards wide and shallow enough to walk across with barely a wetting.

After dining on beef curry in an alley restaurant, I walked empty streets back to the "New Palace." In the hallway, I was hailed by a tired whore who typified the city she inhabited. My room was no better. Next door, a drunken man brayed in a grating voice at a prostitute, complaining that he'd paid for two hours and wanted a second run. I felt sorry for the woman who had to endure his crassness.

Cities could be cesspools, filled with people less than they might be. As an escape from the dreariness, I read *The Nation*, then doused the light and slept.

The Drowned House

Plaa Yai Kin Plaa Lek
(A big fish eats the small fish)
The strong oppress the weak

At dawn I was awakened by a ruckus outside my door. Heavy boots were clumping down the hallway and fists were banging on one door after another. There were shouts and the sound of running feet, and my first thought was that a fire had broken out. I looked around the room to see what I could gather up quickly to make my escape.

Then it was my door's turn to be shaken in its jamb. As I opened it, four armed cops burst in, shining bright flashlights at me and everything in the room. A stocky sergeant in his early 40s, strode up to me and demanded, in English, "What your name?"

"Why do you want to know?" I replied in Thai.

He seemed taken aback at hearing me speak Thai. The others stopped their search and watched me warily. The sergeant's manner softened and he asked, in Thai, "What work do you do?"

One of the cops was standing on my copy of *The Nation*.

"I'm a newspaper reporter."

That threw him. "Sorry, sorry," he said.

With all the whores' customers traipsing in and out, I hadn't gotten much sleep. That and my irritation at the disturbance combined to push me further than it was prudent to go. But I didn't care.

"What's going on?" I pressed him. "Why are you disturbing *farang*s at this hour."

"It's, uh, the Year of the Tourist," he said, hesitantly.

"Last year was the Year of the Tourist. You're two months late."

"We're just trying to protect tourists," he insisted.

"By searching their rooms at 6 a.m.?"

"Sorry, sorry," he repeated, backing out of the room. "Go back to sleep."

Fat chance. I needed a cup of something. There was no hot water and, although the ceiling fan laboriously churning the air had left me with a head cold, I showered under a cold tap. By the time I emerged from my room, everything had calmed down. No one seemed perturbed so it must have been a common occurrence. I stumbled downstairs and saw through the restaurant's open front that the morning was overcast with hints of fog and deliciously cool air. The proprietor was lounging behind his wooden desk.

"What were the cops looking for," I asked crossly.

"Money," he said wryly. I smiled and he added: "Who knows? Drugs, gamblers, gunmen, anybody who's guilty of something and has a bit of money."

I sat at a wooden table near the entrance as the metal accordion walls were pulled aside, screeching like nails on a chalkboard. Nursing a cup of Thai coffee, I settled in to write. Nearby, a group of elderly Chinese men, obviously friends for a lifetime, were kibitzing, laughing and calling out to passing pals to join them. I'd witnessed the scene innumerable times in Bangkok but something about this one was different. It took me a moment to realize they were speaking Thai, not the Tae-chiew dialect used by most Chinese immigrants. They had probably been born and grown old in Thailand, allegiances to the old country severed in all but observance of a few vestiges of their original culture. They were discussing the situation on the border with Laos, making observations, passing judgments, jeering at a friend's contrarian views with a disgusted "*aeooww.*" When a friend drove up and had trouble backing into a parking space, they shouted advice and roundly abused him, laughing all the time. Their infectious cheer took the edges off the town's dour geometry.

Sipping the dregs, I hefted my bags, pleased with the reduced weight, and threaded my way through the market to find a gift for the barge couple. They would, out of courtesy, refuse to accept money, the gift they could best use, but fruit was always welcome in Thailand. Tangerines were in season so I bought four pounds and began walking towards the seawall. A scrawny, gap-toothed man wearing a huge grin blocked my path. It took me a moment to recognize him as Jamrat's friend who had scandalized the teenaged girls in Baan Kaew.

"Hello," I said. "What are you doing here?"

"Looking for work," he said. "Do you have anything for me to do?"

"Can you paddle?" I joked.

"Sure," he said, eagerly, "how much?"

"Oh, sorry, bad luck. I only have one paddle."

His face fell. "Oh well, I'm too old anyway."

I gave him 10 *baht* for breakfast.

He brightened immediately. "You want to go to a brothel?"

"It's 9 a.m.!"

"Yeah, cheap."

"No thanks."

"I can get you a special price." I changed the subject. "How's Jamrat?"

"He's here somewhere," he said, looking around. Uh-oh, if I met him, I'd never get out of here. "I'll find him," he offered.

"O.K., you do that but I have to be on my way," I said hastening for the stairway. "Good luck in finding a job."

"I'm sure he's nearby," he said, still scanning the crowded market.

Before walking the gangplank, I hailed the couple and the old man called from the interior, his voice muffled by the hull. I stepped on board and he and his wife emerged, their feet blackened by bilge.

"Do you have a problem?" I asked.

He sighed. "The caulking is old. We're sinking." I would have expected an anguished cry but instead he laughed uproariously.

"Can you get it recaulked?" I asked.

"Too expensive," he said without a trace of complaint.

"But you'll lose the boat."

"No, we'll keep bailing it out until the monsoon arrives."

"And then?"

"We'll ride the river up the bank and tie up. When the water drops, the boat will come down on land. The hull will rot faster but we're not going to need it much longer anyway; we're getting too old to walk the gangway." His wife smiled in affirmation.

I produced the tangerines and they were delighted.

"Oh, good, good," he said. "These last a long time if we keep them in the cool hull. Oh good."

Tangerines cost under 20 cents a pound but the way the couple was exulting, one would think they were coated with fine Belgian chocolate. My friends must have been abysmally poor, yet they were un remittingly generous.

"Why don't you take a few with you," she said. "To eat along the way."

"Thank you, but I have too much gear already."

We continued to talk as I loaded the boat. Bidding them goodbye, I pushed away. The current grasped my boat in its hand and pulled me away from Nakhon Sawan. I paddled for the middle of the Chao Phya where its tributaries joined. As I moved away from shore, I heard a bullhorn voice from atop the seawall. "Hey, *farang!*"

It could only have one owner. Quickly scanning the tiny objects along the parapet, I saw a stocky body and a thick arm waving to me. I could just make out the gap-toothed man grinning beside him.

"We go boom boom! O.K.?"

I waved and kept paddling.

It seemed strange after all these weeks to say goodbye to the Ping. I felt a moment of nostalgia for attending its birth at the headwaters and its death and absorption into a larger entity here. It was a reluctant melding. The rivers ran side by side for more than a mile, the brown Nan on the left and the green Ping to the right. The line dividing them was so distinct I could have run a knife along it. Finally, in a curling of whirlpools, the two began to blend, the brown obliterating forever any hint of the pure green Ping's former existence. From here, they truly flowed as the Chao Phya River.

"Chao Phya" is a royal title but scholars disagreed on why it had been applied to a river. Foreign maps of the 19th century refer to it as "*Menam,*" the Thai word for "river" which translated literally as "Mother of Waters." Although foreign cartographers misnamed it, their designation demonstrated recognition of its vital contribution to Thailand's growth.

The nation's most important waterway, it has been the principal stage for its historic, economic and cultural development. On this north-south royal road I now traveled, not in royal robes, but in beggar's rags.

Downriver from Nakhon Sawan, modern Thailand collided with its past. On the left bank, a concrete seawall rose 45 feet above the water, an iron ladder leading to the top. Curious, I tied the boat to the bottom rung and climbed to a wide expanse of concrete, huge warehouses, and no sign of life. Rounding the corner of one building, I surprised a watchman. Scowling, he looked to the main gates before addressing me.

"The gates are locked. How did you get in here," he demanded.

"From the river." He did the usual double take and then demanded that we look. As had happened so many times before when looking down on the bobbing boat, his expression changed.

"You came over from Nakhon Sawan?"

I savored these moments because I knew what would happen next.

"No," I replied. "I came down the Ping from Chiang Mai."

"You paddled all the way from Chiang Mai?" he asked.

"Yes."

"How many days?"

Having lost track, I quickly calculated.

"Forty days."

"Forty? Wow!"

Now we could talk. He told me the wharf was part of a gigantic scheme to return the river to its former role as goods transporter. Large barges would carry bulk cargoes–rice and gypsum–up and down the river relieving the overtaxed highway system of some of its burden. It was refreshing to see the river regaining a portion of its former importance.

"How far upriver will they go?" I asked.

"They're building a small port at Taphan Hin [about 25 miles up the Nan River], and another on the Ping."

Alas, the project, funded by the World Bank, would founder for lack of water to permit upstream navigation. Ironically, this space would be rented to a trucking company to use as a transfer terminal, the facility catering to the very industry it was meant to supplant. I paddled on.

A short way downstream, along the right bank, wooden frames penned scores of logs into rafts. Barefoot men walked along them, wielding branding hammers to imprint the owner's name into their butt ends.

It was a scene from my childhood. My father had been a log scaler on Northwest rivers, pacing along the logs to measure their length, thickness, and defects to determine the usable board feet and, thereby, their sale value. Ten thousand miles away and 20 years later, these men were doing the same. I tied up the boat and walked the raft with them. They were pleased to hear that even in a country they perceived as rich, logging was essentially the same.

Their operation was a remnant of huge 19th-century timber operations. Having cut most of the forests in Burma, British loggers looking for new timber concessions found rich stands of teak and other quality woods in northern Thailand. Elephants hauled the enormous trees to the banks of the Ping, Wang, Yom, and Nan Rivers where the current carried them downstream. Logjams and low water often stranded the logs until monsoon rains loosened them, sending them farther on their journey. A tree could take five years to reach the marshaling points at Sawankhalok, Nakhon Sawan, and other towns where they were assembled into rafts. Steam-powered tugboats would tow the rafts to Bangkok sawmills or to wharves where they were loaded on ships bound for Europe.

Now, with the teak forests virtually depleted, these men handled *Takhien Thong* (Hopea Odorata), *Mai Daeng* (Shirea, often called rosewood), *Makha* (monkey pod tree), ironwood and varieties of lesser value. Because dams blocked the major rivers, the logs were trucked to Nakhon Sawan and dumped into the Chao Phya where the men marked and rafted them. A diesel tug would tow the rafts on a seven-day journey to Bangkok for sawing or shipment to foreign ports. Many times, I'd watched 150-foot-long rafts plowing slowly past my river house, blocking the cross-river passage of ferry boats. Small blue tents erected fore and aft housed the men tending the raft. A government logging ban a year later would reduce even this simple operation.

A half-hour downriver, I saw my first water hyacinths, examples of a good idea gone wrong. When King Chulalongkorn visited Java in the 1890s, his consorts were so impressed by the hyacinth's beauty that they returned to Thailand with clippings. They were planted in palace ponds but soon escaped into the canals and rivers, choking them and blocking boat passage. Each rainy season, farmers hacked away at the plants, sending them downstream to the sea or, more often, into a neighboring canal where they became somebody else's problem. Boatmen cursed as their propellers chopped away in a futile bid to bull their way through it, and city fathers wrang their hands, all to no avail. Here, in the upper Chao Phya, it grew sparsely, stray pieces with purple flowers. To the un initiated, it seemed one of the more attractive flowers in the tropics.

To my relief, the sandbars were gone. The river's depth meant I could iron out corners to shorten my travel distance. Or so I thought. On outside bends, the government had erected breakwaters to keep the river from devouring its own banks. In a former age, such erosion would not have caused a problem. According to physics, no land had been lost; whatever was carved from the outer bend was deposited on the inner bend. But these were modern times and property ownership was a matter of grave concern. While there were no complaints from inner-bank landowners about their burgeoning estates, outer-bend residents railed against nature, erecting barriers to keep the robber river at bay. Large-scale engineering projects had ultimately had done more damage to the river than nature, eventually turning it against humans and causing greater catastrophe than if it had been left to flow where it wanted.

There were other signs of urban reach. From a signboard high on the bank, I learned that Nakhon Sawan was the headquarters for the local branch of Alcoholics Anonymous. Then, I encountered a huge sign like those at a golf driving range. Written on it in huge numerals was "380." I thought it was a distance marker, until my map told me I was 280 kilometers (175 miles) from the sea. But when "379" (235 miles) appeared a kilometer later and "378" a kilometer after that, it became apparent that I had a lot farther to go than I thought. I had long ago scrapped the idea of reaching the sea in 48 days but an extra 60 miles required at least another five days of paddling.

Just downstream, a government dredge was at work. I tied up to its stern and climbed aboard. The pilot house chart table held detailed nautical maps of the river, the contour lines showing its depth at key points; the depth gauge read 16 feet. With its hydraulic legs anchored to the river bed, the dredge's bucket arm swept back and forth, shaving another three feet from the river's bottom. A 12-inch pipe sent the sand to shore where mini-Himalaya were slowly rising. I mentioned having seen numerous dredges upriver.

"Yes, most of our work is repairing the damage they cause," the Captain said. "They dig where they want to and it changes the river's regimen. The land upstream and downstream erodes to fill in the holes they have created."

"And the water is so silty the fish die," added the engineer.

"Can't the dredges be stopped?"

"Nobody in Bangkok is interested and everyone else is frightened of influential people. Construction is big business and it needs sand and gravel."

With the start of a building boom in the cities, the river was under siege. I wished them luck and pushed on.

The land was leveling out as I moved south. By the map, Nakhon Sawan was 77 feet above sea level. If the sea was 227 miles south, it meant the river was dropping at only four inches per mile, a barely perceptible gradient. It was no wonder that the river meandered, no longer flowing north to south, but east and west as well, exploring the far edges of the valley, more and more snakelike in its slithering progress.

It was on an eastward passage that I came to a small village on an inside bend where the banks barely rose above the waterline. A few hundred yards downstream, an old broken house sat like a bather amidst half-drowned tree skeletons. I pulled for a small landing. On it, a man, bare-chested above his *pakoma* squatted, casually observed me as he dragged smoke from a crumpled cigarette. When I asked him the location of the phu yai baan's house, he pivoted his body to point his cigarette at a house perched above the mudflats.

"Is he home?"

He shook his head. I settled in for a wait. He regarded me calmly, quietly sucking on his cigarette, careful to blow the smoke away from me. He asked me what I was doing and I told him.

"Where you've been, I'd like to go," he said. "Where you're going, I've been, and don't want to go again," pointing his cigarette first up the river and then down the river and then shaking his head. He had an odd habit of accompanying every question and statement with elaborate hand and head gestures as if miming to a deaf person.

"You don't like Bangkok?"

"Too many people, too much noise, can't breathe," he said, gasping, choking, and looking severely distressed. The water lapped quietly at the dock pilings but aside from the crackling of tobacco when he took a drag, there wasn't a sound. After a long pause, he said, "Except for the

Emerald Buddha..."

"What about it?"

"That's a good reason to go to Bangkok," he said. "To pray at the Emerald Buddha."

The kingdom's most sacred image, the seated Emerald Buddha–in truth, carved from jadeite–rested on a pedestal high above the worshipers in Bangkok's Wat Phra Kaew. Had it been huge and imposing, it would be easy to understand how it could awe a nation, inspire a war for possession of it, but it stood only 16 inches high. There was something charming about its allure, that for Buddhists it was not necessary for an image to be enormous to be sacred.

"How many times have you visited it?"

"Three," he said, holding up three fingers.

"Will you go again?"

An emphatic single nod of the head, and he lapsed into silence. We'd been on the dock for 15 minutes without a sign of the *phu yai baan*.

"Maybe he's gone for the night," I said, looking towards the house the man had indicated.

"No, no, he'll be back," he said, smiling.

"I wonder where he's gone," I mused.

"To the dock," he said with a smile.

For god's sake. "You mean...?"

"Uh," he replied.

I realized he was feeling me out before committing to offering me hospitality but I was annoyed with him for stretching the joke so long. I must have shown it because he said, "But we had a chance to talk. At the house, there are too many people. Here, we can get to know each other better."

True. I *waiied* him.

"*Sawasdee, Khun Phu Yai Baan* (Honored Headman)," I said, bowing low.

"*Sawasdee, Nai Farang* (Mister Foreigner)," he replied, mimicking me and laughing hugely.

I hoisted my pack to my shoulder and when we stood, I realized how tiny he was. He led the way towards his wobbly stilted house, half hidden in a mangrove. The house was like the derelicts surrounding it: weather-beaten, sinking into the mud and collapsing under its own weight.

His wife was on the back porch roasting coconuts while three children under 12 brought more from a small palm grove. They seemed shocked to see us, exactly the reaction the headman had hoped for because he said, "look what I found on the dock."

The headman suggested that I bathe, his pantomime reaching comical proportions and performed, I suspected, for the benefit of the children who giggled at his antics. The shore was muddy and I'd hoped to avoid walking across it to reach the river but the headman told me there was only enough water in the well for drinking. This would be the first night I'd bathed in a river that no longer flowed green and clean. Since morning, I'd counted nine dead dogs and one cat floating in the river and I was neither enthusiastic about the water nor the mud but I guessed I could survive a plunge.

Dinner was served on the first dining table I'd seen in weeks. Dessert was the freshly-roasted coconuts, rubbery but permeated with a pleasing smoky flavor. Having finished dinner before the rest of us, the headman's 12-year-old son excused himself and went out to the porch. As I was nearest the door, I could hear him whispering anxiously to himself in English, "what is name...no, what is name you...no...what is you name..." I poked my head out the door, startling him.

"Say it aloud," I said in Thai.

"What is your name," he said in English.

"Perfect." He beamed.

"My name is Sa-teeb," I told him, using the Thai pronunciation. His brows furrowed in consternation as he whispered the words to himself over and over like a mantra that would suddenly reveal some hidden truth. I noticed that he did with his face what his father did with his hands: transform all thought into visible form. Eventually, a light bulb illuminated. "My name is Sa-teeb, right?" he asked in Thai.

"Yes."

"Oh, good," he said, congratulating himself.

"What is your name?" I asked and the brows furrowed again. His mouth worked furiously while in a nearly inaudible voice he worked to decipher the words, like someone nibbling his way down an ear of corn a kernel at a time.

"Thanet," he said tentatively.

"Good." He grinned, then his face lit up with a new thought.

"Wait here," he said and darted into the house. He returned a moment later clutching old copies of the English-language *Bangkok Post*.

"Can you translate them for me?" he asked.

I asked him to select the stories that interested him. He leafed through to the movie listings which were filled photographs of the stars.

"Here," he said, pointing to a picture of Sylvester Stallone, of the rippling muscles. "Rambo. Right?" he asked, looking up at me. I confirmed it and then spent a pleasant half hour noting which movies he selected for translation. As I expected, he bee-lined for the action films. Most of the Western movies imported into Thailand were filled with bloody mayhem, dominated by uncomplicated heroes and plots. Thai movies were a pastiche of romance, comedy, heroism, dastardly villains, pretty girls, a few ghouls, and pathos, generally all in the same film. Heroes were portrayed on gigantic billboards holding terrifying weapons; even the heroines waved pistols. It reflected a dark side of the Thai psyche, where beneath sunny smiles, nasty things happened to ordinary people. Newspaper front pages were covered in blaring headlines and photographs of crime victims, usually in some state of undress, the wounds and nudity partially obscured by screened masks, the heaviness of the screens dependent upon the censor's mood at the moment. There was no clear explanation for the Thai ability to hold two conflicting beliefs. Buddhism seemed to recognize society's innate savagery and propounded teachings as a means of keeping the barbaric at the gates. Prophets don't write commandments against sins that don't already exist in a culture.

As we talked, heavy drops plopped on the tin roof, the scent of rain wafting in the door on a stirring breeze. Throughout the night, drops that had caught in the coconut fronds would splat heavily on the roof, but no rain fell.

In the morning, in humidity with a palpable weight that pressed us to the earth, the headman told me of his village's decline.

"Before, we had 80 'roofs'," he said, spooning curry over his rice. "But then, a lot of people moved to the city. The government changed the boundaries and we shrank."

"What had they done in the old days?"

"This was a big port. The boats anchored here and farmers brought their rice for loading. Outsiders, city people, set up the docks and storage barns. We were almost a town."

"And then the highway came...?"

"Yes," he said. "They didn't need us any more so we became a simple *moo baan* (village)."

He seemed more resigned than resentful. Time and fate had dealt him a bad hand but he lived in peace because he didn't need much to keep him going. I had always assumed that headmen were wealthy but this one was barely scraping by. That no other villager was doing well took some of the sting out of his poverty.

"The children are smart, and they do well in school," he said, voicing the poor man's age-old hope in his children's future. "Of course, they'll probably find jobs in the city. Maybe we'll have to go live with them when we get old." A bright thought suffused his face. "The whole village will go to Bangkok if the flood waters rise again," he said, wryly. "We lost a house last year. Just went floating off down the river one night."

"Is that the broken one I saw downstream?"

"Yeah," he confirmed. "It didn't make it too far because it got tangled in some half-submerged mango trees."

"Anybody hurt?"

"No. The owners had closed it up some time before and moved to Nakhon Sawan to find work. It was so old, I don't think they expected to live in it again. That house caused me a lot of problems."

"How?"

He laughed. "Because in the provincial records, our village was supposed to have 37 "roofs". When the house floated away, there was a question of whether we'd really lost one roof since it didn't travel beyond the town boundaries. It was a house but it wasn't a house and they didn't know what to do about it."

"I can imagine the bureaucrats' consternation," I said.

"Yeah. If it had gone another 100 yards, it would have been in the next village and they would have had to deal with it." He chuckled at the absurdity of it all.

"How was it resolved?"

"Oh, they decided to forget about it. It is still registered as part of this village. I guess they hope it will sink so they can remove it from the rolls."

Breakfast over, I filled my canteen with water that foamed. I decided to take no chances, dropping two purification tablets into it. I'd rather endure the strong chemical taste than risk ingesting a bundle of highly-colorful microbes. As I pushed off, the headman went into an elaborate pantomime to farewell me, but by now I knew his sense of humor and realized he was mocking himself. Some villages I was reluctant to depart, and this was one of them.

An uneventful morning put me into another long eastbound stretch, pleasant paddling because the sun, hidden by clouds, was not in my eyes. Kilometer posts clicked slowly downwards. Dogs sniffed in the bushes—a rich olfactory repository of ever-changing scents—or chased each other along the beach, darting in and out of the water. Dogs roamed most villages, the most relaxed canines I'd ever seen, seldom barking at any-one, even strangers. A cat, the first live one I'd seen, calmly observed me from the riverbank. Cats enjoyed less favor among the farmers. Sin had cats but on sufferance, because they caught rodents. From here south, cats would become more visible, keeping their distance from the water, but occasionally perching primly atop a post, watching the world go by.

At noon, I paused at Payuha Khiri, a large rice port. Tied up at wharves set on 20-foot pilings, huge barges received rice transported from upcountry farms by canal and road. It would be floated to Ayutthaya and from there it would travel to Bangkok by truck. Considering the short distances between the cities, it seemed an odd arrangement but appar-ently the economics permitted it. No one stuck to tradition if it lost them money.

Beneath the docks, bare-chested teen-aged boys squatted around something I couldn't see clearly. When a ribbon of blue smoke rose from the center of the huddle, I realized they were dragging on a *bhang*, a thick bamboo smoking pipe. A moment later, the sweet aroma of marijuana floated past. They invited me to join them but I waved and paddled on. On the dock above them, a young man rocked on his haunches, gazing calmly at something in the far distance. His right hand clutched a plastic bag; a thinner addict, I guessed. Stevedores worked hard for little pay and drugs were often an integral part of their lives. They weren't going anywhere, so they might as well enjoy what little they had. Since Thailand was a communal society, addicts weren't loners. They shared lives and resources with their friends.

Just below Payuha Khiri, a man shouted derisively, "Put an engine on it; you'll go faster." It was not the last time I would hear the curt statement, nor the snide tone. It was a sharp reminder that I was no longer in the polite North where people understood me when I suggested that the engine noise would drown out birds and other sounds. Here, they were mystified. Neither did they comprehend me when I said I was more interested in the journey than in the destination. Of course, they'd been looking at the river for centuries; it was no longer new. But so had the northerners and they had lost none of their appreciation of its beauty. Life was different here, I concluded.

In the afternoon, everything disappeared, kilometer posts, depth markers, buoys, the sun. The river was contributing only a half-mile an hour to my progress and making me work for the rest. A stiff upriver wind chopped the surface into hundreds of whitecaps, negating the river's downstream pull. With black clouds building in the distance, the wind became a gale; waves began breaking over the bow, filling the boat. After struggling for an hour, I gave up. When I saw a woman on the riverbank, I asked her where the *phu yai baan* lived.

"Why?" she asked suspiciously.

"I'm looking for a place for the night. I thought he could advise me."

She didn't answer but pointed towards a house a short distance away. I paddled to shore and tied up. As I was walking up the road towards the house, the same woman approached.

"You can't stay here," she said.

"You talked with him?"

"He's away."

"When will he be back."

"I don't know, but you can't stay there."

"How do you know?"

"I'm his wife."

I couldn't have it on much better authority. I thanked her and turned back to my boat but then, she changed her mind. "You can stay," she said. Although perplexed by the crossed signals, I followed her.

The couple shared an old farmhouse with two children and a clowder of cats. A tabby lounged on the porch amidst her three frolicking kittens. Two pre-teen children jumped up when I appeared in the yard, hanging on me to ask questions. I've always enjoyed those children whom adults dismiss as precocious and, therefore, impolite. Their still-suspicious mother relaxed when she saw her children warm to me and laugh at my lame jokes.

Her husband, Surapong, appeared a half hour later, a gentle man with a welcoming smile, smaller than his wife by a few inches but at ease with the world. My appearance in the village seemed not to surprise him at all. He listened to the children question me, occasionally asking one himself, demonstrating the inspiration for their lively inquisitiveness. Before dinner, he sat with Sittichai, 12, going over his homework, quietly making sure that he understood everything. The looks that passed between them betrayed a mutual respect. Goy, eight, was a cheerful scamp who tried to help her big brother with his homework but was too young to contribute much. Father and son both bore her interruptions with gentle words and without condescension.

Why the scene should have impressed me, I wasn't sure. Perhaps I was moved by the way the four related to each other. Thai children were often treated as miniature adults rather than as beings with their own whims and perceptions. They were indulged until they entered school. After that, they were expected to toe the line and were given little opportunity to develop their own personalities. The emphasis was on smoothing rough edges so they would fit snugly into a societal mold. Their entertainments were not designed to help them explore their own creativity but to enable them to function in an adult world. In Bangkok, I'd often attended children's parties where the performers were cabaret singers and nightclub artistes. The parents applauded the show while their children fidgeted, unable to comprehend what was going on. The objective was not to amuse them but to acculturate them. If nothing else, it prepared them to cope with boredom.

Even when children approached adulthood, the pattern didn't change. Grown sons deferred to their interfering mothers with a submissiveness that would have earned them derision by their peers in the West. No one thought anything was unusual about the arrangement. After all, Thailand was a top-down, paternalistic society and the children were only being subjected to the types of pressures their parents daily endured without complaint.

As we were talking, Uncle Pranom walked in. He was a geeky looking man, thin with bandied legs and a narrow face decorated by a scraggy Groucho Marx mustache and horn-rimmed glasses. He seemed a bit out of place, like a city person come to visit.

"Are you from here?" I asked.

"Yeah, my mother and father were born here."

"But you lived in Bangkok...?"

"Nope. I don't like Bangkok."

"But you seem different from the other villagers..." and even as I said it, I knew where the difference lay. "Did you work overseas?"

"Israel. For two years," he said.

"As what?"

"A cook; I make a great chicken curry." It was unusual for a Thai to praise himself but he must have mistaken my raised eyebrows for disbelief because he said, "I'll make some for you," and rushed out the door. Half an hour later, he was back with a hot bowl of *gaeng luang gai*, a yellow curry dish. He was right; it was delicious.

While his wife set the table on the floor, the headman produced a bottle of *lao khao* (rice whisky), and a bottle of Krating Daeng (Red Bull). I agreed to join him in a libation but soon began wondering about my wisdom when I saw him pour the Krating Daeng into the white whiskey bottle. This was going to pack quite a wallop. To its credit, the Krating Daeng took a bit of the rawness off the *lao khao*, but didn't reduce its potency. Eventually, the alcohol triumphed over the caffeine, and, slurring my words, I went to bed.

The Monk and the Bargirl

Kracher Kon Rua
(To put [a fish] into a bottomless basket)
An unfrugal person wastes his money
by investing unwisely

Despite the potency of the headman's concoction, sleep came and sleep went at five-minute intervals. I'd seen the grandfather clocks but hadn't paid them much attention; they were part of every farm household that could afford one. Their appeal to a people unconcerned with time had always mystified me. A living room could be bare of furniture except a wooden clothes cabinet with window-pane doors but along one wall would be a grandfather clock, either ticking or long dead. They were often given as gifts and could be found in *wats*, homes, and even ice cream parlors. In ornate gold letters, the glass door noted the occasion, date, and donor. The lettering nearly obliterated the clock face behind it, as if time-keeping were an ancillary function. They stood stolidly, the chromium pendulum sweeping back and forth, scything the days into hours and minutes.

This farmhouse had three. Ticking loudly, they stood against three walls of the living room where my sleeping mat had been placed. Assured that I was comfortable, the family had doused the fluorescent tube, bade me good night, and taken refuge behind a locked bedroom door. Leaving me with the clocks.

At 9 p.m., the right-wall clock's intoned a Big Ben dum-dum-dum-dum refrain, followed by nine melodious chimes. Right, I thought, no more pealing for another hour. Five minutes later, the clock on the left wall tolled nine p.m. Since I was not yet asleep, I wasn't disturbed. But then, five minutes later–at 9:10, by the first clock's reckoning–the one on the center wall struck the hour. This was a bit much but I consoled myself that at least I'd have 50 minutes before the first one struck again. As the last reverberations were receding, I hunkered down in my sleeping bag and began to drift off.

At 9:15, the right-wall clock chimed the dum-dum-dum-dum refrain for the quarter hour, just loud enough to rouse me. And, of course, at 9:20, the left-wall clock did the same, echoed five minutes later by the center clock. And so it continued all night. As I blearily watched dawn lighten the room, I could barely hold up my head. I kept reminding myself that I was a guest, and that my hosts would hardly be pleased to find their cherished clocks reduced to kindling by a glazed-eyed *farang*.

"How did you sleep?" the wife asked, on emerging from the bedroom. My mind boggled for a polite answer. "Fine, thank you," I muttered.

I was rolling up my sleeping bag when Pranom walked in with a fragrant minced pork omelet. How could I remain unhappy when assailed by such a pleasant aroma? He had also wrapped a second one in a banana leaf for my lunch. He told me how much he hated sand and how easily it got into the food he cooked in Israel. "Here, we only have dirt," he said with a note of pride. "It doesn't taste any better but at least it doesn't break your teeth."

The day promised to be another blazer. As I lashed gear into the boat my hands twinged with pain. Wrapping each finger around the paddle shaft like bird talons around a perch, I set off into a murky morning. A bell-like *stupa* with its lotus bulb finial poked above the coconut palms, telling me I had crossed the pale of 13th-century Sukhothai culture into that of the Ayutthayan realm that had ruled Siam from the 14th to 18th centuries.

Just beyond, the water was covered in writhing white velvet. I paddled cautiously through a surreal riverscape: tens of thousands of downy white mayflies (*cheepa khao*), dead or dying on the water after laying their eggs. The feeble struggles of those still living had alerted clouds of black and white swifts that swooped down to pluck them away. The insects coated everything, a pale flocking on house walls, tall grasses, bamboo mooring poles, boat engines. It was as though overnight a snowstorm had blown through Thailand, an event it would never experience.

An hour later, I found myself surrounded by dredges filling barges with sand for shipment to Bangkok. These barges were of the old breed, with graceful teak hulls voluptuously rounded like a Rubens maiden. Each barge was owned by a single family that lived on board and hired its vessel to rice or sand shippers. When full, a dozen owners would pay a tugboat captain to tow them in a train to up- and downriver destinations. As picturesque as they were, the teak boats were the dinosaurs of the barge fleet. High upkeep costs were consigning them to history, retired as the water began to rot their costly teak planks, replaced by steel barges requiring little maintenance and holding twice as much cargo.

As I passed one, a woman invited me into her home on the stern, a roofed area just aft of the cargo hold. Lacking a rear wall, the cramped living area was exposed to the elements. Weathered black-and-white photos of long-dead ancestors posed stiffly in their best clothes on the forewall, watching scenery the barge had just passed. Wedged into the frames were tattered, blurred color photos recalling family visits to important shrines. In one, a family sat on the floor of a *wat*, arranged around a smiling monk seated on a chair, everyone peering solemnly at the camera. The rest of the wall was taken up by a round, pink-framed clock, and kitchen utensils hanging from nails.

A shy, sad woman, Somying insisted that I stay for lunch. "My husband is ashore buying supplies but I know he will enjoy talking with you." While she cooked, I explored the barge.

To the right of the door leading to the hold stood a clothes cabinet-a metal frame covered in a pink plastic sheet printed with bears and bunnies. On the left was a kitchen cabinet with mesh doors to bar the flies. A small shelf held a television and, beneath it, a corroded car battery that supplied the DC power. A wire led to the antenna, a metal sculpture that looked like it had been crumpled by a collision with a low bridge. The family slept above the cabinets in an alcove that extended over the cargo area. The hold was sheltered from the rain by a corrugated iron roof draped over a water pipe framework. When the roof was in place, the barge looked like a roll-top desk.

As Somying sliced vegetables, her baby slept in a loosely-woven, thick-yarn hammock gently rocked by the river's motion. Many Thai children had grown up on these boats, gradually taking over their parents' roles as they matured. Education laws had changed much of that. When the barges tied up at a *wat*, the children trooped down the gangplank each morning to a nearby schoolhouse. When the barge carried their parents upriver for a new load of sand, the children stayed behind with relatives or friends. These fragmented families were yet another instance of the long separations caused by poverty.

Somying's chores were complicated by the lack of a fore or aft deck on which to work. When the hold was fully loaded, the decks were awash in six inches of water; from all appearances it seemed about to sink. High doorsills kept the water from invading the living area. We talked about life on the boat and she confessed that she missed her children.

"But they are getting an education," she said. "That's good because there won't be any work for them on the boat when they grow up." I thought of the old couple living on their decrepit barge at Nakhon Sawan.

"Do you suppose you'll always live on the barge?" I asked.

"Paw ("father", referring to her husband) wants to..." she said.

"And you?"

"I have relatives in Roi Et (a Northeastern town)...or maybe I'll live with my children when they grow up."

"Which would you prefer?"

"I don't know. I love my children but they'll probably live in Bangkok."

"And?"

"Too noisy, too dirty."

"What about Roi Et?"

"We don't know anything about farming. And we have no land."

Anyone of a higher economic class would have spoken of "retiring there" but she and I both knew that for poor people, there was no hope of retirement. With no social security, and nothing of the cushions available to elderly people in developed countries, they were left to depend on their children. In the past, child mortality had been so high that couples bore many children to ensure that at least one or two would survive to support them in their waning years. Only by eradicating childhood diseases and demonstrating that their children would outlive them had the government induced farmers to have fewer offspring. Now, Thailand had one of the lowest birth rates in Asia.

"If we can make ourselves useful, maybe we can find some room in my sister's house. We don't need much."

It seemed strange that she should be looking to old age. She was not yet 30 but she accepted the inevitable decline towards death. Sunset years were not to be anticipated as golden rewards for decades of labor. They would simply be filled with sickness and pain that could be partially alleviated by the solace of Buddhism. Between now and then, anything could happen: accidents or illness against which she and her husband had no health insurance. Work was the measure of whether or not one survived; were the mishap debilitating, there would be no workman's compensation or welfare payments.

As we talked, her husband, Somkuan, returned. It always amazed me that, in a society where jealousy was a part of marriage, husbands could arrive home to find me talking with their wives and never suspect that I might be a rival. He greeted me warmly and while his wife put away his purchases, he sat down to talk. He'd grown up on this barge and assumed ownership after his father died. He had met Somying in a riverside market in Bangkok while she was visiting an aunt. He courted her and soon after, she moved onto the boat. I didn't ask but assumed she was a common-law wife. The lack of a marriage certificate was not important as long as the children's births had been registered so they could attend school.

"How soon will you leave for Bangkok?" I asked.

"We're being roped together now."

"How long is the journey?"

"Eight days." I thought I'd misheard him. It seemed too long for the 160-plus miles, especially since they would be traveling day and night. But then, near Bangkok they would be affected by the sea tide pushing up river. In my riverside house, I'd often been awakened by straining engines, their vibrations traveling through the water and up the house columns. I'd lie awake for the long hour the boats took to pass. It would have made more sense—and saved diesel fuel—to wait for the tide to turn, but none ever did.

The ropemen had reached our barge, the last in a train of eleven. We gathered up the dishes and I descended to my boat. Curious to know how rapidly they moved, I paddled alongside and quickly outdistanced them.

Mid-afternoon, after taking five-and-a-half hours to cover 10 miles,

Manoram came into view. I was making good time. If I knocked off a few more miles today, I could reach Chainat the next day. It bothered me that I was giving more thought to covering specific distances than to the scenery and the people, but the heat–now in the mid-90s with humidity nearly 90%–was killing me. I recalled my initial resolve that when the trip degenerated into counting miles, I would opt out. Even then, I knew I wouldn't; I seldom have the wit to drop out of anything. I have walked out of, perhaps, three bad movies in my life. I pushed on.

That evening I discovered humility. Or would have if I hadn't felt so offended. I guess my string of successes in finding accommodation had grown too long and I'd become spoiled. Now, my luck ran out. I'd hoped to reach Wat Singh, but late in the afternoon a powerful wind, like a hand in my face, began shoving me backwards. When I saw a *wat* roof thrusting above the trees, I angled for shore.

Tying the boat to an exposed tree root, I climbed the bank to find myself in a thick stand of Bo trees thrashing in the wind like a rag shaken by a growling dog. Across the road was a lovely wat without a retaining wall, its buildings bunched together in a pleasing arrangement. Marking the path to the main hall was a shrine that had once been a river boat; the back of a Buddha image was visible through the pilothouse window. Passing a half-completed pavilion, I nearly collided with a monk bent-over to protect himself from the wind, his orange robe flapping and in danger of leaving his body altogether. Like a sailor hurriedly gathering storm-billowed sail, he clasped folds of cloth to himself and seemed startled when, above the shrieking wind, I shouted, "Where can I find the abbot?" When he lifted his arms to point to a small *viharn* at the back of the compound, his robe began to unravel. Clutching himself, he ran to the lee of the ordination hall.

At first, I thought the *viharn* was empty, until I heard a rattling coming from behind a huge Buddha image that serenely gazed down on me in the dim interior. Illuminated by a lantern, the abbot was sitting on the floor, surrounded by manuscripts written on palm leaf sheets bound accordion style. He must have sensed my presence because, without looking up, he said, with more than a note of irritation, "*Haa alai?*" (What do you want?).

"The *luang paw* (abbot)," I said, although it was clear from his age and demeanor that it was he.

"Why?" he barked. I explained my need for accommodations.

"Stay in a hotel," he said brusquely, still not deigning to look up. Perhaps he wasn't aware that I was a foreigner although my accent should have given me away. I knelt down so he could see me.

"A hotel?"

"There are some down the road," and he waved me away. I'd never heard a monk speak so rudely but it was clear that I'd been dismissed and there was no appeal.

My gorge rose. It wasn't that he owed me anything, it was that he had been so callous, making me feel like a beggar. It didn't help that I was a beggar and I was stuck. I went in search of a nearby village but there wasn't any. I briefly considered heading downriver to find another village but the wind was kicking up white-capped waves that made it dangerous to set out again.

Up the road near a group of houses a beautiful young woman was washing clothes. "Is the headman's house nearby?"

"We don't have a headman," she said.

"Where's the nearest hotel?"

Frowning, she thought for a moment. "In town, two miles that way," she said, pointing up the road. And what would I do with the boat? "Keep it here," she said, smiling.

Much as I disliked it, that seemed to be my only course. As I was putting my gear in her house, her husband and two friends appeared. When I suggested chaining the boat to a tree, they insisted that I move it to the safety of the house, and decided the matter by hoisting it out of the water, laying it on their shoulders, and carrying it inside.

For 20 *baht*, her husband drove me to town on his motorcycle. I told him I was looking for an ordinary hotel but he interpreted my wish a bit too literally, dropping me at a ramshackle wooden building that, had I been on my own, I would never have mistaken for a hotel. It had no sign, no indication even that people lived there.

The door was opened by a frowzy woman who growled, "What do you want?"

"A room."

She regarded me sourly and then opened the door wide. I followed her shambling footsteps down a dark hallway, arriving at a door that looked like a battering ram had split it; Band-Aid slats stapled together its broken panels. She fiddled with a tiny lock that clasped a huge, rusted hasp. Its hinges shrieking, the door swung open uncertainly. On the ceiling, a dead electric fan seemed ready to pull loose from its moorings and impale whoever lay below. The bed was shrouded in a sheet across which romped Charlie Brown's dog, Snoopy; the hard pillow was covered in twill. Down the hall, the bathroom had no light, the water jar held soap scum, cobwebs stitched together the corners of the room, the squat toilet stank.

"60 *baht* ($2.40)," she said. It was exorbitant but this seemed to be the only hotel in town. Why should there be others? From what I could see, there was nothing to visit. Maybe I'd fare better with a restaurant.

On the corner down the deserted street was a dingy food shop. A sleepy youth in a ragged T-shirt and holed pants, shuffled up to stand swaying by the table. He regarded me with bleary eyes.

"What do you want?" Those cheering words, yet again.

"A menu," realizing as I said it that it was an improbable request.

He stared at me for a long moment then turned and plodded into the murk at the rear of the restaurant, his rubber sandals scuffing along the bare concrete. I surveyed the interior. The wooden table was wobbly and the metal stool was missing a leg. A square of newspaper, rolled into a cone and fastened to the socket with a rubber band, shaded the bare light bulb. Into the pool of light hopped a cat, scrawny and also missing a leg. It yowled incessantly, demanding that I feed it.

I heard the waiter rummaging in a desk for something, the menu, I assumed. Long minutes passed before his shuffling footsteps began anew, but instead of coming towards me, they faded to silence somewhere farther back in the shop.

"*Phii* (Elder)," he hollered to someone, "Where's the menu?"

Muffled reply. He returned to my table.

"No menu," he said. He seemed about to topple over. I thought he might be drugged but realized he was just very tired.

"Is this a restaurant?" I asked, impatience getting the better of me.

He stood a moment longer, and then began shambling towards the rear again. I thought he had been insulted by my irritated question but then recalled that Thais often don't understand sarcasm when it is delivered with a smile. I realized he was on his way to find "*Phii*" for an answer to my question.

"Hey *nong* (younger), *mai pen rai* (no problem)," I shouted. "I'll try elsewhere." I heard him stop but couldn't see him. It was entirely possible that he had fallen asleep on his feet. Things were beginning to assume comic proportions. Baan Kaew, home of Jamrat, had been dying but at least its people had a pulse. This town was in a coma.

Farther down the street, an open-front restaurant bore a metal banner. In its peeling paint, I read the words "E-sarn BKS" (Northeastern Bus), although there was no sign of a bus. I thought place was deserted until the owner hailed me from the back, then walked up to me to identify herself as "Su." At the sound of our voices, waiters materialized from the upper floors.

"Do you have food?"

"Sure," she said, "Where are you from?"

"America."

She frowned. "America, huh," she said, annoyed.

"Why?"

"I wanted to go there to open a restaurant."

"And...?"

"The American Embassy wouldn't give me a visa."

"Did they say why?"

"Because I didn't have enough money."

"They said that?"

"No, they said I needed a...what do you call it...guarantor just to visit it, but I know the real reason."

I waited.

"They only let in rich Thais."

Her hard-edged voice begged an argument, but I wasn't about to debate the merits of the U.S. visa system because I didn't understand it myself. It did seem like people with money had no problem getting in. Many went as students and then disappeared underground, usually in L.A. "Robin Hoods," they were called. Some made it, others ended up in the underbelly. Most eventually returned (or were deported) to Bangkok. The U.S. Consulate claimed to act according to set rules but their decisions often seemed arbitrary, turning away deserving people and admitting rascals.

"Can you be my guarantor?" Su asked, her hard smile suggesting she already knew the answer.

"I don't live in the U.S. so I wouldn't qualify," I replied, then changed the subject. "What kind of food do you have?"

"Everything. You want American Fried Rice?" Ugh. American Fried Rice was a legacy of the Vietnam War era and it was awful. It was essentially Thai fried rice minus its delicate flavor and with the addition of pebble-like peas, and slices of local hot dog of uncertain pedigree. Lubricated with ketchup, it was topped by a greasy fried egg, runny side up. I opted for steamed rice and mixed vegetables.

The restaurant began filling. The clientele was coarse and already half-drunk. They shouted at each other across the room, or stumbled to other tables to harangue someone about something. Soon, they began plopping down heavily at my table and discoursing on this or that. Some of them had worked in *Sa-oo*, and harbored an intense dislike of their bosses.

"All *khaeks* are cheats," one scoffed.

"*Khaek*" is a pejorative term applied indiscriminately to Malays, Indonesians, Indians, Pakistanis, and Arabs. One of the first comments I heard on arrival in Thailand after telling someone I had lived in Nepal was the stock phrase: "If you are carrying a stick while walking and you see a snake and a *khaek*, hit the *khaek* first." Here, the interpretation was different.

"If you don't provoke a snake, it won't bother you," one said.

"And the *khaek*?"

"He makes trouble for you without provocation."

By suggesting that every country harbored a few dishonest people I got him to narrow his derision to "some" Arabs but the prejudices were too deeply ingrained. I was struck by the contrast between these rough men and the pretty, soft-spoken waitresses, not one of whom was over 18 and all of them waif-like. How the hell did they deal with these oafs?

But as I constantly discovered, there was always a diamond among the roughnecks. This one appeared at my elbow as I was eating, introducing himself as Chuan, a sixth-grade school teacher.

"And what do you teach them?" I asked, expecting the usual subjects.

"Not to destroy the environment," Chuan replied. I stared at him in mild shock.

"Thais are destroying everything around them, just to make money," he continued. "And their selfishness makes life difficult for every one else." On further questioning, he revealed a solid grasp of environmental problems-forest destruction, air pollution-but he left out rivers. Why wasn't river pollution a priority?

"Oh, because they are dirty for only a little while and then the floods carry everything away," he answered. "Forests are gone forever." I thought he was going to cry. It must be torment for him to be surrounded by men who would have strip-mined a forest to buy themselves and their friends a drink. I didn't argue with him about the rivers. He was a lot farther along in his understanding than most people; why ruin it? His next question disarmed me.

"What do you dislike about Thailand?"

The question was usually asked the other way around and foreigners with proper manners were expected to exult in describing its beauty and people. He seemed to expect me to speak otherwise. I bit, just to see how he would respond.

"I dislike corruption, influence that puts people above the law and allows them to hurt others. And destroy the environment." He nodded pensively. A thought occurred to me.

"Are you from here?"

"No, Bangkok."

"Why are you here?"

"I wanted to live upcountry, among the people." The "people" were rapidly becoming pissed out of their minds. I wasn't sure this was the "upcountry" he had envisioned.

"And how is it?" I asked.

Chuan considered before replying. "Well, Bangkok is very polluted. The air here is cleaner." He didn't sound convinced. Our tablemates were becoming louder and interrupting us whenever a thought struck them. Bleary questions drooled from their mouths, demanding answers. We gave up trying to converse.

Alcohol is one of the banes of Thai society. The predominant abusers are men; women generally abstain, at least in the open. Liquor is the glue of male bonding, an integral part of most social interaction. That bond means that solitary drinkers are rare and one never sees a drunk asleep in a ditch or a doorway; his friends usually get him home. And though when inebriated, the men are garrulous they seldom get into fights. When they do, it is bedlam. It often starts in a restaurant when a drunk on his way to the toilet, inadvertently bumps into another drunk's chair. Words are exchanged and a fight ensues. It is never for the sheer joy of fighting, but in defense of honor slighted.

Here, the drunks were becoming atavistic as the evening wore on. One would roll away from my table and another would sit down to blow a whisky blast, nonsensical question in my face. The glazed eyes told me the inquiry did not originate in a functioning brain. Neither did my answer make it back to that brain. I felt like setting a timer on the table and saying "time's up, next?" as they rotated between the stool and their own table where their friends lolled and poured down more Mekong whisky.

And then, my attention was diverted.

"May I sit here?" asked a slender young woman, sitting down and looking back over her shoulder.

"Sure."

"That man won't leave me alone."

To avoid provoking anyone, I didn't look. She was pretty enough to attract admirers.

"Where are you from?" I asked to pull her eyes away from her tormenter.

"*E-sarn* (Northeast). Why won't he leave me alone? He's married."

"He's drunk. He'll probably forget you're here."

She snorted. "Not likely. He's been pestering me for three nights. He'd better stop." A hint of menace suggested that one would be unwise to push her into a corner.

"What's your name?"

"Bao," she said, now focusing her attention on me. I had taken her for about 20 but she said she was 29 and divorced. We talked about her life–her mother was caring for her son in the Northeastern town of Korat–and how she'd come here to escape rural poverty.

Eventually one of the tables decided to head for a brothel and the noise level dropped so we could hear ourselves.

"Do you have a girlfriend?" Bao asked.

"Not at the moment."

"I'll be your girlfriend," she said, pertly.

"O.K.," I said. Keep it light.

"No, you don't want me as a girlfriend," she said, sullenly.

"Why not?"

"Too dark."

I'd heard this so many times from Thai beauties. Their culture had told them that light skin was attractive and dark skin ugly. Nothing would dissuade them from believing it. Within her cultural context where her primary life goal was to secure a husband to support her and a family, the belief narrowed her chances, no matter how beautiful she might be. I told her I thought she was lovely but she knew better. I let it ride. But, momentarily mollified, her focus shifted.

"Do you want a beer?"

"Why not," I thought. It was the end of a tough day and it had been weeks since I'd had one. It might mellow me after my encounter with the abbot and the landlady.

"A small one," I said.

"No small ones, only big."

Thai beer has a high alcohol content and I wasn't sure how much my system could tolerate after such a dry spell. She saw me hesitate.

"I'll help you drink it." I should have taken that as a warning but I somehow missed the signal.

"Sure," I said and she brought it herself. The way she dove in suggested she was no stranger to it. The next exchange told me she was also no ingénue, unfamiliar with the techniques of dealing with men. She spent a long moment looking at her feet. "My sandals are so old." Pause. "These belong to Su." I said nothing, waiting to see if the conversation was headed where I thought it was. "I need my own." Still I sat silently smiling. "Would you buy me a pair?" Bingo. Crux point. I could close down the conversation now or follow it to its inevitable conclusion.

It was either the beer or hormones because I heard myself say, "Sure, why not." Mr. Nice Guy. The road to ruin is strewn with such statements. I boarded the roller coaster to see where it would take me.

Grabbing my arm, she pulled me out to the sidewalk. Yelling to her friend, Ying, to join us, she towed me two shops down. I was curious to see how she'd play it; whether she would try to convince me she was a simple, low-maintenance woman by buying a modestly-priced pair, or if she would go for broke, test my soft spots, get me now before I got away. I'd seen this too many times. Watch, listen, hope I was wrong.

"I like these," she said, trying on a red pair. "Only 18 *baht* (75 cents)." So far so good.

"O.K." I said, happy with the low price. Then, she turned to Ying.

"You get a pair, too." Uh huh. A so-called "nice" Thai girl would have been mortified to ask a strange *farang* to buy her something. Asking him to buy something for her friend was even more reprehensible. Bao had to be a bargirl. To her credit, Ying seemed embarrassed, caught between her friend's wishes and her chagrin at asking me for something. She tried on a couple of pairs, then giggled and said she couldn't find the right size. Bao pulled her away and said, "Let's go back to the restaurant." Without a backward look, she exited, leaving me to pay the bill. The older woman clerk smirked at her back, then at me for being an idiot.

But how does one explain male behavior in such circumstances? They know they are regarded solely as providers yet they play the charade because it might result in a bit of tender flesh being pressed to theirs. I was no different from the rest.

As I re-entered the restaurant, I heard her would-be suitor belaboring her about walking out with the *farang*. "What's he got that I don't? It's just because he's got money." I'd heard this from many poor males as the reason why women preferred foreigners to Thais. The Thai women always contended that it was because the *farangs* treated them better and were less likely to take off when they got pregnant or times got tough. Perhaps the men were right: maybe it was only a matter of money. But who could blame the women? Theirs was a precarious lot. The poor ones didn't have many rights and Thai men in the lower economic orders were notoriously unfaithful, abandoning families if something young and nubile came along. A woman had to secure her future while she was still attractive. But I wasn't about to get involved in a domestic altercation.

I rejoined the group. Bao returned, flounced down, and glared at the wall. Ying glanced nervously over her shoulder as the young man abused Bao with a drunken rant about how ungrateful she was and that she had hurt him by ignoring him. If he was really in earnest about wooing her, he was not making a very solid case. I talked with the others.

Bao ordered another beer. Bad sign, I thought.

"I'm going to leave town for a few days," she said to no one, a statement borne of white heat. Then, she fixed me in her gaze.

"Where are you staying?" Not until she asked did I realize I hadn't an inking what the hotel was called. I described its location.

"Dirty," she decided. It was hard to disagree. "Stay here tonight," she said. Her eyes glowed as she looked at me for the first time in half an hour. This was getting interesting. She ordered a third beer, carefully splitting it half-half with me. A turbid river was beginning to flow around my brain.

The bill came and she sat calmly while I digested it. 190 *baht*. This was breaking my budget but I didn't really care. As soon as the waiter returned with my change, Bao became chatty and attentive.

"Let's go play snooker," she said. "You too," she said to her two friends and Chuan. This was an old power play by Thai bargirls and one I'd always found annoying. She wasn't just spending my money as rapidly as she could but demonstrating to her friends how she could manipulate a gullible man. She would push the line as far as possible. If the man protested-an affront to his image suggesting he was incapable of supporting a woman-she would feign innocence and bafflement. He'd feel like a heel. So, if I understood all this, why was I sitting here? Why wasn't I cashing out and heading home? By this point, it wasn't a question. As with Jamrat, I was caught up in it, curious to see if my instincts were right. And if they were wrong, I wasn't about to turn down spending the night with her. Maybe it was nothing more than knowing a dingy hotel room awaited me; perhaps it was recompense for night after night of behaving properly in the villages and monasteries. Whatever it was, I was in for the ride and she knew it.

We walked down the quiet street, the four in their cups singing loudly, exploding with hard laughs. Halfway along, Bao pulled me to one side. Looking at me ardently, she demanded 500 *baht*.

"What? Why?"

"I don't have any money."

"Neither do I."

"Lie."

"No, when I'm in the countryside, I don't need much money."

This seemed to make sense to her. She was silent for a moment. Then, "I have to buy medicines for my cough," she said, coughing dramatically. "Give me 100 *baht.*"

I made a show of rummaging in my pockets and then pulled out a bill and handed it to her. As we arrived at the door of the snooker hall, she said, "I love you. If anyone asks, I'll tell them I'm your wife."

"Why would anyone ask?" I asked, but her look told me she had her reasons. And then she tried again, "Give me 200 *baht* and I'll pay for everything."

"Everything what?"

"Just everything," she said with a sly look. I had about 300 *baht* to get me three days down the river, and some small bills back at the hotel. I handed her 200 *baht*, which she accepted with great display, and walked off with her friends. Chuan and I played snooker and then joined them at the table. Bao had ordered a banquet, plus beer and whiskey. For someone so small, she had an insatiable appetite.

"Are you tired?" she asked, looking at me with a gaze either loving or inebriated.

"Yes," I said, and realized I was.

"Let's go."

She dragged me out the door and down the street, her friends tumbling after us. Abruptly, she decided we should have a nightcap. For most *farangs*, a Thai nightclub is ghastly room drowning in stygian darkness, mercifully so because when viewed in daylight, it resembles a garish warehouse. Dayglow pictures hang on the walls, colored lights illuminate the bandstand, the only light in an otherwise midnight room. Fortunately, the gloom hides the cockroaches clinging to the undersides of the table, occasionally poking their heads over the edge, looking for scraps. The band is comatose, loud, and off-key and the singers are chosen for their chubby pulchritude and skimpy costumes, but not for their voices which quaver out of tune and are made more painful by a loud, reverberating sound system. But then, the patrons—men in their early 20s–are hardly there for cultural appreciation. Their attentions (and money) are taken by the girls who circulate, sit for a while, wander elsewhere with their girlfriends, while the men slowly get blotto. It is a dismal experience at best, fun the first time and an endurance run from then on.

"I'm out of money," I protested.

"No need. We have the whiskey," she said, producing the remains of the bottle, "and a big bottle of soda," she added to clinch the argument.

Great.

It turned out better than I expected, perhaps because I was beyond rational thought and because Bao draped her leg over mine as we sat on rickety folding chairs at a polished aluminum table. Of course, the waiter placed the bill before me and everyone got up to dance. It was small but left me with only two 50-*baht* bills.

I hadn't realized how noisy the nightclub was until we emerged onto the quiet street. It was near midnight and only my libido kept my energies from flagging entirely. I was in a somnambulistic groove and would go where it led.

Or where Bao led, which was down the street where, once again, she demanded money. Without waiting for an answer, she thrust her hands into my pockets and extracted the two remaining 50-*baht* bills. Thereupon, her demeanor changed. Given the events of the next half hour, she must have deduced that she had milked the cow dry.

We climbed to the restaurant's upper floor, fingers to her lips as she tiptoed as best she could considering her condition. Although my body was heavy–more from fatigue than alcohol–I was surprisingly clear headed. She led me into a large room in which several others slept, pushed me down into a deck chair, and lay down nearby. I brushed away mosquitoes and tried to get comfortable, a small corner of my brain alert should she decide to complete her seduction of me once everyone else was asleep. As I was concluding that a dirty room was better than a cramped chair, the roar of a motorcycle split the night air. Bao became anxious. She tugged me out of the chair and shoved me into Tui and Su's room.

"Sleep on the floor and don't make any noise," she ordered, almost in panic. "Here," she said, thrusting a pillow at me before rushing out the door. In the darkness, I heard Tui, miffed at the commotion, mumble "ahiya" (literally, "monitor lizard" but an epithet roughly equivalent to "shit").

I waited for a quarter hour, slapping at mosquitoes, unable to sleep. Screw it, I thought.

"Tui?"

"Uhhh?"

"We're not going to see Bao again, are we?"

"She's having problems with her boyfriend."

"Right. I don't want to play anymore."

"Uh."

"I'm going back to my hotel."

"That's probably best."

I stumbled down the stairs and into the street, dark except for a few dim lights. Behind me, the nightclub still poured music into the street. I began walking, to get as far from it and the whole damned town as I could. The farther I walked, the better I felt.

Spitting Fish and the Four-cent Ticket

Yiap Rua Song Khaem
(Stand in two boats)
Ingratiate oneself with both sides
and be trusted by no one

As the morning light seeped in the window, I was awakened by a banging on the door. For a moment, my fuzzed brain thought that Bao had seen the error of her ways. Silly boy. If she had come, it would be to demand more money. I opened the door to find the sour-looking proprietress.

"Money."

"You woke me for that?"

"Money," she insisted, her voice grating. I was tempted to tell her to go away but she didn't seem inclined to budge. I was irked that she would think that I'd skip out on the bill; couldn't she tell the difference between deadbeats and do-rights? Perhaps not. And given the people I'd met the previous evening, who could blame her. Extracting some small bills from my pack, I turned to see her peering behind the door.

"What are you looking for?"

"Women."

"What women?"

"Bargirls."

"And if you find one, you'll object?"

"No, you pay more."

This had to be a house rule. In Thailand, it's the same price for a single or a double. I nudged her out of the room, showered, and went to find breakfast. I was disgusted with myself for the previous evening, not for moral reasons but because it had thrown out of balance an equilibrium I had worked so hard to establish.

It was a small matter to find a motorcyclist to take me to the river. There, the beauty greeted me with a big smile. "Your boat's already in the water," and handed me roast chicken and warm rice neatly wrapped in a banana leaf. Once again, just as I was writing off a place and damning its inhabitants to hell, someone did something nice for me. I thanked her for her kindness.

I pushed off under a leaden sky, yet suddenly all was right with the world: I was back in the watery milieu where I felt most comfortable. It was odd that I should regard clinging to water as grasping a tangible substance, yet I did. The small world defined by the boat's contours was mine alone, a familiar refuge where *my* rules prevailed. I could go where I wanted, when I wanted, the boat willing. One nice aspect of travel is that when you have a bad experience, you simply leave town, leaving all the bad behind. It is the bedrock philosophy of the road.

Mid-afternoon, I approached the last dam between me and the sea. I was hugging the shore, considering whether to stop in Chainat or paddle another four miles to the dam, when I was startled by a rustling in the bamboo. Something plopped into the water beside me and, seconds later, a small otter head emerged from the water. Squeaking at me, it hared for the muddy bank and disappeared among the bushes. It was my third wild mammal of the journey; nice to see that something wild was surviving this close to civilization. I took its appearance as an omen that I should bypass Chainat and push for the dam. As the town passed my port stern I paddled leisurely, thinking I had ample time to reach the dam. But I had forgotten that I would have to traverse dead reservoir water. By the time the dam came into sight, the sky was orange and the sun was resting on the treetops. I tied up 200 yards above the dam and walked to it.

The first to be built on the Chao Phya, the dam had been completed in 1957 as part of the Greater Chao Phya River Scheme designed to irrigate the Central Plains. The Scheme was inspired by a 1948 Food and Agriculture Organization pronouncement that Thailand's future lay in supplying the world with foodstuffs to alleviate shortages in Europe and Asia caused by World War II. To improve rice yields, a gigantic program of dams and canals was devised with the Chao Phya Dam as its centerpiece. I entered the dam administrator's office to find the damkeeper and lockkeeper hunched over some charts.

"I want to take my boat through the locks," I began.

"Sure," he said. "Where is it?"

"There," I replied, pointing upstream.

He squinted. "I don't see anything."

The evening light was beginning to wane but the boat was still quite visible in the distance.

"Right there. By the bank. Just below the trees." I directed his gaze as he and the lockkeeper peered out the window. They went out on the terrace with their binoculars.

"Oh. That," the damkeeper said finally. "I thought it was a log."

"Me too," agreed the lockkeeper. I shrugged.

"How should I proceed?" I asked, looking down at the lock just below the administration office.

"Oh, it's too late tonight. Bring it down in the morning and we'll run it through," said the lockkeeper.

"O.K., I'll just l leave it where it is."

"No, no, can't do that," said the damkeeper, solemnly. "The boys."

"What boys?"

"The boys from the city come out to drink whiskey on the riverbank. They will '*yoong*' ("mess" is the closest English word) with it. Keep it at the landing in front of headman Paitoon's house."

"Where is that?"

"Back up the river. Around 800 yards."

Nuts. I thanked them and walked upstream. Two delightful five-year-old girls stood on the bank exchanging excited "oohs" and "ahhs" about the boat. When I began untying it, they pelted me with questions (where are you going? why is there water in the bottom of the boat? what's in the back locker?...). I told them I was going to Paitoon's landing. They decided to race me, their brown legs pedaling as they sped up the tree-lined dirt road. They were at the landing when I got there, breathless, a fresh supply of questions tumbling out.

Headman Paitoon said he'd be happy to watch the boat. With the two little girls in tow–they insisted on holding my hands as they skipped along–I walked back to the dam. They seemed disappointed that I wouldn't take them to town so they could ask me more questions. When I suggested that their mothers might be wondering where they were, they looked at each other, shocked at the realization. "Bye, bye, Mr. *Farang*," they said, skipping backwards and waving as they hied for home.

A *songtaew* carried me the four miles into Chainat where I found a small hotel and dropped into a very pleasant sleep.

The next morning, I had hoped to visit the Chainat agricultural station to learn more about the *chamung thanu* (archer) fish. Central Plains farmers are plagued by a brown leaf hopper which lays eggs on young rice plants. The larvae invade the stems, weakening them so the heads fall into the paddy water and drown. The archer fish spits water five feet into the air, knocking the hoppers off the plants, and devouring them when they hit the water. At harvest time, the farmer nets the fish for food, grim reward for its services but a village protein source. In experiments at Chainat, a half dozen fish had cleared a large, hopper-filled plot in less than a week. I wanted to see the fish in action, but it was Saturday and the agricultural station was closed.

It was also a holiday. The previous afternoon I had been startled to see what appeared to be 15-foot-tall birds standing on the riverbank. It turned out the city was celebrating its annual Straw Birds Festival. Townspeople and villagers had fabricated large local and exotic birds from straw, displaying them in a provincial competition. In a grassy expanse near the river, gigantic birds, stood on pick-up trucks, awaiting the judges' arrival. Their plumage and colors were life-like, and the artistry was superb. I passed a pleasant hour wandering among the exhibits, some of them equipped with sound systems to replicate their songs, others with complicated mechanisms which caused them to flap their wings. When the crowds began to swell, I headed for the dam.

A god's-breath mist hung over the reservoir and spray hissed from the spillway as my *songtaew* moved along the long dam crest, some 80 feet above the lower river. Three decades of muddy water pouring through the multi-arched dam's two dozen gates had softened its concrete to the warmth of adobe. The earth colors complemented the sheets of white water crashing through the gates and sliding across the concrete apron that kept the river from eating away its foundation. A fisherman waited just below the spillway, his boat, body, and long bamboo pole static against the thundering water.

Built when boats were the workhorses of the kingdom's transportation system, the Chao Phya Dam was the only one in Thailand equipped with a lock. Planners conceded the demise of the boat age when they elected not to place navigation locks–or even fish ladders–in subsequent dams. For a boy raised on the Columbia River, where even the highest dam had locks and ladders, it was odd to see a river so compartmentalized, with boat traffic confined between concrete barriers.

Shaped like the crossbar of a "T", the lock was slotted across the southern end of the dam, parallel with the bank. Forty feet wide, it could hold two rice barges side by side, a total of 12 barges in its 80-yard length. This morning, the lock was empty. Two gatekeepers in baggy khaki uniforms and glossy billed caps of the sort worn by trainmen, lounged on a railing, smoking.

"Are you operating this morning?" I asked.

"You have a boat?"

"Yeah," and I pointed back up the riverbank where the reddish hull rested. They half-turned to look.

"Sure, we're running," said the older one.

"When can I come down?"

"Whenever you want." I liked them; no crisp, authoritarian self-importance about their positions; service without fuss. I began the long trek up the riverbank to the boat.

"Ticket," the younger one called after me.

"Eh?"

"You need a ticket," he said, nodding towards a booth. Inside, a prim lady sat as though in theater box office awaiting the first patron.

"How much?" I asked her.

"Does your boat have an engine?"

I pointed to myself. "I'm the engine."

She tore a handsomely-printed ticket from a book. "One *baht*."

"Four cents?" I thought. Did I mishear? When I pushed the *baht* across the counter, the ticket slid across to my hand. I thanked her and began walking away. On a thought, I returned to her window.

"How much if I'd had an engine?"

"Two *baht*."

This was obviously not intended as a money-making venture; even two *baht* barely covered the cost of printing the ticket. The gatekeeper motioned me over, tore the ticket along the perforation, and pocketed the counterfoil. "Keep your boat above the dam until we're ready. When the gates open, paddle in." The older man signaled to a workman on the upper gate who leaned on a capstan spoke and slowly walked around and around. Water began crashing into the lock.

By the time I paddled down, the upper gates were opening. I entered a long, narrow trough, the gates boomed shut behind me, and I was lost in a cavernous, roofless hall. The water level fell so slowly–perhaps five feet a minute–that I was unaware of my descent until I noticed the wall's wetted portion broadening. I rode a slow elevator thirty feet to the bottom, mindful of how small I was in the gigantic lock. I wasn't even aware that the ride had ended until I heard, then saw the enormous gates before me creak open, a birth channel into the lower river, the final stretch to the sea.

I should have expected that the lower river would be a letdown–the river below previous dams had been sluggish–but this was utterly devoid of current. Overboard went all hopes of getting home in a week. Even thoughts that the homeward journey would be a triumphal passage, reward for all the work I'd already put in, were jettisoned. But I wouldn't get there by complaining about it. I shoved a paddle in the water and pushed backwards.

On the left bank a beat-up pick-up trundled along a dirt road, the speaker bolted to its roof blaring an advertisement for "*Dra Plaa Sam Plaa*" (Three Fish brand) fish sauce. The droning voice was so loud that it nearly drowned out the cries of "Stop, stop"" from a gaggle of girls in school uniforms running along the bank. I nudged into the shore.

"We ran all the way," one said, breathless, amazed by her feat.

The 12-year-old girls daintily arrayed themselves on the grass, giggling and whispering, careful not to soil their uniforms, politely overlooking the fact that even at this early hour, I was a perspiring mess. I wondered what they could find interesting about my journey.

They conferred among themselves while I waited. At last came the first question, in Thai: "Do you know Michael Jackson?" The others leaned forward eagerly to hear my reply. Of all the questions I might have expected, this was not among them.

"Urrh, I've seen him on TV..." This statement impressed them deeply, as though I'd touched divinity. The interrogation on pop American culture continued, my ineptitude in answering becoming more apparent. To my relief, a quiet moment came and I jumped in with my own questions.

"Are you all from Chainat?"

The leader earnestly went around the circle, introducing them, consulting with each to ensure she had her facts right. One was from Bangkok; her father had been assigned to work at the dam. Since such assignments could last a lifetime, she considered herself a Chainat resident. Because she came from Bangkok the others seemed to regard her as elite.

As I suspected, they knew nothing about the river. "*Klua* (frightening)," one said.

"Why?" I asked, wondering if it had to do with ghosts.

"It is so strong," she explained, her eyes wide. "And big."

"Can you swim?"

They looked at each other. Only one could swim. Sort of. But not very far. In a broad valley filled with rivers, canals, and lakes, it seemed odd that none of them could swim. Little girls splashed in the water but abandoned it around age ten, leaving the childish pursuit to the boys who dove and cavorted as long as the sun was up. But even this boyish horseplay ended by age 14. One almost never saw adults swimming in the river; it just wasn't done. For a people who considered themselves aquatic, it seemed strange.

Curious to know how their aspirations differed from those of upcountry girls, I asked them their plans for the future. I was surprised they had none of the wide-eyed wonder or fear of Bangkok I had encountered upstream, just disinterest.

"It's noisy and dirty," one said. "Too many people," said another. Clearly, its detriments outweighed its merits. They had no lofty goals and seemed content to stay in sleepy Chainat for the rest of their lives, working as "schoolteachers, civil servants, or nurses."

"Why those jobs?" I asked, assuming they wanted to help their fellow countrymen.

"Security," one said, "you get a pension after retirement." "And free health care and your children get free education," added another.

Several of the girls came from farming families which could rely on no safety nets. After growing up with uncertainty, it was easy to understand why they would embrace a job that removed some of the insecurity from life, not to mention that once in a tenured government job, they could count on working there until they retired at age 60. Their only worry was about being assigned to a distant town because it would put them too far from their families.

My question, "could you live on a farm like your parents?" was met with wide-eyed incredulity. They struggled for answers but what it came down to was that while they didn't look down on farmers acquiring their mandatory four (soon to become six) years of education had set them apart from ordinary farm girls. I sensed no soul-searching about life's path, just a happy acceptance of whatever came their way.

Without overture, they jumped to their feet and dashed away, trailing laughter and calls of "Good luck," and "Come back again," and "Don't forget us."

All day, a flirtatious river teased me, pulling me along for a moment and then stopping. Its timing was perfect; just as I was tiring, the current would run again, sometimes imperceptibly, with no surface disturbance, only a house or tree on the bank moving past to tell me I was mobile. It was now 150 yards wide and not more than 10 feet deep. On the left, a yellow silt beach ran 80-100 yards to high banks. From their crest, solemn houses peered through wispy veils of bamboo at the distant river.

Soon, the sun was sinking and it was time to begin the search anew. Several abandoned barges littered the shore and I toyed briefly with the idea of sleeping on one. Just ahead, a wooden boat moving slowly across the river and the set of the passengers and the paddler told me it was a ferry. As I watched, the paddler turned and waved to me, a quiet gesture that enticed me to head for shore to talk.

Well-bronzed and tall for a Thai, Chalor had surprisingly youthful skin for a man of 64. He had been a farmer most of his life, but had retired and given his land to his first son. Another son in Ayutthaya was "*deh foon*" ("kicking dust" i.e. unemployed). He didn't elaborate but I gathered that the second son was a bit of a disappointment. Chalor had been paddling the ferry boat for seven years, 30 passengers a day for one *baht* each.

He agreed to look after my boat, and gave me directions to the headman's house. The silty sand slid away under my feet as I crossed the wide beach and climbed a tall bluff. A long lane overhung by flowering bamboo ended at a canary yellow house surrounded by heavy construction equipment, an anomaly in a village that otherwise seemed devoted to farming. At the house, the wife welcomed me to what would be one of the more bizarre nights of the journey.

A good-looking man named Thongdaeng, about 25 or so, greeted me. He seemed taken aback when I spoke but recovered to say, "I've never met a *farang* who could speak Thai." He then launched into a meandering story about a foreigner he'd once met in a tea stall in his hometown of Roi Et in northeastern Thailand. The foreigner wanted to order orange soda but didn't know how and in fact didn't know anything at all. When Thongdaeng repeated the same convoluted, pointless story three times in the next 10 minutes, I knew he was in an advanced state of inebriation.

"Come on. I'm going to take you home," he slurred. "For dinner," he added. "We'll come back tomorrow morning."

"Why tomorrow morning?"

He regarded me blearily, rocking as he worked on the answer. "We can't get back for..." he screwed up his face and regarded the sky, tried counting on his fingers and gave up, "...many hours."

"Where is your house?" I asked, looking towards the dwellings partially shielded by the bamboo.

"I told you," he said, offended. "Roi Et."

"But that's 250 miles away!"

"Yeah," he belched.

"At least six hours by road! That means we'll be eating at midnight!"

This computation was clearly beyond him. He stared at the ground which was probably moving in rhythm with his body. Finally he muttered, "Yeah. Let's eat here," he nodded at his sagacity.

"No," he suddenly said. "Let's go eat in Chainat. I'll get my motorcycle," and he began to stagger off.

"Why don't we wait for the headman to decide," I suggested and while he was considering it, the headman drove up. From his erratic driving, and the graceless way he stumbled out of the cab and immediately fell to the ground, it was clear that the pair had been tippling for the better part of the afternoon.

"*Sawasdee, khrap,*" the headman said, clasping his hands together while lying on his side in the dirt, partially visible beneath the cab door. Thus was my introduction to one of the more disconnected characters I've ever met.

His wife rushed over to help him up. The only sober male in the yard leaned over to explain, "He's drunk and not too quick on the uptake but he has a good heart." This assessment would be offered several times through the evening, always in a confessional, almost conspiratorial manner but never with embarrassment or malice. They were just stating a fact that was pretty well established from the moment I met him.

It took three recitations as he swayed, glazed eyes locked on mine, before he grasped my story. Even then, I wasn't sure he understood because he pointed to Thongdaeng standing next to him and, weaving in tandem, said, "We're like brothers," and slung his arm around his good friend's shoulders, nearly knocking them both over. They stood unsteadily like this for a moment. Suddenly, the headman stood stock upright. "Your boat," he announced. He peered around the yard.

"Where is it?" he asked no one.

"The river," his wife said.

"Where's that?" He seemed completely disoriented but I wasn't entirely sure it was the whiskey.

She pointed west with her chin.

"Let's go on your motorcycle," he said to Thongdaeng. "You too," he said, throwing his arm around my shoulder, somewhat of a high reach that took a try or two to accomplish.

"I'll walk," I said.

He didn't object. The motorbike was so small that his bum hung over the taillight. They wobbled down the road, visiting both sides of it repeatedly and narrowly avoiding collisions with the bamboo before disappearing around a bend. I wondered how they would navigate the steep trail down the 20-foot cliff. A whoop, a rapid acceleration, a whump, and sudden silence, followed by a string of epithets, told me they'd chosen the short route.

I emerged from the copse as they were disentangling themselves. Leaving the motorbike behind, they began shuffling across the sand, arms locked. Halfway across the beach they were already yelling at the ferryman on the opposite shore to come back.

When Chalor pulled up, the headman explained very solemnly and carefully that he wanted him to look after my boat.

"Yes," said the boatman with great dignity. "I already told him I would."

"Oh," said the headman, non-plussed. "Oh, that's o.k. then," and turned abruptly, careering across the sand, Thongdaeng behind him, business finished, on to the next item on the agenda. If only they could recall what it was. They were nearing the cliff before they remembered me.

"Hey. Foreigner," the headman hollered. "Come on. Drink whiskey."

"I'll be there in a moment," I replied, and turned to talk with Chalor.

His horn-rimmed glasses were tied to his ears by strings and his face was dominated by a full set of large, white teeth. His thick hair was dyed jet black and he covered it with a straw hat, but he seemed, by contrast with the other two, a patrician.

"It might be better if we put it on the other side of the river," he said. "If you paddle it across, I'll bring you back."

Without the baggage or the pressure of finding accommodations, the trip was extremely pleasant. I liked the ferryman. He seemed as calm as the waters he paddled. On the opposite shore, in the shadow of a tall, narrow monastery, he ran an appreciative hand over the boat, nodding his approval.

"It used to be a lot nicer before it was blistered by sun and battered by rocks," I apologized.

"But it is solid. It doesn't fill up with water like a Thai sampan." True.

We leisurely made our way back across the river. In the short span as the sun plummeted towards the other world, the sky had aged from pink to salmon, bathing the *wat* behind us in ethereal light; a perfect evening. We parted and I trudged across the sand and up the bluff to the headman's house.

Despite its bright yellow paint, it seemed to be an ordinary farmhouse. Closer inspection, however, revealed it to be as shambling as its owner. The family, including half a dozen aunts and uncles, sat under a partially-completed roof. An old man well into his dotage sat waiting for dinner. "How many children do you have?" I asked.

"Eight," he said with pride.

"How many of how many?"

"Six boys, two girls," he said, equally crisply.

"And how many grandchildren?"

His face clouded and he was lost in thought. Finally, he scratched his head with the loose gesture of farm men, and looked at me blankly. "Lots," he said, and the conversation ended.

I showered and changed. "The Transformation" made its impact when I emerged from the bathroom.

"Oh," said Mrs. Headman, "we thought you were an old man." Had I been on the river that long?

I was invited to sit at the table, a large round disk of rough concrete that would normally cover a septic tank. The headman and Thongdaeng had disappeared. As other relatives questioned me, I became aware of two big eyes staring at me from the shadows.

"Are you married?" asked the wife.

Instead of my usual story that my wife was a teacher and our two children were in college—a lie preferable to the amazed questions and clucking that generally greeted my admission that I was a bachelor; at my age?— I said I was single. I would regret my honesty.

"Oh, good," beamed the wife for reasons I didn't immediately fathom, although the moon-like eyes in the margins of my field of vision seemed to wax with increased luminosity. The eyes assumed a face and a body that walked past me and into the kitchen. The wife leaned over and whispered, "She's 22 and not yet married." Uh-oh. Suddenly, I was aware that everyone was watching me and every word was freighted with oblique meaning.

Comic relief came to my rescue as the headman and Thongdaeng stumbled into the circle of light. "Ah, whiskey," he said, producing two bottles filled with a cloudy liquid. I agreed to take a smidgen which they interpreted to mean sloshing the glass full to the brim. I'd be dead in an hour if I drank it all so I took just a few dainty sips. The reaction was mixed.

"No, no,.." said the drunken duo, shaking their heads disapprovingly.

"Good, good," said the womenfolk, nodding, my abstinence a point in my favor. I wasn't sure I wanted to earn points but I knew I didn't want to be lying legless under the table.

Years of experience in dealing with awkward situations had honed the wife's instincts for distraction because just as her husband was beginning to berate me for drinking so sissy-like, she announced that dinner was ready. Diverted from my full glass, the pair began emptying theirs in anticipation of the meal.

As we waited for it to arrive, the headman leaned towards me and bellowed, "Have you ever met a headman as drunk as me?" I assured him it was no contest; he won hands down. He seemed quite pleased.

Dinner and daughter appeared. She was marginally pretty but it was easy to see why the house hadn't been overrun with ardent swains. Like her parents, she was simple although it was difficult to ascertain how bright she was because during my entire stay, she didn't utter a word. She just kept looking at me with those big saucer eyes, her every movement and my response carefully noted by the relatives.

As the daughter returned to the kitchen, her mother leaned over to whisper, "She cooked it all by herself. Is it good?"

I was hungry but if that was the deciding factor, I'd flee. I nodded enthusiastically.

"Can you eat *Plaa raa?*" the mother asked. A foreigner's ability to eat stinking, fermented fish, a Northeastern specialty, was as much a mark of his adaptation to Thailand as his ability to wolf down handsful of chilies. I was decidedly more adept at the rotted fish than the chilies. Even then, I generally smiled a fishy smile as the stench worked its way up my nostrils, and gagged if I didn't swallow quickly.

Fortunately, I'd misheard the word. The daughter set before me a steaming bowl of broth containing foot-long eels (*plaa lai*). Eels are tasty but the devil to de-bone and the bowl's arrival ignited a debate. As he saw me trying to fillet it, the headman began shouting, "The bones are edible, the bones are edible," and the women chorused "no they aren't, no they aren't." It quickly turned into a tug of war with me as the rope. The more I irritated the headman (who, admittedly, was beyond more than momentary irritation at this point), the more I fell into the good graces of the matchmakers. I had no idea where this was headed but it was boding ill. I crunched into the bones but before I could take a second bite, the mother snatched it away from me and began skinning off the flesh. She tossed the slender skeleton under the table where a half-dozen dogs and cats immediately began hissing, snarling, clawing and snapping over them.

I fully anticipated that large chunks of my legs were about to disappear. An elderly aunt on the opposite side put a stop to it by picking up a water pitcher and absently sluicing the darkness beneath the table, ending the fight but drenching my pants.

The wife was tussling with the bones of the second eel when the headman reached far across the table–nearly falling into a large bowl of green chicken curry–snatched about four inches of spine and popped it into his mouth. "See," he said triumphantly, crunching loudly. "O.K.," I said. "Let's make a deal. You eat the bones and I'll eat the meat," my riposte delighting everyone, including him. I was sinking farther into a morass of approval.

Other dishes arrived and then the daughter joined us, sitting a quarter of the way around the table to my left. It was appalling to feel those eyes on me, bold looks that didn't go unnoticed by the others. Instead of quelling her as would happen in most households, the relatives seemed to be encouraging her. Mom talked endlessly about what a nice girl she was and was I sure I wasn't married?

As we were finishing dinner, daughter disappeared. She reappeared 10 minutes later, face powdered white and wearing a pink babydoll negligee. Now what? I thought. Before I had time to react, she flounced up the stairs.

"Well," said the headman unnecessarily, "time for bed."

"You'll sleep upstairs," said the wife, not to my surprise.

I was guided to an upper room containing nothing but a queen-sized mattress the thickness of a gym mat, enclosed in a large mosquito net tethered to the corners of the room by plastic string. On the mattress were two, envelope-sized pillows the softness of stone. I crawled under the net and made myself comfortable. The family withdrew. A faint light pored through the open French doors leading to a balcony that had never been built.

The house gradually settled down for the night but for some reason I felt that every ear was straining my direction. I lay on one edge of the mattress, facing outward. As I was beginning to drowse I felt the mosquito net quietly rise and someone slip onto the mattress beside me. I froze, instantly awake.

In the old days, it was traditional for a headman to offer a guest a woman for the night as a form of hospitality. But those days had faded with the large-scale invasion of foreigners in the 1960s. It was possible there were still remote towns where such practices persisted–and this was definitely not a normal family–but would they actually go so far as to offer their daughter to a stranger? Perhaps it was her idea, which was even worse. This would not be regarded as a one-night stand but the beginning of a ten thousand-night stand.

How could I escape without rousing everyone's ire? I waited for a soft hand to reach across to me. But it didn't. Perhaps it was waiting for my hand to make the first move. Even better. Just as I thought I would not be able to sleep, the hand's owner began breathing gently and I realized she was asleep. Off the hook. I decided to let sleeping daughters lie, and drifted off myself.

Dawn arrived. It was Valentine's Day. I recalled the villagers of Tha Sala planning their celebration. The coincidence of the holiday and my present pickle seemed a cosmic joke perpetrated by callous gods.

Long inhalations and exhalations of deep sleep came from the other side of the mattress. Moving almost imperceptibly, I scrunched my way around until I could see the sleeping figure, a maneuver that took nearly ten minutes. Screwing up my eyes, I peered into the semi-darkness at the shoulder-length black hair. And the white T-shirt. And black pants? Oh my god, I thought, almost laughing aloud, it was the 20-year-old son. I was so relieved that it didn't occur to me until later to wonder what he was doing in my bed. When I did, I realized this was his bed and I was the intruder.

I lay for several long moments poleaxed with relief, then headed downstairs where, to my surprise, I found the headman was up and sober. He was doing his accounts and from his struggles, it was apparent that alcohol didn't affect in the least his inability to total up figures. My arrival gave him an excuse to toss aside his pencil and sip coffee with me. He earned most of his income, he said, by doing earth-moving jobs around the province. Most of his equipment was of the tractor and backhoe variety but he had a small Caterpillar bulldozer that was apparently in great demand.

The previous evening Thongdaeng had promised me a breakfast of *pathongkoh* and hot chocolate but there was no sign of him. Instead, the headman's wife placed before me a huge bowl of *khao tom* (rice soup) with slabs of dried, salted fish, and insisted that I eat it all. Even on the best of mornings, boiled rice in plain hot water is a chore to devour but I tucked into it dutifully, perhaps as expiation for my errors of the previous evening. Halfway through, the daughter appeared but her saucer eyes were clouded and seemed not to recognize me. I never saw the son again.

As I was beginning to slosh from the congee, Thongdaeng appeared with the *pathongkoh* and hot chocolate. With the fuss he made about the effort involved and his delight in serving me, one would have thought he'd ridden the entire 12 hours home to Roi Et and back to fetch them. Then again, everyone here was so loopy, it is entirely possible that he did. I ate a second breakfast and smiled gratefully.

I spent the next hour trying to walk off the liquid weighing heavily on my abdomen. I toured the village, taking pictures of bamboo fences surrounding gardens or cows or buffaloes or houses. At one point, I was accosted by a traveling salesman of patent medicines, questionable nostrums and debatable remedies; nowhere among them was the "*Buat Hai*" packet with the huge-headed man. As I looked at the tiny bottles with their quaint labels, the wife appeared at my elbow.

"Oh, this is just what the headman needs." I couldn't make out what the yellowish clear liquid (which resembled–and smelled–like nail polish remover) was meant to accomplish, and the illustration of a stick figure brandishing what appeared to be a tomahawk was not much help either. "Pay the man 35 *baht* and I'll take it back to him," she said, disappearing as quickly as she had appeared. I paid and the man flashed a conspiratorial smile at me as if we were the only ones in on a joke I couldn't fathom.

My boat was waiting on the shore next to the ferry. Downstream, I heard a motor and, squinting against the sun, saw Chalor standing near a short, squat woman. As I approached, I saw that the noise came from a small motor Chalor used as an irrigation pump to suck water from the river; his wife was training the hose on a riverside garden.

"*Tua lantao*," (peas) he said when I pointed at the bushy plants. His wife covered her dumpiness in a faded sarong. In contrast with his beautiful, white teeth, hers were stained red from betel; only three were visible. The pair talked quietly to each other, like old friends, each laughing at the other's comments.

As the Nile laid a thin layer of transported soil on its shores, the

Chao Phya each year nourished its banks. When the monsoon flood waters receded, the couple planted vegetables. The peas were remarkably green but Chalor said that the upper field was dying because the 150-foot hose wouldn't reach it and at 400 *baht*, a 100-foot extension would have been too expensive. I suggested that he dig a hole 150 feet from shore, line it with cheap plastic sheeting, and fill it with water pumped from the river. He could then move the small engine inland to draw water from his new pond, and send it the remaining 100 feet to the drying peas.

"Good idea," he said, brightening. He explained the plan to his wife but she just nodded and murmured "uh, uh," a perpetually jovial woman who accepted whatever life doled out.

Chalor had ferried his early morning passengers to market and then towed my boat from the temple across the river. As we walked to it, I asked him how he'd come to live here.

"I was 25 and had been a soldier fighting the Japanese. When the war ended, I got married. My wife's family offered us some land here so we became farmers. I built our house with wood I cut from the forests that ran along the riverbanks. There were lots of trees then. Not like now."

We talked about our lives while he sat cross-legged in his boat, smoking. He asked if I'd slept peacefully. After a moment's hesitation, I said "yes." He chuckled softly, probably guessing that it hadn't been a quiet evening.

"Sorry about the mess," he said, nodding towards my boat. I'd forgotten to remove a small bag of trash and a dog had gotten aboard, torn the bag, and scattered the contents. Chalor had gathered most of the trash–and likely tossed it into the river–but the dog's dirty pawprints were everywhere. I tried to pay him for guarding it but he waved me away, his big white teeth brilliant in a shy smile. I pushed off.

Disappointing the Tailors

Naam Thuam Paak
(Water floods the mouth)
An awkward moment when telling the truth
can cause you problems

Lazy river, hazy sky. In a featureless landscape, my field of vision was filled with long stretches of dun dust and ochre bluffs. Tenacious grass tufts that had gained footholds on a sandy shore 300 feet wide were cropped by sandy cows herded by small boys whose shouts rang across the empty plain. Leaving their cows to graze, they ran down the beach, trailing a tiny kite made of bamboo, string, and old newspapers glued together with boiled rice. If their yells and laughter could have lifted it, it would have sped skyward. But the wind was ephemeral and the moment they stopped running, the kite fell to earth. In the kite season—still a month away—a burning zephyr would puff paper wedges aloft to quilt the sky with color.

Here, villages were attenuated, their single-story gray, lemon yellow, robin's egg blue, or lime green wooden homes extended a half-mile along the high bluffs. The homes were set firmly on the ground, suggesting that their owners did not fear floods. The house walls facing the river were made of folding doors that allowed cooling breezes to blow in. Clouds of dense foliage, the canopies of ancient trees, shaded the village from the hot sun. Here and there, thick clumps of bamboo combed the sky with pale yellow fingers.

Buddhist wats squatted on a village's upriver end; their buff walls–

running several hundred yards–were often the first indication I was approaching a village. In the center, the wall would be broken by a tall arched gate, pointed like the steep roof of the *wat* it framed. Whereas architects in the north opted for squat monasteries that hugged the ground, these Gothic chapels mimicked praying hands, slender fingers rising high into the sky. From their roof peaks one could have gazed a dozen miles across the countryside were it not for the dust haze.

In the afternoon, the sun crushed me. On the right, the cliffs had crept to the water's edge. Bathed in perspiration, I hugged them in order to pass beneath an occasional cooling tree. As I neared an eroded cliff, I heard voices floating down from above.

"Paw," an elderly woman's lazy voice asked. "What's that *farang* doing?"

The tree branches dipped close to the ground but not low enough to conceal two pairs of legs. From the thick leaves, I heard the man drawl wearily, "*Ap dat,* mother. *Farangs* like to *ap dat.*"

His reply was so unexpected that I burst out laughing. So that's what I was doing out here: "sun bathing." Of all the odd explanations for my journey, this one capped them.

Mid-afternoon, I passed several fishermen in small boats built of galvanized iron sheets stitched to wooden frames. I was about to ask what they were trying to catch when a six-inch long fish leapt into my boat. Since it hardly seemed worth keeping, I reached down to toss it back in the river...and drew back a bloody hand. What appeared to be a fan-like dorsal fin, was instead a series of small, sharp blades. Blood flowed copiously from my hand. I wrapped it with a cloth and tried again to pick up the fish...which chose that moment to flop towards the bow and out of reach. In lunging for it, I nearly upended the boat, the paddle falling overboard and floating away. While paddling with my hands to retrieve it, I heard a splash. The deck was empty. I stanched the blood, muttering imprecations at the departed fish. So much for being a Samaritan.

The current picked up. Small, comforting "V"s streaming downriver from bamboo poles and water plants gave some hope of an easier passage but the sun was setting and it was that time again. On the right bank, men repaired a wooden boat that was more holes than hull.

"Where's the *phu yai baan*'s house?"

One man pointed downstream.

"How far?

"100 yards," he said, without hesitation.

I beached and began walking. Daeng, a quiet boy of 12, joined me. A hundred yards passed, then 200. Half a mile later, I arrived at the door. I hadn't expected people to know distances on water, but on land? Of course, no one was home. I was working out what to do next when Daeng said hopefully, "you could stay at my house."

"Thank you, where do you live?"

We walked another quarter mile to it but his father and mother were away for the day. His grandfather and grandmother sat beneath a tree and although they approved, I wasn't sure the parents would appreciate their son's springing a surprise like me on them. The sun was now very low in the sky.

"I'd love to stay, Daeng, but it would be better to talk with your parents first. Do you know when they'll be back?"

He thought a moment. "Maybe after dark?"

They would probably offer shelter in order to avoid embarrassment, but the house looked poor and I didn't want to put them in an awkward position. And if they didn't agree, it would be too late to find other lodgings.

"I think I have to move on," I said, and Daeng's face reflected his disappointment. What to do? "I'd like to take your photo so I can remember you," I said and he became excited. He ran into the house to change and I found myself pacing, watching the sun sinking. "Oh no," I thought when I heard water splashing, "he's taking a bath. I'll be here forever." But he finished in record time and in clean T-shirt and shorts and wet, slicked-back hair, he posed next to his bicycle, a big smile on his face. I took down his address and promised to send him the photo later. Then, I plodded the three-quarters of a mile back to my boat.

"Did you find the house?" one of the boat repairers asked.

"Yes, but he wasn't home."

"No, he went to Chainat for the day."

"Thanks," I said, wondering why they hadn't said something before.

It was panic time again. I paddled hard, scanning the banks but the broad beaches separating villages from the river held no one who might direct me to a headman's house. Beaching the boat, trekking to a farmhouse and asking directions every 100 yards would eat up valuable minutes of daylight. Just as I was resigning myself to sleeping on the riverbank– not a bad option since it seemed soft–a man called to me from behind a screen of tall grass. His disembodied voice told me that the headman's house was "beneath the raintree just above the beach."

Of course, on reaching the cliff, I discovered that the house was 200 yards farther in. As I walked a dusty road, strolling villagers stopped to ask me questions. They were inordinately proud of their village, telling me it was "*Pattana chalern maak,*" (very developed). They were so gentle that I relaxed, realizing that were the headman unable to put me up, I'd surely find an invitation elsewhere. With the evening light filtering through the bamboo trees, I slowed to enjoy the walk.

The headman wasn't home but his son-in-law, Suwit, told me I was welcome to stay. I settled in and had just begun to ask Suwit about the village when a blocky young girl careened off the doorframe and bounced into the room, stopping dead when she saw me. Without missing a beat, she said, "Oh good," and bounced out the door.

"My daughter," Suwit said, proudly. "She's 11."

A moment later, Duangjai ran back in clutching a notebook and pencil. Flopping down on a stool in front of me, she smoothed the notebook on her lap. With pencil poised, she fixed me in her dark eyes and began an interrogation. I'd been asked thousands of questions but no one had ever taken notes.

After the half-dozenth question, the answers to which she carefully wrote in Thai, I asked her why she was recording my words.

"Work," she said.

"Work?"

"I have a school project due tomorrow."

"And I'm it?"

"Yep."

"What's the subject?"

"Aquatic life."

"That's interesting."

"Yeah, we're supposed to write about fish. I didn't know which fish to choose but then you came."

"Sooo, how do I qualify as a fish?"

"You don't, but the teacher and the kids will be so interested that a *farang* rowed a boat here that they won't notice that you're not a fish."

This one will be a handful when she gets older, I thought. Her father beamed approvingly. Her questions answered, she left the room to write the report, cautioning me that she might be back with more questions.

Suwit told me that the village was *champ chanalert* (Number One) among all villages in Singhburi province. "It won an award last year."

"For what?" I asked.

"It was the only village in the province where everyone paid their taxes."

A rare distinction, indeed. The authorities must have been stunned.

A TV in the corner announced that M-16-wielding bandits had ambushed a tourist boat in the Kok River near Chiang Rai, killing a British woman. The police had used helicopters to track the robbers. You could be sure that if tourism–the leading foreign exchange earner–were threatened, the police would be galvanized to action. The robbers didn't stand a chance.

"There's no crime here," Suwit assured me. "Everyone is happy." From what I'd seen, he was probably right.

Suwit and his wife were schoolteachers but he had taken a course on public water systems in order to supply drinking water to the village's 300 "roofs". Each household had a water meter and paid monthly fees. I could hear the pumps hammering away outside, raising water into huge tanks to provide good water pressure.

The headman returned but after welcoming me, hurried off to a village meeting, leaving us to enjoy a delicious dinner. When I headed for bed, the water pump was still thumping away just outside the wall of my room. I reflected that I'd slept on 40 mats, floors, and plots of ground in 45 days. Each place had a different set of sounds, nearly all of which interfered with sleep. Not only had I forgotten what my own bed felt like. I'd forgotten the flavor of Western food and the sensation of English on my tongue. I missed simple things like muesli and milk, my cat Squeak, music, and conversation with friends. To make matters worse, my feet were beginning to fester again and my hands hurt from the moment I woke until I fell asleep. Basically, I was tired, bone tired. I needed about 24 hours of sleep to feel fully refreshed. Maybe tonight I could make a bit of a dent in my fatigue.

Almost mockingly, the water pump clumped and hissed all night.

Suwit's daughter was even more animated at breakfast, if that were possible. Her mother asked about her report.

"I'm only going to show it to father," she said, petulantly.

"I know the assignment was supposed to be about fish but don't you think you're taking liberties in describing Steve as a fisherman?"

"He caught a fish yesterday. Didn't you," she said, adamantly.

"But he jumped into my boat," I protested, laughing.

"So?" she said, defiantly. So, I was a fisherman; I'd been called worse. Had I said I was studying fish, villagers would have comprehended the purpose of my journey. It made more sense than the fumbling reasons I provided.

The air was cool and the current was strong so I paddled all morning. I halted when a rotund woman in her 50s hailed me from a high bank 30 feet above the river. *Uan* ("Fat", a nickname she accepted as a simple statement of fact), handed me a glass of cold water as I completed the climb up the bluff. As we approached the house, out the door walked her husband, a scrawny beanpole to her hydrant fleshiness, yet another odd couple.

We discussed farming and the seasonal rise and fall of the river. "You're lucky you live so high above it, safe from the floods," I said.
"No!" they said simultaneously, and showed me where a flood had climbed four feet up the house posts. "The waters stayed more than a month," the wife said. "They killed the rice crop and about a dozen fruit trees."

"When was this?" I asked.

She frowned, as if the wrinkles would trap a date falling out of her brain. "Oh, several years ago," she ventured. Then, she brightened. "Eh, it was the year mother died. Five years ago," she said emphatically.

Her husband claimed that they had also lost land to the dredgers. "They cut so close to shore that pieces of the bluff kept falling into the river," he said. It didn't stop until the provincial government banned dredging and the companies moved upriver to Chainat. But farming was never an easy road. While their land and flooding problems had abated, they found it difficult to raise crops without their children to help them. "They make more money in the city," Uan said, without complaint.

"What if they had stayed here?" I asked.

"It would have been difficult," Uan said. "Our fields are very small."

It was a familiar story. A tiny parcel of land divided among three children yielded insufficient income to support a family, however small. With shrinking forests, the traditional approach of clearing new land was no longer an option. Fortunately, with Bangkok now experiencing an economic boom, children flocked to the city to find better-paying jobs, but left behind a farming tradition and knowledge that had been built up over eons. In Chiang Mai valley, I had found villages entirely populated by elderly people whose fields lay fallow for lack of workers to till them.

"Who will farm your fields when you get old?" I asked. They shrugged and sighed. "Maybe relatives will come from upcountry to help us," he said. They didn't talk much about it but it was clear they were concerned about the fate of lands held for generations, soil bound up with their history as a family. As we strolled and talked, she pulled tamarinds and papayas off the trees and stuffed them in my pockets, so that by the time I was ready to leave, I was laden with enough fruit to last several days.

The sky was broiling and I was lazing my way downriver when I heard a bell chiming the noon hour. Odd, I thought, Buddhist monasteries ring the hour only at 8 a.m. and 6 p.m. And these bells were more like gongs; richer, more resonant as though a friar were tolling the Angelus across the Loire. Then I heard scratching and realized it was a very old record being played on a very old phonograph. Rounding the bend, I came upon a bizarre sight: a cathedral rising high above the right bank. In design, it seemed more Spanish than French, with beautifully-executed, delicate lines. It was such an anomaly in the Thai countryside that I stopped to investigate.

It was boarded up, its doors locked and its belfry empty. I went around the side, looking for a door, and found...nothing. A church had obviously stood here, its foundations were still visible but aside from an iron circular staircase leading to the belltower, nothing remained but the facade. Boys kicked a soccer ball across the former sanctuary, running over when they saw me.

"What is this?" I asked.

"*Bot krit*," (literally, a "Christian ordination hall", i.e. church), said one, bouncing the ball on the concrete floor. At that moment, a Thai dressed in priestly robes strolled up to introduce himself as Father Somchai. Catholics? In the middle of Buddhist farming country?

He laughed. "This village was founded 100 years ago by two Buddhist families. Several years later, two French missionaries arrived and the families converted." He swept his arm across the skyline. "There are several Catholic villages in the area."

"And the church?"

"Built in 1938. The facade was added in 1949. Now, only the facade is left."

"And the rest?"

"Destroyed by the 1983 flood. We built a new church in 1986. Over there," he said, pointing to a gray building surrounded by mango trees.

The rest of Pahalithai was exactly like any other Thai village. Had I not known it was Catholic, nothing–aside from the church and the monk dressed in black, rather than orange, robes–would have tipped me off. The priest accompanied me to my boat, asking about my journey, hands clasped behind his back like a French cleric. It was as though I had taken a strange turn through a reality warp and entered a curious enclave.

Then, as usual, a short step took me from the divine to the droll. I was looking for a place away from the heat, to write down the morning's events. I found it just downriver at a car ferry landing where, a short way up a dirt road a corrugated-iron coffee shop leaned against a big tree. The iced coffee was over-sweetened with thick condensed milk but it was cold. I no sooner opened my notebook when a chunky cop plunked down heavily on the stool beside me, and began a disjointed diatribe on the relative merits of Thailand and America. He extolled Thailand and Thai life and wondered if we had anything to match it in the U.S. He was impossible to ignore since he virtually shouted at me four inches from my face. Having established that Thailand was far better than U.S., he asked:

"When are you going back?"

"I don't know."

"When you do, take me with you," a statement delivered not as a request but as an ultimatum. Then, his partner walked in, sat down and proceeded to bark out questions of a word or two as though interrogating me. Name? Country? Profession? Coming from? I felt like I was completing an immigration arrival card. Finding it impossible to concentrate or contribute to this inane conversation, I smiled, paid, and left. Near the ferryman's booth, I sat beneath the tall tree, trying to re-organize my scattered thoughts.

Then the kids showed up, four of them, filled with vim and curiosity. I gave up trying to write and instead spent a pleasant half hour talking with them. They were describing their plan to build a bombproof kite with plastic bags and nylon string, when a car drove up to the landing. Four inebriated men stumbled out and swaggered over, enveloping me in fumes and idiocy. They thought it funny to talk gibberish as if they were speaking English. When I failed to understand, they would switch to Thai and I'd answer in Thai. Then the charade would begin again, over and over, the same routine. Would the ferry never come?

The kids retreated and from a distance, ridiculed the men for being so drunk. My tormentors just waved them away and continued to pelt me with nonsense. The more they jabbered, the more the kids jeered at them until finally, one man shambled up the road to drive them away. But they weren't a bit afraid. While giving ground, they continued to laugh and taunt him. I had to admire their spunk; I wished I could do the same. In the end, the sun did him in and he collapsed into the back seat of the car.

The ferry pulled in and the men piled into the car but it took the drunken driver several attempts to start the engine. He eventually succeeded, but it was still in gear and began lurching towards the ferry, with him hanging onto the steering wheel as to a saddle pommel. The car bucked so violently that he inadvertently turned the wheel and the vehicle headed for my beached boat. Oh, jeez, I thought, it he hits it he'll destroy it. But the car kept turning, missing my boat but putting him in great danger of plunging into the river.

Instinct must have kicked in because it occurred to him to brake. The car hopped twice more and stopped with one wheel in the water. The men sat inert for several minutes before the driver bellowed "*alai wahh* (what's this)?" in anger at the car. His friends began berating him, not for bad driving but because he had neglected to let them out before he drove into the river. The ferry operator, a slender woman in her 20s, just looked at them, disgusted.

The quartet barely managed to get the car on the ferry without driving it off the far end. They were shouting humorous insults at each other as the boat pulled away, leaving me in silence. I tried to write but my mood was shot. The page was still blank when the ferry returned. The woman left it idling and came to sit beside me.

"Jerks!" she said.

"What happened?" I asked.

"They decided to see if they could drive off the minute I touched the shore. But I have to reverse to slow down or I'll slam into the bank. Luckily, I saw what they were doing and shouted at them. They braked just before they ran off the front of the boat and were crushed between the bow and the bank. I hate drunk people," she said, with considerable heat.

I commiserated with her and we talked a while. Then she asked: "Would you like a ride? Free," flashing a merry smile.

In the pilot house, she stood at the helm beneath a calendar displaying Mt. Zermatt in its winter coat. Her father normally operated the ferry, she said, but he was ill. She'd traveled back and forth with him since she was a child so knew what to do. She seemed fragile, but she spun the wheel and pulled on the throttle with the strength of someone twice her size. It was easy to imagine her scolding the drunks, cowing them into obeying her.

The memory of the cool air blowing off Mt. Zermatt faded quickly once I was back in my own boat, working my way down the river's griddle-hot surface. The mountain's freshness didn't kick in until mid-afternoon when I was treated to a small upriver gale. I was beginning to understand the correlation between the sun/clouds and the wind. When the clouds hid the sun, the wind picked up; when the sun re-emerged, it dropped. The sun played peek-a-boo all afternoon. When the feeble current disappeared, I gave up. Rounding a bend, I came upon a huge monastery on the right bank that my map identified as Wat Chaiyo (Victory Monastery). As there were no houses near it I pulled for the opposite bank where an older man was tending a boat. He asked me the usual where, what, how, etc. and when I told him I was searching for the headman's house and a place to stay, he immediately said, "Stay with me!" When I agreed, he began chortling "Oh, good, good, good. We can talk together. Oh, good luck to me. I'm so happy." His intensity and good cheer were mildly alarming, reminiscent of Jamrat's "today's my lucky star." But when he rushed to unload my gear and move it up the beach, I followed him. His clothes and his battered boat told me he wasn't mannered or manored. Since most of the people with whom I had stayed had been relatively affluent, this could be an interesting departure.

Thong-in lived 200 feet from the river in a stilted house. Beneath the living quarters was a workshop with 17 sewing machines where his employees stitched clothes on sub-contract from a Bangkok garment manufacturer. It was evening but several workers were still hunched over their machines, working feverishly in the meager light provided by two fluorescent tubes. Thong-in's wife shouted in frustration at one worker but when she saw me, she abruptly stopped, looking at her husband for an explanation.

"I brought home a *farang!*" he announced as if he'd just netted a fish. His wife wasn't quite sure what to do with the catch.

"Get him a glass of water," Thong-in ordered. She re-tied her faded floral-print burgundy sarong–something Thai women often did when flustered–and scurried to the kitchen.

"You'll sleep upstairs," Thong-in said. We climbed to a living room bare...except for three grandfather clocks. Oh no, I thought, but I was now committed. Dropping my belongings, I prepared to shower in a corrugated iron enclosure beneath the house. I was about to dispense with my sarong so I wouldn't have to dry it when I heard tittering and saw small eyes peering through the cracks between the ceiling boards. I kept the sarong.

Dinner was basic fare–a yellow curry and some vegetables–and Thong-in's wife hovered anxiously, watching me eat. Several times she apologized for the meagerness of the meal, embarrassed that they were serving an honored guest so badly. I smiled and assured her that the food was excellent, which was true, but she wasn't convinced.

Joining us was their son-in-law Somsak. He ran the sewing operation and while he was economical with his words, one sensed his quiet competence. As we batted at clouds of flying ants that kept falling into our food and water, we talked about their small business. Thong-in, loquacious but never boring, told me he'd been a farmer before getting into the garment trade.

"I grew rice, supported six children. My wife and I could earn about 12,000 *baht* ($480) a year but there were expenses: 4,000 *baht* ($160) for fertilizers and 1,000 *baht* each ($40) for two field hands."

"Sounds tough."

"Oh, we grew our own food but you can raise rice only a few months a year. What do you do when the fields are empty and there is no rain? You sit. Or go to Bangkok to work. That's what my wife did. She got a sewing job in Bangkok and that's when I got the idea to set up my own operation here."

"Why here?"

"Well, we tried it in Bangkok but we couldn't afford the rents. We did much better here, but it wasn't until Somsak got involved that it really began to grow. He's really smart."

Somsak flushed under his father-in-law's praise but it was clear from the catch in his voice that the old man was indebted to him for keeping their heads above water.

"Do you ever miss farming?"

"Nah. I miss the water buffalo and the cool breezes and the fruit trees but not the work. It's very hard."

"And my boat," he said as an afterthought, smiling warmly. "I did like you did once."

"Really?"

"Once, before the Chao Phya Dam was built, I bought a boat in Kampaeng Phet and several of us paddled it downriver, looking for work. It was the rainy season so the river was really flowing but we made it from Nakhon Sawan to here in a day and a night, paddling without stopping. What a great trip!"

And what a hell of a feat! It had taken me eight days to make the same distance. Even aided by a river in floodtide, running non-stop, and with several paddlers to share the work, it was a long journey. We talked about various points along the river and I reveled in finally finding someone who understood what I was doing and didn't think I was insane.

As we talked, I was observing the house and its occupants. There was a striking contrast between the dynamics of a poor family and that of the affluent one for whom money buys time and space. Here, many people were crammed into small quarters, unable to escape each other, and the stress took its toll. They tended to yell at each other, as though pretending they were separated by great distances. Beneath their graciousness was a palpable frustration and more than a hint of suppressed violence.

Tempers flared, sharp words were exchanged, especially with the children. "Eat or mother won't love you," and similar endearments were shouted at the toddlers. It was the fear of the future that I'd encountered elsewhere along the river.

Their concerns were legion: costs of new objects, theft, losses, breakage. Any malfunction was regarded as a dent in the future, eating up cash already allocated for something else. I was seeing poverty up close and thanking my stars I only had to experience it for one night.

"How much rent do you pay in Bangkok?" Thong-in asked. All ears strained for my answer. I mentally adjusted it downwards, knowing they were poor.

"3,500 *baht* ($ 140) a month" I lied, half of the true rent.

Astonishment. "3,500 *baht?*! That's really expensive."

"But I share it with someone else," I added hastily. "That cuts it to 1,750 *baht.*"

"Still too much. We stayed in an apartment in Huay Kwang (in northern Bangkok) for only 1,000 *baht* ($40) a month," they said, shaking their heads. I'd seen these apartments: a grubby room with a single fluorescent tube on the ceiling, windows covered with anti-burglar bars, holed screens (if any), and six people sleeping on thin mats.

Here, the family received pieces for blouses and other garments from a Bangkok supplier and assembled them under the house. Somsak rode a bus and then a *tuk-tuk* to Bangkok ten times a month to deliver the finished goods to a middleman who then shipped them overseas. When I asked about problems, he exhaled forcefully, saying "*yuh*" (lots).

"It's tough to find good workers willing to stick with it."

"How long do they stay?" I asked.

"Two, maybe three days. Then, they disappear. How can we run a business when never know how many employees we'll have each day? It's impossible to meet deadlines."

"How much do you pay them?"

"A lot. Two *baht* (eight cents) per piece." I couldn't even imagine working for that amount but if he thought that 1,750 *baht* for an apartment was costly, he probably regarded two *baht* he paid the workers as extortion. It might explain why the employees were unmotivated, working for him because they couldn't find better-paying jobs. It was hard to regard Somsak as an exploiter and his lifestyle was hardly extravagant. It sounded like he was operating on very tight margins and even these small fees cut into his profits. With fabric and labor, the blouses cost around 30 cents to make and sold for at least 25 times that amount in Europe or the U.S. I thought about the times I'd priced shirts in department stores and thought the workers well paid.

Thong-in excused himself. "I have to go sleep in the boat."

"Aren't the mosquitoes bad?"

"They're terrible," he laughed. "But if I don't sleep in it, someone will steal it. I'll watch yours too," he added. People with nothing stealing from people with nothing.

Everything conspired to deny me sleep, and they came in multiples of three. All night, three geckos–one less than 10 feet from my head– bellowed "*too-kae, too-kae*." Just as the presence of the tiny, chirping house lizards portends good luck, Thais consider it good luck to hear the foot-long tookae to call seven times in a row. These geckos' good fortune stemmed from their inability to reach the magical number which would have given me time to clear my head, locate them, and bludgeon them. Instead, the miscreant generally quieted just as I was zeroing in on him. Then he'd move to another location and begin again.

And then, there were the grandfather clocks. This time, I decided to silence them. Creeping stealthily, I opened each clock's glass panel and stopped its pendulum. Then, I set my watch alarm for 5 a.m., ample time to re-start and reset them.

Somewhere around midnight, three hounds in the next yard got into a horrific fight, snarling and howling as they removed large chunks from each others' hides. Everyone awakened and began yelling at the dogs, making even more of a din. Somebody tossed rocks that missed and clashed against the cymbal-like corrugated iron fence. Finally, someone on the balcony poured a bucket of water on them and the curs ran yipping into the darkness. Peace settled over the village once again.

But not for long. At around 3 a.m., there was a tremendous crash and cursing from downstairs. Lights came on and the family pored down the staircase to confront the sprawling figure of Thong-in's son, drunk and shouting. He was looking for his wife who had apparently run away from home in Bangkok after an altercation. Assuming she'd come here, he had caught a late bus, downing Mekhong whiskey along the way. When he couldn't find his key, he'd tried climbing over the metal fence, waking the entire neighborhood. He was alternately cursing and crying as the family tried to hush him.

"Be quiet, you'll wake the *farang*."

"*FARANG*! WHAT *FARANG*?"

"The *farang* sleeping upstairs."

"UPSTAIRS?" Uh oh, I knew what was coming next. He clumped up the stairs, missing several along the way, and poked half his body under the mosquito net.

"HEY, *FARANG*! COME DRINK WHISKEY WITH ME!"

I muttered several English replies which, thankfully, he didn't understand, then smiled and tried to dissuade him. But he was insistent, repeating, "COME DRINK, COME DRINK, GO PARTY" over and over. I stayed put, and his mood switched from bleary affability to wrath.

"WON'T GO DRINKING WITH ME. I'M NOT GOOD ENOUGH TO DRINK WITH, EH?"

Supine and half-naked was not the most advantageous position for dealing with the situation. I was throwing on clothes as family members appeared, clutching his arm and dragging him away. He was still shouting.

"PEOPLE LOOK DOWN ON THE POOR. THEY THINK THEIR COMPANY ISN'T GOOD ENOUGH..." and similar sentiments. Were the incident to occur in the States, the neighbors would be calling the cops. But Thais are reluctant to confront someone, even drunks, with the bad news that their behavior is upsetting people.

The family finally got him downstairs where he began yelling about how no one cared about him and why had his wife run away and why wouldn't the *farang* go drinking with him. The family's reaction was not to console him but to deflect his ire, laughingly joshing him for being drunk and stupid. He continued to rant until Somsak went out to talk with him. The result, however, was damned little sleep for anyone.

At 5 a.m., my watch alarm beeped and in my bleariness, it took me a while to recall why I had set it. Just as I was remembering, I heard the household stirring. I zipped across to the clocks and began running them through the hours, clutching the chimes to muffle their tolling. I was no sooner back under the mosquito net than someone exited from the bedroom and went downstairs. My heart was pumping and I was wide awake, with no hope of further sleep. The myth of the peaceful countryside is just that, a myth.

At breakfast, nobody mentioned the night's ruckus. The conversation was about money. Thong-in wanted to know if I could help them get a better price for their piecework.

"I'm a writer, not a businessman," I said.

"Ask one of your friends, they must know," Thong-in insisted.

"Really, I don't know anyone in the garment business."

It was obvious from their expressions that I was lying. How could I live in the city and not know someone in the garment business? Why was I refusing to help them? their faces asked. The atmosphere became unpleasant. I lamely said I'd see what I could do. They gave me their address.

"Give me your telephone number in Bangkok and I'll call you next time I'm there," said Thong-in. No, I thought, I don't want you to. Why did I hesitate: they had provided hospitality, so why was I reluctant to return the favor? Because a lot of people had provided hospitality and I envisioned them all descending on my apartment, expecting to stay and be entertained.

This had occurred many times after up-country trips. In several instances, they had stayed a week and I was soon overwhelmed, in part because, while I wasn't rich, I seemed so by comparison with their simple lives. They looked at everything in the apartment, asking its price. I didn't think they were about to steal anything but the disparity in incomes put us on two levels and made it difficult to converse.

Their stays had also made me aware of my dual nature–urban and rural–and the vast differences between then. Outside their village setting, we really didn't have a lot to talk about. While I was thankful for their help, I preferred to pay for my meals and move on, ending the association on my departure. Was this the attitude of someone who was truly grateful to them or someone who took advantage of others? What are a traveler's obligations to a gracious host? I didn't yet have an answer, but just as I had no compunction about assuming a false persona to cocoon myself and maintain privacy, I had few reservations about severing a connection once I left a village. Many of my hosts I would visit at a later date and take a gift, but I preferred to maintain the distance between us. There were just too many of them and too few of me. I gave Thong-in a phony number.

Somsak wanted to show me Wat Chaiyo so we piled into their

small motorboat and headed across. The monastery was huge but not ostentatious. It had been simply decorated, letting its bulk speak for itself. Four enormous overlapping roofs sheltered what the abbot claimed was Thailand's largest seated Buddha image. Incense swirled and the air reverberated with the clack of *siamsi* sticks used in divination. Petitioners shook cans filled with bamboo sticks half the thickness of a chopstick and with a number written on one end. When a stick fell out, the seeker took it to a rack at the back of the hall. There, he matched the stick's number with one of two dozen numbered slips of paper. Printed on the paper was a prediction about his coming days, a fortune cookie without the cookie, a chance draw in the great fate lottery.

I shook the can and number 17 clattered to the floor. The slip of paper told me I'd be going on a long journey that would bring me wisdom and riches. So far so good on the wisdom; I had my doubts about the riches.

As I was leaving, I placed some money in the donation box and was rewarded with pleased "oohs" and "aahs". It occurred to me that supporting their *wat* was one way of repaying my hosts for hospitality, a valuable lesson I would employ in other villages.

Still, it was with relief that I re-boarded my boat, and waved goodbye. Thong-in's family clearly regarded me as a savior. Rich and connected, I could help them out of the morass of poverty. And I was going to disappoint them.

God chose to smite me for my lack of compassion. I had paddled three miles when the wind god put his hand in my face, and shoved me backwards. Black clouds scudded across the river, trailing spume. When I smelled rain, I pulled for shore.

At a landing, a few drops plopped around me and then stopped. Would it or wouldn't it? An older woman was gathering freshly-washed clothes into a bright blue basin.

"Is it going to rain?"

"Yes."

"Hard?"

"Very hard."

I scanned the sky again. Overhead, the sky was pale. Rain looked highly unlikely but I knew better than to challenge local prognosticators. I recalled too many days when I'd leave the house under a threatening sky, clutching my umbrella. My maid would say "why the umbrella? It isn't going to rain." And it wouldn't. On other days, I'd head out into what passes for blue sky in Bangkok and the maid would warn, "better take your umbrella." The first few times, I scoffed. And got drenched. Then I learned: don't question, just do as she says. I never have figured out how she knew.

This one knew. Finding the landing too high, I paddled the boat to shore and stepped into knee-deep sucking mud. Sucking my slime-coated legs from the muck, I climbed the bank to find myself at a primary school set on stilts. I had just ducked into the open area beneath it when the skies opened up, pelting the earth with fat drops, running in torrents, soaking everything.

Settling in for a long wait, I slumped into a squat, my back against a pillar, and began writing. With me were three young boys who, very late for school, were waiting for a break to slip into class unnoticed. Twenty minutes later, the rain stopped as suddenly as it had begun.

The afternoon was death. Even considering my lack of sleep, the boat felt incredibly heavy, as though I were paddling a refrigerator. I shifted my weight forwards and backwards but nothing alleviated the drag. At one point, I plunged my arm into the water and ran my hand along the boat bottom certain that a 400-pound barnacle had attached itself to the hull. I finally struggled into Ang Thong after six hours, having covered only eight miles.

Ang Thong had no waterfront, no promenade or walls. At a shanty so well secluded under the bridge that I nearly missed it, I came upon a disheveled man in his 20s who appeared to be supporting himself by fishing. He talked with me in whispers, his eyes darting furtively; odd behavior and, come to think of it, an odd place to be living. He agreed to look after the boat.

"What's wrong with this river?" I asked him. "Why does it feel like it is backing up?"

"It is backing up."

"How?"

"The ocean."

"We're 115 miles from the ocean!"

He shrugged.

With Bangkok's low elevation, the tides pushed ocean water

upriver twice a day, quite swiftly at times. Many guests at my riverside house had asked, "which way is the ocean?" and been surprised that it was the opposite direction from the river's flow. Ayutthaya, 89 twisting river miles from the Gulf of Thailand, was only 11.5 feet above sea level and there the river was tidal affected. But Ayutthaya was still 26 miles downstream. Could the ocean's power reach this far north? If so, I'd have a very long, very hard pull to the sea, all work and no help from the river. Once again, I began mentally ripping up schedules.

Before sending me in search of a hotel, the fisherman peered over the parapet. Assured that the quay was deserted, he pushed me gently on my way and quickly ducked back into his hovel. I wondered briefly if it was wise to put the boat the care of an fugitive, but then dismissed it. If he was on the lam, he certainly wasn't going to make a clean getaway in a teak tub like mine.

At a small backstreet hotel, I settled in for a long sleep, thankful I wouldn't have to contend with dogs, drunks, or clocks. That the bed had last been occupied by an elephant, with a deep depression into which I kept falling, was a minor irritant by comparison. Perhaps with a full night's sleep, I could stop ticking off the miles and get back into the spirit of the journey. The map told me that in one more day, I'd reach Ayutthaya; four days and I'd be in Bangkok. After that, I could coast to the sea.

I was dreaming. With the oncoming tide, the boat was becoming heavier, not lighter. I kept hearing Sirichai, the boatbuilder, saying "but just put a motor on it and it'll go very fast." He might be right. It wouldn't be the first time I had been tempted to put an engine on it. A jet engine.

Muttering Ducks

An Ninthaa Kaalee Muan Thee Naam,
Mai Chork Cham Muan Ao Meed Maa Kleed Hin
(Water poured into a river leaves no trace,
a knife struck on a stone makes no mark)
Sticks and stones may break my bones,
but words cannot hurt me

Early on a murky morning, I threaded my way through a maze of alleyways to reach the river. When I hailed him, my mysterious boat guard peered from his doorway and, as before, spoke in hushed tones. But when I gave him 50 *baht* for guarding the boat, he was so surprised that he thanked me in a normal voice. Catching himself, he scanned the parapet with worried eyes. Definitely on the lam, I concluded.

As I pushed off, the sky cleared and the wind went my way for a change. The shallows were filled with magenta lotuses, a bright-blue king-fisher perched on a log, and crow-pheasants whooped softly as they hunted insects in the tall grass. In my mania to reduce weight, I tossed my spare paddle amidst them.

Then, windows opened in the grass walls. Through them, I could see kilns; curious, I pulled over to take a look. Clayish soil, water, and rice husks (for porosity) were being poured into large rectangular pits where men in muddy T-shirts and faded sarongs walked around and around, mixing the quagmire with their feet, a technique as old as the pharaohs. Pressed into wooden frames, sun-dried, and then baked in the kilns, the gooey mass was transformed into bricks and tiles. It was probably in pits like these that artisans had fashioned the building blocks for the magnificent temples and palaces of Ayutthaya, Siam's capital from 1351 to 1767.

Here, I also encountered my first "long-tailed" boat. On the stern, a car engine mounted on a pivot sent its power to the propeller via a 10-foot shaft. The pivot allowed the driver to swing the shaft in a 240-degree arc, enabling him to maneuver the boat in the hundreds of narrow canals that branched to either side of the river. Unfortunately, the benefits were offset by the engines' unmuffled roar that ripped the calm air like a chain saw.

The air was also rent by hecklers shouting "Hey, look at the dumb *farang!*" and "Hey, *farang*, put an engine on it; you'll get there faster". Why their derisive comments should have annoyed me, I wasn't sure; cities everywhere produce similarly disaffected young men. It would be easy to suggest that I was irritated because I no longer received the special treatment I'd experienced in the North, but it was more than that. Their jeers echoed what I interpreted as an altered perception about their surroundings.

Here in the Central Plains, I was discovering that the river was regarded as an impediment to travel, a sewer for urban garbage, and a source of sand for building projects. While upriver farmers never forgot how their "Mother" nourished them, it seemed that townspeople had turned their backs on it. Such was my assessment on a hot and sweaty day but I would be the first to admit that I was tired and irritable. In a sour mood I plodded south through the blistering afternoon, ignoring the loudmouths.

At Wat Chulamani the river divided, with most of its water flowing southwest into the Chao Phya Noi (Little Chao Phya) that rejoined the main river a dozen miles south. For several millennia, the Little Chao Phya had been the river's main channel but in 1857 engineers dug a three-mile-long shortcut to the southeast to provide Ayutthaya with additional water. I turned left into the newer strait.

After days on a river stretching 150 feet either side of me, the 80-foot-wide shunt seemed intimate. Big leafy trees filled with twittering birds dipped their branches almost to the water's surface. They shaded Thai-style houses–the kind rarely seen today except in picture books–stilted wooden homes whose steep roofs rose to pointy gables and curlicue eaves resembling elf shoes. For more than an hour, I paddled quietly down a serene river bathed in golden light filtering through the trees. At the Baan

Wat Mai landing, I tied up and walked a hundred yards downstream, hoping to find the village *kamnan.*

Set a quarter-mile from the river, Wat Mai was an island floating in a ocean of rice plants that ran to the horizon. In the open water along the field's edge, a straight-backed, bare-chested man in a *pakoma* paddled a small sampan. Before reaching me, the stately figure abruptly turned right and entered the standing rice. Within a few strokes, only his head, shoulders, and paddle were visible above a sea of green that undulated gently in the evening breeze.

Halfway down the road to the *wat*, a bespectacled elderly man peered into the distance, as though watching for a friend on his way to visit. Like him, I stood with my hands clasped behind my back.

"What are you looking at?" I asked, perplexed.

"Oh, nothing," he said, somewhat embarrassed.

"But you're gazing so intently into the distance."

"New glasses. I wanted to see what I could see that I couldn't see before."

"And?"

"Nothing's different."

"So why did you buy them?"

"Because I couldn't see when I read." Ah. I explained the difference between near- and far-sighted.

"Can you read easier, now?" I asked.

"Oh yes. Before, my arms were too short. Now, they're just right."

"So the glasses are doing their job."

"Yes," he said, folding them and placing them in his pocket, immensely relieved that he hadn't spent his money for nothing. Only then did he react to my presence. "What are you doing here?" he asked.

I told him, then asked, "Where's the *kamnan*'s house?"

He looked up the road and began to put on his glasses, thought better of it, and put them back in his pocket. "There. About a mile back upriver," he pointed.

"Oh, that's a long walk."

"That's o.k."

"Of course it is, you're not doing the walking."

"No," he said, "What I meant was, he's not home."

I'd had so many conversations like this that they were beginning to seem normal. At least, he'd saved me the walk. I thanked him and started to leave.

"The assistant *kamnan* lives right there," he said, indicating a house wedged between the road and the river. "But he's not home either." Here we go again, I thought, but then he added, "he's down at the store. I'll walk you there."

Our stroll ended at the village cooperative store. It was a modest operation, less a profit center than a dalliance with the idea of commerce since the customers easily outnumbered the goods decorating the shelves. The moment my friend introduced me, a young clerk reached into the refrigerator and pulled out a Vitamilk soy drink and refused to take payment.

I was introduced to Damrong, the assistant *kamnan*, an unprepossessing man. He immediately offered me lodgings and only later thought to ask me where I'd come from and how I'd gotten there. I replied by pulling out my maps. We spent so long discussing the journey that when we finally emerged into the balmy air it was dark and I had to fumble along the muddy riverbank to find my boat. Then, once underway, I couldn't locate Damrong's landing until I heard a mumbling that I recognized as the hundreds of ducks I'd seen in a pen beneath his house.

As I entered with my gear, Damrong apologized for the mess. "My wife is usually in charge of these things but she's gone to Bangkok with my son."

His was a classic Thai house. Teak panel walls angled gently to a steeply-pitched roof. The room lacked a ceiling which allowed one to see the roof laths and the undersides of the baked clay tiles that covered it. The broad planks of the teak floor had been polished by myriad bottoms, but it was what lay on the floor that caught my eye. Strewn before a chugging refrigerator and glass-fronted cabinets were dozens of wood slabs in various stages of carving, as well as sketchbooks, pens, and brushes.

"You're an artist?" I said.

"Well, I'm a schoolteacher," he replied quietly, "but I like to draw. And carve wood."

As we sat on the floor, he quietly slid a sketchbook before me to inspect. His drawings of classical Thai motifs–the flame-like *kanok* being the most common–had been beautifully rendered, the work of a consummate artist. The carved panels were masterworks. As he traced the patterns, explaining their symbolism, his calm voice revealed extensive knowledge and a deep love. But as he talked, I gradually became aware of a sub-tone of sadness, as though he were talking to me across a broad river of pain. Although it was unsettling, I didn't press him to explain.

He'd studied art in a local high school, and later in a Bangkok art college. "An artist's life is difficult," he said, "so I returned to Ayutthaya, took up teaching and helped my father manage his farmlands." Evenings were spent cross-legged on the floor, first applying hammer to chisel and then, when it became too dark to see clearly, hunching over his drawings.

Eventually, we ran out of conversation and my eyes wandered around the room. They settled on a black-and-white photograph of a teen-aged boy who resembled Damrong at a younger age. It sat high atop one of the cabinets, in a wooden frame so ornately carved that it seemed en-shrined. Damrong followed my eyes and silently got up to take it from the cabinet.

Sitting cross-legged opposite me, he rested his forearms on his knees and clasped the photo in his hands. He seemed to struggle with some emotion. "My son," he said, looking at the photo, then glancing at me as if expecting me to ask him to elaborate. I waited.

"He was 16. My first son. I taught him everything I knew about painting. He was a natural artist, better than me."

He paused so long that I finally asked, "Where is he now?" already anticipating the answer.

"He was always complaining about headaches. Doctors prescribed medicines but the aching seemed to get worse. We didn't have enough money to take him to a doctor in Bangkok..." He paused, struggling. "We had money," he said, almost angrily. "I didn't think the headaches were anything to worry about. He was a growing boy. He stayed up late study-ing in bad light. I sometimes get headaches if I work late." He fell silent again.

"About six years ago, something happened, something burst," he continued. "The doctor said it was an aneurysm. He died the next day." He continued to stare at the portrait, his anguish evident. At last, he set the picture aside and looked at me with a resigned smile.

"We already had two daughters and then we were blessed with another boy, three years after my first son died."

"Have you taught your daughters?"

"I tried. They weren't interested."

"And your youngest son, is he an artist?"

"He's only three," he laughed. "And he loves to draw. Maybe...Maybe." His bittersweet smile melded past sorrow and future hopes as if, for him, time wasn't a continuum but a single point in the present.

He sat quietly for a few moments and then turned to his work–probably his normal response when assailed by conflicting emotions. I slipped into my sleeping bag and began writing in my journal. My last image of the evening was of him hunched over his notebook, sketching delicate patterns with a thin-nibbed pen. I wondered how I might channel my sorrow were something similar to happen to me, and realized that his grief was simply beyond my experience and imagining. Once again, I understood how smoothly my own life had passed by comparison.

I'm certain that ducks sleep, but the 400 under Damrong's house muttered all night, the droning vibration waxing and waning continuously, and disturbing my slumbers. It was the snoring that I found particularly bothersome, in part because I couldn't pinpoint the source. Damrong was asleep in the bedroom and the sounds seemed to come from beneath the floorboards. Who could be sleeping in the four-foot space between the house and the ground?

Bleary-eyed, I got up with the sun and went outside, ostensibly to check on the boat, but in truth to see who was making all the racket. The moment I stuck my head beneath the house, two large, honking geese charged me. Only the mesh fence saved me from multiple stab wounds. I have no idea how they made the noise but snoring geese were a new addition to the repertoire of night sounds seemingly designed to keep boatmen from sleep.

Shortly after dawn, Damrong left for school and I set off into another beautiful morning, enhanced by the snugness of the narrow river. The breeze in my face was cool, the overhanging trees shaded me, and sunlight filtered by the leaves tatted the water with lace. At the end of the shunt, the river broadened and I found myself at the northeastern corner of the island that holds Ayutthaya, Thailand's royal capital until 1767. The island was another impressive example of Thai river engineering.

In 1350, a smallpox epidemic had rampaged through Suphan Buri, a dozen miles to the west. In search of a healthier site, the town's ruler, Prince U-Thong, marched his army east until they reached the Lopburi River at a point where it formed an oxbow that embraced a lobe of land. Flowing south a few miles east of the island was the Pasak River. U-Thong's soldiers dug a short conduit to carry the Pasak's waters into the Lopburi, then excavated a two-mile north-south channel to form the eastern shore of the island, creating a moated city measuring 1-1/2 miles by 2-1/2 miles.

I turned left, determined to paddle down the northern canal to the Pasak's eastern channel, a route which would take me into the town market. I began easily but soon became mired in plastic bags, bottles, rusted tin cans, styrofoam, and other debris floating in a disgusting miasma black with rotted vegetation not unlike the swamp U-Thong had fled. I considered pulling the boat through the shallow section but it was so polluted I was convinced my feet would dissolve the moment they touched the muck. Instead, I turned around and paddled back to the Chao Phya and down Ayutthaya's western shore.

The river provided a superb panorama of the city's monasteries and monuments, majestic even in ruins: first, Wat Thammaram with its tall *prang* (monumental spire) and noble proportions; then, the corncob-like spire and old halls of Wat Raja Plii. I then passed the superb Wat Chai Wattanaram, built in 1630 by King Prasat Thong on the ruins of his dead mother's former palace. Despite its shattered wood-coffered roofs and its fragmented Buddha images, its stout central *prang* and attendant spires dominated the shoreline.

The river then turned east past more monuments. St. Joseph's Cathedral had been constructed late in the 17th century by Thai Catholics converted by Jesuit priests. Next to it was my favorite Buddhist monastery: Wat Buddhaisawan. It had been erected in 1353 by U-Thong on the site of the palace where he had lived while the spires of his new capital were rising around him. Its halls and cloisters were clustered around an enormous *prang* that seemed like a small mountain towering over the city's southern flanks.

Near Phom Pratu Chakrai Noi, a watchtower on the old city wall, a plump, saronged woman called out: "Hey *farang*! Come have a glass of cold water!" I paddled over. In her 40s, Somsri ran a small shop selling the fruit preserves that she and her daughters bottled. She had a no-nonsense attitude I liked.

"Where are you trying to go?" she asked, hands on fleshy hips.

"Bangkok."

"Not today, you aren't," she said, pointing to the water hyacinth sprigs now moving briskly upstream. She was right; even with the most vigorous paddling I would make little progress. I tied up at her landing, watched closely by her mother and mother-in-law who hovered over me, concern folding their faces as they listened to us talk. Bent with age, they looked like sisters, even in the way they scurried about. Though their culture differed from mine, they belonged to an archetype that defied nationality: quintessential grandmothers.

"When we saw you out there paddling in the hot sun, we felt so sorry for you," the mother said. The other nodded vigorously and then added, "we got hot just watching you."

Somsri asked me about the trip so far. I related how far I had come expecting the usual "ohhs" and "ahhhs" but she was singularly unimpressed.

"You need a rest," she said. "Leave the boat here and spend the night in town. We can watch it."

I shouldered my pack and walked to the road where I caught an ancient *tuk-tuk* (motorized trishaw) that poked its way along the perimeter road that ran just inside the royal city's ancient walls and into the chaotic market.

One of Asia's stellar kingdoms for four centuries, the Ayutthayan empire once extended deep into Malaysia and encompassed major portions of Laos and the eastern half of Cambodia. At its height in the 17th century, it had a population of one million, exceeding that of contemporary London. In 1767, however, the city was destroyed by Burmese invaders who burned it, stole most of its gold, marched its elite and its artists to Burma in chains, and reduced its population to 10,000. For 150 years, the ruined city had been inhabited by ghosts. Today, it is a minor provincial capital, its monuments attracting tourists but few businesses. The bulk of its citizens huddle along the former eastern wall.

I alighted from the *tuk-tuk*, asked someone for a hotel, and was directed to the "U-Thong." It seemed fitting to stay in a hotel reflecting the glory of the town's founder but it turned out to be grotty and cockroach-infested. However, when the innkeeper flung open the door of an upper story room and I found myself looking through big windows at the river, I decided to stay.

At the post office, I mailed another six pounds of gear to Bangkok, primarily surplus food. Kind clerks helped me pack each item securely, refusing to charge me for what turned out to be a very elaborate wrapping job.

While waiting, I met a university lecturer from Texas. Jim was taking a circuitous route home after spending a year in New Zealand writing a book about politics and the media. We discovered several commonalities, among them the fact that we occupied adjacent rooms at the hotel. After wandering through the old town and dining at a rice barge that had been converted into a restaurant, we sat on the U-thong's balcony, watching the river, drinking and talking. It had been five weeks since I'd conversed in English and it felt good to wrap my tongue around familiar words.

In the course of the conversation, I admitted that I was having a bit of an attitude problem for which I couldn't entirely blame the heat and my fatigue. I was disturbed by the environmental abuse, about blatant disregard for a river I'd come to love, and for a failure by Thais to recognize that it was still the nation's lifeline, and not a relic of the past.

"I'm also rattled by the pointless roar of unmuffled long-tailed boats and the people yelling at me from the riverbanks. I know I should laugh it off instead of letting it irritate me."

"Well, you have been on the river for a long time," Jim ventured.

"But I've been in *Thailand* a long time...and I used to think that I wore Thai culture like a second skin," I countered. "But in the past couple of weeks I've become increasingly irritated, ready to blow off people who really haven't done anything wrong, or blaming them for screwing up their beautiful river. I keep forgetting I am an outsider. Or rather, I'm always aware of it and the alienation bothers me. It makes me forget how nice most people have been."

In the end, I realized it was something I would have to work out on my own, and soon the conversation turned in more rewarding directions. It was a pleasant evening in which we explored our reasons for traveling, and the lure of the open road that ended at unknown but tantalizing destinations. When the beer began to work, I let it do its stuff, enjoying the peace and watching the river with someone of my own culture, comfortably bridging a gulf of incomprehension.

The alcohol and the semi-soft bed were therapeutic and I was up at 6 a.m. to take full advantage of the outgoing tide. Jim knocked on my door just as I finished packing, and we went to the market for Thai coffee and *khanom krok*, a succulent hot coconut-milk sweet. Jim wanted to see the boat, so we caught a *tuk-tuk* to Somsri's house.

The laughing grandmothers had removed the boat's floor boards.

"We put them under our beds so no one would steal them," one said conspiratorially, clasping my hand and squinting up into my face.

I readied the boat and was preparing to leave when Somsri began filling the bow with preserves, bottle after bottle.

"Oh my god, I'll never be able to eat all these," I said, overwhelmed by her generosity.

She didn't even pause. "Give them to your friends in Bangkok," she said, setting down the last of a dozen bottles.

I thanked her, the grandmothers brought me another glass of ice water, "just to get you started," and I pushed off. My last image before the current caught me was of Jim's already overloaded arms being burdened with more jars of preserves.

Two hours of hard paddling brought me to a cluster of mosques—four within 500 yards–and no Buddhist monasteries. I thought the Muslim presence odd, since Ayutthaya had been a Buddhist center, but then I recalled a story told me by a Thai professor.

On commission from Ayutthaya's King Narai in the 17th century, the French had built a series of riverside forts between the royal city and the Gulf. The forts had long-since disintegrated but the professor said he had pinpointed their locations by looking for Muslim communities. His lead was a note in French chronicles that most forts had been manned by North African mercenaries, many of whom had settled and raised families. Muslim cemeteries often provided proof that a garrison had been stationed nearby. While I was musing on history, the tide turned against me. On the left bank stood a beautiful wooden pavilion sheltered by raintrees. Since it was useless to paddle, I tied up and climbed its wooden stairs.

The raintrees shaded a path that led to a derelict monastery covered in broken tiles and enclosed in walls yellow with age. The concrete coating on the *chorfa*–the so-called "sky tassel" that decorated the roof gable–had crumbled, leaving the rusted reinforcing rod to point at the sky, and giving the place a pleasing air of decrepitude. I thought it abandoned until I saw orange swatches moving in its courtyard, saffron cloth enveloping the skinny limbs of elderly monks. They seemed to know I was there but didn't come to disturb me. I lay back to enjoy the cooling breeze. With my eyes closed, it felt like an afternoon on my river house porch when I lay reading, the busy river moving past my door. Farther inland, a train lowed, another lonely traveler. Lulled by the peace, I drifted off. When I awoke, the current had shifted.

I paddled all afternoon before searching for accommodations along the right bank. But what had seemed from a distance to be a village turned out to be a few ancient factories and scattered houses. I was losing the light again and cursed myself for not having called it a day an hour earlier. Downriver on the left, a monastery presaged evening food problems but I had no choice. By the time I re-crossed the river and tied up at the landing, it was nearly dark.

I squinted to read the faded gold lettering on the red sign: Wat Cheungrian. Amidst its broken-down wooden buildings, I found the abbot who took one look at my boat and decided we had to haul it onto land and into the *wat*. Waving away my objections, he ordered the monks to heft it out of the water and stagger 200 feet to an outbuilding.

In search of dinner, I walked along an unlit road leading from the monastery gate towards several food stalls. The first two were closed but there was a light in the third. Just as I reached it, a large man darted out of the dark behind me and grabbed my hand. I was too startled to react.

"Come eat with us," he said, a gentle smile in his broad face.

"Thank you, but..."

"We have lots of food."

"We who?

"I'm the *kamnan*," he said, with nothing in his demeanor to suggest it.

"Oh," was all I could manage.

"It's my daughter's wedding. We'd be honored to have you join us."

Still clasping my hand, he led me down the road to a compound fenced with bamboo that held a dozen wooden houses perched on stilts. In the dirt courtyard, the guests sat on creaky metal chairs at squeaky metal tables, the chorus nearly drowning out conversation. Streamers ran from house to house and Christmas lights twinkled in the banana trees. Women walked in and out of the underhouse area that served as a kitchen, bearing pots filled with delicious curries. In my haste to find food, I hadn't showered and looked a mess but nobody seemed to mind. Wed in the morning and now enjoying their marriage feast, the happy bridal couple escorted me to a table, brought me orange juice, directed others to fill my plate, and treated me as a royal guest.

Fathers teased and joked: children chased each other around the moving mothers. Elderly men sat to one side, drinking and talking quietly, watching with contented smiles the chaos swirling around them. The mood was so infectious that I soon forgot how filthy I was and plunged in. As I ate, a ladle would snake in from one side or the other, dropping sumptuous viands onto my plate, the women vying to see how far ahead of me they could stay. Several times I begged off and was laughingly chided for my poor opinion of their cooking. The tall, bulky *kamnan* waddled about like a seigniorial lord, hands clasped behind his back, looking for empty plates, calling to women to fill them. Several times he paused to ask me, "Are you full yet?" Half an hour later, my overflowing plate looked like I hadn't even begun.

When at last my host excused me to return to the *wat* to sleep, a dozen pre-teen girls began twittering, "We'll escort him back." The *kamnan* shook with laughter. "O.K., but don't keep him up talking. He's tired and you have school tomorrow." The girls danced around me. "Oh good, you can help us with English!"

We sat in the riverside pavilion and they quizzed me on English words. They were surprisingly proficient, absorbing everything I told them, repeating it perfectly moments later. Eventually they tired and reluctantly started for home. When I presented them with jars of preserves, one young girl thrust something into my hand, saying, "This is for good luck," before turning and scampering after the rest. In the distance, I heard them repeating the words I had taught them.

I stepped into the light which streamed from the abbot's window. In my hand was a fuzzy pink cat the length of my thumb. Tied on the bow of my boat, it would ride to the river mouth as a talisman.

It had been decided that I would sleep in the abbot's room. As I stepped in the door, my eye lit on two big grandfather clocks. Oh no! But then something behind the glass doors caught my eye. As I neared them for a closer look, I heard the abbot say, "I'm a light sleeper." A thick cloth was tied around each chime so it emitted only a faint clunk when the hour was struck. Bless him.

The Barge People

Rua Lom Mau Jord, Taa Bord Mau Kae
(The boat sinks before reaching port;
am aging man becomes blind)
Just when one thinks he is safely home,
calamity can strike

The abbot meditated before the window, his silhouette dark against trees made gauzy by the soft dawn light; a morning of peace and I with no patience to savor it. Beyond him, the river was running strongly and I was stuck indoors. How long would he remain lotus-like? Perhaps hours. And the monks would be away on alms rounds, miles from returning my boat to the river. I might as well relax.

But the abbot had heard me stirring.

"I told the monks to hold off *bintabaht* until we got your boat in the water," he said, quietly. I thanked him for his thoughtfulness. He smiled serenely and returned to wherever he had been.

Ten monks and I arrayed themselves around the boat and, with a shout, we lifted it and set off. Dropping it in the water, they collapsed against the tree trunks, laughing and wiping perspiration from their faces with their orange robes. Two small girls and a boy of four watched me loading gear and then came a whispered order, "Give it to him!"

I turned to see the boy looking at the girls and then at me in open-mouthed confusion. "Give it to him!" the elder girl hissed in the exasperated manner only young girls can muster.

He finally thrust forward the box he'd been holding. "Dad said to give this to you," his big sister said. "It's lunch."

I recognized it as leftovers from the wedding feast. Wonderful! I thanked them and asked them to thank their father for his generosity.

"Now run home. Your mother will worry," I heard the abbot behind me say. The girls rushed off, leaving the boy behind. His eyes grew wide as he realized he'd been abandoned. Wheeling around, he trotted after them, whimpering. The abbot chuckled.

"Come back to visit," said the abbot as I pushed off. Under his breath, he probably added "without the boat" since the portage had tired everybody.

It was a soft morning, the light of a waxing sun pervading the cool, tranquil air and portending a beautiful day. I paddled, drifted, ate a Chinese pastry. But as I chewed, I became aware that I was now drifting backwards. Damn! Only 9 a.m. and the tide had changed. An obdurate river was determined to make me work all the way to the sea. I settled under a tree near Bang Sai to wait it out.

Lower Chao Phya boatmen venerate a god resident at a riverside shrine across the river at Lante. The tiny house holds a statue of a *javet*, a male god attended by wooden cows and buffaloes said to be his servants. The engines of passing boats often stop functioning as they near it. The drivers don't waste time trying to repair them but paddle straight to the shrine to offer chickens, ducks, whiskey, flowers, candles, and incense. According to boatmen, the engine re-starts immediately. Were it not for the long cross-river paddle, I would have made an offering to induce the *javet* to move my boat downriver.

Mid-afternoon, the current changed and I set off under a blazing sun. Passing speedboats kicked up tall wakes that washed over the gunwales designed to protect me from waves. So far, my boat hadn't done anything it was supposed to do. For the next half hour, I angled the bow back and forth to split the wakes coming at me from every direction, pointing at one bank, then the other, but making little forward progress. In the end, I elected to paddle and ignore the sloshing bilge. If the boat sank, so be it.

Eventually, the sun slunk over the horizon, pulling a shroud behind it. I crept along the western shore, hoping someone might call me over, but no invitation came. Two miles later, I moored at a *wat* whose abbot wanted to haul the boat out of the river. I politely but firmly said "it would be fine where it was" and he did not press the issue.

From a distance Wat Gai Tia ("Short Chicken Temple") had seemed modest, but up close, I saw it included several elaborate *kuti*s clad in glossy ceramic tiles and boasting walls of latticed glass. Dropping my gear in one, I went in search of dinner. As I entered the adjacent village, a strapping 18-year-old introduced himself as Chali and offered to help me find a restaurant. Very dark, he looked part African; could he be a descendent of the 17th-century French mercenaries?

"My father was an American GI," he said, quietly.

"Your father lives in the village?" I asked. On retiring, many GIs stationed in Thailand during the Vietnam War had returned to take up residence, supporting their families on their pensions.

"No, in America," he said quietly. From the way he said it, it was clear he'd been abandoned, the fate of many Thai children fathered by American soldiers. Casualties of war.

"But my mother does," he said, brightening. "She'll fix you dinner." Not only was I uncertain how his mother would react to her son's bringing home a stranger on short notice, I wasn't sure how she now felt about Americans. Once, in a village long ago, a middle-aged woman had spat venom at me so ferociously that I jumped back, thinking she was about to attack me. Others pulled her away. "She's crazy," they whispered. She'd been a bargirl near one of the upcountry U.S. airbases. Her soldier boyfriend had promised to marry her but one morning, she awoke to find him gone. She later learned he already had a wife and family in a midwestern town. The revelation had sent her over the edge, and seeing me had triggered bad memories. Luckily, Chali's mother beamed when she saw me, readily inviting me to join the family for dinner.

When Vietnam fell, many Americans voiced concern that Amerasian children, especially those sired by African-American fathers, would be killed. It hadn't happened there nor in Thailand. With their vaunted tolerance, Thais embraced nearly everyone. Chali was not an outcast; in fact, he appeared to be a leader, as much for his calm demeanor as for his size. He was completing engineering studies and would take the examination for the Air Force the following month.

He was not alone. An African-Amerasian comedian well-known across the country, played on his blackness in costume and hairdo, but not for his material. He didn't need to because he was accepted as Thai.

After one African-Amerasian woman gained fame as a sprinter, sports officials combed the villages looking for similar children to groom, believing that their larger builds would strengthen Thai Olympic gold hopes. When Tiger Woods achieved fame, he was instantly embraced, regarded as more Thai than American, and bestowed with honorary citizenship. With the quiet conversation and delicious dinner the evening passed pleasantly.

Back at the *wat*, I found my roommate, Bhikkhu Charanyu, watching the evening news on TV. At the river, I washed clothes and bathed with the announcer's voice droning in the darkness. By the time I returned, the *bhikkhu* had switched off the set. I bedded down on the *kuti*'s cold tiles but, once again, sleep was hard won.

When I'd first met him, the monk had struck me as a bit odd. Although I'd told him I was a Christian, he now lectured me on my duties as a Buddhist and instructed me in the proper way to sit and hold my hands while meditating. Eager to please him, I did as he instructed, but soon I began to fade. Halting the conversation would have been impolite, so in elaborate charade I feigned fatigue, my lids drooping, my body rocking back and forth as though I were about to drop into a coma. Soon, he began mimicking my movements, his words slurring. My god, I thought, I'm a mesmer! Finally, he said, "It is best to sleep," laid down, and was gone in an instant. I wasn't far behind.

But he had left the radio on, which he apparently did every night. The program was an endless drone of Buddhist scriptures and sermons by a series of monks, all of whom seemed to be fighting winter colds. Every few minutes, I'd be jolted awake by a monk clearing his throat or coughing into the microphone. Unfortunately, only at 4 a.m. did I wake to sufficient consciousness to silence it. Listening for the monk's steady breathing, I crept to the radio, turned it down...and slept until dawn.

At first light, the river already running upstream. The monks offered me breakfast but I wanted to push on, even against the current. On a hot, humid morning, with frequent pauses to wipe condensation from my glasses, I paddled to Pathumthani. While eating Chinese buns in the market, I wrote and watched the river, willing it to change direction, Canute on the waterfront. It was probably my imagination but it seemed to run faster upriver than downriver. "Where does the water go?" I wondered.

While chatting with boatmen, I saw the river pause. For a few long moments, it remained static, moving neither upstream nor down. Then, it imperceptibly shifted, and quickly picked up speed, a remarkable transformation that took less than five minutes. The moment I realized it was on its way, so was I.

It flowed strongly all afternoon, carrying me 12 miles in 4-1/2 hours. As the light was waning, Pakkred hove up on my left and a bent spire separated itself from the palm trees on the right. It took me a moment to recognize it as the leaning *chedi* at Wat Paramaiiyakavas ("Grandma's Wat"), so named by King Chulalongkorn for his grand-aunt who paid for its restoration in 1884. One of my favorites, its tilted spire pointed Pisa-like down a narrow channel, one of six *lat* (shortcuts) that ancient engineers had dug across oxbows in the meandering river to lop 47 miles from the journey between Ayutthaya and the ocean. It was one of the few times I applauded river engineers; they had considerably reduced my paddling time.

The channel was one-third the river's width and through it sped dozens of long-tailed boats, their unmuffled exhausts shattering the peace. The drivers looked neither right nor left as they churned tall wakes, swamping sampans paddled by elderly women who could have been their grandmothers. Three times within half an hour, they poured so much water into my boat that I had to stop and bail to avoid sinking. Then came a wave so powerful that it pulled the waterlogged sponge from my hand; I watched it sink into the murk. Now I had no way to empty the boat and the lockers were beginning to fill.

At that point, I lost it. Screaming oaths, I paddled to the bank and picked up a large rock. When the next boat neared, I yelled at the driver and threatened to pummel him. He slowed and veered away, no doubt perplexed by this raging foreigner but having no idea what might have provoked him. Like some wronged David, I stood there, furious, the stone hanging from my hand.

What was happening to me? Where was the culturally-sensitive man who had started this journey a few short weeks before? What was he doing threatening boatmen with rocks? A welter of emotions washed over me: anger with them for their selfishness, shame that as a rational man, I had let them get to me. But I couldn't be the only one irritated by them! I looked around to see that even the elderly women paddled on, unperturbed by the wakes. I was the only one objecting. I dropped the stone. Better to put the energy to something useful. After scooping out bilge with a canteen cup, I began paddling, and concentrated on house-hunting.

At the end of the shunt, I re-entered the main river and passed a community whose houses rested on pontoons or on stilts. Their front "yards" were bamboo frames filled with vegetables, floating gardens that absorbed the shock of the waves. I asked one gardener where the headman was, not certain there would be one this close to Bangkok.

"That's him, standing next to the green house," he said.

But the headman regarded me suspiciously, big city wariness written all over his face.

"Why don't you paddle back upstream to the *wat*?" he said when I asked about accommodations.

"Too hard," I said. Realizing he wasn't about to offer me a room, I said "Never mind. I'll move downstream and see if I can find another *wat*."

He relaxed. "If you go back upriver a bit, you'll find my house, the blue one." Then, as an afterthought, he added, "May I ride with you? It'll be shorter than using the road."

As I paddled, I outlined my journey thus far. His response surprised me.

"May I interview you?"

"Interview?"

"I'm a stringer for the Nonthaburi paper," he said. "A bad reporter," he chuckled.

"Why?"

"I had a scoop sitting right in front of me and I almost missed it." We both laughed. He drew a pen from his pocket and had jotted most of the details by the time we arrived at his home. After greeting his family, he took me to a wooden house next door.

"Hope you don't mind, I use it as a storeroom," he said, unlocking the front door.

Stacked everywhere were thousands of the small wicker baskets that vendors fill with the *plaa tuu* (mackerel) they sold in the markets. Basket weaving seemed to be a local industry because a dozen adjoining houses were similarly crammed floor to ceiling with baskets. While I bathed in the river, the headman's elderly mother re-heated several curries. I ate by myself on the floating verandah that pitched and rocked as boats passed.

Deciding that I would be too hot in the storeroom, the mother laid a mat on the verandah and I bedded down there. Of course, I had shown my usual perspicacity at choosing lodgings. The family also operated a floating filling station. Long-tailed and cargo boats pulled in every five minutes to be tanked up with diesel, revving their engines to maneuver into position. The business finally closed at 2 a.m. but until early morning, long-tailed boats paused every half hour, their drivers shouting and shining their searchlights, hoping to rouse someone to fuel them. I also discovered that the house was directly beneath the flight path of jets taking off on overnight flights to Europe.

I awoke to a morning muggy and hot. The headman and his grown children had left for work before dawn in order to beat the traffic so I got away early, a rare privilege. I pulled out into a current coursing upriver to its source like a maddened, migrating salmon. Early explorers had begun at the ocean and moved upriver towards the headwaters, whereas I seemed to move upstream in order to reach the sea. And the strong wind in my face didn't help. But, creature of habit, trained by the boat to its ways, I dug the paddle into the water and pushed on. It took three hours to cover the two miles to the new Pathumthani Bridge and another three to reach Nonthaburi.

Nonthaburi, the seat of the province immediately north of Bangkok, was an old market town slowly being absorbed by Bangkok's urban creep. It was distinguished by two landmarks linking it to a former age: a tall clocktower, and an elegant two-story wooden city hall painted leaf green. Although the huge complex comprised several buildings ranged about broad courtyards, it had a delicacy lacking in most official buildings. Thin pillars, narrow cladding boards, and long covered walkways connecting the upper floors lent it a pleasing airiness. Its high ceilings dated it to a period before electric fans, when bureaucrats were cooled by river breezes blowing through its tall louvered windows. It was a relic from an era which blended esthetics and functionality, before economics dictated design.

Running along the quay was a broad promenade, a luxury the riverine city of Bangkok lacked. It was lit by tall lampposts from whose standards hung life-sized metal durians, the smelly, spiky fruit Thais (and I) eagerly await each monsoon season. Durians had been the town's mainstay crop, the high prices they commanded–often $40 each–financing the construction of the provincial hall and other buildings. That was before riverside land became too valuable and developers leveled orchards to build tract houses.

Drenched with perspiration, my *moh hom* shirt adhesed like a blue skin, I stopped in the noisy market to buy a new sponge and two pounds of sweet tangerines. While a vendor dropped my purchases into a bag fashioned from old newspapers, I watched the river. It was still running swiftly upstream and the thought of getting back on it was exhausting. I decided to wait it out.

Anchored at the downstream end of the promenade was a floating restaurant. Tying the boat to one of its pontoons, I climbed to the wooden deck to find I had it virtually to myself. The kindly proprietor approached, asking the usual questions about my journey, then said, "You know, you're standing in a museum."

I glanced around. Nothing distinguished it as such; it looked like an ordinary floating restaurant and I said so. He drew me to a pillar on which hung a framed, badly-damaged sepia photograph. In it, courtiers stood expectantly around two men resplendent in uniforms and seated on thrones.

"The kings of Thailand and Laos."

"Here? In this restaurant?"

"No," he laughed. "In the Mekong River. It was in the 1950s and they were signing a treaty for something. This barge was specially built and anchored exactly midstream between the two countries. It was a big event."

"How did it get here?"

"After the ceremony, I persuaded the mayor to sell it to me. Said I'd make it into a museum and a restaurant to honor royalty. I dismantled it and brought it here by train."

"Uh, where's the museum?"

"Ahhhh," he exhaled. "Never got around to that. There wasn't much to display anyway. Except the picture. It's more than can be found anywhere else to mark the occasion, so I guess it qualifies as a museum. Wish I could remember what the treaty was about."

When he was called away to the phone, the staff crowded in to ask about the boat and my trip. For the next hour, I drank cold water, ate freshly sliced watermelon, pineapple, and papaya, and chatted. When the river stopped, then turned, I set off, hoping to make the outskirts of Bangkok by nightfall. Once below the city, I'd be on the final leg with only a short run to the sea.

But, as usual, fate intervened. Four strokes into the mainstream, my paddle snapped at the edge of the metal sleeve. With the longer portion, I paddled back to the restaurant where the waiters hauled me aboard, concerned that I was alright. When I asked where I might find a machinist's shop, two of them removed their aprons and led me through the streets to a shop awash in black oil and strewn with metal scraps. The only viable splint was a foot-long section of very heavy water pipe. With it, the paddle would be off-balanced by the additional weight on one end but the journey was nearly over and I couldn't damage my hands any more than I already had.

The constant wetting which had rotted the wood had also swollen the shaft. When hard hammering wouldn't dislodge the wooden portion inside the old sleeve, he drilled it out, shortening the paddle by eight inches. I'd be forced to lean over the gunwales to grab water but it handled better, with less flex. In a half an hour, I was on my way again.

While we'd been working, the river had changed its mind about going to Chiang Mai. It now turned and headed for the sea like a harassed man who has just discovered that he left his house keys at the office.

It was evening when I reached the Krung Thon Bridge on Bangkok's northern boundary. Downstream, the sun illuminated the bridge and the city skyline backdropped behind it, creating a lovely panorama. I should have been elated about returning home but all I could think was, "This is a city. Where am I going to find shelter for the night?"

Anchored just below the bridge was a bevy of old rice barges that boatmen had turned into homes. Seated on the stern of one, a man smiled in sympathy as he watched me struggle.

"Thirsty?" Thida asked.

"Dying," I gasped.

He disappeared inside and returned a moment later with a mug made of surgical steel and filled with cool water.

"Where are you going?"

"Nowhere, at the moment."

"Need a place to stay?"

I was surprised by the directness of the offer. I'd always wanted to spend a night aboard a teak barge. "Yes," I said, enthusiastically.

A decade before, the barge had been retired after long service hauling rice up and down the river, and Thida's father had bought it. In the West, it would have been considered impolite to ask its price, but this was Thailand.

"40,000 *baht* ($1,600)," he said. "And another 40,000 to refurbish it."

He'd done a beautiful job. The barge was not opulent but it had been crafted with love. Thirty-five feet long and 12 feet wide, its polished railings glowed in the late afternoon light. The stern area normally occupied by the tillerman had been enclosed in woven bamboo screens that slid on grooves mitered into the teak planks. Through the door, I stepped onto a floor of thick teak planks laid over the hold to form a living room.

"Sorry about the mosquitoes," he apologized, swatting at one. "The hull leaks. They breed in the bilge."

A naval lieutenant, Thida commuted daily by bus and boat to a minesweeper at the Bang Na naval station near the river's mouth. His family lived as squatters, walking narrow gangplanks to haul household water from onshore taps and stringing electric lines to accommodating waterfront houses. We retired to the stern to watch the sun insert itself between the sawtooth buildings on the opposite shore. I mentioned my surprise at his quick invitation to spend the night.

"I don't normally pay attention to *farang*s on the river," he said. "They're usually playing. You looked like you'd been out there a long time."

We were talking of the joys of residing by a river when we were interrupted by revving engines. "My father and sister," he said as a pair of motorized sampans stacked high with soft drinks, pastries, fruit, and other snacks slid up to the stern.

Every morning at 6 a.m., Pratueng, Thida's father, traveled to the market to buy foods for the day's circuit. His 30-ish sister helped her mother bake pastries and sweets she would later sell with black Thai coffee she heated on a small on-board charcoal brazier. At 9 a.m., father and daughter set off in separate directions to spend the day selling snacks door-to-door along the shore. They knew my former river house and we agreed that, yes, they'd probably sold me fruit or pastries at one time or another.

While she prepared dinner, Thida's mother suggested that I shower. Anchored beside the barge was a dock that floated on bamboo bundles. Wrapping myself in a sarong, I dropped down to it, clutching my towel and soap. There, I hesitated. The barge was moored in a backwater so filled with debris that the river was obscured by a layer of rotting vegetation, Styrofoam, tin cans, and motor oil. If I peered closely, I'd probably see a dead animal floating among the water hyacinth. It was then that I noticed the toilet squatting on one end of the platform: four sheets of corrugated iron and a free-fall flush. That morning, I had developed a subcutaneous rash all over my body that itched and burned. Initially, I put it down to the heat but when it persisted I concluded that it had come from bathing in the river at Wat Gai Tia. I gazed at the river. Should I jump in and get it over with? No, why be foolish? With a metal pan, I scraped a hole in the garbage and before it could close, sluiced a panful of river over my body.

I slept on the bow next to a fish tank equipped with an aerator that hissed and bubbled. The tank seemed such an anomaly, a body of water sitting a few feet above the body of water in which the fish normally lived. The fish weren't complaining. They might be imprisoned by glass walls but at least the water was clean.

The night was surprisingly quiet, allowing me to hear clearly the hum of mosquitoes devouring me. City lights hazed the sky. Not a star was visible. No wonder city people often seemed out of touch with Nature.

Buddha Lessons

Khon Dii Tok Naam Mai Lai, Tok Fai Mai Mai
(A good man will not drown when he falls into the water,
and will not burn when he falls into the fire)
Live morally and you won't get into trouble

Day 55, the day of my long-anticipated return to Bangkok, didn't begin quite as magically as I had expected. For one thing, all the punishment I'd inflicted on my body had caught up with me. Rural areas often get the bad rap as cesspools of contagions, and yet I'd been healthy until I reached the city. Now, my skin burned and itched from the river water. Overnight, a pain in my right shoulder had migrated to my left. I had diarrhea.

More disturbing were my hands. On awakening, I reached for my glasses and although my eyes told me I was grasping them there were no tactile messages; from wrist to fingertips, my left hand was numb. I should have given it a rest for a day or two but I couldn't. In Nonthaburi the previous afternoon, I had telephoned a friend who volunteered to meet me at the foot of the Memorial Bridge at 10:30 to relieve me of more gear; it didn't seem right to be a no-show. Wrapping my claws around the paddle, I set off into water the color of cafe au lait.

I had only two miles to go but the upriver current was so strong that I could progress only by paddling without pause. Each time the paddle left the water, the incoming tide pushed me upriver. Dozens of long-tailed boats raced by, chopping the river to midsea turbulence, the waves sloshing into the boat.

At 9:30, I reached my old riverside house with the boat three inches deep in bilge. This was to have been a triumphal moment, the completion of a circle, the return to the journey's genesis, but I was fighting just to remain afloat. I moved the boat into the empty space beneath the porch on which I'd sat dreaming about this journey so many years before. With one arm, I hugged the boat snugly against a supporting pillar to avoid being swept upriver and so the waves couldn't dash the hull to pieces. With the other arm, I bailed, relieved that sensation had returned to my left hand, a gratifying sign that the damage wasn't permanent. When the boat was as dry as I could get it, I tried to climb to the porch but the bucking waves threatened to smash the boat. Instead, I turned and set off into the maelstrom once again.

To my astonishment, I arrived at the bridge at 10:15. Photographs show me drained, my face lined by fatigue and dehydration, my hair drenched with perspiration, and my sweat-soaked shirt plastered to my body. Also waiting on the dock was a cameraman from Channel 9 and a photographer from Matichon newspaper alerted by the headman's story in the Nonthaburi paper.

"Can you paddle in again like you're just arriving?" asked the photographer.

Fighting my way through the waves and harassed by long-tailed boats, I circled and paddled in again. As I completed the circuit, another reporter turned up and asked me to repeat the action for his photographer. And another. And another. By the fifth round, I was wasted. A boatman who, half an hour earlier had nearly capsized me, handed me a cold soft drink. God was just after all.

Eventually my friend left with my excess gear and the newsmen departed to file their stories. Exhausted, I decided to wait for the tide to turn. The boatmen who had been giving me such grief now decided that I was a celebrity and fell over themselves to feed and water me. In the next hour, I drank four bottles of cola, and ate a plate of rice curry and two bunches of bananas. One man even bailed out my boat, at one point shouting at another boatman when his wake sloshed water over my gunwales.

The city had an unsettling effect on me. When later I reviewed my slides, I was surprised to see that of 3,200 shots, only four were of Bangkok. After two months in the countryside, the jangling chaos was too harsh. All I wanted to do was get away. When the tide turned, I jumped in my boat and began to put as many paddle strokes between me and the city as I could.

Once past the Krung Thep Bridge and into the suburbs, I felt better. The air filled with the effulgent blue light of a spring day. I looked at the sky because then I could avoid seeing the rotted plastic bags I snagged on every other paddle stroke. Downstream from the lyre-like Rama 9 Bridge–the last one before the sea–human habitation thinned and nipa palms covered the shore. Evening was approaching and hope of finding lodgings was receding. When Wat Dhammaraj appeared on the left, I pulled for it. Tying up in an estuary, I asked for the *luang paw*, and was directed to the *viharn* which lay across a broken courtyard awash in brackish water.

The solitary man sitting calmly before the Buddha image seemed too young to be the abbot, but when he looked up, I saw the quiet confidence of someone in charge. His bright eyes fixed on mine as I briefly outlined who I was and where I was going but he cut me off by saying "...so you need a place to sleep tonight. Fine. But tell me about the journey so far."

I was prepared to dismiss him as another abrupt abbot but he listened and asked good questions, forcing me to think about what I'd gained from my journey. For the first time—and perhaps impelled by the realization that the adventure was nearly over–I was able to back away from my daily concerns and begin to digest what it had all meant. Sitting with him, I was at peace. All the annoyances of the previous week seemed miles away as I chronicled my trip and sifted through the various experiences. Although I was recalling the good things and glossing over the bad, I sensed that he was aware that I was still wrestling with experiences and feelings I couldn't yet fathom.

As I listened to his calm voice, I became more curious about the abbot. He was clearly mature far beyond his years. At a break in the conversation, I asked his age.

"31," he said.

"It's a rare achievement for someone to have attained such a high position at such a young age." He shrugged.

"I was a gambler and a troublemaker. Then, one day after my 17th birthday, I realized that hellraising wasn't giving me any pleasure. I became a monk instead. I thought I'd stay here a few days and then return to the other world."

"But?..."

"I felt something here that I'd never felt outside. A sense of fulfill-ment my life up to then had never given me. And then when the old abbot died, the other monks elected me abbot so I'm still here. Until I die, I guess," he said, laughing softly as though amazed that such a thing could have happened. But he seemed embarrassed to be talking about himself.

"Let's get you settled," he said, rising to his feet. He assigned me to a *kuti* with another monk. Our conversation had lasted so long that it was dark and I resigned myself to going to bed without dinner.

"Here," my roommate said, pushing a plate of fried rice towards me. "I sent the *dek wat* (temple boy) to the market for it. I hope it's all right." Unwilling to dine in front of a man forbidden to eat, I thanked him and moved to the verandah where I wolfed down the rice, amazed at how delicious it was. I then prepared for bed. Although my body was tired, my mind grappled with a welter of thoughts. Many hours into the night I finally dropped off.

Just before dawn, I awoke to a dog fight in the courtyard. Unable to sleep, I rose and found that, once again, my left hand was numb. It would remain insensate for the rest of the journey. The cause was obvious, so was the remedy: stop paddling. Two days from now, I could.

The still-dark courtyard was under eight inches of water. I splashed across it to the mango tree to which I had tied the boat. Over-night, the incoming sea had filled the slough with trash and filthy water, but in the dim light, the boat seemed to glow. Peering into the darkness, I saw it was covered in white splotches and it didn't take much searching to find the source. From tree branches directly overhead, dozens of roost-ing chickens had voided themselves all night. When the breeze shifted, I got a full whiff of the mess but there wasn't much I could do about it in the dark.

Just upstream was a ferry landing and even at this hour it was alive with commuters. To one side, a small stall served piping hot Thai coffee. I sat and sipped, watching the passing show, glad I didn't have to be part of it. Factory and port workers stood groggily on deck as the boat made its slow journey across a sluggish river. Women headed home from market, their twin baskets holding unsold vegetables and their families' breakfast.

My calm was interrupted by a stout, 30ish woman plunking heavily onto a stool beside me and panting, "Good, I've found you."

"Found me?"

"My brother told me about you." I stared at her, perplexed.

"He read the story in *Daily News* yesterday," (so quickly?) "Then, he saw you at the dock. I wanted to get these to you before you left."

Wrapped in a graying, folded newspaper were five custardy pastries.

"You must be hungry after all that paddling so I made these for you. Eat," she commanded.

I bit into one; it was heavenly. "You made these yourself?"

"I'm a cook at the grade school," she said bashfully. "How are they?"

"Wonderful!"

She beamed. "I'll bring you some lunch later."

I protested but she was adamant. "You did something no Thai would do."

"No. I just had more free time than most Thais."

"No, Thais aren't brave like you. You are *geng*." That word again. I thanked her and, she got up and hurried towards the school. I shared the rest of the luscious custards with the shopkeeper, realizing that it was chance encounters and small kindnesses like these that had given me the most joy. They, not the great monuments and other touted attractions, were the core of any meaningful journey. And I'd had plenty of them.

When the river failed to turn, I lingered at the *wat*. The abbot was busy so I wandered in a courtyard still under a foot of filthy water irides-cent with the rainbow sheen of gasoline. The river was slowly claiming the *wat*. Black mildew crept up the yellow walls. Constant damp had rotted roof beams and loosened tiles. Drowned trees reached bare branches to the sky. Even the dogs and cats were afflicted with mange and skin lesions. Unfortunately, they were friendly and if I stood still for a moment, one would wander up to rub itself affectionately against my bare legs. Not that I looked any better than the beasts. The eruptions on my thighs and feet matched those on the animals; the same flies that crawled on the dogs, lit on my open wounds. I dwelt in a leper colony.

At noon, the custard lady ran up with lunch neatly wrapped in plastic bags and newspaper. Breathlessly wishing me luck, she rushed back to the school. An hour later, as the tide was turning, a novice approached me.

"Abbot wants to see you."

Seated as he had been the previous evening, the abbot greeted me, inviting me to sit down. While we talked, he reached into a long lacquered box at his side.

"Here," he said, withdrawing a necklace of sandalwood beads resembling a rosary. He laid it over my outstretched hand, saying, "Think of each bead as a personal discovery you have made. See if you can get them to join in an unbroken circle." Holding the necklace in my clasped hands, I *waiied* him.

Back at the river I found that my boat was even whiter than in the morning. The abbot was distressed. "Oh, I forgot about the chickens. We should have put it by the ferry landing." As I stepped into the boat with a sponge, he gently pushed me aside and began swabbing the boat with a corner of his orange robe which grew progressively whiter and less fragrant. When I tried to help, he said, "go get your things." No wonder he'd been elected abbot.

When I returned, he'd finished. "I think we've gotten most of it," he said, exiting so I could get in. Standing in the boat, I *waiied* him long and solemnly, grateful that he had given me some new ideas to ponder. Then, I pushed into a draggy current made more sluggish by the debris.

Soon, I was looking at Bangkok's backside. Two miles below the *wat*, the river looped back on itself around a large thumb of land called Rajburana. Cutting across the "fingernail" was another klong lat: I was surprised to see an enormous ship pass its far end. Dug in the reign of Rama I (1781-1809), this shortcut canal had reduced a nine-mile journey to 700 yards. But when waterfront gardens in Bangkok began dying from salty water, the watergates at either end of the canal were bricked up and it was never used again. Although the huge ship had seemed so close, I would not meet it again for another hour. I began encountering other ships, and was pleased to note that despite their size, they created low, long-amplitude waves that lifted me gently and set me down again.

Entering Bangkok's congested Klong Toey harbor I was dwarfed by the orange hulls of huge ships that would have steamrolled and sunk me without a trace had I gotten in their way. Vessels were being unloaded along the wharves while others, anchored mid-river, were disgorging their cargoes onto a dozen teak lighters that hugged them in double ranks. To stay out of their way, I moved to the inner bend where the mangroves had been lacquered in glossy black oil ejected from ship tanks.

From a small dock, I heard someone shout, "Sa-teve Wan Beek," and saw a man tattooed from neck to ankles waving a newspaper; others beckoned me over. The front page of *Thai Rath* showed me at the Memorial Bridge about to sink and looking a sweat-soaked mess. Some claim to fame. The tattooed man and his friends were giving me a thumbs-up and shouting *"geng, geng!"* Someone passed me a cola. One woman remembered nearly every detail of the newspaper story including the fact that I was from Oregon, a state I doubt anyone had heard of the day before. It was with great reluctance that I pushed on.

I knew I'd pay for delaying my departure from Wat Dhammaraj; just how dearly, I soon found out. The breeze stiffened, bending the palm trees like limbo dancers and feathering their fronds. The sky blackened until only a sliver of yellow light remained between it and the horizon. Then the wind slammed into me, pelting me with fat raindrops. Making no headway, I strained just to hold my position, cursing the skies, flailing the river for its undying refusal to give me a break. Although I was only 12 miles from the river mouth, my plans to reach it the following day were shredded like clouds in a gale.

Decision time. I was four miles from Phrapadaeng and the wind showed no signs of abating. Sleep on the deck here or push on? Obstinately, I pushed on. Then, like a miracle, the sun dropped below the black clouds and suffused the river with golden light, revealing dozens of small peach-colored clouds floating like fleecy sheep against the inky vault. In a different frame of mind, I would have reveled in it but I was too busy contending with the waves. When the river bent to the right, the wind shifted and paddling became easier, yet each time I raised the paddle, the droplets blew into me, soaking my clothes.

No *wats* or houses appeared, only warehouses and ships moving like phantom mountains up and down the channel. When night dropped like an iron wall, it became so dark that I couldn't locate Phrapadaeng, and through my water-streaked glasses could barely make out the dim lights of four car ferries crossing the river in staggered pairs. Since they couldn't see me I had to dodge them, relying on sound to guess where the landing might be. When two tugboats flicked on their bright lamps, blinding me, I shouted and they shifted their beams, lighting my path. When a reversing ferry nearly pinned me to the landing, a tugboat blew its fog horn. The ferry decelerated and I slipped to safety.

Hanging on to a dock fender while commuters looked down on me, I debated pushing on for Wat Phra Chedi Klang Nam, a few miles downriver...and quickly rejected the idea. Too many large ships and long-tailed boats were moving up and down and across the channel. One close call was enough for the evening.

On the other hand, neither could I remain in a vehicular ferry lane. When someone shouted that the passenger ferry was 500 yards downriver I paddled on. As I reached it, I saw a copy of *Thai Rath* being waved above the crowd; strange, the power of the printed page to galvanize people. My question about securing the boat was met with general consternation.

"I'll ask the police," someone said and rushed off.

Uh oh, I thought, but the man was already gone. Chaining the boat to a piling, I set off for the police station.

When I walked in, the duty cops were gathered around the sergeant's desk, poring over the newspaper. Reading my mind, a policeman said, "The first thing is to find a place for the boat." After a brief discussion, they decided I should paddle to the house of a woman named Lek, owner of the ferries. Where was the house? A half mile upstream, naturally, against the current. When I reached it, seven men lugged the boat out of the water and into a shed. Once again I marveled that there is never a shortage of volunteer manpower in Thailand; it was one of the country's great natural resources and was generally offered willingly.

Back at the police station, a man identified himself as a reporter wanting to write another story on me. While he pondered an angle, the duty officer telephoned around town, then loaded me into a pick-up truck for a drive into Phrapadaeng. And through it. And onto the main highway. Where the hell were they taking me? And then I saw. The flashing neon lights identified it as a short-time motel, the kind where husbands take their mistresses for trysts. "The owner is going to put you up for free," the sergeant said with a huge grin. I smiled weakly.

The short-time motel was typical of thousands around the country. The entrance door to each room opened directly from a courtyard which served as a parking lot. Each parking space had a thick curtain which could be pulled around a car, concealing its occupants from view while they scrambled into the motel room and into compromising positions. Few positions could be as compromising as mine. What if this were the angle the reporter was seeking?

As in every country, there is a scurrilous tabloid press that will do anything for a circulation-boosting article. I recalled a story told me by John Everingham who had scuba-dived under the Mekong River to snatch his Laotian girlfriend from beneath the noses of the Communist Pathet Lao. Using a second mask, John and Keo had swum back underwater, a major accomplishment given the river's width and the fact that Keo had never before dived. Exhaustion had put her in the hospital for three days. While John was talking with her, a reporter sneaked into the room. The next day, a photograph of the pair–she lying in a hospital bed, he on a chair beside her–appeared on the front page of a Bangkok tabloid under the headline, "Rescued Lao Girl Rushed to Hospital after 3 Nights Love with Foreigner." I locked my door. Despite the chill of the air-conditioner and an unending series of blue movies on the overhead, control-less television, I slept soundly.

I awoke stiff from the air-conditioning. In the windowless room that admitted no light nor provided any indication of morning's arrival, I should have been disoriented but some diurnal impulse roused me. My watch read 7 a.m. I'd been spared the notoriety of newspaper headlines–- "River Runner Recuperates in Sex Motel"–but nonetheless, I peeked around the door for hidden photographers before I emerged.

Coffee lay a half mile away along a busy highway enveloped in din and fumes. I wasn't the only one feeling the effects of the pollution; other coffee drinkers looked glum, reluctant to face another day. Recalling the morning laughter in villages above Chiang Mai, I mused that such were the rewards of urban progress.

The previous night Lek had been somewhat dubious about my leaving the boat at her riverside house, but this morning she was all smiles. "We saw you on Channel 9 last night," her daughter-in-law explained.

The current was headed north so I ordered breakfast at a small food stall and to my surprise found that Lek had already paid for it. An elderly Chinese newspaper vendor appropriated me as his private property and began collaring everyone who came by with the words, "Hey did you see Channel 9 news last night? Well, this is the guy," and then stepped back to bask in reflected glory. Borrowed fame is a strong lure. But I was having fun. The big push was over and the journey to the sea was short. I would savor the remaining hours.

My interlocutor kept badgering the other diners, zeroing in on a taciturn *samlor* driver who was trying to concentrate on a plate of rice. The vendor would make a comment and then prod the driver with "Right?", "Huh?", and other interjections, blinking incessantly as he talked. Each time, the driver obliged him with a quick up-tilt of his head, but without breaking stride as he conveyed rice from plate to mouth. When the vendor finally left the shop to peddle papers, the *samlor* driver pushed aside his empty plate and asked me:

"Do you know about the time the French Navy shelled the fortress?"

From my history readings, I recalled an 1893 incident involving the French who were vying with the British to become Thailand's colonial masters. I told him briefly what I knew.

"Do you want to see it?" he asked. I hesitated. "Free," he added, but it wasn't the price that bothered me. I've always had reservations about piling my heavy *farang* body into a flimsy trishaw pedaled by a man with puny legs, but he insisted. Rationalizing that I was lighter than I'd been two months earlier, and that the streets were level, I climbed in behind him.

We wound through lanes lined by shophouses to arrive at a citadel overlooking the river. It was one of a half dozen 19th-century forts that had been filled with bronze cannons engraved with the names of the Chinese, British, and American firms that had cast them. In the 1830s, when Thailand was still known as Siam, King Rama III stretched a stout chain across the river which could be raised and lowered by capstans to bar a ship's passage—another remarkable engineering feat considering the weight of chains and the width of the river. To keep an enemy within range of shore batteries, dozens of old junks were loaded with stones and sunk in the middle of the channel. Just upstream, the Siamese anchored several rafts laden with firewood. Were an enemy ship to breach the chain and evade the cannons, Siamese soldiers would ignite the rafts and allow them to drift downstream into the invaders. The French had ignored the fortress, the chains, and the rafts, knocking them out with several cannon shots and proceeding upriver to Bangkok unhindered.

The fortress had fallen on hard times. Stucco peeled away in sheets and mildew attacked the brick foundations. The stalwart garrison had been replaced by emaciated post-teen men who wore the red-rimmed eyes of glue sniffers. They were so zoned out that they paid scant attention to us.

Daeng pedaled through back streets for another hour as we discussed the river and the town's history. Eventually, we looped back to the coffee shop where I bought him a soft drink. He left, wishing me luck on the remainder of my journey and I sat to write the morning's events, plunking the notebook in a pool of spilled rice vinegar whose pungent tang would subsequently assail my nostrils each time I opened it.

Shortly before noon, the tide turned and I pushed once again into the flowing stream. I wanted to spend my last night in Wat Phra Chedi Klang Nam, a monastery rich with symbolic associations. Since it was a short way downstream, I drifted, letting the breeze caress and cool my sun-drenched body. Not until mid-afternoon did I reach the entrance to an estuary.

As its name, "Stupa in the Middle of the River" suggested, the monastery had once occupied an island, initially sharing it with a small cannon-studded fortress. Because the island was near the river mouth, the *wat* became a beacon to Thais traveling to and from distant nations. Beginning in the 1880s when King Chulalongkorn sailed abroad on state visits, royal passengers would disembark to pay obeisance to the wat's Buddha image. In the 1920s, the river's course shifted to the east and the right channel silted up, anchoring Phra Chedi Klang Nam to the western bank, but until the 1950s, ships continued to pause at the *wat*. When airplanes superseded ocean liners as the preferred vehicles for royalty, the ritual ceased. Since I was a boatman it seemed proper to end my journey on a reverential note by spending the night here.

I mired the boat on a mudbank and walked 200 yards to the *wat*. Monks were leaving the great hall after a sermon but two of them led me inside. The elderly abbot was slightly hard of hearing and it took a moment to register what I was asking. Then, divine intervention intervened. Two monks laid before the abbot a copy of the morning's *Matichon* newspaper containing my story and four photos and other monks crowded around, comparing the photos with the live specimen before them.

The abbot may have had trouble hearing but he was quick-witted, instructing several monks to fetch my belongings, others to sweep out a *kuti* and still others to find bath water for me.

By the time I finished washing my clothes, the monks were busy with other matters so I walked to the river, sitting on the bank to watch it flow by. It was a river different from the one I'd watched coursing past my rocking chair. Familiarity had bred love; from an adversary, it had become an intimate friend. It looked so broad, so benign, so utterly bland but I now knew better than to dismiss it by its looks. On my Bangkok porch, I had come to know something of its moods and seasons. Now, I knew its origins, its history, its moods, its thoughts.

I had flowed along its lifespan, attending its birth at a rock face where it fell as a pure, sparkling stream. I had seen it mature, not into a proud elderly gentleman but into an old man who had served his purpose and now slumped heavily towards its inevitable end. I now understood what it had murmured as it flowed past my porch: faint memories of its vibrant youth; bone weariness from the weight of the silt it carried, like a snake engorged and made lethargic by all it had ingested on its journey south.

I also sensed the pain of its decline. Having been despoiled by people who no longer regarded it as vital to their lives but as an exploitable resource and a repository for their garbage, it moved towards the sea a spent force, an accumulation of the foul places it had visited. Innocence, hope, maturity, depravity, decay, and death. I didn't have to be Siddhartha to recognize that the same currents flowed through my own life.

I had also aged; I was exhausted, and as battered and gouged as my boat. The journey had been physically demanding–each day discovering new muscles, coping with the heat, battling a recalcitrant tide–but I had been drained as much by protocol as by paddling. Two months of seeking shelter each night, bedding down on so many different surfaces, speaking nothing but Thai–becoming public property just at the moment when I wanted to slink away and be alone–and always having to be on my best behavior, had been tougher than I'd anticipated.

I hadn't always responded positively to adversity–I'd been churlish and short-tempered when I should have laughed it off–and that bothered me. Much of it could be attributed to the heat, the monotony of paddling, and extreme fatigue but, in general, it told me that I was a different traveler than the carefree boy fresh out of the Peace Corps, 20 years before. I had less tolerance for people; I had a great need to be alone. That surprised me. I thought I had recognized that I was, and would always be, an outsider, unable–and unwilling?–to be truly a part of Thai culture and society. But, it seemed, I'd only accepted it intellectually. This journey had given my sense of alienation palpable contours.

In large part my mental fatigue had been my own fault. I had laughed off villagers' suggestions that people downriver were *jai lai* and *jai dam*, but I'd unwittingly succumbed nonetheless. Their fears had wormed their way deep inside me–my own *nguaks*–often obscuring my deeper recognition that I'd enjoyed a wealth of felicitous encounters with remarkable people. I had seen the daily obstacles they dealt with, the difficulties of farming in unfavorable circumstances, and the poverty in which many of them lived. I had come to admire them for their ability to cope cheerfully with adversity, and for their ingenuity. The ancient *muang fai* irrigation systems, their farming implements, fishing traps and techniques revealed long hours of patient observation and the wit to fashion local materials to achieve the objectives of feeding and sheltering themselves.

What had begun as a journey about a river, became a journey about people. Although I often shunned them, they had welcomed me with over-whelming generosity. Most moving was that those who had the least, shared the most. And when I would later return to their villages I would be welcomed as an old friend.

They had understood what I was up against and had tried to en-sure that nothing bad would befall me. I could now see that their warn-ings were meant not to discourage me but to prepare me to meet the chal-lenges. I thought of all the willing hands and backs that had strained to lift the boat out of the water and carry it over obstacles, or across a dusty monastery courtyard to a locked building, safe from harm. They could have left it in the open, let me take my chances on having it stolen; who was I to them? Yet everyone had worked to safeguard me, even the over-zealous police.

And, like the Buddha amulet given me by the Chiang Dao abbot, they continued to watch over me even after I left their village. Pig farmer Yen's words as he handed me a scrap of paper with his address scrawled on it–"Write to us when you get to Bangkok because we'll worry about you"–were repeated all down the river. It was as though I were family, not a stranger who had one day appeared on their doorstep. This is what would endure in memory, not the bad moments and the loudmouths. As normally occurs when one reviews the past, bad memories would be overwhelmed by the good ones.

Would I do it again? Yes. When I wasn't wilting under a noonday sun. I was in the best shape I'd been in for years. I had lost 15 pounds, my body was solid, my back strong, my stomach flat; I bounced when I walked down the street. The major damage had been to my hands. They were talons, good for wrapping around a paddle, pen or fork, but not much good for anything else. My numb left hand would regain feeling several days after I returned home but it would take eight painful months before my hands would become supple again. Next time, I'd use a lighter paddle...and a lighter boat.

In short, the trip had been meaningful in a manner far deeper than I had originally envisaged. Years of short stays in Thai villages had taught me a fraction of what I had gained here. I learned about what happened to people, rivers, and villages, as they grew and matured, valuable lessons I could not extract from books. And I'd become a boatman, much to my amazement and to the amusement of anyone who had witnessed my struggles in the early days.

Perhaps most important, I'd succeeded where others had warned that I would fail. It isn't often that one does something no one else on earth has ever accomplished. It felt good, even if I didn't entirely understand why.

While I had been talking to myself, the sun had been slowly sinking behind me, its orange glow caught in the wavelets buffeted by a rising wind. I returned to the *wat* and was surrounded by young monks brimming with eager questions. In turn, I asked them about their perceptions of the river. They knew that Buddha had reached enlightenment while seated lotus-like on a riverbank, but the Chao Phya had little significance to them, symbolically or otherwise. Many had been born in the villages through which I'd passed, and had chosen to become monks for the educational opportunities it gave them. We found common ground in the fact that we were all so far from home.

Crossing the Bar

Fon Sang Faa, Plaa Sang Nong
(The rain says goodbye to the sky,
the fish says goodbye to the pond)
To take one's leave

On Day 58, the whitewashed chedi, blushed by the rising sun, glowed above me as I set off with four monks on their morning alms walk through the adjoining village. It was my form of meditation and, like them, I walked barefoot, silent, a pilgrim, the touch of firm earth on my soles a marked contrast to the liquid road that had carried me here. By bearing food donations back to the *wat*, I made merit, and my efforts were rewarded with an invitation to breakfast.

Once packed, I spent an hour washing the boat, lovingly rubbing what was left of its shellac skin to as much of a sheen as it would take, stalling, dawdling, unwilling to set upon the river for the final push to the sea. But at 11:30, the tide shifted. Slipping the key into the lock for the last time, I pulled once again onto the conveyor belt that would carry me to the sea. The light was now hard and bluish, the hot air moist as if the sky were perspiring, its sweat and mine conjoining.

The journey that had focused my entire being on a single objective for two months was about to end. Seeking a sense of completion and to thank the river gods for their protection, I paddled across to the Paknam market where I bought a spray of beautiful mauve orchids and a dozen incense sticks. In the middle of the river, I arrayed the orchids on the bow and stuck the incense sticks into the anchor chain hole. I lit them, and began another of many conversations I'd had with the river. I thanked it for allowing me to accompany it on its journey, and for conveying me safely to the sea. As my last words trailed off, I opened my eyes to see that the incense sticks had disappeared down the chain hole and that fragrant smoke was rising from the interior of the boat. I quickly poured water into the bow and the smoke ceased.

How ironic to think that I could have made it this far and then go down, not by drowning, but in flames. Was the river trying to tell me something? Had I inadvertently put a hex on the boat by some act I had performed, compromised the peace that should await me as I entered the wide green sea?

And then it struck me. One last task awaited me.

I'd had lots of time to think about the burden of owning a gun. I now understood myself well enough to know often I'd misread situations, jumped to conclusions, said or did something I later regretted. Owning an object that in a single second could alter my life was a responsibility I no longer wanted. Removing it from my bag, I dropped it overboard. With a sploosh, it disappeared into the brown water and a great wave of relief washed over me. In future, I would seek other ways to avoid succumbing to my fears.

Pinpointing the river's mouth was nearly as difficult as locating its source. Where did a river merge with the sea? The channel widened, angling away on both sides but never extending perpendicular to the river to signal that I had crossed the bar. To give myself a sense of completion, I paddled farther out than necessary. Far out on the horizon bobbed a marker buoy. Two hundred strokes on, I laid my hand on the cold metal, next to the numeral "33." Then, I lifted the blades from the water, and laid the paddle on the thwarts, tacit recognition that my journey was over.

I sat for a long while, listening to the waves plash on my hull, the wind nudging me while seagulls screeched overhead. It was hard to accept that I'd paddled my last stroke and that the river and I would soon part company. It would be lifted to the skies and pushed north in fluffy clouds to fall in the mountains, reincarnated and primed to begin the journey again.

My own river would flow elsewhere. And on another day, I would contemplate what it had all meant. For the moment, the beads on the sandalwood necklace were still individual beads to me. Ultimately some questions would be answered, others would be explored on new rivers. Perhaps the beads would eventually meld into an unbroken circle.

A rising wind told me I had more immediate concerns. I had begun the adventure symbolically by drinking a bit of the waterfall. Here, the water was so foul, I merely dipped in a finger and tasted it. Thick brine. I had truly arrived. Paddling around the buoy, I pointed my bow north and headed for shore.

Epilogue

It took 13 years to write this book. I was stymied by what I perceived as a need to know more about rivers before I could write about them. Thus, for a dozen years, I read incessantly and, for three months, ran the other three tributaries of the Chao Phya. And then I learned how to kayak and joined expeditions down the Mekong River from its source in Tibet, and paddled a dozen rivers elsewhere in the world.

Today, I'm not sure I understand anything more about them than I did when I first thrust my paddle into the upper Ping. Yes, I now understand the logic of a river, can foresee what it will likely do when it encounters an obstacle. But the cosmic forces that impel it are still a mystery that leaves me in awe, the feeling one gets while sitting beneath a vault of stars and becoming lost in its miracle and of one's insignificance in a grander plan.

I also needed to understand why I had been distracted by inconsequential events and people, minor irritations that had clouded my appreciation of the lower river. In the end, all I could deduce was that the problem was me, not them. I realized that I prefer the solitude of the hills to the noise of the plains, and shun cities for the beauty of villages and traditional lifestyles.

In the end, the irritations faded, leaving only the enriching recollection of a grand experience. The journey gave me a focus I had lacked. And a storehouse of memories that are mine alone...mine and those of the myriad villagers with whom I shared them along the way.

Conversion Table

From Thai to English systems:
Rai (Land measure); 2.5 *rai* = 1 acre. 6.25 *rai* = 1 hectare
Sawk (The distance from the elbow to the fingertips) = approx. 18 inches.
Li (Chinese distance measure); 3 *li* equal 1 mile.

From Imperial to metric systems:
1 inch = 2.54 cm.
1 foot = 30.48 cm.
1 yard = 0.9144 meters
1 mile = 1.609 km.
1 square mile = 2.59 km.
1 pound = 453.59 grams
1 ounce = 31.1 grams
1 quart = 0.946 liters

From metric to Imperial systems:
1 centimeter = 0.3937 inches
1 meter = 39.37 inches
1 kilometer = 0.612 miles
1 square kilometer = 0.386 miles
1 kilogram = 2.205 pounds
100 grams = 3.5 ounces
1 liter = 1.05 quarts

Value of the Thai baht in 1988: 1 US dollar = 26 baht

Glossary

Bhikku: A Hindu term often used to describe Buddhist scholars.

Bintabaht: Early morning walk by Buddhist monks through villages to receive food and alms from parishioners. By this means, the monks provide ordinary Thais a means of making merit to ensure they return in a future life as a higher being.

Bot: Hall in a *wat* reserved for monk gatherings and ordinations.

Chamung Thanu: Archer fish, capable of spitting water into the air to knock leaf hoppers off rice stems and into the paddy water where they are devoured by the fish.

Chedi: A monument built over the remains of a revered monk or into which the ashes of a well-known family have been sealed.

Chinchok: A finger-long house lizard that feeds on mosquitoes and makes a chirpin
g count. Houses filled with chinchoks are considered blessed.

Cholaprathan: A concrete irrigation dam, smaller than a hydroelectric dam, and usually maintained by the Royal Irrigation Department.

Chorfa: Literally, "sky tassel", this graceful, bird-like decoration extends from the ends of the over-lapped roofs of a Buddhist *viharn* and *bot*. It represents the *garuda*, the bird-like creature that carries the Hindu god Vishnu. The installation of the final *chorfa* on the roof signifies that the structure has been completed and consecrated.

Durian: A fruit with a spiky rind. Regarded by aficionados as divine, and by those offended by its strong odor as foul.

E-sarn: The northeastern region of Thailand holding its poorest land and, consequently, its poorest people.

Farang: Literally, "French" but applied to all Caucasians.

Geng: Clever, used to describe very able people.

Jai Dam: Literally, "black heart". Person with bad intentions.

Jai Lai: Literally, "evil heart".

Jalakhae: Crocodile

Javet: A male river spirit in human shape venerated by boatmen.

Jek: A pejorative Thai word for a Chinese; also a Thai name.

Kamnan: Headman, usually over a large village. In some instances, he is senior to the *phu yai baan*'s heading each moo in a village.

Keng: Barking deer (*Muntiacus muntjak*), a small, unfortunately tasty, deer that, although officially protectedis a favorite of poachers.

Khaek: A pejorative Thai word for Hindus and Muslims.

Khanom: A category of pastry that includes baked goods, sweets, and desserts.

Khao Tom: Boiled rice. Congee.

Khun: A word used in informal conversation before names of people of either sex who have no title or rank, in the manner of the English Mr., Mrs., or Miss, as in "Khun Somkid"

Kuti: A monk's single-room hut, usually on monastery grounds. Used as accommodation and a meditation chamber.

Kwang: Common deer (*Cervidae*).

Laab: "Minced" but used to indicate a group of Northern, Northeastern Thailand (and Laotian) minced, and often highly spiced, meat dishes at one time eaten raw but now steamed.

Lamyai: Longan. A ping-pong-ball sized fruit with a thin but tough brown skin encasing a sweet, translucent meat. Grown primarily in the North.

Lao Khao: Literally, "white whiskey", equivalent to "white lightning" in coarseness and potency.

Likay: A market form of the palace dance-drama, usually with its own repertoire. Often bawdy, always entertaining.

Luang Paw: Abbot of a Buddhist monastery.

Luuk Thung: Literally, "song of the rice paddy". A folk song celebrating the virtues and heartbreaks of country living.

Matum: Bael fruit. A hard shell surrounds a sticky interior. Generally cooked in syrup or prepared as an herbal tea, using the dried shell.

Moh Hom: A loose shirt worn by farmers, invariably dyed dark blue, and worn by both men and women.

Moo: Ward, as in an administrative district within a large village.

Muang Fai: An ancient irrigation dam and diversion channels built of local stone and wood.

Mun: "It" or "thing", normally used when discussing objects or animals. Can be used colloquially as the third-person singular but is extremely disrespectful, except when used in informal situations with close friends.

Naen: Novice Buddhist monk, generally in his early teens.

Nai: Equivalent to "mister".

Pakoma: A sarong or loincloth, usually checkered and worn by men. Or used as a towel or a tote bag and even a hammock.

Pathongkoh: A deep-fried, Chinese-derived pastry generally eaten in the morning.

Phii (rising tone): Ghost or spirit.

Phii (falling tone): Elder brother or sister, or someone exceeding one in rank or age.

Phra: A monk.

Phu Yai Baan: literally, "big man of the village" i.e. headman.

Pia Kadot Sii Namtan: Brown Leaf Hopper, an insect pest that infests and destroys rice while it stands in the field.

Plaa: Fish.

Plaa Raa: Fermented fish, used as a savory, primarily in the Northeast. Foreigners who can stomach the pungent paste are considered "*geng*".

Prang: A corncob-shaped monument inspired by those in Angkor Wat and often containing the cremated remains of revered monks. In Buddhist mythology, it represents the 33 levels of heaven.

Rai: A unit of land measure equal to 0.4 acres.

Ramwong: A graceful group dance in which men and women dance in pairs but do not touch. The dancers move slowly around a wide circle while performing sinuous hand and arm movements.

Sa-oo: Thai term for Saudi Arabia where many Thais worked for high pay, primarily on construction sites during the 1980s.

Sai Nam Loan: A small concrete irrigation dam.

Samraut: To survey or study.

Sawasdee (pronounced sawat-dee): Thai word of greeting.

Som-tam: A fiery dish from the Northeast whose ingredients include shredded young, raw papaya, tomatoes, chilies, dried shrimp, and often small salted land crabs.

Songtaew: Also called a baht bus, it is essentially a passenger compartment placed on the bed of a pick-up truck. It is the universal form of public transportation in the provinces and in big city back lanes.

Stupa: The Sanskrit name given to the mound of earth covering a relic of the Buddha. Generally called a *chedi* in Thailand.

Teen Chang: Literally "elephant footprints", used to describe indentations in rock and said to have been left by the ancient spirits of elephants.

Too-kae: Gecko. The onomatopoeic name for a foot-long lizard that inhabits the dark areas of houses and jungles, the name based on the cry the reptile makes.

Tuk-tuk: A three-wheel motorized taxi rickshaw.

Viharn: The meeting hall of a monastery; usually its largest building.

Wai: The traditional Thai greeting to those older and senior to one. The hands are clasped, prayer-like before one's chest, the fingertips touching the chin.

Wan phra: The weekly Buddhist holy day set according to the lunar calendar. In the morning, parishioners go to the viharn of the monastery to present food to the gathered monks who preach sermons and chant scriptures. A joyous communal meeting without the solemnity associated with similar religious gatherings in other faiths.

Wat: Monastery. The term encompasses everything lying within the precincts defined by the outer compound wall that encloses meeting halls, the ordination hall, belltowers, monk's quarters, pavilions, manuscript libraries, and occasionally, schools.

Save by ordering direct from
Wind & Water Books

<u>*Siamese Bestiary.* Kristiaan Inwood, Wind & Water, 2002.</u>

In the 1970s, writer/artist Kristiaan Inwood moved to a jungle house where, inspired by the birth of his first son, he recorded the beauty of tropical Thailand. This foray into Nature's wonder, into marriage to a delightful Thai, becoming a father, and inhabiting a culture foreign to his British upbringing, is knit together by the author's wry humor and his wealth of exquisite drawings.

"...a beautiful book...soundly recommended." —*Growing Point, UK*

— *Hard cover with dust jacket. 104 pages. US$17.95 (originally US$24.95). Add shipping and handling: N. America: $10.45; Asia: $8.00; Europe & Australasia: $9.10.*

<u>*Bangkok Then and Now.* Steve Van Beek. AB Publications. 2002</u>

Explore one of Asia's great cities through photos taken at the beginning and end of the 20th century. The text examines daily life, scores of newspaper stories from 1900 tell us how to stay healthy (cholera belts were essential), and chronicle the notorious hat snatchers and their geckoes, and the tram drivers who placed horserace bets by tapping their footbells.

"Written with remarkable wit and tied together deftly with the magic string of a skilled storyteller." —The Nation

—*Hard cover with dust jacket. 140 pages. $19.95 (bookstore price: US$29.95). Add shipping & handling: N. America: $15.80; Asia: $11.55; Europe & Australasia: $13.70.*

The Chao Phya, River in Transition. Steve Van Beek, Oxford University Press, 1995. The Chao Phya River has been a key contributor to Thailand's history and culture, nourishing a rich rice bowl, serving as a vital highway, and protecting its cities. Although more important today than ever, the river is being altered in ways detrimental to its future. This beautifully illustrated work offers a insight into the River of Kings, shaper of the Thai nation and people.

"A fascinating excursion into history, culture, economics, and religion" —*Bangkok Post*

— Hard cover with dust jacket. 212 pages. US$24.95 (originally US$70). Add shipping and handling: N. America: $16.85; Asia: $12.30; Europe & Australasia: $14.60.

Photocopy this form and post or fax to 662 653-8973

Slithering South

_____ copies x $11.95 + _____shipping = _____

Bangkok Then & Now

_____ copies x $19.95 + _____shipping = _____

The Chao Phya

_____ copies x $24.95 + _____shipping = _____

Total shipment US$_____

Name_____

Address_____

City_____ State_____

Country _____ Post Code_____

Tel: _____Fax:_____

E-mail _____

Send cheques endorsed to Wind & Water Ltd. in U.S. dollars to our Bangkok office: Amara Court, #C-6, 645/49 Petchburi Road, Bangkok 10400, Thailand. Or contact publisher@windandwaterbooks.com